The Floating Borderlands

The Floating Borderlands
Twenty-five Years of U.S. Hispanic Literature

Edited by
Lauro Flores

University of Washington Press
Seattle and London

The stories and poetry in this volume made their original appearance in the
journal *Revista Chicano-Riqueña*, initiated in 1972 and in 1986 renamed
The Americas Review: A Review of Hispanic Literature and Art of the USA.
The Americas Review is published by Arte Público Press, Houston,
under the direction of publisher Nicolás Kanellos.
The University of Washington's publication of selections from the journal
commemorates the journal's twenty-fifth anniversary.
Credit and permissions information can be found at the end of the book.

Publication of the color sections is made possible, in part, by support
from the University of Washington Graduate School and Ted Rodríguez.

Library of Congress Cataloging-in-Publication Data
The floating borderlands : twenty-five years of U.S. Hispanic literature /
edited by Lauro Flores
p. cm.
ISBN 0–295–97746–9 (alk. paper)
1. American literature—Hispanic American authors.
2. Hispanic Americans—Literary collections.
3. American literature—20th century.
I. Flores, Lauro, 1950–
PS508.H57F58   1998   98–23924
810.8'0868—dc21   CIP

For Christine Yuodelis

East, West,
West, East;
flor de loto,
flor de lis...

Contents

Memory Makers

Prose

Poetry

New Navigators of the Floating Borderlands

Prose

Poetry

Illustrations

The Floating Borderlands

Introduction

> *Tonight we shall eat the assumptions of ourselves,*
> *of our house and where we are going.*
> *Tonight we shall embark on the Floating Borderlands*
> *toward our liberation.*
>
> —Juan Felipe Herrera

Students in my literature courses have occasionally heard me speak about the scarcity of U.S. Hispanic texts extant in 1970, when I finished high school and began my undergraduate studies.[1] At that time, I tell them, it was not unusual—perhaps it was even inevitable—for Chicano Studies instructors to include in their reading lists two basic items: *El laberinto de la soledad* (*The Labyrinth of Solitude*), the seminal essay issued in 1950 by the Mexican poet and Nobel laureate Octavio Paz; and *Pocho*, José Antonio Villarreal's first novel, initially published in 1959 and reprinted by Doubleday in 1970. The former was usually chosen because it devotes one chapter—the first one of the book, to be precise—to the *pachucos*, the Chicano zoot-suiters Paz saw during his stay in Los Angeles in the 1940s. Ironically, it was in those very youths that he located the paradigmatic embodiment, the "essence," of the Mexican character: a tragicomic figure riddled with contradictions and confusion, and quintessentially defined—according to Paz—by an extreme inferiority complex. The latter, *Pocho*, so the story went for some time, was supposed to be the first Chicano novel.

As is now common knowledge, the arguments advanced by Paz in his *Labyrinth* were soon subjected to close scrutiny, challenged on multiple grounds, and eventually repudiated by various scholars.[2] In similar fashion, the claim regarding the historical primacy of Villarreal's *Pocho* was ultimately discarded in the face of the evidence produced by later research.[3] By then, however, other texts had emerged as alternative choices for planning Chicana/o culture and literature courses and for the configuration of the appropriate syllabi.

Historically, though, the fact remains that in the late 1960s and early 1970s, U.S. teachers and scholars confronted twin challenges: a compelling need to unearth those Hispanic texts that had been written, and in many cases published, in previous epochs, but which for a variety of reasons had fallen into oblivion; and an imperative to promote the creative activities of the new and emerging Hispanic authors. In this sense, it was particularly crucial to provide an appropriate forum for their burgeoning expression.

The historic Quinto Sol Publications house, which, along with its journal *El Grito*, was founded by Herminio Ríos and Octavio I. Romano-V. in Berkeley, California, in 1967, was an important pivot for this forum among Chicanos. With

3

the dual challenge outlined above in mind, Quinto Sol printed the first anthology of Chicano literature, *El Espejo/The Mirror* (1969), and also instituted the now legendary Premio Quinto Sol, the annual award mainly responsible for hammering out the initial profile of a contemporary Chicano literary canon. I believe this is a fair assessment of Quinto Sol's role, despite the controversy that has arisen when critics have questioned the authenticity of the contests and the consecration of some works.[4] Significantly, and not coincidentally, however, the authors who won the first three Quinto Sol awards—Tomás Rivera, *...y no se lo tragó la tierra* (1970); Rudy Anaya, *Bless Me, Ultima* (1971); and Rolando Hinojosa-Smith, *Estampas del Valle y otras obras* (1972)—were chosen for the present anthology.[5] Also included are Estela Portillo Trambley and Luis J. Rodríguez, winners of a Quinto Sol honorable mention in 1972. Rodríguez was honored when he was only seventeen and has gone on to become one of the more powerful voices on the U.S. Latino literary stage today.

A few years later, in 1976, Hinojosa-Smith's second novel, *Klail City y sus alrededores*, would receive the prestigious Casa de las Américas prize in Cuba. This event irreversibly placed Chicano literature—as a distinct cultural expression, different from both Mexican and Anglo-American articulations—on the international literary map and forced the recharting of the landscape of world literatures.

In the meantime, in 1972, the year Hinojosa-Smith's first novel won the Quinto Sol prize, Nicolás Kanellos and Luis Dávila had founded the celebrated journal *Revista Chicano-Riqueña* (*RCR*) at the University of Indiana. The journal was originally conceived by its creators as a multicultural medium that would help to bring together Chicanos, Puerto Ricans, and other Latino writers of the United States, and which would also facilitate the dialogue between Latinos and the *latinophiles* who coexisted in this country. With these goals clearly stated in the editors' *Nota preliminar* in the first issue, *RCR* broadened the cultural-nationalistic parameters that defined the scope of Southwest-based journals like *El Grito*, whose valiant efforts and invaluable contributions focused almost exclusively on works written by Chicanos.

The first issue of *RCR* included the reprinting of "Bromeando" (Joking), a narrative piece discovered by Kanellos in an old issue (1927) of *El amigo del hogar*, a local newspaper[6] published in Harbor, Indiana, and a brief essay, "Los hijos pródigos," written by Luis Dávila specially for the *Revista*'s inaugural issue. While the reprinting of "Bromeando" revealed Kanellos's early concern with the recovery of the Hispanic literary past (an interest of his that has continued and evolved over the years), Dávila's essay conveyed the need of Midwest Latinos to establish a sense of cultural purpose and identity in the early 1970s. Dávila speaks of the "terror" that possessed Latinos "upon recognizing that [they were] cultural vagabonds, courageous but raggedy, rolling about through the softly hostile environment of the United States," in a land that, contrary to the Southwest or Puerto

Rico, he says, they could never claim once belonged to them.[7] "No importa," says Dávila, "pues vivir por acá tiene ciertas simetrías con el vivir en Aztlán o en la Isla [It doesn't matter, because living here has certain symmetry with living in Aztlán or on the Island]." And, he continues, "we have decided to invent and believe in a region where also our dreams can fit." Although not fully articulated by him, a kernel of the *floating borderlands* notion, which constitutes the heart of this anthology, was already present in Dávila's meditations at that time.

Thematically, "Bromeando," the piece rescued from oblivion by Kanellos, also explored a similar concept. The problems it humorously conveyed are a commentary on Mexican refugees' various attempts to cope with the clash of cultures they confronted while "floating" in a strange and often hostile land. The appearance of "Bromeando" in the first issue of *RCR* was important, among other reasons, because it pointed up the diversity of the Mexican community of East Chicago, Indiana, and because it registered contemporary social attitudes and diverse aspects of the Mexican oral tradition. In other words, the boundaries usually separating traditional realms—geographical, social, and genre—become blurred in it.

In the fall of 1979 *RCR* moved to the University of Houston, where it continued to thrive and rapidly established itself as the major platform for Hispanic artistic expression. A year later, the partnership between Dávila and Kanellos dissolved, leaving Kanellos as the sole head of the review. Numerous journals with aims similar to those voiced by *RCR* were launched at various times and in different sites of the country. Virtually all of them vanished almost as fast as they appeared, while *RCR* prospered as the most consistent, durable, and prestigious publication of its kind.

Once in Houston, Kanellos also established his own publishing outlet, Arte Público Press, which has since become the major publisher of books by Hispanic writers in the United States. Confronted with the pressures and demands that eventually arose out of this venture, Kanellos enlisted the assistance of Julián Olivares and José David Saldívar in the spring of 1984 and delegated to them all responsibilities related to the publication of the journal. At this juncture, the format of the review was slightly altered and a subtitle, "A Review of Hispanic Literature and Art of the USA," was added to the masthead. Under the direction first of Olivares and Saldívar, and later Olivares alone, the production of special thematic issues became a regular feature of the journal. It was also under the leadership of Olivares and Saldívar that, in the spring of 1986, *Revista Chicano-Riqueña* abandoned its old name and became *The Americas Review* (*TAR*). The change was not capricious or arbitrary, as the editors explained in the transition issue (14:1). Although, demographically, the dominant U.S. Hispanic groups were, and still are, the Chicanos and Puerto Ricans (the *raison d'être* of the review's original name), during the decade following the founding of *RCR*, "the increased presence of Hispanics in the USA, notably with greater presence of other Hispanic groups whose creative expression also needed to be seen and heard," made it necessary to re-examine, to re-define, and to expand the scope of the journal (in fact, the addition of the subtitle, as mentioned above, was already an indication of the ongoing metamorphosis of the publication). Thus, the change in names was only the next logical step in a process of continuous renovation and readjustment that has permitted the journal to keep striving to accomplish its mission to serve the broad needs of an increasingly heterogeneous Hispanic population. The new title was the editors' symbolic act "to publicly embrace all U.S. Hispanic groups in creative brotherhood." Saldívar moved away from Houston shortly after this change, and Olivares took charge as senior editor of *TAR*, with Evangelina Vigil-Piñón as assistant editor, posts they continued to occupy until 1994 and 1995, respectively.

Now, as the journal reaches its twenty-fifth anniversary, it is again under new editorship and has migrated once more—this time to the University of Washington. In some people's minds (the myth-oriented, to be sure), the journal has finally come full circle and has returned to the original Aztlán, the legendary "place of many lakes" that the *Mexica* people left behind when they made their trek south in quest of the promised land. To commemorate the journal's move to the Pacific Northwest, the University of Washington Press has invited me to prepare this anthology featuring the "best" works published in *RCR/TAR* over the last quarter century. A risky and problematic proposition, without a doubt, but one I enthusiastically undertake.

* * *

Every anthology is arbitrary in some measure and inevitably reflects the editor's taste, judgment, and preferences, as well as prejudices and biases. Any attempt to distill twenty-five years of literary production in some four hundred pages involves the certitude that some worthy works and authors will be left out. This is especially unavoidable when the material at hand is copious and remarkably diverse. *The Americas Review* publishes creative works (mainly poetry and short fiction but also an occasional novel excerpt or a play script), essays, literary and cultural criticism, interviews, and reviews—in English and Spanish. It also features art work on a consistent basis.

While the art dimension is handsomely represented by the sixteen images included in the inserts, this anthology is devoted almost exclusively to two literary genres: fiction and poetry. That said, I must admit, apropos of the multiple meanings encapsulated in the very title of this book, that some works—Juan Felipe Herrera's "Outside Tibet," Rane Arroyo's "Blonde as a Bat," Richard Blanco's "Teatro Martí," Inés Hernández Avila's "Coyote Woman Finds Fox at the Street Fair at Port Townsend," among others—escape the narrow genre definitions we are accustomed to use. These works "float" across those boundaries and challenge traditional notions and customary borders as is obvious in the themes and motifs they display.

A similar observation can be made regarding the images produced by artists like Carmen Lomas Garza as José David Saldívar eloquently argues in his recent book *Border Matters* (1997), a proposal that advances a more open and encompassing notion of cultural studies vis à vis traditional literary approaches. In Saldívar's view, Lomas Garza practices a spatial poetics which suggests a return to visual storytelling. In these social commentaries, "she rearticulates domestic [gendered, social] and geopolitical spaces" and "thus helps to establish in Chicana painting what has become over the course of the 1980s and into the 1990s the project for narratives by Chicanas." A parallel "reading" of Lomas Garza paintings and Denise Chávez's "The Closet," for example, will illustrate this point well. On a different plane, Lomas Garza's works are hybrid artifacts in the sense that they rely on forms which combine high art with popular crafts, elements and techniques. A similar observation can be made about Patricia Rodríguez's works.

Once the parameters for organizing this book were narrowed down, the criteria for selection became relatively simple. Naturally, my desire always was to produce an extensive and truly representative—but manageable—sampling of the diverse authors, themes, and styles that *TAR* has published over the years. I also hoped to achieve an accurate portrayal of the evolution of literary expression during the last two and a half decades. But the point of departure, the true basis for selection was the aesthetic worth of each piece, independent of any other considerations. In an attempt to maintain maximum objectivity, I secured the assistance of several readers, most of whom had not had a previous association with the journal and were not acquainted *a priori* with the authors under consideration. I believed they would be able to weigh the value of each work on its own merits. Nonetheless, I alone assume full responsibility for the final selection.

After the bulk of the material was chosen on the grounds described above, my next task was to determine the format into which it would be arranged. The options were diverse, ranging from the traditional half poetry/half prose fiction type of anthology on one end to the thematic volume on the other. After much pondering, I decided to divide the book into three sections which, in my opinion, reflect the three stages that characterize the development not only of *The Americas Review* but also of contemporary Hispanic literature in this country. The parallel is logical if one considers the vital role the journal has played in this historic process. It is not an exaggeration to say that *RCR/TAR* has been instrumental in redefining the U.S. literary landscape over the last two-and-a-half decades.

The first section, "Nationhood Messengers," assembles those "pioneer" writers who achieved notable recognition between, roughly, 1970 and 1984. These authors were responsible for the initial attempts to provide a cultural "definition," as each of them perceived it and as it pertained to the particular group they identified with—Chicana/o and Nuyorican, in the main. I must note that although some of the writers I have chosen to include in this anthology were published relatively recently in *TAR*, their serious professional activity and the recognition they achieved in some cases (Floyd Salas, for example) date back to the 1960s.[8] A second point worth making here is the fact that this group does not constitute a "generation," at least not in the strict sense of the term. For example, grouped together in this cluster are authors like Rolando Hinojosa-Smith (1929) and Juan Felipe Herrera (1948), who are quite distant from each other in terms of age and perspective. The majority of these writers, especially the poets (Alurista, Lorna Dee Cervantes, Ricardo Sánchez, Miguel Algarín, Lucha Corpi, Tato Laviera, Miguel Piñero, etc.), were for the most part "intuitive" writers who lacked formal training but who were instrumental in opening up a wide range of possibilities for a new type of expression, which included among its many innovative features the utilization of code-switching and the incorporation of *caló* and other vernacular forms of speech in the production of what was truly an avant-garde form of art. Finally, it must also be noted that the vast majority of the authors in this group are male, which accurately reflects the literary and social milieu of that first stage of our contemporary development.

The second part, "Memory Makers," constitutes a group of authors who serve as a bridge between the "pioneer generation" and the fresh voices who are now beginning to make themselves heard and who are included in the third section. While some of the second group began to publish sporadically before the 1980s, it was not until the middle of the decade that they moved to the forefront and were fully recognized and valued as "serious" writers. In some cases (Sandra Cisneros, Alberto Ríos, and others), they are graduates of prestigious MFA programs such as the Iowa Writers Workshop.[9] They have cultivated their craft and produce polished works, which in general are close in form to mainstream Anglo-American literary norms. Logically, then, the majority of them write almost exclusively in English. The vigorous desire of some of their predecessors to defend and preserve the Spanish language, which they perceived to be part of their cultural heritage and identity, begins to change drastically at this juncture, roughly around 1984. Also notable is the fact that in the main, contrary to the situation prevailing in the previous stage, the most salient of the writers belonging to this group are women: Julia Alvarez, Ana Castillo, Sandra Cisneros, Denise Chávez, Helena María Viramontes.[10]

The third and final cluster, "New Navigators of the Floating Borderlands," includes those writers whose strong voices are now beginning to be heard and who, given the quality of their works to date, will undoubtedly achieve prominence in the first decades of the twenty-first century. There is not a cohesive generation bond in this case either. Some authors are very young indeed (Rigoberto González, Ramón García), while some more mature writers are only now seeing their writings begin to have an impact in the literary milieu (Kathleen Alcalá, Daniel Chacón, Arturo Mantecón, Dan Orozco, Beatriz Rivera, Juan Armando

David Acosta Posada, etc.).

In determining the format of this book I also had in mind the manner in which this collection could be useful for courses devoted to the study of U.S. Hispanic literature, both at the secondary and the post-secondary levels. Thus, although the "generational" or chronological approach is favored if one chooses to follow the strict organization of the book, I feel that the variety of themes included in each of the sections should make it possible for instructors to tailor the readings of their students according to specific curricular needs and goals. Some of the more obvious thematic nuclei are: family relations; the farm laborers' existence; indigenous roots; the immigrant experience; memory and autobiography; urban space; gender and sexuality; women's issues; language and culture; etc.

Here I should acknowledge that *TAR* has on occasion published works by non-Hispanics and by Latin-American authors who do not fully identify with or are not yet part of the historical U.S. cultural map and dynamics—writers from South America who reside in this country on a temporary basis or who, for a host of reasons, are here physically but still live spiritually, and in some cases also professionally, in their place of origin.[11] The sporadic inclusion of those authors is part of the broader dialogue in which our journal has attempted to engage lately and is also a manner of opening up a broader horizon for the new writers developing in our midst. But promoting those authors certainly falls beyond the parameters of the central mission of *TAR* (A Review of Hispanic Literature and Art *of* the USA). For this reason, their works were not considered for inclusion in this anthology, regardless of their aesthetic quality.

* * *

When I first accepted the position of editor of *The Americas Review* from afar, I did so with a bit of trepidation. After all, the monumental role the journal had played up until then weighed heavily on my shoulders. My trepidation was followed by a burst of enthusiasm, which—when I was confronted with a lukewarm reception and little administrative support from the University of Washington—transformed into dismay. It was at that critical moment that Michael Duckworth, acquisitions editor for the University of Washington Press, having learned about *TAR* and my new role in it, first conceived the project that has resulted in this anthology. He approached me with his idea and provided me with the opportunity to bring it to fruition. His patience, advice, and friendship have been invaluable to me.

In addition, I want to recognize the many friends and colleagues who, in various ways, have also been part of this project. Juan Felipe Herrera helped me to chart the structure of the book and also provided me, in part, with the main title and the subtitles for the divisions of the book. Tony Geist, colleague and friend of many years, also contributed to the conception of the format, read my first ideas, listened to my arguments with patience, attention, and affection, and completed the title of the third section. Alicia Gaspar de Alba allowed me to use parts of her poem "The Waters of Grief" for the epigraphs. Dan Orozco and Mauricio Carrera unselfishly assisted me in the beginning stages of the project. My *sobrino* Rigo, *escritor de mucha garra*, listened to my ideas and gave me his critical and uncompromising feedback. Emy Manini performed the bulk of the typesetting of the manuscript and deserves my special gratitude for her generous, dedicated, and excellent labor. She was assisted by Marla Valverde and Marcelo Pellegrini; my appreciation goes to both of them and also to everyone in CARTAH, the Center for Advanced Research Technologies in the Arts and Humanities at the University of Washington. A subvention from the University of Washington Graduate School, as well as the support of Ted Rodríguez and Torero's Restaurants, made it possible to use color in the illustrations; my gratitude to Dean Marsha Landolt and her staff. Marilyn Trueblood, my in-house editor, provided many suggestions that helped to improve this manuscript.

I thank my colleagues Julián Olivares, Yvonne Yarbro-Bejarano, and Erasmo Gamboa for reading my initial notes and for giving me their invaluable insight, friendship, and encouragement; Farris Anderson, Julius Debro, Arturo Madrid, and Tomás Ybarra-Frausto for their support; Fulgencio Lazo for his art, which has enlivened the cover; Nicolás Kanellos for letting me reprint most of the material initially published in his journal; Susan Bergholz and Charlotte Sheedy for giving me access to the works of the authors they represent; Elsa Flores for allowing me to include Carlos Almaraz's "Greed;" Julio Martínez, Suzanna Moroles, Robert Stanfield and the Owings-Dewey Fine Art Gallery, and the National Museum of American Art. My wife Christine and my children, Rafael and Leonor, put up with my late night hours and my frequent neglect. Lastly, I must thank all the writers and artists who have generously allowed me to include their work in this anthology. Without them this book would not exist. To all of them, ¡muchas gracias!

Lauro H. Flores
University of Washington

Notes

1. The informed reader will immediately recognize the problematic nomenclature I employ here. When referring specifically to "Mexican-American" authors or culture, or to this demographic group in general, I employ the word *Chicana/o*. When the reference includes other groups as well I use *Latina/o* or *Hispanic* without distinction. Although "Hispanic" is a loaded and controversial term, it forms part of the subtitle of *The Americas Review*, the journal that anchors this anthology. In addition, it allows for gender inclusion while making it possible to avoid the cumbersome utilization of slashed words.

2. For an example see Carlos Blanco Aguinaga's "El laberinto fabricado por Octavio Paz," first published in *Aztlán* 3:1 (Spring 1972, 1-12) and also included in *De mitólogos y novelistas* (Madrid: Turner 1975, 5-25). As I make the last revisions of these notes, the news of Octavio Paz's passing reach me. He died April 19, in Coyoacán, Mexico, at age 84. A whole epoch of Mexican cultural history goes with him. *Pax*.

3. A chief example is the *Recovering the U.S. Hispanic Literary Heritage Project*, housed at the University of Houston and headed by Kanellos since 1992.

4. According to critics, the Quinto Sol editors wanted the American public to accept as reflective of Chicano culture certain works that were actually a reflection of their own conception of that culture. See, for example, Juan Bruce-Novoa's "Canonical and Non-Canonical Texts," in *The Americas Review* 14:3-4, 1986.

5. The years indicated here pertain to the granting of the awards. In each case, the book was published by Quinto Sol the subsequent year.

6. *El amigo del hogar* was founded by Mexican political and religious refugees and published in Indiana between 1924 and 1930. Kanellos notes that it was the main vehicle of information for the Mexican community of East Chicago, Indiana, during that time: "*El amigo del hogar* is a product of one of those urban centers which Américo Paredes has termed 'Mexiquitos' [little Mexicos], that is, the Mexican *colonias* of the large industrial cities which received the migration of Mexican-Americans from the Southwest, the former *braceros* from Mexico, and the political refugees of the Mexican Revolution."

7. All the works mentioned here as appearing in the inaugural issue of *RCR* were published in Spanish. The translations are mine.

8. Salas's first two novels, *Tattoo the Wicked Cross* (1967) and *What Now My Love* (1969) were published by Grove Press. *Buffalo Nickel*, his most recent book, was released by Arte Público in 1992.

9. Sandra Cisneros, unfortunately, was not available for inclusion in this book. Neither was Gary Soto, another important author who has also published in *TAR*.

10. To my mind, the landmark that came to signal this transition was perhaps Sandra Cisneros' *The House on Mango Street*, first published by Arte Público Press in 1983. Two other books which were also indicative—each in its own controversial and contradictory manner—of the renewed and dynamic presence of "Latino" literature in the U.S. literary landscape at almost exactly the same moment were Richard Rodriguez's *Hunger of Memory* (1982) and Danny Santiago's [Daniel James] *Famous All Over Town* (1983). These were followed by a stream of relatively successful works: Cherríe Moraga, *Loving in the War Years. Lo que nunca pasó por sus labios* (1983); Ana Castillo, *The Mixquiahuala Letters* (1986); Denise Chávez, *The Last of the Menu Girls* (1986); Gloria Anzaldúa, *Borderlands/La Frontera* (1987); Luis J. Rodríguez, *Always Running. La Vida Loca: Gang Days in L. A.* (1993); and other notable titles published during the decade 1983-93.

11. I am referring here, for example, to international graduate students who come to pursue a degree in this country, or to those writers who have immigrated to the U.S. after they have already achieved relative fame in their own countries of origin and who often continue to publish the bulk of their work in those countries. Nobody would think, if I may use a hyperbole to illustrate this point, of including Carlos Fuentes or Fernando Alegría in an anthology of this type.

Nationhood Messengers

We are writing the waters of grief,
the tides of language that
tossed us out of the country
of our innocence.
                    —A. Gaspar de Alba

The Captain

The morning after we arrived I went for a walk in the forest which surrounded the chalet. There had been a light drizzle in the night, but now the sun shown brightly and the droplets of water glistened as they clung to the trees. I had listened to the light rain for a while, and the fatigue of the war had drained away and I had fallen asleep. It was the first soft, warm bed I had slept in since my last visit home over a year ago. I slept well, but I awakened early. I was accustomed to awakening early, because on the front the artillery barrages always came early, presaging the movement of troops or attack. But this morning there was nothing, only silence. Outside my window the birds chirped in the trees. The aroma of freshly brewed coffee tinged the cool, fresh air.

I decided to walk alone before breakfast. I put on an old pair of tweed trousers and a heavy wool sweater which my wife had knitted for my birthday, then I made my way down a dark hallway towards the rear of the chalet. The Fuhrer's suite also occupied the rear wing of the chalet, and as I passed by an open door, I glanced in and saw him sitting at a small table by the window. He wore a dressing gown, and he was having his morning coffee as he read a newspaper. He looked up and smiled and nodded. I drew myself up to salute, but he had already returned to his paper.

He had appeared shortly after we had arrived the night before. He had made a short talk, toasted us, and told us to enjoy ourselves. There would be no meetings. We would take our dinners together, but that was all, the rest of the time was ours to do as we pleased. There was a spa, he said, a large game room adjoining the dining room, a comfortable den with plenty of recent newspapers, and of course there was the forest. He made a point of encouraging us to walk in the forest. There were good trails for walking and beautiful meadows full of spring flowers.

We were warriors, he said, and we had fought hard for our common goal, so now it was time to rest and enjoy this island of peace away from the war. The Eagle's Nest he called it. He made a toast, smiled, thanked us for our adherence to his cause, then he disappeared. A tall, blond woman who had stood quietly in the background accompanied him.

"He is looking well," someone commented.

We nodded in agreement. We had heard rumors about his health, but those were dispelled when we saw him. He seemed in good spirits. His hair and moustache were neatly trimmed, and his uniform was impeccable.

As I passed the open door I noticed a huge mirror which covered almost one complete wall and which reflected the rest of his suite: a wide bed, a valet polishing his boots, a fireplace at the far end of the room, and at another table near the fireplace the same blonde woman whom I had seen the night before. She glanced up, saw my reflection in the mirror, and I thought she frowned. I proceeded and found my way to the rear exit where a door opened onto a large terrace. There were tables and chairs, and at the edge of the retaining wall a telescope. I walked to the edge of the terrace and looked down at the dense green forest which surrounded us. In the distance I could see the smoke of the village where we had arrived by train the night before. Below me, along the slight grade which dropped into the valley, but within the fence compound, there were many small meadows. They were bright with the flowers of spring. I could not remember a more beautiful sight. At that moment, the war seemed so far away. The only reminder of the war was the sight of the guards stationed around the perimeter of the compound.

I lighted my pipe and wandered into the forest. Underneath the canopy of trees the sun shone in patches and glistened and dazzled in the drops of water which clung to the leaves and in the mist which rose from the ground. Squirrels chattered in the trees. Bluejays and blackbirds hopped from branch to branch, calling shrilly to the stranger who had intruded in their sanctuary. Up ahead I saw a red fox disappear into the dense undergrowth. A female hunting, because it was followed by two cubs.

It could not be more beautiful, I thought as I walked aimlessly towards the meadows I had seen from the terrace and then turned at the fence and worked my way towards the road which led from the gate to the chalet. Even the guards at the gate had been pleasant last night. They had not asked for papers, merely saluted and waved us through when the driver said we were the Fuhrer's guests for the weekend. We were received with open arms by the servants. The cooks were waiting for us with a late dinner. They were jovial and served the meal in good spirits. The wine flowed freely, good French wine which none of us had tasted since before the war.

I did not personally know most of the officers. We were all positioned along the eastern front and we knew each other through the war reports, but we were not staff or generals so there was no reason for us to know each other. As a matter of fact, there was only one general in the group. Fat Lips I'll call him. He was the one who toasted the Fuhrer the loudest and longest. Long after I went to bed, he was still drinking. And there was Frank. We had been at the military academy together. It was good to see him again. We had talked briefly about old times, showed each other photographs of our families: he had two girls, I had one.

But why were we here? Frank had questioned me. Why had we been chosen?

We were not part of the Fuhrer's group, we weren't politicians, and except for Fat Lips we weren't generals. We did have good records as officers. During the early days of the eastern offensive my men had proven themselves as brave, capable soldiers. We had taken the northern flank, capturing thousands of prisoners, and I had been made a hero of sorts. But the days of heroes quickly passed. The cold had come and the movement had bogged down. The war grew dismal.

I pushed those thoughts from my mind, sniffed the fresh, spring air and paused to light my pipe again. I had found the road that led to the chalet. I recalled the fragrance of the coffee, a luxury we rarely had on the northern flank. I was hungry. I looked forward to sitting down and eating a hearty breakfast. "Why be concerned about why we were invited?" I thought aloud. "We are here, let's enjoy it." For me it was the first break from the front in over a year. As I walked toward the chalet I thought of my wife and wished that she could be with me. Even for the officers, the letters were few and far between. The enemy was bombing the cities now, and I worried, for her and for my young daughter.

As I approached the chalet an army bus rumbled up the road. I stepped aside to let it pass. I thought perhaps more officers were arriving, and was surprised to see women in the bus. One of them was the Fuhrer's woman. The other women, evidently from the village, smiled and waved and I waved back. For the most part they were handsome women, village peasants with round, pleasant faces. One in particular caught my eye. She was a young woman, perhaps eighteen. She smiled and looked directly at me as the bus drove past. When the bus stopped in front of the chalet, the other officers came out to greet the passengers. I joined them. The meeting was pleasant, with a great deal of laughter.

Fat Lips helped a heavy-set woman off the bus and she responded by giving him a hug. Everyone laughed. My friend Frank reached out to assist a woman who reminded me vaguely of my wife. When the young woman who had caught my eye stepped down she looked directly at me. She held out a small valise, I took it and offered my arm. At the door the servants took the bags, everyone was happy. Inside, the cooks, seemingly delighted with the arrival of the women, were waiting to lead us into the dining room.

The only woman who did not come with us was the Fuhrer's woman. I paused at the door and looked back. She was still standing by the side of the bus. The Fuhrer had joined her. He stood by her side, seemed to lean slightly towards her to ask her something, then he smiled and looked towards us as we entered the chalet. He hooked his hands in his belt and seemed to rock back and forth, looking very pleased.

Breakfast was a delight. There were fresh eggs and bread from the village, lots of coffee, and of course the company of the women. They were typical peasant women, broad shouldered and heavy bosomed. They had plain but warm faces, and they seemed pleased to be with us. The usual reservation and aloofness of the German woman was missing. They were the first female companionship most of us had known in a long time. They listened to our stories and jokes and laughed. We all laughed, even at the old jokes we had heard before.

The women told us their names, but very little else about themselves. They insisted on hearing about us. We were the saviors of the homeland who had come to rest in their forest. They were there to serve us, they said. Of course it was what we needed, to talk to women—warm, clean women who leaned forward and listened intently as we unburdened ourselves.

Someone, Fat Lips I think, ordered brandy after breakfast. We drank it with our coffee and the talk became more lighthearted and animated. Toasts were made. The women of the village were praised for their beauty. The war was praised. The Fuhrer was praised. He was a magnanimous person to have us at his Shangri-la, the Colonel said. With him as a leader we would conquer all our enemies. The lull in the war was only temporary. Everybody cheered. The women drank with us. Their faces grew ruddy and pleasant with the brandy and excitement.

Else, the woman who seemed to have chosen me, sat with me at breakfast. Now as the Colonel stood to propose a new toast she drew closer to me and took my hand beneath the table. I trembled and looked at her. Her hand was warm. She leaned closer to whisper that she would like to leave the party. Her breath was sweet on my face. When I looked into her eyes she returned a look of admiration and invitation.

I was surprised at first, then tremulous. I had not felt my blood pulse to the closeness of a woman for a long time. In war a soldier learns to harden himself against loneliness. He learns that the heart must be cold and immune to the death in the fields around him. But when she held my hand I felt like a young man again, like a lover who walks hand in hand with his girlfriend in the park in time of peace. Maybe that is why we had come here, to be rewarded for our soldiering with an interlude of peace. Still I could not help but remember my wife, my young daughter, all my comrades who couldn't be with us on this island of peace, my men who had died on the bloody fields of war. I thought of all the times I had told them to go out and die for the Fatherland. I saw the frozen bodies which had fallen along the road as we pushed eastward . . . and now it was spring, spring in the forest, a moment of peace.

I looked into Else's eyes and she encouraged me. I felt a need for her, felt the need to take her in my arms. I was hungry for companionship, eager to tell this young woman the events which had become part of my life since the war began; I wanted to free myself of the death and suffering I had seen, and she as a woman could provide that freedom and release. They were the same things I would tell my wife if she were there.

"I know a place in the forest," she said as if she read my thoughts, "a meadow where we can take a picnic lunch. If you would like to go?"

"Yes," I answered.

She smiled and slipped into the kitchen and when she returned she was carrying a picnic basket. She handed it to me, then she picked up a blanket from a couch and led me out of the chalet and into the forest. The others were also wandering into the forest to enjoy the bright, sunny day.

"There are beautiful meadows just below the chalet," Else said. "Come, I know one that will be dry from last night's rain. It is a beautiful spot."

I followed her and she led me down towards the meadows I had seen earlier that morning. We came to a sunlit meadow where she spread the blanket. We were alone. The others had found their own quiet places in the forest. The only visible sign of life was the sprawling chalet at the top of the promontory. When I looked up I thought I could see the Fuhrer and his woman on the terrace, but it was too far for me to be sure.

"Come, sit down," Else beckoned. She opened the wine and we sipped. She uncovered the basket and there were delicious cold cuts of cheese and liverwurst, a loaf of bread, and winter apples which I hadn't tasted since the war began. We ate and laughed. The wine grew warm as the day grew warm, but we didn't care. We were happy. Else teased me and hand-fed me small pieces of cheese and apples.

When I could eat no more I stretched on my back and enjoyed the sun. "Come," Else coaxed me, "you said you were hungry. Now eat." She held a thin slice of apple in her lips and leaned over me and placed it to my mouth. I took it, nibbled at it, our lips brushed, then I pulled her down and kissed her. She responded, covering my mouth with her warm lips. At that moment I needed her more than I needed anything. "The sun is warm," she said. In the bright sunlight her white body was flushed. For a moment I could only look at her, and admire her beauty. Then she smiled and reached out to touch me, and I pulled her close.

She laughed softly when I lay quietly by her side. "Why are you in such a hurry?" she asked in her teasing way.

"Because I was afraid you would vanish . . . I was afraid that this is a dream which will fade," I answered. "And because I haven't been with a woman in over a year. My wife—"

"I know," she said as she caressed me. She ran her hand up and down my naked body, letting her fingers wander softly and aimlessly, needing no words to arouse me again. Then she laughed as I kissed her and ran my fingers through her long, silky hair. She held my face in her hands and looked up at me with her bright blue eyes.

"You are a tender lover," she said and smiled.

"And you are a beautiful woman," I answered, but the thought came that it was my wife I had yearned for this past year, and it was she I seemed to hold when I made love to Else.

Maybe she saw or sensed my mood in my eyes because she said softly, "Let today and tomorrow be ours. Let them be special to us." She kissed me and I returned her kisses. Yes, I thought, let these two days be ours. We dissolved into each other, like innocent children exploring the beauty of our warm bodies, pausing to sip wine and nibble the fresh cheese and apples. We came together again and again in the warm, spring sunlight.

In the late afternoon when we lay quietly, side by side, enjoying the sun, the reality of the war came back to me. Even on this island of quiet and peace, I thought I could feel a quake in the earth as I sensed the rumble of heavy artillery far in the distance.

"Tell me about your wife," she said to draw me out of my silence, and I told her about my wife and young daughter.

When the sun began to set and the afternoon grew cool we walked back to the chalet. At dinner I spoke briefly to Frank. He seemed very happy. He said that he and his woman had also spent the day in the forest. There was only one ominous note at the end of the day. The Fuhrer dined with us, but he sat at the far end of the table. He didn't speak to us as he had the night before. There was a distracted look in his eyes, a frown on his forehead. From time to time he would look up at us and shake his head. His woman, who was dressed in a striking gown, touched his arm and when he looked at her he smiled briefly, then the frown crossed his face again.

The next day Else and I didn't stay for breakfast. With basket and blanket in hand we headed early in the morning for our meadow. We had been blessed by another warm day and we were happy. We ate and sunned and made love. At one point during the day I asked her who the woman with the Fuhrer was, and she simply replied that it was the Fuhrer's woman.

"What does she do?" I asked.

"Her job is to please the Fuhrer," Else answered.

I asked her if she had noticed the Fuhrer's countenance the night before at dinner, but she said that was something not to be talked about. When I pressed her for the reason she said it was because it was rumored that the Fuhrer could not make love to women like other men, and that is what caused his distress.

It was then that I looked up at the chalet and knew it was he on the terrace. I remembered the telescope and the view of the meadows from the terrace. I took the blanket and pulled it over Else, and when she asked why, I said it was because I felt a chill in the air. The rest of the day my thoughts were troubled. I wondered again why we had been invited to the Fuhrer's hideaway, and I could not help but look up at the chalet from time to time and see the small, nervous figure of the Fuhrer pacing back and forth on the terrace.

Later in the afternoon a wind came up and we were forced to return sooner than we wanted. Rain clouds darkened the rooms of the chalet and a strange silence permeated everything. Else disappeared, and when I went to dinner neither she nor the other women appeared. I asked why they had not joined us, and Fat Lips said, "It has to do with the Fuhrer's health."

"We won't see them until we leave in the morning," the Colonel added. We ate in silence, enveloped in a sullen silence which even the French wine could not dispel. I had looked forward to my last night with Else. I had ordered wine and flowers for my room, and I had planned to give her a gift, one of my medals which she had admired. It was a decoration for valor, and I wanted her to have it.

The others drifted into the game room, and I could hear the sound of billiard balls as they struck each other. I remained at the table, trying to understand the disquietude which kept nagging me. I missed Else. I knew that, but there was that other thing: the Fuhrer on the terrace, the telescope, and now the women had disappeared. We had all heard rumors about the Fuhrer's strange sexual needs, but those of us who were loyal to him discounted them. Great men have their detractors, we had told ourselves, and after enjoying the pleasant stay for two days I was convinced the stories were lies.

I got up and wandered aimlessly towards my room. I didn't want to be with the others. Perhaps it is just as well the women are occupied with something else, I thought to myself, perhaps I needed the time to be alone. I wanted to write my wife, I wanted to tell her about the Fuhrer's haven and to tell her that the Fuhrer was a good man and now I was sure that with time we would be victorious over our enemies.

As my apartment lay in the same direction as the Fuhrer's, the two guards at the door saluted and let me pass. But instead of turning toward my room I turned toward the exit I had used my first morning at the chalet. A walk would do me good, I thought, and clear away the uneasy feelings which crowded my mind. It wasn't until I was in front of his door that I remembered the hallway would take me past the Fuhrer's room. The door to the room was ajar. I started to walk by quickly, but the sounds of the women made me stop. At first I thought they were having a party. They were whispering and laughing lightly, and I heard the clinking of glasses. I turned and looked at the mirror on the wall, and what I saw made me gasp. I felt the evening meal and wine sour in my stomach and a bitter taste fill my mouth as the image in the mirror swirled before me. He was there, on the bed, and they seemed to dance around him, naked, whispering, teasing. . . .

I shook my head and stepped back, not wanting to believe what I was seeing in the mirror. I suddenly knew why we were here. Stunned and angry I turned away, and as I turned I came face to face with the Fuhrer's mistress and Else. Both were dressed in sheer gowns. Else looked beautiful. Her long, blonde hair fell like silk over her naked shoulders. Her cheeks were red with rouge and her lips bright with lipstick. The sweet fragrance of perfume filled the dimly lighted hallway.

"What are you doing here?" the Fuhrer's woman asked sharply. She tightened her grip on Else's arm.

"I was on my way outside," I answered and looked at Else. I knew where she was going, I knew what she was going to do, and yet there was no shame in her eyes. She looked at me as if she didn't recognize me.

"The girl!" I heard the Fuhrer call. "Bring the girl!"

"On your way," the Fuhrer's mistress snapped as she led Else past me and into the Fuhrer's room. The door closed sharply in front of me.

I felt my legs tremble as I leaned against the wall for support. I felt a nausea in my stomach, the same sick feeling I had felt when I killed my first enemy. I wanted to reach out and pull her out of the room, to protest in some way, but there was nothing I could do. He was the Fuhrer; his word was law. He had brought the war, and he had brought us to his hideaway. Now I knew why.

I don't remember what I did the rest of that night; I know I walked in the trails of the forest. In the dark I felt better. I didn't want to be seen. I walked and wished there were some way to forget the scene in the Fuhrer's room, forget Else's love, the way she looked as she stood next to the Fuhrer's mistress, and I wished I could spit away the bitter taste which kept rising into my mouth. It helped if I concentrated on the war, if I thought about my responsibilities in the field. It helped if I went over the logistics of the war and of my job until I was thinking only of the minutest details which had to do with moving men and supplies and reading charts and plotting movements of troops.

I walked until early morning, then I went to my room, showered and shaved and put on my dress uniform. When I looked in the mirror I had to turn away, and I knew then it would always be difficult for me to see reflections without remembering the scene of the night before. I walked briskly to breakfast, because I was now in a hurry to leave the place. My fellow officers were there, all in dress uniforms, gathered around the table along with the women and the Fuhrer and his mistress. The Fuhrer looked in good spirits; he was talking and joking with the men.

"It has been a most pleasant stay," Fat Lips was saying. "I feel rested enough now to fight this war until doomsday!"

"Ach, let us hope we don't have to fight that long," the Fuhrer answered. Everybody laughed.

I looked at Else. She looked drawn and tired. All of the women looked tired. They smiled and laughed and tried to keep up the pretense, but beneath the make-up their faces were hard and bitter.

"For such a leader we will fight forever!" the Colonel said as he stood, and everyone raised his glass and toasted the Fuhrer and his health.

The men ate heartily, the women only played with their food as they listened to the talk of war. From time to time I looked at Else, but when her eyes met mine she looked away.

After breakfast the Fuhrer thanked us again. He hoped our stay had been a pleasant one. He assured us that a turning point in the war was coming. We were a master race which would not be denied its destiny. We would be victorious. We would rule the world. The officers cheered and stood and saluted as he marched out. "Long live the Fuhrer!" they shouted. "Long live the Fatherland!"

Then we boarded the bus for the ride back to the village. The women rode with us. The men were in good spirits, still praising the Fuhrer, but the women were silent. I looked closely at them, trying to decipher what they felt, what they were thinking, but their eyes turned away from me.

The Fuhrer's car was at the railroad station when we arrived. He was standing in the bright sunlight, talking to a man I assumed was the mayor of the village. When we descended from the bus a small orchestra struck up the national anthem. The women moved away from us quickly. There were no partings. They hurried to their families who stood behind the line of troopers which separated us from the villagers. I looked at the villagers, rural broad-shouldered men who stood silent and stiff, awaiting the return of their daughters. They said nothing as the women were met by their mothers or sisters, but in their eyes I saw a gleam of contempt which I had begun to recognize.

"It has been a good stay," the Fuhrer said to the mayor.

"We are pleased, your excellency," the old man bowed. He held his hat in his hands and twisted it nervously.

"Yes, it has been excellent," the Fuhrer said loud enough for the villagers to hear. Then he leaned and whispered as he pointed to Else. Because I was close I heard him whisper, "The girl. Does she have sisters?"

The mayor nodded. "Yes, your excellency. She comes from a big family. She has two younger sisters. See, they are standing by her."

I looked to where Else stood with her family. The two younger girls that stood by her side were very pretty, but they were very young. I turned and saw the Fuhrer smile.

"Ah, yes, beautiful girls," he nodded and rubbed his hands. The mayor bowed his head. "Well, until the next time." The Fuhrer smiled, saluted us, then turned and walked briskly to his car. He and his mistress boarded it and sped away.

I felt a shudder through my body, my knees grew weak. At the same time the conductor called for us to board the train. My fellow officers waved at the women, but they did not respond. A silence had come over the villagers. The faces of the men were cold and set, as if they had been chiseled from the granite of the nearby hills. I looked at Else and she turned to look at me. She did not smile. Frank touched my shoulder. I was holding up the line. Then I remember I opened my clenched fist, and the medal which had cut into my palm dropped to the black, oily gravel at my feet. We boarded the train quickly and it moved away from the small station, returning us to the war which we had left for that bitter interlude.

A House on the Island

For most of the semester Elena Alvarez drove the class relentlessly, and in the remaining days only Nan and Ricardo were prepared for the end. The young poet had frightened the others from the island.

Is this what you want?
Yes.
Me?
Does it matter? Right now we're good for each other. We're far from everyone.
What are you staring at?
The birds. They're watching us. I can see their outlines through the leaves, and with a little sky behind. They see our flesh, imagine if they could think.
You're not concentrating!
Yes, Ricardo, I am.
. . .well?
Well what?
I'm done.
That's okay. Just stay with me a little longer. Stay the way you are.

The leeside of the island was quiet, warming. A breeze filtered over the palms that line the upper edge of the strand and the water inside the reef lay smooth and blue. On the cove's white beach two figures slept deeply.

Elena tapped the lectern with a pencil until they woke. As usual she began the morning class grumpy, without her first taste of coffee. The wall clock showed six minutes after the hour. "Ricardo, could you close the door? There's too much noise in the hallway." Unlike most Spanish classes, Elena's were held just inside the entrance to the Life Sciences Building, far away from Humanities. Hydra and starfish collected dust in open cases under the windows. "Can you open a few windows, too, Ricardo? The air's stale."

Elena wore dark, fisheyed glasses. She removed them and shuffled back and forth across the sand, snapping impatiently at the two flaccid expressions, one in the first row, the other in the third. Her complexion was soap-clear and smooth above the beige wool-knit dress, plain, severe. A small, intense woman, she seldom relaxed her students until well into the hour. Her wide hips fumed, legs spread apart, feet planted, and she scrawled a few words on the board. *Just stay with me a little longer. Stay the way you are.* Finally an image struck Nan and she displayed it timidly

"Since the bird is in free flight, maybe the poet is suggesting he has no will either. Maybe the bird means. . . ."

Ricardo (bored) and Elena (thinking of real birds) listened from habit. "I think I see it now," Nan continued, "The poet wants to be free."

Elena sighed and after a long pause suggested they forget the poem and explore her island. "This part of the island is deserted. My father and I were the only ones who used to come here. There's nobody for miles around. It might be fun to take a look."

Ricardo threw his books down but Nan wanted to know where they were going. "To my house," Elena replied. Nan begged Ricardo to stay.

"It's no risk."

"Don't leave me then."

He kissed her lightly on the lips. "Come on, let's break the routine."

Nan shrugged. She hadn't stuck it out this long only to be dropped before the semester's end. Mrs. Alvarez had something special in mind. "Wait a minute," and Nan hurriedly applied shadow to her eyes, brushed her hair and cleaned her front teeth with tissue paper. As she rose the chair toppled on a sand crab. Next she pulled on her pantie girdle, adjusting the elastic, twisting the sides, tugging at the bottom. Then she slipped on the pantyhose, dropped her skirt hem and meticulously brushed off the grains of moist sand.

"Hurry up," Ricardo shouted. Elena had kicked off her shoes and was skipping into the shade. Nan perspired easily and quickly dabbed her armpits with talcum. "Hurry, goddamit!" Nevertheless she was genuinely embarrassed at winning a Lancaster, California, beauty title (Rotary Club entry). "Come on! Leave your books. Nobody's going to take them." Her folks came every other Saturday. "Hey, girl, you coming?" She stumbled after him onto firm ground.

"Wait up, Ricardo."

"Grab my hand."

Nan daintily hopped over a fallen palm frond. "She's crazy, you know. Why didn't she just take us over to the cafeteria for coffee? What do you bet we get lost?"

"She knows her way."

"The hell she does. She's already stuck."

Elena had tripped on a coconut, but was up and skipping before they could reach her. "Don't be afraid, you two," she called back. "Just stay close behind. And bring the coconut. We'll have some later on."

Elena was glad the path still existed, though covered now with tree roots and grass. But she worried that it was unused. I always came this way. My father would bring me on Vicente, our one-eyed burro. Poor Vicente. A scorpion got the eye when my brother José, the retarded one, left Vicente alone in the forest. How do you punish a dumb child, father said, and I answered, if it wasn't Vicente's eye, it might have been José's. And he shrugged as if to say José could afford to lose an eye.

Elena spoke as the three rested on a tree trunk. Termites had gutted the core. Nan was busy slapping the insects on her legs, annoyed at the heat, her sweat and Elena's digressions.

After that, Vicente was always falling into traps. He'd knock you over if you stood too close on his blind side. He was next to worthless, so my father gave him to me.

"Did we have to go this way? "Nan said. "It looked much better along the coast. Maybe we'd find a clearing. We might get lost here and I have to make a nine o'clock seminar."

Ricardo remembered their first date. They had gone to a movie before finals, and Nan was tense. He was late in calling for her and they arrived at the theater ten minutes after the film had begun. "I don't want to see it," she said.

"Why not?"

"We'll miss the beginning. Then we'll have to sit through the intermission to catch the first part."

"So let's skip the beginning. We can figure it out."

Ricardo lied that he had read all about the film and would explain the beginning inside.

"Well, what's happened?" she whispered as they sat back.

"I don't know. I lied."

"Lied?" She searched him. "But why?"

"Nobody's going to test you. There's no quiz, Nan."

Silence.

Eventually Elena faced her. "If you want to go another way, go on. There used to be an old man who lived above the rocks at the south end of the beach. He had two sons, fishermen, who were always looking for mischief when the wind was down. There's hardly any wind today. Be careful if you go that way."

"Will you go with me, Ricardo?"

"I'm a coward."

Elena smiled and moved away. The three began pushing through thicker brush, once losing the path, backtracking and starting over again. The low cover thinned out, the trees grew taller and the sunlight barely poked through the dense roof of leaves. The air fumed darker, cooler. Elena led them in silence. The house was at the top of a hill at the end of the valley. This forest was the coolest, most hidden part of the valley. Many islanders were conceived in the forest. (She laughed to herself.) Father had loved nearly all the young women on the island and probably half of them were brought here.

They stopped briefly to drink water from a stream. In her eagerness Nan forgot bacteria, parasites and diarrhea. She drank handfuls in gulps "It's safe," Elena said bluntly. "The excrement always went down the other side of the hill."

Slowly they climbed out of the forest and onto a sloping trail that rose gradually into a lower growth of bushes and more wooded, stiffer branches. The ground became drier. Behind them the steep-sided valley flattened in the distance, stopping sharply at the sea's edge.

Caught in the moment, Ricardo had long ago stopped whistling. He was climbing El Sereno's hills above the old freeway, a polo-shirted kid with a stick for beating tarantulas. At the top he would see the ocean. Nan was hiking barefoot, her soles punished by rocks and an occasional thorn. Her clothes choked her, cut into her waist and thighs. Heat resumed. Sunlight burned into every pore. Exhausted she began to panic. They had left the coolness below. Elena seemed to ignore the change, while Ricardo, his nicotined lungs heaving at every step, doggedly followed his instructor, determined not to lose her.

Nan shouted for them to stop. Delirious, she waved her arms about wildly, screaming that she wanted to go back. Men in the forest. Scorpions, rapists. Her first attack of the runs. Come back! Where are you going? She cried in great sobs for a long while, begging Ricardo to help her. Suddenly she grew quiet. She had to know the time. Yet her watch was on the beach in her handbag. A monstrous fear shook her body. A trap, she thought, and limped after them.

The trail had dipped and Ricardo urged his flagging muscles into a run. Then he walked for what seemed an hour. The shade came in patches from the few trees that hung over the tall yellow grass. Long ago he lost sight of Elena, but found her wool-knit dress thrown carelessly on a dead branch. From far away he thought it was an animal, then a flag. In the crook of his arm he still carried the coconut and around the green shell he wrapped the dress.

Elena saw him stagger into the small clearing. She lay contentedly on a velvety cover of moss under the sway of a large, big-leafed tree.

"I'm over here, Ricardo."

He steered his body toward the tree, stopped and sank heavily to his knees.

"I thought you'd gotten lost," he said.

"I couldn't if I tried."

"Why did you run off like that? Nan's still back there somewhere."

"She'll be along."

"The last I saw of her she looked like she had turned back."

"She won't lose herself. Going back is always easier."

Ricardo had caught his breath but was still too tired to pretend casualness or anything. "But you ran away." He simply stared at Elena's bare body stretched before him. "Why?" Her skin glistened, her long black hair fell loose to one side. "I suppose it doesn't matter now." Suddenly on the green, dark green carpet, Elena's almost diaphanous whiteness moved. Ricardo flushed and turned his head. *Stay the way you are.*

"Don't turn away, Ricardo, I'm resting. It's the best way to cool yourself. Thanks for bringing my dress."

Ricardo fidgeted with his shirt buttons and she helped him remove the shirt and the rest of his clothes. They were quiet as he touched her. At first gentle, respectful. She jerked him to one side, leading him, forcing him closer, driving him quickly with her hands.

No, this is not happening, Nan thought. She lay very close to them, unconscious of her cuts and soreness. She had wandered crazily down the slope and had fallen before entering the clearing. After crawling close, so close she could hear their breathing, she pulled at the moss with her hands and wrenched out great chunks with her fingers. She had not seen them until she had almost touched them.

"Is this what you want?"

"Yes," Elena said.

"You really want me?"

Nan watched Ricardo's back arch as he raised up on his arms.

"Does it matter? Right now we're fine for each other. No one's around. We're far away from all men."

Nan glanced around. Beyond the two bodies more trees and grass. The sky not as blue now. Afternoon blue. Pale, a few clouds. She turned, her fists tightened. Elena constantly moved under his weight.

"What are you staring at?" he said. Elena peered over his shoulder.

"The birds. They're watching us. See their outlines in the sky? They're watching all this moving flesh. Imagine if they could think."

"Hey, concentrate."

"I am, Ricardo, I am."

Nan wept silently. What could she do? What things could she say to that bitch. The story about the house ended here. No house, no goddam house. Never was. What's her excuse? A poem. "Let's go to my house, Nan. No more class, Nan. I'll tell you about my father's island. And the music, the music, Nan. Did you understand it? Have some coconut, it's fresh. More rum? The record's ending. Could you turn it over, Nan? How's your drink, Ricardo? Finished yet?"

"Well," he told her.

"Well what?"

"I'm done. Were you?"

"That's okay."

"It's been a while. . . ."

She heard clearly: "Don't worry. Just stay with me a little longer. Stay the way you are."

Nan crawled away, limp. Elena had sensed her near. Throughout. Ricardo had seen her briefly. Later he left Elena to search for Nan. As it grew dark he followed the stream to its mouth. There Nan waved to him on the beach. Before resuming by the trail she had circled the clearing, castigating herself. She had flung herself at trees and once painfully fell into a spiny thicket.

Ricardo stumbled across the darkened sand and as he drew near she rubbed the chill from her bare arms. Neither would look closely at the other, nor would they touch. Without a word they slumped down in the first and third rows. Bitten, body-sore and sunburned, they closed their books quietly and counted the few minutes till the end of class.

Rolando Hinojosa-Smith

Un poco de todo

En Klail City todavía hay uno de esos parques públicos de una manzana entera con su kiosko en el centro. El parque tiene cuatro entradas y está en frente de la estación de trenes. Los trenes corren de vez en cuando y se llevan los productos agrícolas de la región. Los bolillos (como casi nunca salen de noche) no van al parque a andar o a platicar. La raza, sí, y como el aire es libre, el que no se divierte es porque no quiere.

El parque también sirve pare que los políticos vengan a echar sus discursos y allí, una vez y en otra vida, yo, Rafa Buenrostro y el menor de los Murillo, fuimos a ver qué veíamos y a oír qué oíamos cuando Big Foot Parkinson se presentó como candidato a *sheriff* por Belken County.

En la barbería de los Chagos se decía que Big Foot apenas sabía leer y escribir; que era más pesado que una cerca de nogal; que los Cooke, los Blanchard ricos y los Klail lo controlaban; que la carne de la barbacoa que se daba en las juntas políticas estaba podrida; que no era más bruto porque no era más viejo; que era un caguías; y, así, otras cosas más por el mismo estilo.

Polín Tapia, el pintor, también era coyote en la corte del condado y, de consecuencia, se metía en la política. Con el tiempo se hizo dueño de una Underwood portátil en la cual escribía discursos políticos en español pare los bolillos que entraban a la política. La raza oía a cualquier cabrón leer algo en español y luego luego se ponía a decir que el Míster Tal y Tal hablaba español y que se había criado con la raza, y que conocía a la raza, y que apreciaba a la raza, y etc. etc.

El Big Foot había ocupado a Polín durante esa temporada, poco antes de que hablara en el parque. El Big Foot todavía se dedicaba a hablar solamente durante las barbacoas. Hasta ese tiempo el Polín, como explicaba, no le había escrito los discursos. Era más bien su consejero. Como contaba en la barbería, "Yo le dije que no se le olvidara de mencionar que estaba casado con chicana."

Sí, Polín, pero en la última barbacoa el muy bruto contó ce por be y se emboló todo.

¿A poco tú le escribiste el discurso, Polín?

Les digo que no. Le aconsejé nada más.

Pero que arrojo de pelao, ¿eh?

No. Lo que yo digo: después de Dios, el gringo para inventar cosas.

Eso, chingao.

Bien haya el Big Foot.

Pero qué metidota de pata hizo el domingo pasado.

¿Y qué dirían los bolillos?

Lo de siempre: que no valemos un sorbete.

N'hombre, ¿que qué dirían del Big Foot?

Ah, pos que es muy bruto, ¿qué más van a decir?

El choteo y la plática se siguieron por mucho tiempo hasta que los Chagos anunciaron que iban a cerrar temprano para ir al parque a oír a Big Foot ya que se estrenaba esa misma noche.

Claro, dijo alguien, como Polín le está aconsejando, ahora lo va a hacer bien.

No te creas. El Foot es causa perdida; no tiene remedio.

A ver, muchachos, hay que cerrar. Jehú—ponte a barrer. Así que acabes, apaga las luces y no se te olvide de atrancar la puerta del lado. Ya sabes, pones las llaves en el clavo.

Sí, Jehú, ten cuidado; no se te olvide que tenemos el candidato a *cherife* en Klail.

Eso, chingao.

¡Y qué candidato!

Por fin se cansaron de relajar y cogiendo la escoba me puse a barrer el cuartito y a pensar otra vez en el rancho de don Celso Villalón. Exprimí las toallas, lavé las navajas y sequé las copas del jabón para la rasura. Antes de que acabara llegó Rafa Buenrostro y juntos nos fuimos al parque donde la gente ya se estaba aglomerando.

¿Nos echamos una raspa?

Juega. Mira, allí está el menor. Llámalo.

¡Eit, menor! Vente pá acá. Ándale.

Una de fresa, maistro.

A mí de leche. ¡Córrele, menor!

¿Y cuándo llegaron?

Apenas ahorita. ¿Quieres?

¿Cómo que si quieres? Así no se invita, ¿verdá Rafa?

Bueno, menor, ¿quieres o no quieres?

Sí, venga 1a raspa.

¿Qué color quieres, hijo?

De limón, maistro.

Yo pago.

Maistro, ¿ha visto a don Celso Villalón?

Que yo sepa, no ha llegado.

¿Pá qué lo quieres? ¿A poco te vas de cabrero?

No sé. Eso de coimear con el tío Andrés ta bien y el barrendeo con los Chagos también, pero no sé . . . quiero volver a Relámpago.

No te vayas, Jehú.

Vale más. . . . desde que murió don Víctor no me encuentro bien—un poco desganao, ¿sabes?

. . .

Y tú Rafa, ¿qué piensas?

No sé, Jehú. Ta pelón.

Verdad. . . .

Eh, vénganse ya. . . . Jehú, vi a Mague Farías allá con su amá.

No hagas pedo, menor.

* * *

Las palmeras que rodeaban el parque atajaban las estrellas y el brillo de la luna. Llevábamos tres días de lluvia después de las sequías del verano y se prometía un otoño más fresco de lo natural. La gente se juntaba en grupitos aquí y allí y los chicos correteaban que era un encanto.

Nosotros andábamos pisando los trece o catorce años y esperábamos la entrada al high school como quien entraba en campo enemigo. Los tiempos iban cambiando pero la gente como el tipo de Big Foot seguía en las mismas. . . .

De vez en cuando se ponía alguien de pie y hablaba. La gente oía y aplaudía automáticamente. Después otro y lo mismo. Y así, sucesivamente.

El menor había desparecido para volver con Mague Farías a donde estábamos Rafa y yo. Rafa se hizo a un lado y, como siempre, sin decir nada le tendió la mano a Mague. Rafa me vio y con los ojos me dijo que se iba. Le meneé la cabeza y se quedó. El menor volvió a desaparecer y esta vez se trajo a Fani Olmedo para Rafa. Los veo más tarde, dijo el menor.

Y así, los cuatro, nos pusimos a andar. . . .

Allá por los naranjales, aunque lejos del parque, todavía se podía oír el murmullo de la gente y las voces de los políticos por medio de la bocina eléctrica.

Cuando volvimos por fin le tocaba la hora a Big Foot y nos tocó oír la parte cuando pensaba granjearse con la raza:

. . . Yo casar primera vez con mujer jacana pero ella voy por murio.

(Aplausos)

. . . yo volver casar y yo casar otra vez mujer jacana y ELLA voy por murio.

(Más aplausos)

El Big Foot seguía a la carga:

. . . yo casar tercer vez con mujer jacana y ella tamién voy por murio.

Aquí, siempre, y sin fallar, venía el choteo:

¡Las estarás matando de hambre, animal!

¡Es que no te aguantan, colorao!

¡Te apesta la boca!

La raza comprada y vendida aplaudía y hacía *sh, sh,* para mostrar que ellos, a lo menos, eran educados.

El Big Foot, impasible, seguía con sus hazañas e inventos. . . .

Por fin llegó la hora de irse y me despedí de Mague. Yo todavía andaba algo resentido por la parada que me había hecho la semana pasada: no vino al parque y me anduve solo alrededor del parque hasta cerca de la una.

La decisión de irme al rancho de don Celso Villalón la tomé esa misma noche y así fue que al día siguiente trabajé en que mi tío Andrés y con los Chagos por la última vez.

* * *

A Rafa lo veía en la high y la desgracia del año entrante nos juntó de nuevo cuando su familia se vino a pasar una temporada en el rancho de don Celso: habían matado a don Jesús Buenrostro mientras dormía y su hermano, don Julián, casi se volvió loco de rabia. A las tres semanas dicen que todavía estaba medio loco hasta que vinieron los dos hermanos Vilches que estuvieron hablando con él hasta la madrugada. Al día siguiente, sin avisarle a nadie, don Julián, solo, cruzó el río en busca de los que habían matado a su hermano.

Volvió a poco más de mes y parecía un hombre que estaba en paz con todo el mundo.

A Rafa le tocó estar allí la noche de las cabras, cuando nació Celsito, el nieto de don Celso viejo.

El Big Foot salió como sheriff. No tenía contrincante.

Cara de caballo

Nowhere in the recorded histories of California is there an explanation for why Doña Arcadia Bandini married Abel Stearns. Both were from prominent families, well known and respected in Southern California. But the match of these two people was considered truly a fairy tale.

Don Juan Bandini's daughters were famous for their beauty, and the most beautiful of them all was the eldest, Arcadia Bandini. Don Juan, one of the most powerful and wealthy men of his time, believed he was destined to become a great leader. When the United States took over the northern Mexican territories, Don Juan supported the new government. He believed that California would prosper once the people accepted the new leadership, and he thought his support would one day be rewarded.

A small and dapper man, Don Juan was also highly intelligent and given to sarcasm when matters did not go his way. He possessed one of the largest ranches in Southern California, lands which stretched from the Mexican frontier to the San Bernardino Mountains. At the height of his success, Don Juan was a ranchero whose holdings assured him a position of great respect.

Don Juan was married twice. His first wife was Doña Dolores, a lovely woman of the Estudillo family who bore him five children: three daughters, Arcadia, Isadora, and Josefa, and two sons, José María and Juanito. His second wife, Arcadia's stepmother, was Refugio, also of great beauty, from the Argüello family. Doña Refugio and Don Juan had five children: three sons, Juan de la Cruz, Alfredo and Arturo, and two daughters, Monica and Herma. Arcadia was the oldest of all his children, and Don Juan carried for her a special flame in his heart. She was born at the zenith of his power, and she buried him in 1859 a disillusioned man.

Don Juan was respected as a man of education and of generosity, even during times of personal misfortune. He made two bad investments, the financing of a store in San Diego and a hotel in San Francisco, which forced him to seek loans to cover his family's living expenses. He went to a French gambler, poet and novelist, Leon Hennique, and asked for ten thousand dollars. Hennique gladly gave him the money, but tagged on a four percent monthly interest rate. Don Juan was confident he could repay the loan in a few months with revenue from cattle sales.

But an unforeseen slump in cattle sales forced Bandini to ask Hennique for an extension on the loan. The Frenchman granted the extension but insisted on the deeds to Don Juan's homes as guarantees of payment. As the months passed, more bad luck plagued Don Juan, until he found himself trapped in an economic labyrinth from which he could see no escape. In his panic he made more impulsive decisions, causing his business affairs to decline even further.

During this period of economic crisis, the Bandini family was constantly at odds. Doña Refugio continued to plan one expensive fiesta after another, and Don Juan's sons, acting as if the money in the Bandini coffers had no end, pursued their costly gambling activities. Another kind of friction also appeared. Don Juan's sons had married Mexican women, but three of his daughters had married Anglo American men. Don Juan became convinced that the reason for his bad luck and the disharmony in his family was due to the foreign element, the *gringo* influence that had entrenched itself in his family through his daughters. He was bitter that his daughters had chosen *gringos,* but what hurt most of all was the fact that he had encouraged those unions. He had supported the new government all the way, even delivering his virgin daughters to its men.

Now the Bandinis were on the verge of economic disaster. Charles R. Johnson, who had married the sixteen-year-old Monica, offered to advise his father-in-law. Don Juan resisted, but Johnson was finally able to convince him to sign over a temporary power of attorney. Johnson then sent Don Juan and Doña Refugio to Monterrey on vacation. Arcadia remained alone with the servants on the San Diego estate.

Johnson and his brother-in-law, J.C. Couts, who was married to Isadora, reflected the Anglo attitude towards Mexican men. They considered them incompetent and lazy. But J.C. Couts was, at least, a decent man and he finally convinced Johnson to speak with Abel Stearns about a loan for Don Juan Bandini. Johnson knew Don Juan disliked Stearns because of Stearns's hostility to Mexico and Mexicans. He also knew Don Juan and Stearns had often competed for the best *vaqueros* to work their respective ranchos. Nevertheless, Johnson decided to ignore Don Juan's feelings and he asked Stearns for a loan of four thousand dollars. Johnson described to Stearns the crisis the Bandini family was going through, and he told him that to save Don Juan's land was to save his life. Stearns agreed to inspect the Bandini holdings and consider the loan.

On the morning of April 28, 1851, Isadora and Monica arrived at the Bandini estate in San Diego to inform Arcadia that Abel Stearns was to visit that afternoon. The servants were ordered to prepare a grand feast. The two sisters then lectured Arcadia for not making herself available to men, and they advised her to make herself beautiful for Abel Stearns, who just happened to be one of the richest men in the state. Arcadia listened with half an ear. The two sisters broke off their complaints when Stearns arrived with Johnson and Couts. The three women waited on the porch of the large adobe ranch home. As Stearns approached, he kept his eyes on Arcadia, not even glancing at her sisters when they were introduced. With side-long looks of satisfaction, the two couples left Arcadia and Stearns alone on the porch.

Abel Stearns was born in Mexico in 1799 and came to California in 1829. He was fifty-one years old when he met Arcadia. He was the largest landowner in Southern California, and certainly one of the wealthiest. He was also one of the ugliest men in Southern California. Born a homely man, he was severely wounded in a quarrel over some wine. A deep cut ran through his nose and both lips, giving him a distinct speech impediment. He was called *Cara de caballo*; some people found it difficult to look at his face. This was the man who stood before Arcadia Bandini, a woman so beautiful that he could only gaze at her and whisper *gracias*.

Arcadia stared at Stearns's grotesque face. His disfigurement forced him to breathe heavily and noisily through his deformed mouth. She noticed how large his hands were, his arms ridiculously long. But as she studied his face, she saw a kindness, a promise of a good man behind the physical distortion. Stearns asked her to marry him. He spoke of his wealth and of the things he could do for her family, for her beloved father. He promised to love her forever and to make her the happiest woman in California. Arcadia made her decision. "Abel Stearns, you are the ugliest man I have ever seen. I will marry you and I will be yours to the last moment of your life." Stearn's broken lips formed a smile. He kissed her hand and went off full of excitement to explore the Bandini estate. Arcadia called for her sisters and announced her engagement. "Send for our father and mother. Tell them I am to be married upon their return. Let the people know that Arcadia Bandini will wed Abel Stearns."

And so she did. Two days after the Bandinis returned from Monterrey, their most beautiful daughter was wed to the ugliest man in Southern California. At Arcadia's request, the private ceremony was held in the open plains of the Rancho Alamitos. The newlyweds spent their wedding night in a simple cabin atop a hill on Stearns's Rancho Laguna. The cabin was to become their favorite place, their escape from everyday life.

The years passed and the Stearnses became even more prominent members of Southern California society. To Abel's extreme disappointment, they had no children. Arcadia was relieved, because she did not want to take the chance of passing on her husband's ugly traits to innocent children. To ensure her infertility, she took special baths, ate particular herbs, and drank potions prepared for her by Indians and Mexican women. To compensate for her deliberate lack of fertility, Arcadia made love to her husband as if he were Apollo himself. Abel could hardly believe his good fortune, and he lavished the same affection on his beautiful wife. They made love with such passion and so often that Abel could not understand why they did not conceive a child. There were times when he thought he had committed a grave sin by marrying such a beautiful woman, and that God was punishing him by denying him children. Arcadia's infertility preoccupied him on his business trips, but when he was with her he forgot all their problems and let himself become engulfed by the love of this beautiful woman.

Only once did Arcadia actually tell Abel she loved him. They were in their cabin on the Rancho Laguna, and she began to think about her popularity with so many men and women. She realized it was because she was married to *Cara de caballo*, because whenever she appeared on his arm at fiestas, balls or even on the sidewalks of Los Angeles or San Francisco, her beauty was instantly exaggerated. For all that attention, for the wonderful life he had given her, Arcadia loved him very much. He was seventy years old at that time, and Arcadia was as lovely as when they had married. They made love on the braided rug in front of the fireplace, and their passion was as strong as it was twenty years before.

Abel Stearns died in San Francisco in 1871. He was seventy-two. His body was returned to Arcadia in Southern California. He of course left his entire estate to her, making her the wealthiest woman in California. When she was fifty, Arcadia Bandini de Stearns married a handsome and prosperous young man from Rhode Island, Jonathan Hawthorn Blake. Blake never asked Arcadia her age; to his eyes she was always young and beautiful. The two of them lived contentedly in their homes in Los Angeles and San Diego. They traveled extensively to the Orient and to Europe. At the turn of the century, Arcadia was as beautiful as when she was twenty. Legend has it that she was consulting a *brujo* who prescribed a potion made from ground-up brown insects. She had to drink the potion every day to conserve her beauty and her youth. Legend also has it that one day Arcadia failed to drink her potion, and the next morning her face was transformed into a *cara de caballo*. The few servants who witnessed her transformation lived only long enough to tell the story.

Sheila Ortiz Taylor

Selections from *Imaginary Parents: A Memoir*

Pocadillas

It is Easter morning and I wake up in my Aunt Thelma's bed. The yellow bead board ceiling is awash with light. I have slept profoundly, through the cry of the rooster and the clucking of his consorts. I am safe in my grandmother's house. The house of my mother's mother: Mymama, Della Caroline Ortiz. Mymama.

Aunt Thelma is not in the bed. I follow the smell of coffee into my grandmother's kitchen. Mymama stands at the counter patting out giant flour tortillas. Aunt Thelma is on her third cigarette and her fourth cup of coffee. "Ia, Ia, Ia!" she exclaims, draws me toward her fragrant pajamas and pats my bottom. She and my uncle Earl have no children, live with Mymama and Mypapa, helping with the yard and the chickens and the housekeeping in this tiny frame house near the Los Angeles River.

"You're blowing smoke in that child's face," says Mymama, flipping a tortilla over on the grill with her fingers.

"Ia, Ia, Ia," says my Aunt Thelma again, inhaling thoughtfully, preparing to tell me again the story of my naming. "When you were a little girl and I would say to you, 'What is your name?' you'd say 'Ia, Ia, Ia.'"

"Sheila was too hard," I say.

Mymama nods, hands me a warm tortilla. "This child needs some breakfast."

"Just tortillas," I say, sitting at the long white table on the bench next to my aunt, the table Mypapa built so his thirteen children could all eat at once.

Mymama sets a thick plate before me, with tortillas rolled inside a cloth napkin. Then she takes the butter out of the icebox and puts it before me, hands me a table knife with a red handle. "For you," she says. "I always make these flour tortillas especially for you." I reach up, hugging my way into her warmth and plumpness. My cheek crushes against her cool brooch, the one with the dark purple palm tree on the island, an enclosed but exotic world where I live in the moments when she holds me.

There is a scraping sound from the back porch, then the slam of the screen door.

"Ovaldo," says Mymama, releasing me and wiping her hands on a dishtowel.

He appears in the doorway, her brother, her male double. Both short, brown, low centers of gravity, curly gray hair attempting escape, a certain seriousness, a certain weight, a certain amused light now and then escaping from dark eyes, the eyes of their mother, Teresa Cabares from Morelia, the city of beautiful women.

"Traigo el maíz," he says. Under his left arm he carries a rough bundle of corn wrapped in funny papers, and in his right hand he carries a bouquet of irises wrapped in waxed paper and secured at the stems with a red rubber band.

"Well, how are you, Uncle O.V.?" says my Aunt Thelma without the slightest expectation of a reply. My mother says he is deaf as a doorpost. My father says he doesn't speak English. Mymama has told me he lives in his own world.

His own world is two streets over. He lives there with his daughter Sonna and her husband, two boys, and fifteen cats. In the front yard are decaying cars—doors fallen off, windows out, rumble seats swollen and split—that Sonna has planted with geraniums that cascade out windows and doors and into the yard. Flowers everywhere.

My uncle nods at Thelma as she takes the twin bouquets from his arms, then turns to go. Mymama follows him out, murmuring in Spanish.

At the sink, my aunt rips off the corn husks, rinses corn and husks under the tap. Later my mother will come, and Aunt Maggie and Aunt Frances and Aunt Julie, and they will stand in a line making Easter tamales and laughing and telling stories. My Aunt Thelma whistles as she works, deep and loud like my mother. She is in her own world. I move off to the living room to study Mymama's pocadillas.

Mymama's pocadillas are arranged along three long glass shelves. They are tiny and require frequent dusting. Mostly they are things people have brought her: pincushions and tiny teapots that are really salt and pepper shakers; a ceramic seal balancing a ball on his nose. My mother says they all have a story. I touch the glass dog, the one my Uncle David gave her when he was seven years old and had not yet blown off the two fingers on his left hand with a dynamite cap. I touch the glass dog and hear the marimba band that was playing on Olvera Street when the old glassblower put his lips to the pipe.

Next to this is a chartreuse ceramic ashtray my sister made in first grade by tracing around an ivy leaf and pressing its intricate veins into wet clay. I turn it over to see her initials: ST. An elephant tusk comes next. It is carved in the shape of a snake and has secret drawers lined in green felt that we are not supposed to open. I ease one out to see the tiny game pieces and hear the Chinese music, then slide it closed. A German medal lies next to the tusk. Uncle Arthur captured it and sent it home with a silk pillow that says Guam. I trace the map, hear rifle fire.

Next come three tiny bottles of perfume from Mexico. My great-grandfather Miguel brought these to my great-grandmother, the corn goddess Teresa, when he took his first business trip to Mexico City after their marriage. It is said my great-grandmother was still a child, and that when he asked her what she would like him to bring her, she asked for a doll. I bring the golden bottle up close to my eye; it is half full, sealed tight.

I stop, the bottle warm in my hand. I hear voices. Beyond the front porch I see Mymama and her brother talking together, their heads close. Between them and me, hanging in the front window, are a blue cloth panel embroidered with seven gold service stars and a blue cardboard sign asking for ten pounds of ice.

Convoy

My mother is sitting on the couch examining a dust mop. Across from her sits the Fuller Brush Man. I sit on the Corn Goddess rug between them, playing with a vegetable brush. The Fuller Brush Man's black case is open on the floor. He holds shiny books on his knees. My mother keeps adjusting the neck of her house-dress, which inclines to fall open just below the lace of her slip. The Fuller Brush Man, with his twice-a-year visits, always surprises her. She is often not quite dressed. She must throw a housedress on, appear, as she puts it, "without her face."

But this purchasing of brushes is serious. It requires black cases, shiny books, forms that must be checked off, signed, torn along perforations. These are supplies that must be had. Like the sailors in newsreels, we need things that must be brought to us, against great odds. Like them, we are at sea.

My mother does not drive. My father says it is not necessary. Twice a week my mother pulls me in the Radio Flyer to the Mixville Market. Otherwise, supplies are brought in. On Mondays and Wednesdays the Helms Bakery Man comes in his yellow and blue truck. We climb inside while he pulls out large, fragrant drawers of baked goods. He lifts cookies, coffee cakes, cupcakes, brownies in squares of waxed paper, and places everything carefully in white bags. He keeps his change in a machine on his belt. He flips the lever with his thumb and dimes fall into his palm. We run into the house with our white parcels, laughing, smelling of bread.

Every other Thursday the Date Man comes. He rocks along the dirt road in his Model A truck, dust clouds streaming behind, scale clanking, isinglass windows winking in the California sunshine. We crowd around, fingering plums, dates, grapes. His scale is a miracle of tin, chain, arrow and dial. My mother lifts a cluster of dates, slides them into the brown bag he holds. His dry neck rises out of a high collar. He must be a hundred years old. Old as raisins.

The Fuller Brush Man is younger. His hair is thick and blond. A thick flax-colored moustache covers his lip. From the presence of brushes he has begun to sprout them. He tells jokes, asks my mother if he can take off his coat. It's that warm.

She opens the French doors. I think of the joke my father tells, the one I don't understand, where he lifts me up in his arms, strokes my blond hair, says to my mother, "Must have been the Fuller Brush Man."

And the Skies Are Not

I am standing before an easel, wearing one of my father's soft and sweet-smelling dress shirts backwards. I dip my fat brush into a can of blue calcimine paint and streak it across the top of my rippling paper.

At last I am in school, Allesandro Street School, the only school in the city named for an Indian. I have waited five years for this day, the day when I would walk to school with my sister along the winding streets, down the steep concrete steps, across the red-car tracks, across this territory that the Mexican government granted my great-grandfather, Miguel Ortiz, for an obscure favor performed long ago, land subsequently lost to the family out of a certain characteristic vagueness about property and ownership.

I breathe in the warm chaos of Mrs. Gordon's kindergarten class. Behind me children build rooms out of giant wood blocks, others sing, others recite their alphabet. I paint, streaking my sky, this picture shaping itself from top to bottom.

"What are you doing?" asks the girl next to me in a tone I have never heard before but will in time become familiar with. "Skies aren't stuck up at the top. They come all the way down to here." She bends over, indicating to me the tops of her ruffled socks.

I stop my work, looking from the girl's socks to the top of my picture.

"Does not," says the girl on my other side. I look over gratefully. She has deep dark eyes, straight black hair. Her eyes say it has cost her something to contradict this girl who knows everything. Her name is Hazel Medina. I fall in love with her then and there. Hazel Medina.

"And skin color," says the first girl. "This is skin color for when you make people." She moves a can of calcimine from her easel to mine. I look into the can. The paint is the color of pale seafood sauce. I decide never to paint people. Oceans, maybe. Or desserts.

"Time for music," calls Mrs. Gordon. "Bring your chairs into a circle, here, around the piano." I stand with my brush poised. Hazel Medina shows me how to set the brushes into jars of water. We take off our fathers' shirts and pull chairs up near the piano. Then the first girl pulls her chair up on my other side. She is wearing a new plaid school dress that has a little white apron attached. She smooths it carefully. A large white bow holds her hair in place. The teacher keeps calling her Eleanor dear.

We are halfway through "Little Wind Blow on the Hilltop" when my vaccination starts itching. I look up high on my left arm where a scab has formed. Now that I have looked at it, thinking of anything else becomes impossible.

It looks like a dormant volcano: black, ashen, and very very dangerous. Eleanor dear looks also. She gives a little shudder of disgust, turns back, straightens the little white apron. Red Buster Brown sandals form a grid over her ruffled socks. I examine these socks once more to see if blue sky comes all the way down. Then I check Eleanor dear's arm for a vaccination. Nothing. Then I look out the window.

When we finish "Little Wind Blow on the Hilltop," Mrs. Gordon tells us we have a treat because Eleanor Manning plays the violin. She gestures with her hand and says Eleanor dear as if it were an invitation. Eleanor Manning gets up, smooths her white apron, and accepts an enormous violin case from Mrs. Gordon. This violin case looks like my Uncle Jake's coffin, even to the pale blue velvet inside. I see my Aunt Thelma reaching inside to pick up Uncle Jake's pale, slender hand to pat it in consolation. Eleanor Manning reaches inside and extracts a gleaming violin and a tiny velvet pillow. She puts the tiny pillow under her chin and nestles the violin on top of it. Eleanor Manning draws her bow across the violin and adjusts the tuning. I feel a tiny pain in a back tooth each time Eleanor Manning moves the bow.

The itching in my vaccination becomes more intense. I look over at Hazel Medina, who is staring out the window thinking of home. I glance around the room for evidence this violin playing has set off an itching in everybody's vaccinations. Nobody could come to school without these vaccinations, my mother has said, and yet no one else seems to be driven half-crazy like me.

Eleanor Manning plays "Twinkle, Twinkle, Little Star" through twice, then puts away her violin and then the tiny pillow and hands the case back to Mrs. Gordon. She returns to the chair next to mine, arranges her white apron. Mrs. Gordon says, "Thank you, Eleanor. Wasn't that just wonderful, people?"

At last I scratch this left arm of mine, defying my father's express command: I might scar myself for life if I scratch. Nevertheless, I scratch. Relief and well-being suffuse me. When Mrs. Gordon passes around the triangles, sandpaper blocks, maracas, and tambourines, I reach happily for a beautiful polished block with a padded drum stick. I touch the block softly with the stick in my left hand and send out into the air a melodious tree sound; this is the meaning of the word forest. I glance sideways at Eleanor Manning, violinist. Then I see it: right in the middle of Eleanor Manning's immaculately aproned lap, the guilty cinder of my vaccination. I stop breathing.

The others are all singing "Home, Home on the Range" and hitting wood blocks and triangles. Eleanor Manning sings, her head slightly tilted back, her eyes half closed. I close my own, and join my voice with hers and with Hazel Medina's. We sing through to the end, joy and confusion bubbling inside me, until Mrs. Gordon collects the rhythm instruments and tells us the first day of school is over.

We jump up, run outside. My mother stands in the schoolyard waiting under a eucalyptus tree, the bright California sky floating over her head like a blue banner.

Birthday

I breathe in the fragrant burning wax from Karen Halverson's birthday candles. Her father holds a lighter over the seventh candle. We all bend toward the flickering candles to study the art of Karen Halverson's birthday cake. This is no ordinary cake. This one is store-bought. Even Becky's mother, who records birthdays with an eight-millimeter camera, makes her own cakes and usually her own ice cream. In Becky's front lawn is a permanent circle of brown where we take turns cranking the handle on the ice-cream mixer. Karen Halverson's birthday party suggests a world beyond family and neighborhood.

I gaze into the cake, a sheet cake decorated to look like the swimming pool the Halversons will build next summer. Pink children swim in blue-green frosting. We lift our voices in song. Mrs. Halverson fires off little bulbs from her camera. I am happy, at my first real birthday party. I have come here without my big sister. I stand singing between Hazel Medina and Terry Taylor, my mouth tasting of burning candles and crepe paper. Karen Halverson blows at the candles. Terry Taylor squeezes my hand.

Terry Taylor is pale and blond and thin. My mother likes him because he has been raised by his grandmother. Terry Taylor looks a little bit like my white mouse at home in its wood cage smelling of damp fur and shredded newspaper, though Terry Taylor is always clean and ironed because of his grandmother. I have decided to marry Terry Taylor eventually so that I won't have to change my name. But it is Hazel Medina, with her dark, dark eyes smoldering like extinguished candles, Hazel I love. Oh, Hazel. I squeeze her hand as Mrs. Halverson plunges the ice-cream scoop into half a gallon of Ralph's grocery-store vanilla. Karen holds a big kitchen knife by herself. She runs the knife the length of the cake. The pink skin of the swimmers streaks and reddens in the water, runs as if sharks have attacked. I look into Karen's face, but she is thinking of presents.

We sit down at the long table. The fragrant crepe-paper tablecloth blossoms around me, fills my lap. I press it back, take a pink paper plate from Mrs. Halverson. Cake and ice cream. Neither one smelling like any birthday before this one. I pick up my fork. Terry Taylor pushes his plate back against his cup of nuts and candy and his popper. He might throw up. Hazel has a smear of frosting below her nose like a little pink moustache. The ice cream tastes faintly of machines. I lick my lip, look sideways at Hazel. We laugh. Mrs. Halverson brings Terry Taylor a glass of water. Then it is time to open presents.

Karen gets two plastic purses just alike. When she picks up my present, she says, "Oh, a book," without even opening it. I suddenly feel tired. I am only two blocks from Mymama's house, but it feels like two thousand miles. Terry Taylor is lying back in the wrapping paper, his face like white tissue paper. Hazel Medina brought a card but no present.

We play Pin the Tail on the Donkey. Mrs. Halverson takes a picture of the birthday girl pinning a tail on the startled cat and then we all get to go outside.

We stand a little stunned near the front door, on a grassy hill that slopes down toward a white picket fence and the sidewalk beyond. Then Louis Wheeler sets off his popper and the girls all scream but keep their places in the circle. In the moment when we are all waiting for the next thing to happen, a breeze moves through the stillness and suddenly my Uncle Ovaldo comes into view.

He is moving slowly along Karen Halverson's white picket fence. His old brown hat is pulled down low over his deep eyes. Gray hair kinks out on either side. He looks small down there. His house slippers make a whispering sound on the sidewalk. He is moving methodically, like a duck in a shooting gallery. He looks like he will whirl around and go back to his little house where geraniums bloom out of old cars in the front yard, back where he came from, when he reaches the end of Karen Halverson's fence.

"That's my Uncle Ovaldo," I say.

To my astonishment, they laugh.

"No, really," I say.

They laugh again. Not Terry Taylor and Hazel Medina. But Karen Halverson laughs. And Louis Wheeler. And Joyce Alsauce. And Eleanor Manning.

And when they laugh this second time, I find—after the ice cream and the cake and the singing and the pictures and the games—that suddenly and without warning I am a crazed dog hurtling down the hill toward this dark, deaf man, panting, pleading, "Uncle O.V. Ovaldo, mi tío."

At the end of the fence he does not turn, but keeps on, and keeps on, his house slippers saying shush, shush, shush.

Estela Portillo Trambley

La Jonfontayn

Alicia was forty-two and worked hard at keeping her weight down. Not hard enough really and this was very frustrating for her—never to quite succeed. She wanted to be pencil-thin like a movie star. She would leaf through movie magazines, imagining herself in the place of the immaculately made-up beauties that stared back at her. But in essence she was a realist and was very much aware of the inevitable body changes as years passed. She often studied her face and body in the mirror, not without fears. The fantasy of glamour and beauty was getting harder and harder to maintain. Getting old was no easy task. Why didn't someone invent some magic pill? . . .

Sitting naked, defenseless, in a bathtub brimming with pink bubbles, she slid down into the water to make the usual check. She felt for flabbiness along the thighs, her underarms for the suspicious cottage cheese called tired, loose fat. Suddenly she felt the sting of soap in her eye. Carefully she cupped water in her hand to rinse it out. Damn it! Part of her eyelashes were floating in the water. It would take close to an hour to paste new ones on again. Probably Delia's fault. Her girl was getting sloppy. Mamie was a new face at the beauty parlor, anxious to please the regular customers. Maybe she would ask for Mamie next time. No dollar tip for Delia after this. The soapy warmth of her body was almost mesmerizing. In her bubbly pink realm Alicia was immortal, a nymph, sweet-smelling, seductive, capable of anything.

Heck! She had to get out if she had to paste the damned eyelashes on. She stood up, bubbles dripping merrily off her nice, plump body. She had to hurry to be in time for her blind date. She giggled in mindless joy. A blind date! She could hardly believe that she had agreed to a blind date. Agreed? She smiled with great satisfaction and murmured to herself, "You insisted on nothing else, my girl. You wanted him served on a platter and that's the way you're getting him."

Rico was her yard boy, and at Katita's wedding she had seen Rico's uncle, Buti, from afar. Such a ridiculous name for such a gorgeous hunk of man. From that moment on she had been obsessed with the thought of owning him. It was her way, to possess her men. That way she could stay on top—teach them the art of making her happy. "Oh, I have such a capacity for love!" she told herself. Humming a love song, she stepped out of the bathtub and wrapped a towel around her body gracefully, assuming the pose of a queen. A middle-aged queen, the mirror on the bathroom door told her. There are mirrors and there are mirrors, she gloomily observed. She sucked in her stomach, watching her posture. But the extra pounds were still here and there. Time had taken away the solid firmness of youth and replaced it with extra flesh. She turned away from the mirror, summarizing life under her breath, "Shit!"

The next instant she was smiles again, thinking of the long-waist bra that would smooth out her midriff and give her an extra curve. Then there was the green chiffon on her bed, the type of dress that Loretta Young would wear. She visualized herself in the green chiffon, floating towards Buti with outstretched hand. There would be the inevitable twinkle of admiration in his eye. In her bedroom she glanced at the clock on her dresser. It was late. With rapid, expert movements, she took out creams, lipstick, eye shadow, rouge, brushes from her cosmetic drawer. She wrapped a towel around her head and had just opened the moisture cream when she remembered the eyelashes. Did she really need them? She remembered Lana Turner with her head on Clark Gable's shoulder, her eyelashes sweeping against her cheeks. Max Factor's finest, Alicia was sure of that.

Hell! She rummaged hurriedly around the bottom drawer until she found a plaster container with the words Max Factor emblazoned on the cover. Anything Lana did, she could do better. She took out a bottle of glue, then carefully blotted the excess cream from her eyes and began the operation.

"Hey, slow down!" yelled Rico as Buti made a turn on two wheels.

Rico turned around to check the load on the back of the pick-up. They were returning from Ratón where at the Rangers' Station they had gotten permits to pick piñones in the Capitán mountains. Buti had presented the rangers with a letter from Don Rafael Aviña giving him permission to pick piñón from his private lands. Buti had also signed a contract with the Borderfield Company to deliver the piñones at the railroad yards in Ancho, New Mexico, where the nuts would be shipped along with cedar wood to Salt Lake City. His first profitable business venture since he had arrived in the United States. He had a check from Borderfield in his pocket. He was well on his way to becoming what he always wanted to be— a businessman. From there—a capitalist—why not? Everything was possible in the United States of America. He even had enough piñones left to sell to small tienditas around Valverde, and a special box of the best piñones for his blind date, the richest woman in Valverde. Things were coming up money every which way. He had had qualms about letting Rico talk him into the blind date until Rico started listing all the property owned by Alicia Flores—two blocks of presidios, ten acres of good river land, an office building. That made him ecstatic. Imagine him dating a pretty widow who owned an office building! There was no question about it—he was about to meet the only woman in the world that he would consider marrying. By all means, she could have him. It was about time he settled down.

All that boozing and all those women were getting to be too much for him. What he needed was the love and affection of one good wealthy woman. Yes, ever since he had met Don Rafael things had gone for the better. Only six months before he had even considered going on welfare. Poker winnings had not been enough, and his Antique Shop was not doing very well. He had resorted to odd jobs around Valverde, a new low for Buti. Then, he had met Don Rafael at El Dedo Gordo in Juárez.

At the Fat Finger everybody knew Buti. That's where he did the important things in his life—play poker, start fights, pick up girls, and most important of all—drink until all hours of the morning. It was his home away from home. His feet on native soil and mariachi music floating through his being—that was happiness. One early dawn when only Elote, the bartender, and Buti were left at the Fat Finger—they were killing off a bottle of tequila before starting for home— who stumbles in but this little fat man with a pink head, drunker than a skunk. He fell face down on the floor soon enough. Buti helped him up, dusted him off, and led him to the table where Elote had already passed out.

"You sit right there. I'll get us another bottle." Buti wove his way between tables and made it to the bar. The little man just sat, staring into space until Buti nudged him with a new bottle of tequila.

"Where am I?" the little man asked, clearing his throat.

"In the land of the brave. . . ." Buti responded with some pride.

"Where's that?"

"The Fat Finger, of course."

The friendship was cemented over the bottle of tequila. The little man had been a good ear. Focusing on the pink head, with tears in his eyes, Buti had unloaded all his woes on the little fat man. Buti recounted—he had tried so hard to become a capitalist in the land of plenty to no avail. He tried to look the little fat man in the eye, asking, "Are you a capitalist?"

"Yes," assured the little man with a thick tongue. "I am that."

"See what I mean? Everybody who goes to the United States becomes a capitalist. Now—look at me. Great mind, good body, what's wrong with me?"

"What you need is luck," advised the little man with some wisdom, as he reeled off his chair. Buti helped him up again and shook his head. "That's easier said than done. I know the principles of good business—contacts, capital and a shrewd mind. But where in the hell do I get the contacts and the capital?"

"Me," assured the little fat man without hesitation. "Me, Don Rafael Aviña will help you. I'm a millionaire."

"That's what they all say." Buti eyed him with some suspicion.

"Don't I look like a millionaire?" demanded the little man, starting to hiccup. The spasmodic closure of the glottis caused his eyes to cross. Buti looked at him, still with some suspicion, but decided that he looked eccentric enough to be a millionaire. "Okay, how're you going to help me?"

"First you must help me," said Don Rafael between hiccups, "find my car."

"Where did you park it?"

"I don't know. You see, I have no sense of direction," confessed Don Rafael, leaning heavily on Buti. "It's a green Cadillac."

That did it. A man who owned a Cadillac did not talk from the wrong side of his mouth. "Can you give me a hint?"

Don Rafael had gone to sleep on his shoulder. Now is the time to be resourceful, Buti told himself. How many green Cadillacs can be parked in the radius of six blocks? Don Rafael could not have wandered off farther than that on his short little legs. It would be a cinch, once he sobered up Don Rafael, enough for him to walk on his own speed.

It took six cups of coffee, but Don Rafael was able to hold on to Buti all the way to Mariscal where Buti spotted a lone green Cadillac parked in front of Sylvia's Place, the best whorehouse in Juarez.

"Hey, Don Rafael," Buti had to shake the little man from his stupor. "Is that the car?"

Don Rafael squinted, leaning forward, then back against Buti. "Is it a green Cadillac?"

"A green Cadillac."

"That's my car." Don Rafael began to feel around for the keys. "Can't find my keys." Buti helped him look through all his pockets, but no keys.

"You could have left them in the ignition."

"That would be dumb." Don Rafael kept on searching until Buti pushed him toward the car to look. Sure enough, the keys were in the ignition.

"There are your keys and your car." Buti gestured with a flourish.

"Then, let's go home."

"Your home?" queried Buti.

"Why not? You can be my guest for as long as you like—if you can stand my sister. . . ."

"What's wrong with your sister?"

"Everything—does everything right, prays all the time, and is still a virgin at fifty."

"See what you mean. You could drop me off at my place in Valverde."

They drove off, and it was not until they were crossing the immigration bridge that they heard the police sirens. A police car with a red flashing light cut right across the green Cadillac. In no time, three policemen pulled Buti and Don Rafael roughly out of the car.

"What is the meaning of this?" demanded Don Rafael, sobering up in a hurry.

"You're under arrest," informed a menacing looking policeman.

"What are you talking about?" Buti asked angrily, shaking himself free from another policeman's hold.

"You stole that car," accused the first policeman.

Don Rafael was indignant. "You're crazy. That's my car!"

"That's the mayor's car. He reported it stolen."

"The mayor's car?" Buti was dumbfounded. He would never believe little fat men with pink heads again.

"I have a green Cadillac," sputtered Don Rafael. "I demand to see my lawyers."

"Tomorrow you can call your lawyer. Tonight you go to jail," the third police man informed them with great stoicism. All of Don Rafael's screaming did no good. They wouldn't even look at his credentials. So they spent a night in jail. Buti diplomatically offered Don Rafael his coat when he saw the little man shivering with cold, and even let him pillow his pink head on his shoulder to sleep. Buti had decided there was more than one green Cadillac in the world, and that Don Rafael threw his weight around enough to be rich. Don Rafael snuggled close to Buti and snored all night.

They were allowed to leave the next morning after Don Rafael made a phone call and three lawyers showed up to threaten the government of Mexico with a lawsuit for false arrest. Outside the jail stood Don Rafael's green Cadillac from heaven knows where.

On the way home, Don Rafael gave Buti a written permit to pick piñon on his property for free, thus Buti could count on a clear profit. Don Rafael wrung his hand in goodbye, making him promise he would come up to Ratón to visit him and his sister, which Buti promised to do. Yes, Buti promised himself, he would soon go to Ratón for a social visit to thank Don Rafael for the piñon. He was well on his way to becoming a capitalist. . . .

"Hey, Buti," called out Rico, "you just passed your house."

Buti backed the pick-up next to a two-room shack he had built on the edge of his sister's one acre of land. The two-room house sported a red roof and a huge sign over the door that read "Antiques." After the roof and the sign, he had built himself an inside toilet, of which he was very proud. That had been six years before when he had come from Chihuahua to live with his sister and to make a fortune. He had fallen into the antique business by chance. One day he had found an old Victrola in an empty lot. That was the beginning of a huge collection of outlandish discards—old car horns, Kewpie dolls, wagon wheels, a stuffed moose head, an old church altar. At one time he had lugged home a rusty, huge commercial scale he claimed would be a priceless antique someday. The day he brought home the old, broken merry-go-round that boasted one headless horse painted blue, his sister, Trini, had been driven to distraction. She accused him of turning her place into an eyesore and ordered he get rid of all the junk.

"Junk!" exclaimed Buti with great hurt in his voice, "why all these antiques will be worth thousands in a few years."

Rico had to agree with his mother—the place was an eyesore. After parking the pick-up, Rico reminded Buti about his date with Alicia that night.

"Put on a clean shirt and shave, okay, Buti?"

"Baboso, who you think you're talking to?"

"She's a nice lady, don't blow it," Rico reminded him.

"Sure she is. I'm going to marry her," Buti informed his nephew, who stared at him incredulously.

"She's not the marrying kind, Tío," Rico warned him.

"She's a widow, ain't she? She gave in once."

"That's 'cause she was sixteen," explained Rico.

"How old was he?" Buti inquired.

"Seventy and very rich."

"Smart girl. Never married again, eh? What for?"

"She's had lovers. Two of them."

"Smart girl. What were they like?"

Rico wrinkled his brow trying to remember. "The first one was her gardener. She took him because she claimed he looked like Humphrey Bogart."

"Humf. . . what?"

"Don't you ever watch the late, late show? He was a movie star."

"What happened to him?"

"Humphrey Bogart? He died. . . ."

"No, stupid, the gardener."

"He died too. Fell off the roof fixing the television antenna."

Buti wanted all the facts. "What about the second lover?"

"He had a cleft on his chin like Kirk Douglas," Rico remembered.

"Another movie star? What's this thing with movie stars?"

"That's just the way she is." Rico added reassuringly, "But don't worry, Tío. She says you are the image of Clark Gable."

* * *

After the dog races, Buti took Alicia to Serafín's. It had become their favorite hangout. For one thing, the orchestra at Serafín's specialized in cumbias, and Buti was at his best dancing cumbias. No woman could resist him then. He could tell that Alicia was passionately in love with him by the way she clung to him and batted those ridiculous lashes. As he held the sweet-smelling plump body against him and expertly did a turn on the floor, she hissed in his ear, "Well, are you going to move in?"

"Haven't changed my mind," he informed her in a cool, collected voice.

"Oh, you're infuriating!" She turned away from him, making her way back to the table. He noticed that the sway of her hips was defiant. Tonight could be the night. She plumped down on the table. "I've had it with you, Buti."

"What do you mean?" He tried to look perplexed.

"Stop playing cat and mouse."

"Am I supposed to be the mouse?" His voice was slightly sarcastic. "I've never been a mouse."

"Let's put our cards on the table." Her voice sounded ominous.

"Okay by me."

"Well then, don't give me that jazz about you loving me too much to live with me in sin. Sin, indeed. When I hear about all those girls you run around with . . ."

"Used to run around with," corrected Buti, looking into her eyes seductively. "I only want you. You are the world to me. Oh, how I want to make love to you. It tortures me to think about it. But I must be strong."

"There you go again. Come home with me tonight and you can make love to me all you want to." It was her stubborn voice.

"Don't say those things, my love. I would never sully our love by just jumping into bed with you." Buti was proud of the fake sincerity in his voice. "Our love is sacred. It must be sanctified by marriage."

"Marriage be damned!" Alicia hit her fists on the table. She was really angry now. He could tell. She accused him. "You just want my money."

"You're not the only girl with money. But you are the only woman I could ever love." Buti was beginning to believe it himself.

"You liar! All the girls you've had have been penniless, submissive, ignorant wetbacks from across the river." Her anger was becoming vicious now.

"Wait a minute." Buti was not playing a game anymore. He looked at the woman across the table, knowing that she was a romantic little fool, passionate, sensuous, selfish, stubborn, domineering, and full of fire. That's the kind of woman he would want to spend the rest of his life with. Nevertheless, he took affront. "What am I? I'm penniless not quite, but almost. You could say I'm a wetback from across the river. And you, in your mindless way, want me to submit. Stop throwing stones. We seem to have the same likes!"

She looked at him with her mouth opened. She had sensed the sincerity in his voice. She could tell this was not a game anymore. She knew she had been ambushed, but she would not give in.

"If you love me, and I believe you do, you'll come live with me, or . . ." —there was a finality in her voice—"I simply will not see you again."

"I will not be another scalp on your belt." There was finality in his voice too.

* * *

"Hell!" Alicia slammed the half full can of beer against the porch railing. She hated the smell of honeysuckle, the full moon, and the heavy sense of Spring. She hated everything tonight. And look at her—this was her sixth can of beer—thousands of calories going straight to her waistline. She hated herself most of all. Buti was through with her. He must be, if what Rico had told her was true. He had come over to help her plant some rosebushes and she had casually asked him how

Buti was doing these days. According to Rico, he spent a lot of time up in Ratón, New Mexico, visiting his friend, Don Rafael Aviña, and his unmarried sister.

"Is she rich?" Alicia asked nonchalantly.

"Very rich," Rico answered in innocence, setting up the young rosebushes against the fence.

She didn't ask much more, but knowing Buti, she could put two and two together. He had found himself a greener pasture and a new playmate. He loves me. I know he loves me, but I've lost him forever. She couldn't stand it anymore—the moon, the smell of honeysuckle. She went back into the house and turned on the late, late show on television. She threw a shawl over her shoulders and huddled in a corner of the sofa. She sighed deeply, her breasts heaving under the thin negligee.

She recognized the actress on the screen. It was Joan Fontaine with the usual sweet, feminine smile and delicate gestures. She always looked so vulnerable, so helpless. Clark Gable came on the screen. Oh, no—why him? Even his dimples were like Buti's! Damn it all. She wanted to see the movie. They had had some kind of quarrel and Joan Fontaine had come to Clark to ask forgiveness, to say she was wrong. Joan's soft beautiful eyes seem to say—you can do what you wish with me. You are my master. . . . Alicia began to sniffle, then the tears flowed. Especially when she saw big, strong, powerful Clark become a bowl of jelly. All that feminine submissiveness had won out. Joan Fontaine had won the battle without lifting a finger. Hell, I'm no Joan Fontaine. But Clark was smiling on the screen, and Alicia couldn't stand it any longer. She turned off the set and went out into the night wearing only a negligee, a shawl and slippers. She didn't care who saw her. She was walking—no, running—towards Buti's shack almost a mile away. The princess leaving her castle to go to the stable. It was her movie now, her scenario. She was Joan Fontaine running towards the man she loved, Clark Gable. It mustn't be too late. She would throw herself at his feet—offer him all she had. She suddenly realized the night was perfect for all this!

The lights were on. She knocked at the door, one hand against her breast, her eyes wide, beseeching . . . in the manner of Joan Fontaine.

"What the hell. . . ." Buti stood in the doorway, half a hero sandwich in his hand.

"May I come in?" There was a soft dignity in her voice. Buti took a bite of his sandwich and stared at her somewhat speechless. She walked past him into the room, and when she heard the door close, she turned around dramatically with outstretched arms. "Darling . . ."

"You're drunk . . . ," Buti guessed.

"I only had five beers," she protested hotly, then caught herself. "No, my love, I'm here for a very good reason. . . ." Again, the Fontaine mystique.

Buti took another bite from the sandwich and chewed nervously.

"Don't you understand?" She lifted her chin and smiled sweetly as she had seen Joan Fontaine do it hundreds of times. Buti shook his head unbelievingly. She began to pace the floor gracefully, her voice measured, almost pleading. "I've come to tell you that I was wrong. I want to be forgiven. How could I have doubted you? I'm so ashamed—so ashamed." Words straight from the movie.

Buti finished off the sandwich, then scratched his head. Alicia approached him, her hand posed in the air, gently falling against his cheek. "Do you understand what I'm saying?"

"Hell no. I think you've gone bananas. . . ."

She held back her disappointment with strained courage. "You're not helping much, you know. . . ." Then she bit her lip, thinking that Joan Fontaine would never have made an unkind judgment like that. She looked into his eyes with a faint, sweetly twisted smile, then leaned her head against his shoulder. She was getting to him.

There was worry in his voice. "Are you feeling okay?"

She began to cry in a very unlike-Joan-Fontaine way. "Why can't you be more like him?"

"Like who?"

"Like Clark Gable, you lout!" She almost shouted it, regretfully.

Buti's eyes began to shine. She was beginning to sound like the Alicia he knew and loved. "Why should I be like some dumb old movie star?"

"Don't you see? . . ." she held her breath out of desperation. "It's life. . . ."

"The late, late show?" He finally caught on—the dame on television.

"You were watching it too!" She accused him, not without surprise.

"Had nothing else to do. They're stupid, you know. . . ."

"What!" Her dark eyes blazed with anger.

"Those old gushy movies . . ." He gestured their uselessness.

"That proves to me what a brute you are, you insensitive animal!" She kicked his shin.

"Well, the woman, she was kind of nice. . . ."

"Joan Fontaine . . ."

"Jonfontayn?"

"That's her name. You're not going to marry her, are you?" There was real concern in her voice.

"Jonfontayn?" He could not keep up with her madness.

"No—that woman up in Ratón."

"Berta Aviña?" The whole scene came into focus. Buti sighed in relief.

"Rico told me she is very rich."

"Very rich."

"Is she slender and frail and soft-spoken like? . . ."

"Jonfontayn?" Buti silently congratulated himself on his subtle play.

"Yes. . . ."

Buti thought of Berta Aviña, the square skinny body, the tightlipped smile. He lied. "Oh, yes. Berta is the spitting image of Jonfontayn."

"I knew it. I knew it. . . ." Alicia threw herself into his arms. "Please please, marry me. Oh, I love you so, you beast!"

"Not tonight, baby. We have better things to do. . . ." He pulled her roughly against him, first giving her a Clark Gable smile, then he kissed her for a long, long time. Still relying on his dimples, he picked her up, not without effort, and headed for the bed. She tried to push him away protesting, "Oh, we can't . . . we mustn't . . . not before we're married."

He stopped in his tracks, not believing his ears. "What?"

"Well, that's—that's what she would say. . . ." Alicia smiled meekly, batting the Max Factor lashes.

"Who?"

"Joan Fontaine, silly. . . ."

"Frankly, my dear, I don't give a damn."

He threw her on the bed.

El Pete Fonseca

Apenas llegó y ya se quería ir. Había llegado un domingo por la tarde, a pie. Venía rumbo del pueblito donde comprábamos la comida los sábados y donde no nos hacían mala cara cuando llegábamos todos mugrientos del trabajo por las tardes. Casi estaba oscuro cuando vimos un bulto que venía cruzando la labor. Nosotros habíamos andado jugando entre los árboles y cuando lo vimos casi nos dio miedo, pero luego recordamos que éramos varios y casi no nos entró el miedo. Nos habló cuando se acercó. Quería saber si había trabajo. Le dijimos que sí pero que no. Sí había, pero no había hasta que saliera la hierba. Como había estado muy seco el tiempo no quería salir la hierba y todas las labores estaban bien limpiecitas. El viejo del rancho desde luego estaba contentísimo porque no tenía que pagar por que estuvieran limpias las labores de cebolla. Nuestros papases renegando por que lloviera para que se viniera la hierba y nosotros también teníamos que hacernos los desanimados, pero en realidad nos gustaba levantarnos tarde, y andar por entre los árboles, y por el arroyo matando pájaros con huleras. Por eso le dijimos que sí pero que no. Que sí había trabajo pero que no para el día siguiente.

—Me lleva la chingada.

A nosotros no nos pareció mal que hablara así. Yo creo que vimos como que le quedaban las palabras a su cuerpo y a sus ropas.

—No hay trabajo en ninguna pinche parte. Oigan, me pueden dar un lonchesito. Me lleva la chingada de hambre. Mañana me voy pa' Illinois. Allá sí hay jale.

Se quitó la cachucha de pelotero y vimos que traía el pelo bien peinado con una onda bien hecha. Traía zapatos derechos, un poco sucios pero se notaba que eran de buena clase. Y los pantalones casi eran de pachuco. Decía *chale* cada rato y también *nel y simón* y nosotros por fin decidimos que sí era medio pachuco. Nos fuimos con él hacia nuestro gallinero. Le decíamos así porque en realidad era una casa de guajolotes. El viejo del rancho le había comprado diez casitas de guajolotes a otro viejo que vendía guajolotes y se las había traído para su rancho. Allí vivíamos, estaban bien chicas para dos familias pero estaban bien hechas. No les entraba el agua cuando llovía—eso sí, aunque las lavamos muy bien por dentro, les duró mucho el olor de caca de gallina.

Se llamaba Pete Fonseca y papá conocía muy bien a un amigo de él.

Decía papá que era moy recargue porque siempre andaba diciendo que tenía catorce camisas de gabardina y en realidad así le llamaba la palomilla—el catorce camisas. Hablaron del catorce camisas un rato y luego que fuimos a cenar frijoli-tos con trozos de espem y tortillitas de harina bien calientitas le invitó papá que comiera con nosotros. Se lavó muy bien la cara y las manos y luego se peinó con mucho cuidado, nos pidió brillantina y se volvió a peinar. Le gustó mucho la cena y notamos que mientras estaba mamá cerca no decía palabras de pachuco. Después de cenar habló otro rato y luego se acostó en el zacate, en lo oscuro, donde no le diera la luz de la casa. Al rato se levantó y fue al escusado y luego se volvió a acostar y a quedarse dormido. Antes de dormirnos oí a mamá que le dijo a papá que no le tenía confianza a ese fulano.

—Yo tampoco. Es puro buscón. Hay que tener cuidado con él. A mí me han hablado de él. El catorce camisas se las recarga mucho pero creo que éste fue el que se echó a un mojadito en Colorado y lo desterraron de allá o se le escapó a la chota. Creo que él es. También le entra a la mariguana. Creo que él es. No estoy muy seguro. . . .

El día siguiente amaneció lloviendo y cuando vimos para fuera de la ventana vimos que Pete se había metido a nuestro carro. Estaba sentado pero parecía que estaba dormido porque no se movía para nada. El agua le había despertado y se había tenido que meter al carro. Para las nueve había dejado de llover así que sa-limos y le invitamos a desayunar. Mamá le hizo unos huevos y luego él preguntó que si había alguna casa libre o algún lugar donde meterse. Y que cuándo iba a empezar el trabajo. Y que cuánto se podía ganar allí por día y que cuántos de nosotros trabajábamos. Papá le dijo que todos nosotros trabajábamos, los cinco y que a veces ganábamos hasta setenta dólares al día si acaso trabajábamos unas catorce horas. Después de desayunar se salieron papá y Pete y oímos que le pre-guntó a papá que si había algunas chamaconas en el rancho. Le contestó riéndose que solamente había una dejada. La Chata. Y se fueron hablando por el camino que rodeaba a las casitas y que iba a dar a la pompa de agua.

Le decían la Chata porque cuando muy pequeña le había pegado una enfer-medad como roña en la cara y el hueso de la nariz se le había infectado. Luego se alivió pero la nariz le quedó chiquita. Era muy bonita menos la nariz y todos hablaban mal de ella. Decían que desde muy chica le habían gustado mucho los hombres y el borlote. Cuando tenía apenas quince años dio luz a un niño. Le echa-ban la culpa a uno de sus tíos pero ella nunca descubrió de quién era. Sus papases creo que no se enojaron con ella. Eran muy buenas gentes. Todavía lo son. Después, cada rato se juntaba con diferentes y cada uno le hacía al menos uno. Unos los daba, otros los cuidaban los padres, pero los dos más grandes los traía con ella. Ya trabajaban. Para entonces, para cuando llegó el Pete, tenía dos semanas de dejada. Su último esposo se había ido, ni se enojó con ella, ni nada. Se fue nomás. La Chata vivía en uno de los gallineros más grandes con sus dos hijos. Por eso papá le había dicho a Pete que solamente había una dejada. Hasta nos pareció que le había puesto cuidado pero nos pareció curioso porque la Chata ya tendría sus treinta y cinco años y el Pete pues tendría unos veinte y cinco a los más.

De todos modos sí le había hecho caso a lo que le había dicho papá porque después, cuando andábamos jugando cerca de la pompa, nos preguntó por la Chata. Que dónde vivía, que cuántos años tenía, que si estaba buena. En eso estábamos cuando bajó la Chata a llevar agua y le dijimos que ésa era. Nosotros le saludamos y ella nos saludó, pero notamos que se fijó en el Pete. Le echó el ojo, como dice la gente. Y más cuando éste le preguntó cómo se llamaba.

—Chavela.
—Así se llamaba mi madre.
—Mira, mira.
—A lo macho, y mi abuela también.
—Anda chocante.
—Pero si no me conoces todavía.

Se retiró la Chata de la pompa y ya cuando iba lejesitos, suspiró Pete y dijo en voz alta,

—Mamacita, 'sota linda.

Para que oyera, después nos dijo. Porque según él a las viejas les gustaba que les dijeras así. Desde ese momento notamos que cada vez que estaba cerca de Pete la Chata, aquél le decía siempre en voz alta *mi Chavelona*. Lo decía fuerte para que oyera y yo creo que a la Chata le gustaba que le dijera así porque ya cuando empezó el trabajo siempre cogía surcos cerca de Pete y si el se adelantaba ella también lo hacía. Y luego cuando nos traía agua el viejo, Pete siempre la dejaba tomar agua a ella primero. O le ayudaba a subirse a la troca, o a bajarse. El primer sábado que nos pagaron después de que había llegado Pete, les compró unos paquetes de fritos a los niños de la Chata. Y así empezó.

A mí me gustaba más cuando le cantaba canciones. Pete se había quedado a trabajar, decía él, hasta que se acabara todo. Se metió a vivir con otros dos muchachos en una trailer vieja que estaba por allí. Nosotros íbamos después de la cena a platicar con ellos y nos poníamos a cantar. El se salía de la trailer, se encuadraba hacia la casa de la Chata y le cantaba con todo lo que podía. En la labor también nomás nos acercábamos a ella o ella se acercaba a nosotros y el Pete se soltaba con sus canciones. A veces hasta en inglés *sha bum, sha bum o lemi go, lemi go, lober* y luego en español . . . *Ella quiso quedarse, cuando vio mi tristeza . . . Cuando te hablen de amor y de ilusiones.* A veces hasta le paraba de trabajar y se levantaba del surco, si el viejo no estaba por allí, y movía las manos y todo el cuerpo. La Chata lo veía de reojo, como que le caía mal pero siempre seguía cogiendo surcos cerca de Pete, o encontrándose con él, o emparejándose. Como a las dos semanas se iban los dos juntos a tomar agua a la troca cuando el viejo no la traía y luego se iban por detrás de la troca y luego salía la Chata componiéndose la blusa.

El Pete nos platicaba todo después. Un día nos dijo que si queríamos ver algo que nos escondiéramos detrás de la trailer esa noche y el trataría de meterla a la trailer.

—Ya sabes pa'qué . . . pa' darle pa' los dulces. . . .

Los muchachos que vivían con él y nosotros nos escondimos detrás esa noche y ya después de mucho rato vimos que venía la Chata rumbo a la trailer. El Pete la estaba esperando y apenas se acercó un poco la cogió de la mano y la estiró hacia él. Le metió la mano debajo de la falda y la comenzó a besar. La Chata no decía nada. Luego la rejuntó contra la trailer pero ella se le salió de donde la tenía cogida y le dijo que no cabrón, que no tan pronto. El Pete le estuvo invitando a que se metiera a la trailer pero no quiso y así estuvieron. Que si me quieres, que si te casas conmigo, que que sí, que cuándo, que ahora mismo, que el otro vato. Por fin se fue. Salimos de lo oscuro y nos platicó todo. Luego nos estuvo platicando de otras viejas que se había echado. Hasta gabachas. Se había traído una de Chicago y luego había puesto su negocio en Osten. Allí, según él, hacían línea los cabrones, a cinco dólares el palo. Pero decía que la vieja que sí había querido era la primera con quien se había casado por la buena y por la iglesia, pero se había muerto con el primer niño.

—Que sí lloré por esa vieja, y desde entonces, ni madre. Esta pinche vida . . . ahora con esta Chavelona, ya empiezo a sentir algo por ella . . . es buena gente si vieran. . . .

Y notamos que a veces se ponía a pensar. Luego decía con cierta sinceridad. . . .

—A qué mi Chavelona . . . es muy caliente . . . pero no se deja . . . hasta que me case con ella, dice.

Al tercer día de cuando nos habíamos escondido Pete ya había decidido casarse. Y por eso toda esa semana era todo lo que platicaba. No podía perder nada. Entre él y la Chata y los dos muchachos podrían juntar bastante. También tendría quien le hiciera sus gorditas y el cafesito bien calientito, y quien le lavara la ropa, y, según Pete, cada noche a lo menos un palito. Se ponía a hacer cuentas: a cuatro dólares el palo a lo menos, por siete noches eran veintiocho dólares por semana. Aunque no hubiera trabajo le iba bien. También decía que le caían bien los niños de la Chata. Se podían comprar una ranfla y luego los domingos se podían ir a pasear, al mono, a pescar, al dompe a juntar alambre de cobre para vender. En fin, decía que le convenía casarse con la Chavelona. Y entre más pronto mejor.

Al poco tiempo vino a hablar con papá una noche. Se salieron al camino donde nadie les pudiera oír y estuvieron hablando por un buen rato. Esa noche oímos lo que le decía papá a mamá en lo escuro de la noche.

—Fíjate que éste se quiere casar con la Chata. Se la quería robar pero en qué. Así que mejor se quiere casar bien. Pero fíjate que está enfermo de la sangre así que no quiere ir al pueblo a sacar los papeles. Entonces lo que quiere es que yo le vaya a pedir la mano de la Chata a su papá, Chon. Quiere que vaya mañana mismo. . . . Señor don Chon, vengo aquí, hoy, con la comisión de pedir la mano de su hija, Isabel, para comunión de matrimonio con el joven Pedro Fonseca. . . . ¿Qué tal, eh? . . . ¿Cómo se oye, vieja? . . . Mañana mismo después del trabajo, antes de cenar.

El siguiente día todo lo que se oía era de que iban a pedir a la Chata. Ese día Pete y Chavela ni se hablaron. Anduvo muy quieto todo el día trabajando pero pesado el Pete, como para mostrar que era hombre serio. Ni nos dijo chistes como lo hacía siempre. Y la Chata también se veía muy seria. No se rio en todo el día y cada rato andaba regañando a los muchachos para que le trabajaran más aprisa. Por fin se terminó el día de trabajo y antes de cenar papá se lavó bien, se hizo el partido cuatro o cinco veces y se fue derechito a la casa de don Chon. Pete lo encontró en medio del patio y los dos sonaron la puerta.

Entraron. *Les dieron el paso ya.* Como a la media hora salieron todos riéndose de la casa. *La dieron.* El Pete traía a la Chata bien abrazada. Al rato entraron a la casa de Chavela y ya al oscurecer se cerraron las puertas de la casa y los trapos de las ventanas también. Esa noche nos contó papá como diez veces como le había ido con el pedir de la mano.

—N'ombre, nomás le hablé así con mucha política y no puso ningún pero. . .

El siguiente día llovió. Era sábado y fue cuando en realidad se celebró la boda. Casi todos se emborracharon. Hubo un poco de baile. Se pelearon unos pero al rato se apaciguó todo.

Fueron muy felices. Se vino el trabajo con fuerza. El Pete, la Chata, y los niños trabajaban siempre. Se compraron un carro. Los domingos iban muy seguido de paseo. Fueron a Meison Cidi a visitar unos familiares de la Chata. Esta parecía que andaba bien buchona de puro orgullo. Los niños andaban más limpios que nunca. El Pete se compró bastante ropa y también andaba bien limpio. Trabajaban juntos, se ayudaban, se cuidaban muy bien, cantaban juntos en la labor. En fin, a todos nosotros nos gustaba verlos porque a veces hasta se besaban en la labor. Iban entre los surcos cogidos de la mano. . . . *Aquí vienen los mil amores.* Los sábados iban al mandado, se metían a una cantinita que estaba allí y se tomaban unas cuantas después de comprar la comida. Regresaban al rancho y a veces hasta iban al mono por la noche. La pasaban muy bien.

—Quién hubiera dicho que este carajo se fuera a casar con la Chata y que le cumpliera tan bonito. Fíjate que parece que la quiere mucho. Nomás diciéndole mi Chavelona cada rato. Y fíjate como quiere a los niños. Te digo que es de buen corazón. Pero quién iba a decir que lo era. Si parece puro pachuco. Fíjate como la quiere. Y no se ve descarado tampoco. Y ella, pos lo trae más arreglado que al otro que tenía antes, ¿no crees? . . . Y a los niños, nomás jugando con ellos. Ellos también lo quieren mucho. Y ni quien se lo quite, es muy jalador. Y la Chata, tú sabes que ella también le entra parejito. Se van a llevar sus buenos centavitos, ¿no crees? . . . Hasta que le fue bien a la Chata. . . . N'ombre, yo no sé por qué eres tan desconfiada tú, vieja. . . .

Seis semanas después del casamiento se acababa ya la pisca de papa. Faltarían unos dos días a lo más para que se acabara el trabajo. Nosotros tanteábamos que se acababa todo para el martes y por eso arreglamos el carro ese fin de semana, porque ya teníamos las narices apuntando para Tejas. El lunes recuerdo que nos levantamos temprano y papá como siempre nos ganó con el escusado. Pero yo creo que ni llegó porque volvió casi luego luego con la noticia de que el Pete se había ido del rancho.

—Pero ¿cómo viejo?
—Sí, se fue. Se llevó el carro y todo el dinero que habían juntado entre él y la Chata y los niños. La dejó sin un centavo. Se llevó todo lo que habían ganado. . . . ¿Qué te dije? . . . Se fue. . . . ¿Qué te dije?

La Chata no fue a trabajar ese día. En la labor nadie hablaba más que de eso. Le avisaron al viejo pero dijeron que él nomás había movido la cabeza. Los papases de la Chata bien enojados y nosotros pues casi no. Yo creo que porque no nos había pasado nada a nosotros.

El día siguiente se acabó el trabajo. Ya no volvimos a ver a la Chata ese año. Nos venimos para Tejas y acá, unos dos meses más tarde, papá habló con don

Chon quien acababa de llegar de Iowa. Papá le preguntó por Pete y le dijo que no sabía en realidad, pero que creo que lo habían cortado en una cantina en Minesora, que creo que andaba diciendo que la Chata le había quitado todo el dinero y hasta el carro, que creo que el viejo del rancho siempre sí le había avisado a la chota y que lo habían pescado en Aberlí. De todos modos, ni a don Chon ni a la Chata les regresaron nada. Nosotros nomás nos acordamos de que apenas había llegado y ya se quería ir. Como quiera, el Pete hizo su ronchita. Pero, como dicen, nadie sabe pa' quién trabaja. Eso pasó allá por el '58. Yo creo que la Chata ya se murió, pero los hijos de ella ya serán hombres. El Pete, recuerdo que llegó como la cosa mala, luego se hizo buena, y luego mala otra vez. Yo creo que por eso se nos pareció como un bulto cuando lo vimos por primera vez.

Kid Victory

Fear drains me when I step through the ring ropes and look over at the guy I'm going to fight. I haven't been in a gym in twelve years and don't know if I've still got it.

Muscles ripple on his long, white body. Built rangy like me, but bigger by fifteen pounds at one-forty and twenty-five years younger, I know I'm going to have my hands full.

I turn away so I won't have to look at him and see this guy staring at me from the spectator stands next to the ring, under the wall of dirty windows.

Typical-looking street kid, growing up downtown, he's got on a cream-colored felt hat, sitting right on top of his head like a gangster, a shiny polyester sport shirt and gabardine slacks, polished shoes and vest, with no coat, and a thin mustache touched up with eyebrow pencil to make it show on his white lip.

The boxing club's in a downtown section of Oakland, full of seedy bars, vice cops and whores, black pimps and dope fiends, up on the second floor of an old brick building, right across the landing from a taxi dance, a dollar a tune, and you can rub up all you want. It's an old, high hall just like the taxi dance, with a whole wall of dirty windows facing the one-way traffic on Twelfth Street below.

Two rings and the spectator stands are on the left half of the room by the windows and bare floor, mirrors and punching bags on the right. The locker room and two showers are behind the bags, with posters of past fights all over the walls and a few cracker-box sayings on signs like, "The fighter with a big head will get it knocked off."

The bell rings and I forget The Kid, move out with tingling legs to meet the long-waisted Okie, hands up by his freckled face, coming to get me.

I skip away and around the ring, and when he comes after me, skip back in, pop him with a quick jab, then skip back out before he can counter, and I think I can handle him. No more fear, I'm not as rusty as I thought.

I keep dancing around, popping him with jabs every time he gets in range, sometimes hitting him with a quick one-two and an occasional left hook, don't try to hit him hard, he's an amateur and I'm an ex–college champ, so I relax and take it easy on him. He's too slow for me, fifteen pounds worth. Even at age forty-five, I'm too quick.

I keep moving, throwing light shots that mainly hit their mark, beating him with the jab and a counter right hook to the ribs under his jab, out-punching him. But then he catches me in a corner and charges like a football lineman, and when I cover up with my arms, hits me in the nuts!

"Hey, man! Take it easy! I'm not punching on you!" I say and shove him back, see Art over in the corner laugh, but The Kid frown. It hurt but not that bad even though I'm not wearing a cup and I dance out into the ring again and, when he tries to charge me again, skip away and say, "Take it easy."

But he charges me again, gets me with a one-two and when I cover, hits me in the nuts again.

"Goddamnit!" I say, wincing at the sharp pain, and shove him back with both hands, but can't move because it hurts too bad. Then when he charges me again, without moving away, I dance back into the ropes and spring off them like a sling-shot, stick out a straight right lead, catch him right on the button with a "smack!" and wobble him back, almost knock him down.

To keep from dumping him, I purposely don't hit him with all my strength. I'm just trying to teach him not to cheat, even if he's losing. When I connect, I hear a cry of admiration and glance out at The Kid on the stands, grinning.

But Okie charges in again and catches me with a stiff one-two to the forehead and I dance away and say, "Alright, man, if that's what you want," when the bell rings.

* * *

Though I'm panting hard and trying to get my breath, I walk over to Okie in the corner with Art and say, "Hey! Lighten up, man!"

But he keeps his freckled face turned to Art and doesn't even look at me. Art glances out of the corner of his eye like he doesn't want me in the corner with him and his boy so I walk away, still trying to catch my breath.

I walk around the ring, feeling weak as a kitten, trying to get my wind back, breathing deeply, holding the air in my lungs as long as possible so the oxygen will get into my bloodstream and revivify me, when I see The Kid staring at me with big eyes.

Turning at the neutral corner, I then see this little fighter with a powerful body and blue-toned cheeks, gotta be a bantamweight like me when I'm in shape, glowering at me from the next ring, where he's shadowboxing, from under a heavy head of stiff hair. One eye's squinted as if he's not sure he really believes I'm that good, which makes me feel good.

I haven't boxed in twelve years and I'm only an ex–college champ, but I've kept myself in pretty good shape by running three times a week, more or less, don't smoke and barely drink so I've got it under control and I could have knocked Okie down, maybe out, stopped him on a TKO with that straight-right shot, if I'd put all my power in it. I'm still taking it easy on him, even if he did hit me in the nuts, though I'm panting hard, trying to get my wind back.

But he charges out and hits me in the nuts the first time we meet in the middle of the ring and I skip away, aching and angry, and when he charges in again, stay right there and when he throws a jab hit him with a right hook to the ribs with all my strength and make him grunt and back off, stay away until the pain goes away and he can breathe again.

I look him right in his pale eyes so he'll know what I mean, but after a few seconds, he charges again and this time, keeps his left low to protect his ribs. I feint with a jab at his stomach to keep his left down, then loop an overhand right over his low left and pop him right on the button, stop him right in his tracks, and freeze him straight up.

I could knock him cold with a follow-up left hook, but hold off and wait until his eyes lose their glaze and can focus on me again, then I skip away, tap him on the headgear with light jabs a few times and keep out of his range until the bell rings. Then I walk up to him and grin and throw my arm around him. He's had enough and I don't think of going a third round. I'm too tired anyway.

He jerks his head around, staring at me with those watery green eyes, surprised I'm not mad at him. But it's just a sparring match to me, just fun. I'm not out for his blood, just don't want him to get mine. I feel pretty good for an old man, haven't done badly at all.

I turn away and see The Kid with his head tilted back so he can see better, staring at me with bright eyes, and I'm amazed when Blue Beard parts the ropes for me to climb out of the ring.

"Thanks," I say, but he doesn't smile. He just spreads them with his knee and his hand. Still there's respect in it. Yet, when I walk down the ring steps and Art takes off my gloves and I feel so weak I could melt down and spread out on the floor like a pool of butter, he keeps glowering at me from up in the ring as he shadowboxes, like he's trying to scare me.

* * *

Then The Kid comes down off the stands and watches me punch the bags.

I wish he wouldn't. I'm so tired and out of shape, I can hardly hit the little speed bag. Can't keep my arms up, they're so weak, haven't been used like this in years. I was never good at it anyway. So, after two sloppy rounds of barely getting in twenty punches without missing and having to keep starting over again, I finally get through and go over to the heavy bags, pick an empty one and start working on that with the next bell.

But The Kid follows me over, stands a few feet away, sighting on me from his hat brim, making me feel self-conscious and I have to fake it. I lean against the bag with my body like I'm fighting in close, then, with my hands down, loop sloppy hooks from my sides, like I'm bobbing and weaving with my body, feeling so weak, I'd quit if The Kid weren't standing there, neat and shiny in his dress-up clothes. But I stick it out two whole three-minute rounds, getting slower and slower with each punch, heaving a sign of relief when the bell finally rings.

I turn away so I won't have to look The Kid in the face and notice Blue Beard standing on the other side of The Kid with a smirk on his face.

He shakes his head like I'm over the hill, and when I try to jump rope and can barely get through ten spins without catching one of my feet, he snorts, then bursts out laughing when I trip, trying to start again.

I have to grin myself, I'm so embarrassed, but The Kid looks down at the floor like he's embarrassed, too, and I put the rope away and sit down to rest, too tired to even try anymore when Blue Beard stands right in front of me, looks at himself in the mirror, and starts jumping rope.

Bare-chested, his flat, wide muscles rippling over his whole body, he shows off for me. The rope whirs so fast, it looks like his feet barely touch the floor. Yet, he's hardly breathing, let alone breathing hard, when I was panting like a choo-choo train for one lousy round. His body's so much better than mine at twenty years younger, I guess he can probably beat me and tremble at the thought of fighting him.

* * *

The next day, I barely get dressed in my sweats and out into the gym, here I stand next to Art and start wrapping my hands, when Blue Beard comes out of the locker room, walks over by us and starts shadowboxing in front of the mirror and flexing his muscles.

When I don't look up from my wraps at him, he stops, steps over next to me, puts his fist against my jaw and says, "Hey, Old Man, I won fifteen out of eighteen fights as an amateur before I turned pro."

I gently but firmly push his fist off my jaw and say, "Sounds good to me," then notice The Kid sitting in the stands, watching.

Blue Beard doesn't bother me by calling me an old man. In the gym, anybody over thirty who fights is an old man. And most people think I'm in my thirties because I take care of myself, have a good grain and raw vegetable and lean meat diet, and I'm smooth-skinned and unwrinkled young faces run in my family. Thinning hair and the slightest puffiness on my hips are my only signs of age. I don't mind looking thirty and take pride in surprising people when I say how old I am.

"As a pro, I won my first eleven fights with eight kayos," Blue Beard says.

I look at the little guy. He's my size and weight, in better shape but not built better, just differently, both of us with muscles, but him with wider shoulders, me with a thicker chest.

"That's damn good," I say, guessing he's trying to set me up, get me to brag, too, then choose me, but I'm not ready to fight him yet and I try to keep it polite.

"Damn good, if it's true," Art says and laughs. "But it could all be bullshit. Right, paisano?"

"No, paisano," Blue Beard says and turns away, starts shadowboxing in front of the mirror, next to Art's equipment booth, where his boxing supplies are, gloves hanging from nails by their laces, old headgear, jump ropes, dirty handwraps and smelly old T-shirts.

Blue Beard's not graceful like I am. I'm a better boxer, if twenty years older. His jabs are straight and strong, but awkward, not smooth. He's got me a little scared, though, and I watch him as he jumps. "Whir-snap, whir-snap, whir-snap, whir-snap," the rope goes as somebody else pounds on the speed bag with a "ratatattat" and another guy thumps the heavy bag with a "thud, thud, thud."

"He won his first eleven fights when he first came over from Italy, but he's lost four straight decisions since," Art says. "He's on a losing streak and mean, tries to whip everybody in the gym. Nobody'll spar with him. Stay away from him."

I look at Art. Swarthy and fine-featured, he looked like the movie star Vittorio Gassman when he was a young contender and now, in his mid-thirties, looks like Omar Sharif, the Egyptian actor. His curly hair has turned gray from drinking and smoking and he weighs 205 instead of 147, almost 60 pounds over his fighting weight, when he was called Slim. I appreciate him trying to help me, but I look at Blue Beard and don't say anything.

I know Blue Beard's after me, one of the few guys in the gym his weight who can probably give him a work-out. He's trying to soften me up with his nickel-psychology, scare me, and halfway succeeding.

* * *

Every day, Blue Beard watches me punch the bags, then shakes his head and laughs, and I can see The Kid lower his eyes and turn away. So I train hard.

I never see The Kid work out himself, though, and one day, when I'm punching the big bag, Art walks by and I stop him and ask, "See that kid over there. Does he fight?"

"He's got no balls. Been hanging around here for six months now and never so much as punched a bag," Art says and tilts his head to one side, watches me pop the bag with left jabs, then sneers and says, "That's no way to jab. It's all arm, you don't have your weight in it. Step in when you punch so you get power."

I step in and hit the bag with a stiff left and he says, "Throw three," and when I do it quick but without much power, he says, "Naw, naw," and shakes his head and walks away. I see Blue Beard smirk and The Kid look down.

But I keep at it and stay off the liquids and watch what I eat and come every day and start getting in shape. Soon, I can go a whole round on the speed bag without missing, popping it like a machine gun, and can do it three rounds in a row. When I finish, I look around and see The Kid staring at me, grinning.

I get it down on the double-end bag, too, after a month. I dance around it and hit it with lots of jabs and quick, long-armed combinations jab-cross hooks. And there's The Kid looking at me from under the brim of his hat, not saying anything, never working out himself, just watching me.

* * *

Blue Beard and Okie are in the ring waiting for the bell when I walk out into the gym from the locker room, where Art's taking a piss and jiving with some guys back there. I think of going back to tell him, but he knows Okie's up there—it's his fighter—and I change my mind with the bell. I want to see this. There's bound to be fireworks, with two bad actors in there.

Sure enough, they meet right in the middle of the ring and start slugging. Blue Beard throws a jab and Okie, taller by three inches, catches Blue Beard with a one-two and Blue Beard then cuts loose with both hands and hits Okie with four looping hooks, backs him into the ropes, and swarms all over him, hits him with some solid shots to the head, jolts him, and I look around for Art but only see The Kid looking at me.

Blue Beard keeps punching and wobbles him, though Okie manages to slide down the ropes and get away. I hope Blue Beard will lighten up on him like I did, and I look around for Art again, but only see The Kid.

Blue Beard stays on him, drives him back, catches him in a corner and hits him with another solid shot, wobbles him again, and I know he's going to knock him out, unless Art shows up. I don't want to butt in if I can help it. Managers don't like that.

I look around again but only see The Kid and Blue Beard's manager, Dago. But he just stands down below his corner, looking up from his round face, gray hair combed straight back, long red nose hanging down, and his belly sticking out, not even moving when Blue Beard hits Okie really hard with an overhand right and staggers him. I get the urge to jump up there myself. It's true, then, what Art said, that he's mean. But this is only a work-out, not a professional fight, and when he catches Okie with two more hard shots and Okie's hands drop, leaving him defenseless, and he takes another shot to the face, I jump up the steps and shout, "Back off, man! Back off!" and when he keeps punching, leap through the ropes and run across the ring and grab his arms.

"Lighten up, man! You'll hurt him!" I say.

But when he looks over his shoulder and sees that it's me, he spins around and hits me with a hard left hook to the jaw.

I jump back right away and hold up my arms.

"Leave him be, man! You got him!" I say and skip back out of range as he charges in again and barely get away when Art jumps into the ring and grabs him.

"No, paisano," he says and holds onto him.

Blue Beard stops struggling but says, "You better get out of here, Old Man, or you're next."

I'm tempted to take him up on it. But I jumped in there when neither of them were my fighters and he feels justified, so I turn around and step back through the ropes, then go down the stairs and look up at him from outside the ring.

He watches Art lead Okie through the ropes in his corner and down the steps, then turns to me and says, "You want some, too, Old Man!"

I stare up at him. We must be the same size, five-five, and the same weight. I'm down to 119 all the time now, and even 117 after a work-out. So, I'm in fair boxing shape, and when he sticks out his blue-hued chin and glares at me with his little brown eyes, and says, "Do you?" I feel the blood rush to my head and I say, "Yeah! I want some!"

"He just stopped Okie in the first round, man. What's the matter with you?" Art says as he unties Okie's gloves.

"He hit me, then added insult in injury by choosing me, acting like he can take me, like I'm afraid."

He loosens the laces on a glove, then jerks it off.

"He'll try to kill yuh, man. He doesn't like you buttin' in like that."

"I don't care," I say.

"You're crazy?" he asks and jerks the other glove off.

"I don't like what he did to your boy," I say and avoid looking at Okie.

Art squints. There's always a little dark spot, like a speck of dirt on the inside corner of one eye, like some permanent scar tissue from boxing.

"Don't get hurt over it," he says and I'm surprised. I always thought he'd like to see me get it, since I never acted afraid of him, twenty wins as a pro or not. I could always see a grudging kind of respect for me, but now he's actually trying to protect me.

"I'm stronger now, Art," I say. "I learned how to shift my weight forward, too, even when I punch fast. I hit a little bit, myself. I want to give it a try."

"You sure or crazy?"

"Sure," I say just as Blue Beard calls out, "You chickenshit or you gonna fight?" and I answer, "Fight!" and nod at Art.

He steps over to Dago and says something, and Dago says, "Your boy comes in to get in shape. My boy comes to earn a living. Your boy can fight or not. My boy fights."

Art turns back to me and says, "Alright. Go get your gloves and headgear. Make sure you wear a cup. And when he comes at you, run!"

* * *

I go back to the gray locker room with the old peeling wallpaper, take off my sweatshirt, so I'm down to a loose-fitting green tank top which will give me plenty of room in the arms and cut down on sweating and fatigue, get my gloves and headgear, but sit down for a moment between the battered green lockers.

What am I doing it for? For Okie? He hit me in the nuts because I was better than him. To punish the little beast, Blue Beard, for being a killer? Maybe, but I'm no cop, and it wasn't any of my business.

Mainly, I'm doing it for myself, I figure. Because he chose me, threatened me, same as said he could kick my ass, and I'm going to see if he can or not. It's pride, I have to admit it. I set myself up as a Good Guy by jumping in the middle of his fight when it was none of my business, technically, and now I'm so scared I'm weak, feel like laying down on the massage table and not going out there. I don't even know if I can last the round better than Okie, who, if anything, is in better shape, and Blue Beard's out to get me for butting-in now, not just on general principles anymore. So he'll be twice as mean as he was to Okie, which means trouble.

The bell rings ending a round. I should go in and get my gloves on. But I'm not ready. I try to steel myself, first. I'm stronger now and faster than both of them, have more grace and talent, if not power and drive. If I'm older, I'm smarter. If I can only keep from getting tired.

I know another thing. I'm not the only one afraid. Art was so good as an amateur champion, other managers wouldn't let their fighters fight him. And he looked like a contender when he turned pro, with 20 straight wins and 17 knockouts, until a real contender knocked him out in his twenty-first fight. Then a week later, when he was discouraged to find he could get it, too, a ten-round middleweight main-eventer dropped him in the gym, and he slapped his gloves against the canvas and cried and never fought again. I'm not the only one scared.

When the bell rings again, I stand up and go out to the ring, as ready as I'll ever be, and Art's frowning.

"Look, if he traps you and presses on you, take a half-step back with your right foot, twist your body sideways so you're holding his body off with your left shoulder and arm, and your right arm's free, drop it down to your hip and turn back and drive an uppercut to his gut. That'll take some steam out of him."

"Thanks, Art." I say and know I'll need it. I can see The Kid watching me from the stands, his felt hat down low, his eyes looking up past the brim, probably thinking I'm crazy to get in there with Blue Beard after he stopped Okie.

* * *

I need everything I've got. Art has to wash down my mouthpiece and doesn't stick it in my mouth until after the bell rings, and when I turn around, the little beast is already charging down on me, his face a scowl in his black headgear, and scares me to death, then smacks me right in the left eye with a right hook and sends a flash of painful light through it, then cuts loose with a barrage of punches to my face, trying to knock me out before I can even get out of the corner.

They sting but they don't stun me. I'm not dizzy. I still have my senses and try to stick out a jab to keep him off.

But he backs me down the ropes like he did Okie and catches me in a neutral corner and cuts loose again, going for the kill.

But this time my head's down and my hands up and I catch the shots on top of my head and on my shoulders and, inside his wide hooks, cut loose with a short left hook, all my shoulder in it, that catches him right on the chin and stuns him.

His eyes widen and he stops punching, stares at me, gives me a second to slip out of the corner. I don't realize it's a mistake until I skip out into the ring, where I can see him still just standing there. Meaning, I could have gotten him then if I went all-out and had the confidence I wouldn't punch myself out and could last the whole three rounds. But I couldn't take the chance. I didn't want to be a sitting duck, if I didn't get him.

It's too late now, and when he comes charging out of the corner, screaming, "Yaaaaaaa!" I skip away like a water mosquito.

Art waves at me to slow down, I'm wasting energy, but I've just escaped with my life and I'm not about to sit there and let him hit me. I'm going to stay away from the little beast. Even Blue Beard waves at me to come on and punch on him, too, trying to make me fight.

But when he traps me in the corner again and hits me with a good right hook to the head, I counter with a left hook over it and catch him right on the chin and all my fear vanishes. I'm in a fight now and I don't care.

Then when he screams and charges the next time, I step in with all my weight like Art showed me and spear him right on the chin with a left jab and snap his head back. When I see I can keep him off with the jab, I stand right in the middle of the ring and fight him every time he charges. I make no attempt to skip around, just stand there toe to toe with him so I won't get tired, and try to beat him to the punch with a stiff jab every time he rushes in, keep pumping it in his face and hold him off until the bell rings.

* * *

"Did he hurt you with that first punch?" Art asks in the corner.

"The punches hurt but he didn't stun me," I answer between deep breaths.

"Well, you stunned him and should've finished him then. Now, he's strong and even meaner. Keep sticking him with that jab and move away."

"I'm too tired to run, Art," I say and take a deep breath to ease the ache in my chest. "I better stand in the middle of the ring and fight him."

He squints that eye with the dark speck in it again and then says, "Alright, but remember to keep that left going. Don't forget to shift your weight so you can get momentum in those combinations."

When Blue Beard charges me in the corner at the bell for the second time, I slug it out with him and drive him off, then, my hands down at my sides, I'm so tired, I hit him with three, quick right-hand leads. I see his eyes widen when I hit him and know the shots hurt. I do belt for my weight, partly because of the quickness and accuracy and also because I've got big hands for my size and long-armed build, with big knuckles on them like a sledgehammer.

But I've discovered his main weakness and I use it with my jab the rest of the round and mostly keep him off. But he keeps driving in even after I hit him and gets me with a couple of smashes to the face and blood trickles out my nose. I'm too tired to fight back and I'm afraid he's going to knock me out.

Thank God the bell rings and I turn back to my corner, feeling like I can't last another second. His superior body is getting to me now, age is telling. I need the rest bad.

* * *

"You alright?" Art asks.

I take a deep breath, blow it out, and say, "Just tired," and take another deep breath. But I notice after the third one that I'm catching my wind. The tiredness is going away. I feel better now than I did after the first round.

Art wipes the blood from my nose, washes out my mouthpiece and barely gets it in my mouth when the bell rings and the little beast comes charging at me again.

He scares me all over again. But this time, I pop him with a one-two, left-right, right in the face and snap his head back. But he screams, "Yaaaaaa!" and charges me anyway, and though I stick my left in his face, he keeps coming and drives me back to the ropes, pins me on them with his arms and elbows, presses against me with his whole body. I'm sure he's going to get me now. I can't even move, but I make myself turn and take a half-step back along the ropes, like Art said, keep him off with my left shoulder and arm, then drive a right hook to his gut, make him grunt and get time to get off the ropes.

He charges me right away again though and pins me on the other side of the ring, the same way, keeps me pinned so I can't turn and step back. He's wearing me down. He's going to get me. I shift my weight to the left like I'm going to try and get off that way and when he presses against me, shift my weight back to the right, shove his right shoulder with my right glove at the same time, and slide out along the ropes to my right and get away from him.

I'm exhausted but I pop him with two jabs from the middle of the ring when he comes at me and keep him off, but drop my arms, I'm so tired, and he screams and throws a looping right hook at my open chest. I'm too weak to get my arms up in time to block it, so I just twist my body and catch the punch on my shoulder muscle without even trying to lift my arms, then shoot a quick, loose straight right lead out with just my arm and catch him in the face, surprise both him and me when he blinks and stops punching like he's stunned.

I see he's hurt. It's my only chance, do or die and right now, otherwise he'll get me for sure. I throw it once, twice, three more times, knock him back against the ropes and chase him down them, catch him in the corner and won't let him out. This is the last round and I fight with every bit of strength I've got.

He cuts loose with both hands when I come in and bangs me good, stuns me, makes my legs buckle, but I trade straight shots with him, right and left crosses, with both hands, and mine are cleaner and in a tighter pattern inside his, getting him right on the chin, while his are only hitting my headgear.

He wobbles, his knees buckle now, and he ducks down and covers his face, so I drop my hands to my hips and fire with ripping hooks to the body, take his head shots, but beat him to the punch and get more powerful punches in, pound on his body, going to take this strong man out, when he suddenly catches me right on the button with a looping right and everything blurs into slow motion, like I'm under water. I can hear the ocean roar.

I think I'm going down. My legs turn to mush, but I keep punching instead of grabbing or covering up or trying to get away. I keep catching him to the body, feel the punches thump into his ribs and dig into his guts, and the wooziness passes, and he suddenly grabs his stomach with the gut shots and falls to his face on the canvas and rocks back and forth in pain.

I can't believe it. I've stopped the little monster when I couldn't go another second. As Dago rushes into the ring to pick up his fighter, I step out of the ring and float down the steps and bounce around on the floor like I'm on a pogo stick, way up on Cloud Nine, spacey as in a dream when The Kid suddenly appears next to me and raises my glove and says, "My man! My man!"

* * *

I can't believe it either when The Kid comes out of the locker room a few minutes later dressed in a tight-fitting black bathing suit that shows his pale white legs, low-topped white tennis shoes, and a short-sleeved woolen dress gaucho.

"Where you going?" I ask.

"To fight," he says.

"With who?" I ask but he walks over to Art without answering and Art hands him a pair of gloves and starts putting another pair on Okie.

"Would you put these on me?" The Kid asks.

"You sure you want to do this?" I ask, wondering why Art would let him box when he's never even punched the bags.

"I like the way you put away that little Dago."

"Yeah, but—" I say and stop. I don't want to get in trouble for butting in again. One fight over that in one day is enough. I'm glad Blue Beard's in back, taking a shower. But I am worried about The Kid, especially if he's doing it for me.

"Got a mouthpiece?" I ask, after I put my sweaty headgear on him.

"Borrowed this," he says and points with his glove at a cheap model on the table that could fit anybody. I wash it off and put it in his mouth, then watch him go up the steps, through the ropes, and into the ring, where he turns and looks at me with a scared face, then turns away.

I look at him up there in his swimming suit, bare-legged clear to the balls, and feel responsible. I look at his pale legs and his pale face and try to look into his eyes, but he keeps his face turned and moves slowly out into the ring when the bell sounds.

Sure enough, as soon as Okie gets in range, he starts windmilling like a six-year-old kid, sloppy but hits Okie a couple of times and keeps him off. He even backs him around the ring, until he starts puffing and slows down and drops his arms, his face white like he's really winded. Then Okie walks in swinging, catches him with three smashes to the face, makes me wince, they're so hard, and I'm even glad when he drops down and grabs Okie's legs. At least, he made Okie stop, though everybody in the gym starts laughing.

He lets go of Okie's legs and stands up, but Okie doesn't even step back, steps right in without giving him a chance, and The Kid starts swinging wild with looping punches again, hits Okie on the cheek with the first one, and makes him step back and shake his head like it stunned him.

But Okie charges in again, slugging with both hands, knocks The Kid back against the ropes and starts pounding on him so bad, The Kid drops into a ball and grabs his legs again. But Okie keeps punching on his head and when I glance over at Art to say something, The Kid lifts Okie off his feet.

Everybody laughs again.

But when The Kid puts him down, Okie leaps on him with two roundhouse punches to the head and knocks him back a couple of steps, makes him duck down into a ball again, and keeps punching on him, instead of letting him up, keeping his legs back so The Kid can't grab them.

I keep waiting for Art to jump up there and make Okie step back, but Art doesn't move and nobody else says a word either, and I finally yell, "Stop!"

But when Okie keeps punching and The Kid's rocking back and forth in his ball like he's going to topple over, taking all those head shots, blood streaked across his face, I jump up onto the ring apron and say, "Okie! You're supposed to step back."

But Okie keeps punching on him without even looking at me, and I slip through the ropes and grab his arms and pull him off, shove him toward Art, who's finally come into the ring, grinning.

I feel really bad. The Kid's nose is bleeding and his eyes are glassy.

"Come on," I say. "Let me get that headgear and gloves off."

I take them off and put them on the table by the ring, then put my arm around him and walk him back to the locker room, saying, "It's okay, man. Everything's okay."

I feel responsible. He did it to imitate me. But I have skill, if not much experience, and he doesn't have either. I stay back there with him until he gets his clothes off and gets in the shower, where the water can refresh him. I see he's soft, without muscular definition, though he's not fat.

I walk out in front, snub Art for not stopping it, and sit down on the bench by the ring, wondering what I'm doing in a pro gym where all the guys are out for blood, not for the sport like me. They're in an entirely different league. I wonder if it's worth it. I almost got my ass beat by that little beast trying to save Okie and now Art lets Okie beat up on The Kid. I make up my mind right then to take my shower and pack my gym bag and get out of there for good, go back to my alma mater gym, where it's all about proving yourself, not killing the other guy. I pull my locker key out of my pocket to leave for good when The Kid comes walking out of the locker room with his felt hat on, gabardine slacks creased, polyester shirt rippling with shiny highlights and his shoes glimmering.

I stand up, wondering what I can say to make him feel better, and hold my breath when he crosses over to Okie on a big bag.

He smiles with tight lips like he's trying to be brave, then bows from the waist and shakes the tip of Okie's bag glove with his fingers, then shakes Art's hand, smiles and bows, and starts toward me.

"Hey, look, man," I say. "You keep coming around and I'll train you. I'll teach you how to throw a good jab and a one-two that will stop Okie in his tracks. I'm really sorry I—"

But The Kid holds up his hand like an Indian signifying peace and says, "Don't worry about it, Old Man," and turns and, instead of slinking out the door, defeated, like I feared, he starts strutting out like he had just won his fight, hopping up on one toe with every other step like street kids do, swinging his arms, his head up high, tall as his hat and just as proud, with that beatific smile on his lips.

"Well, I'll be goddamned!" I say, shaking my head, then look at my key, toss it up, catch it in my hand and stick it back in my pocket.

Miguel Algarín

El jibarito moderno

when he dances latin,
he crosses his legs
right over left,
left over right,
light as a bright feather
el jibarito turns on and off
like the farthest
star in the milky way,
when he smiles his upper lip
covers his vacant gums
where his teeth have melted
just like my sugar teeth
dissolved into the chocolate
that made me fat in childhood,
el jibarito moderno
travels light
maybe he's afraid of gravity,
y eso,
hay que velarlo cuando
un bomboncito appears
in the atmosphere,
muchacho,
vélalo y cuídate
porque el jibarito conquista
con su liviana apariencia
y su estoy asfixiado look
that melts the temperature
of la damita in blue,
cuídate, cuídate
porque el jibarito
derrite y consume
sin que te des cuenta,

es como el viento
en una tarde caliente
que acaricia y seca
aliviándote el calor.

Paterson

Valley city
sitting and stripping
the river water of purity
your Garret mountain castle
hides the blooming death
of your concrete, tar valley floor,
latino signs yelling salsa
campbell soup seduction
into an identity that is less
than plastic, on the other side of gray,
in the swirl of slimy green blue waters
boiling multi-colored red, green,
blue, white fishbreaking light,
in the swirl of young green leaves cut into pieces
creating caves of credit privacy,
in the watery spume of a valley stripped of purity,
    city as man
    Paterson as city,
credit bound people
filling the streets like the nausea
of the giants filled Dante's inferno,
Hamilton thought it up,
        credit I mean,
he thought it up, the abstract
of bartering is to use paper
for purchasing objects needed,
      thank you Alexander,
muchas gracias!
for confusing simple exchange need
with subtle enslaving credit for all
that's bought
        but Paterson as City
        and City as Paterson
brings good news death
to the man left out of the will,
      oh the pain of broken wings
      when the convenience of credit

breaks speed, adds weight
and blends will into submission,
     the other night I dreamt
     of buying heaven on credit
but when my friend Chino told me he was
Alexander Hamilton's bill collector
I switched rather than fight
     the force of credit made power
by the willing Alexander
     posing his upper torso,
letting out torrents of persuasive
sound layers that showed Congress
how to straighten out its sea of debt,

thank you Alexander!
for showing us how to come to terms
with our credit skin cancer.

do u remember

do u remember
the parody of trembling laughter
through the parks clouded by moonlight
    shadows, do u remember
        the rain
    and the thunder
        mushrooming
        huracanes
    do u remember
        under our feet
life sprouted on wet dark
        earth, do u
          remember
the dew of dawn lightening
    while your guts tightened
        the irony grew
    out of asphalt
          and found its
          way into
          neon
    celluloid
    and vinyl cuts
          of memories
    running amok
          on wheels
    burning dinosaur bones
and some roaches
    rolling down a '47 chevy

cornfields thaw out

cornfields thaw out
    belted cross the land as
midwestern thunderclad clouds hover
        in omaha, the meat-packing houses
pack mexicans—mojo's what they call us
    while warm tortillas
        shake off the cold at noon
      down dodge st., down way down Q st.
            into the southside salsa
mornings boil dew
          and the stench of slaughtered beasts
    engulfs the nostrils
    and the thought of carnage prevails
nothing much is different in this barrio
    big foot and bigotry squatted
since then no buffalo hooftracks can be stalked
      even pheasants are weary
      of cowboys plucking feathers
      to adorn their stetson tops
and rabbits dread the wheel
      more than their ancient foe
    coyotes howl and german shepherds bark
      the moonfull spring is
    here, for a while only
for a short, short while
    trees will bloom

Jimmy Santiago Baca

Sun Calendar

After the play of the universe
the player threw down to earth
the mask of the sun.

Through small holes it breathed
and cooled in the mud.

It spoke to an Indian's heart,
"Bring your obsidian knife
and carve out the dialogue

of eternities ago,
and chart out the present,
outline the future, when at my feet

the earth will lie in broken shards
and the sun will come
to retrieve his mask."

When the craftsman's blade
chipped out every age
whole populations read
its definition and fled:

all their belongings behind,
the fruit trees unpicked,
fresh tides of cornfields withered
and no one knows where the people went.

We Knew It

We knew it,
but not this bad, lord no.

In Texas, the land wrinkled up
squinting at the sun,
and in the Midwest them fine fat rows
got thin as an old woman.

That heat came on
angry as a wet hen
and when the heat hit the cold,
lord, lord. Some darkening it got
and put that sky damn black.
Started over that way. I seen it come, hail
big as golf balls and small apples.

Tucker's farm looked like someone
took an ax and hacked the 'bacca leaves
right clean. Stalks looked like stakes.

Es all like that. Doggonit, leaves
stacked three feet deep in the road
from Allen's fields. They was worried
about Allen's heart. He just stood there
looking out the window.

I came out round that pond back there.
I said no need to go mo,
by god, James' field was plum flat.
It turned, came round Whitfield's store
stomping corn and ragging leaves.

Left women crying in their kitchens,
I tell you, es all they could do es cry.
Took half of Compton's crop
and Poe didn't have no insurance.

I went up by Harold's meadow,
one we cleared some years ago
back behind them woods. Melvin was there
drinking by hisself. I didn't need to see no mo.

I went on down to Hock's store
and filled me a jar with whiskey,
Everytime that wind hit, blew chairs
off the porch and knocked the porch swing
against the wall: I'd take a drink.
Lord no, didn't need no rain and wind like that.

Barbara Brinson Curiel

María la O

1

When I was born
my mother named me for a song
whistled by a passerby.

I turned eight.
She showed me
the kitchen
of a rich man's house.

My daily wage
fed her legitimate children.
She ran water
through the coffee grounds
a second time
for me.

2

Secret smiles led to words, caresses.
I walked out of my mother's house.
We went to the priest.

I had no wedding ring.
He pierced my ears with
two circles of gold: arracadas de oro.

At the inn
sweet pork glistened fat from our lips.
Mario's eyes shone across the table.

In our rented room
stone walls echoed soft words,
open-mouthed kisses, palms caressing muscled backs.

His lips against my ear, I squirmed:
a speared fish,
I trembled,
the dust was shaken from our mat.

3

Wake up marido.
Fields of dark flowers
bloom beneath your hair.

Last night's wood
has blistered
into ash.

Your sand dollar nipples
sleep
beneath my hands.

Morning sun's bright halo surrounds us.
Insect shadows
weave through your fingers.

You are a silk man between my thighs.
We kiss,
our mouths taste the same.

4

From the doorway
I watch him
walk to work.

His arms and neck shine.
His veins trace a memorized path.

A stonemason,
walls rise beneath his hands.

I take in sewing,
seeding roses on tablecloths.

At night, his whistle
gets home first,
his shadow warms the doorway.

Once he brought me a new-born lamb
so I wouldn't be alone.

But at night,
searching for each other in dreams,

we crushed the lamb
between us.

In the morning,
its neck twisted straight,
Mario buried it in the yard.

5

A devil
perches on Mario's chest,
wings shadow lungs.
Its tongue on my love's tongue,
it sucks his breath.

His heart reaches
through his ribs for air.

He walks to work,
his back straining
for a breath.

He can hardly lift his tools,
so the patrón sent him home.
He sleeps all day,
works nights in a bar.

His face has turned grey.
His eyes search
for new sleep.

6

There was no work,
no food.
His lungs strained harder
against his heart.

Mario sold my gold earrings.

For awhile longer
we eat,
but only sweet potatoes,
onions.

The revolution
has bone-seeded the fields;

it has sewn arms
and legs onto itself,
become a lover
to women in black.

My teeth are stubs of chalk in my mouth.

Mario grinds his teeth in his sleep;
dreams of hell,
doesn't see our wood fence
splinter into the road.

7

Looking for a wedding ring,
I found an incomplete circle of brass.

My mother wrote from El Paso:
my stepfather had a job on the railroad,
"meet us in Oklahoma."

Her cold arms of words
pierce me like fish spines.

My love's cold arms hold
Death to his breast.

The straight steel arms of the train track
will embrace me,

carry me to railroad yards,
to fields of

Texas cotton,
Michigan cherry,
California grape,

to the city's concrete bed,
to an open road.

Lorna Dee Cervantes

Heritage

Heritage
I look for you all day in the streets of Oaxaca.
The children run to me, laughing,
spinning me blind and silly.
They call to me in words of another language.
My brown body searches the streets
for the dye that will color my thoughts.

But Mexico gags
"ESPUTA"
on this bland pochaseed.

I didn't ask to be brought up tonta!
My name hangs about me like a loose tooth.
Old women know my secret,
"Es la culpa de los antepasados."
Blame it on the old ones.
They give me a name
that fights me.

Refugee Ship

like wet cornstarch
I slide past *mi abuelita*'s eyes
bible placed by her side
she removes her glasses
the pudding thickens

mamá raised me with no language
I am an orphan to my spanish name
the words are foreign, stumbling on my tongue
I stare at my reflection in the mirror
brown skin, black hair

I feel I am a captive
aboard the refugee ship
a ship that will never dock
a ship that will never dock

You Are Like a Weed

You are like a weed
growing from a plastic lawn
   and I, the gas station,
   brick-layered, manicured.

  "Pop in the coin
   and come on and
    Pump Me!"

And oh, I'm a sell-out
and a shopclosed babygotnogas

and you are like a weed
in the middle of Times Square.

Oh baby, you're so GREEN
and I'm so laid out.

Blue Full Moon in Witch

I come to you on an angel's moon,
when heat off foam rises to a crest,
on sheets of stainless sea, on
shallowed ice on shattered diamond leis,
where above it all an arctic cauldron lies
and covers us in woven halo gems.
Spring still forms and shudders crystals.
Since before the hail there is this ring.
Before the rest there is this missing
fractured light in the captioned
reruns of our dreams. I want you
and my heart still licks
its heaven. I want you
and heaven pulls its ring.

From the Cables of Genocide

Who gave you permission to detonate
this neutron bomb in my heart?
My imploding senses reel
in the leftover scent of you,
squirrel, plural wrecker, acorn
masher. My laurel leaves
wither to ash, the clot
of my rose, a dirt devil
in the branches of my veins.
Proven destination, where are you
now? Does the blood still flow
camellias like a slap when I see you
crossing my backyards, the alleys
where we met, where we kissed
red stars? Moon of my moon,
let me wish you. Let April
catch in the throat of our beating
white flags. Let me not be
the only fool standing.
The only gas breathed
is you.

On Love and Hunger

*You can want to do nothing and then
decide instead to do this: make leek soup,
I mean. Between the will to do something
and the will to do nothing is a thin,
unchanging line: suicide.*

—Marguerite Duras, *Leek Soup*

I feed you
as you hunger.
I hunger
as you feed
and refuse
the food I give.

Hunger is the first sense.
Imagination is the last.
You are my sixth sense,
imaginary lover,
missed meal.

Food is the first choice,
first flaw, fatal
in its accessibility,
fearless on the tongue
of mean denial.

First word,
first sight.

Food is love
in trust.

Lucha Corpi

Lamento

a María Auxilio

La gran encina derrumbada
está besando la tierra
con sus ramas extendidas.

Bajo el sol inclemente y frío
las golondrinas velan el cuerpo
de un clavel que ayer apenas
se mecía junto al río.

* * *

El viento, viejo villano,
quiere robarnos su nombre.

¡María Auxilio!
¡MARIA AUXILIOOOOO!

¡Que fuera a morir así
como un clavel junto al río
bajo los cascos de piedra
de un caballo enajenado!

¡Que fuera a morir así. . . !

Ella que había crecido
con su mano de mujer recia
las más tiernas primaveras
en donde el lecho y la ausencia
asfixiaban al perdido
entre su red de amapolas.

Ella que desde el lecho
del ultraje y la ignominia
se levantara muy de mañana,
cargando la noche a cuestas,
para que así aprendiéramos
que aún de una mancha solar
puede brotar una estrella.

* * *

Viene volando la noche
y yo quiero detenerla

    Geranio de rojo llanto
    una mujer de la raza
    al anochecer ha muerto.

Viene volando la noche
y yo quiero detenerla

    Chicano de brazos fuertes
    carga su cuerpo vencido
    para que no lo cubra la noche
    con su manto de amapolas.

Viene volando la noche
y yo quiero detenerla

    Barrio mío que hoy le lloras
    no dejes que el viento
    deshoje su viejo nombre
    y hunda en la ausencia
    su tiempo y su victoria.

Viene volando la noche
y yo quiero detenerla

    Hermana
    tira la senda de un verso
    al paso de su recuerdo
    para que no muera del todo.

Invernario

En los ojos que observaron
la tormenta avecinarse
había calles empedradas
y trigales todavía húmedos
por la lluvia de la noche,
un triángulo de sombra
entre dos casas blancas,
un viejo campesino con su violín
envuelto en periódico
en camino a la feria del pueblo.

Me observé en esos ojos
como quien mira en el mar
su imagen fragmentada,
por la corriente indómita
y la ve convertirse
en coral
y sombra
y pez
en roca
y mineral fosforescente.

Desde entonces
aprisionado
entre el demiángulo del ojo
y el origen del cantar
como un suicida impenitente
me acecha mi deseo
por sus brazos.

Fuga

Cansada de llevar en los ojos
resplandor, muro y silencio
y al oído
un rumor de alas y lluvia,
entre adiós y puerta inesperada
me decidí por el fuego
y en su promesa de agostos oportunos
mi corazón ardió
una noche de invierno.

Crucé la insolente geometría
que tus manos construyeran
en las agrestes latitudes de febrero.

Tu milagrería de tigres al acecho lancé
a la insubordinada ecología del viento.

Lavé el sabor temible de tu piel
de mis labios.

Cautericé motivo, causa y sentimiento.

Borré tu mirada de mi cuerpo.

Y clausuré las puertas de la historia
para no recordar más tu nombre ni mi nombre.

Afuera
en el invierno de los dioses
con mano temblorosa destapé el silencio.

Conjuré las semillas del fuego.

Las sentí palpitar en mis sienes, en mis pechos.
En el espacio abierto de mis dedos eran

sangre

    trigo

      y luz de junio.

Eran la noche y sus mil ojos

    crepúsculo

    dolor

      y canto

y la espiga tendida en el campo

    acantilado

    delta

      y pez dorado

secretos de estrellas en la arena

    escama

    espuma

      y sal

y el lamento melancólico de la ballena
anunciando la amplitud ecuánime
de un equinoccio boreal.

The Last Wow

the blue eyed gypsy is gone.
once again i am alone.
there is no song. there is no poem.
gypsies must move on
or else they won't be gypsies long.
the last wow . . .
            the last ajúah . . .
have been said.
the drops of dew, sweat and love
fell on each other one last time.
siamese souls of love
                 cannot be
dissected with words
without real blood erupting
as if invited by a knife.
—i want to travel some more,
abroad . . . here . . .
              do some growing up.—
i refused (my ears refused)
to listen anymore,
            to be a witness
to the tears of anguish
spoiling the beauty of your face
which is by now a permanent fixture in my mind.
i chose instead to listen
to the song we call our own
and relive the moments
of one of our many honeymoons . . .
—tanto tiempo disftrutamos de este amor,
nuestras almas se acercaron tanto así
que yo guardo tu sabor
pero tú llevas también, sabor a mí.—

the zodiac,
        the many horoscopes we read
each other, the gemini and the saggittarius,
they approved of our love
and made such sound
            and healthy predictions.
the lines in the palm of my hand
               confirmed
the duality of my joy,
our joy.
numerology, the number seven,
echoed in envious applause our heaven,
the find each was to each other.
inside a church
          when we received
               holy communion together
we thanked god for our love/sin.
we had settled
        major differences
which, futuristically speaking,
had our meeting and falling in love
in the realm
of possibilities
that happen only
          on a zillion to one basis.
how is it then
        that now
          a last wow
              brings sudden death
to our love just as it flowered,
challenging tradition
and daring to establish itself
on the testing grounds of immortality?
i sing some more in the silence of my mind
trying to escape the sadness of the moment:
—yo no sé si tenga amor la eternidad
pero entonces como aquí
en tu boca llevarás sabor a mí.—
the last wow.
what is a wow?
          you and i already know
but does the creator of the first wow

centuries ago
        mind our reversion to use
his shout of joy
          brought about by spiritual explosions
dispersing sensuously all the feathers
in our bodies. . . ?
wow is our personal no-meaning sound
manifesting our happiness.
—you are so final.
can you leave the door open?—
you said . . . gypsies have been known to return.
i said to myself,—ghosts do not bother with doors.
those who are already inside need no doors.—
the last wow
        is a mortal blow
which somehow
takes love/life away.
the last wow is the last everything.
the blue eyed gypsy is gone.
once again i am alone.
there is no song. there is no poem.
gypsies must move on
or else they won't be gypsies long.

—pasarán más de mil años, muchos más.—

Inés Hernández Avila

Luminous Serpent Songs

For Beto*
from Port Townsend
September 13, 1993

Eight seasons past today
You shed your skin for the last time
Luminous your spirit crossed over into grace

I have not many words for you
I give you my heart instead
Feel with me the songs of promise
Smell the sweet grass, sage and *copal* I burn in abalone
Sit amongst the brother sister deer awhile
and rest a moment on your journey

I roll a cigarette of many lands for you to share
I will begin this smoke you will finish
Here I place it in the shell of shimmering auras
like the sunset you gave to me this evening
as I walked and saw your face up in the sky

From far over these original lands
my love, my husband, is singing songs for you right now
sacred songs, *Yoeme* songs, with all his heart
I can hear them over the mountains
through these trees that rustle so
His love meets mine meets you in wonder
at the simple movements of the serpent
who is filled with the light of wisdom

I'll play *Flaco* for you, too,
You loved the *bailes y la música tejana*
As I listen to the melodies the night wind tells me
how much you have to teach us about loving and letting go
about being in a good place in spite of separation
about being brave in the face of pain, in the face of parting

I sway a little, dance a little for you, with you,
standing outside in my *Trique huipil*,
looking up at the tree that speaks
where I place the ashes of the smudge I have burned for you

You are up there in the heavens *hermano*
but somehow I see you coming back soon
I see you as a little child again
someone's little son

May you be blessed where you are
and may you be blessed always on your return

*Alberto "Beto" Mestas was a beloved community member in Sacramento, California, who died in 1991 from a brain tumor at the young age of thirty-six.

Coyote Woman Finds Fox at the Street Fair in Port Townsend

For Kathy Fox

Coyote Woman strolls with apparent casualness through the Sunday street fair, but her whole self is alert for the sign she seeks, for her intuition has sent her out on this fine day. Suddenly she finds an image that draws her in. She is transported to the Sangre de Cristo Mountains where Guadalupe/Tonantzin has appeared in the blues and fuchsias of the glistening evening sunset and spread herself across the montaña's face. As Coyote Woman returns to Port Townsend, she wonders who could have made such a fine journey possible, when who, but Fox appears. Friend and helpmate artist that she is, it is she who has made EarthMother appear in the same resplendent hues on Kodacolor paper. It's not as durable as ayate but it does Coyote Woman good. The image was what she was looking for anyway, to place just so in her studio in the woods.

"'Blue Woman,' I name you," Coyote Woman says to her sacred Kodacolor, "and you will inspire me in my own creations," she adds, smiling her famous smile, shaking her long dark hair with signature abandon. Fox, as usual, finds amusement in her friend's inclination to primal discovery, but she knows that Coyote Woman can't do without her, so she just laughs.

Once they arrange to meet later, Coyote Woman moves on to sniff around the other booths, sauntering through the crowds, dealing a while with fellow artists, enjoying the breeze on her face, keeping an eye out for mischief, and listening to the musicians of Sanya Huayra bringing the continent together even again with the Andean rhythms and songs EarthMother creates for her own pleasure, emanating into being the pulse and vocables of her intonated mistresspieces.

As she wends her way to her cabin to write, Coyote Woman finds the Deer brothers have come to visit. Smiling to them, she breathes deeply and sighs, saying, "It's a good day. Come in, share a glass of juice with me. To Fox who gave me Blue Woman's portrait, to you who have come to gossip with me, and most of all, to me, for today I am a fortunate woman!"

Juan Felipe Herrera

Photopoem of the Chicano Moratorium 1980/L.A.

Photo 1. Pilgrimage

The march is holy. we are bleeding. the paper crosses unfold
after ten years. stretching out their arms. nailed. with spray
paint. into the breasts of the faithful. followers. they bleed
who we are. we carry the dead body. dragging it on asphalt
america. we raise our candle arms. our fingers are lit. in
celebration. illuminating. the dark dome of sky. over Whittier
Boulevard. below. there are no faces. only one. eye. opening its
lens. it. counts the merchants locking iron veils. silently
secretly. as we approach. their gold is hidden. they have
buried diamond sins in the refrigerators. under the blue
velvet sofas. they are guarding a vault. of uncut ring
fingers. the candles sweat. who tattooed the santo-man on our
forehead? Rubén Salazar. we touch the round wound with saliva
the clot of smoke. a decade of torn skin. trophies. medallions
of skull. spine. and soul. spilled. jammed. on the grass. gone
forever. beneath the moon-grey numbers of L.A.P.D. August 29
1970. running. searching for a piece. of open street. *paraíso
negro*. pleading to the tear-gas virgins. appearing over the
helmet horns of the swat-men. iridescent. we walk. floating
digging deep. passing Evergreen cemetery. passing the long
bone palms shooting green air. stars. as we count the death
stones. burning. white. rectangles. into our eyes. processions
have no gods. we know. they know. the witnesses. on the sidewalks
the thirty-two-year-old mother with three. children. no
husband. by the fire hydrant. the bakers. the mechanics leaning
on the fence. spinning box wrenches. in space. the grandfather
on the wheelchair saluting us. as we pass. as we chant. as we
scream. as we carry the cross. a park with vendors appears
ahead

Photo 2. Oasis/We Gather/Audience/Wide-Angle

We drink tropical waves. unknown lips of sun &
fragrant oils slip. down our backs. *nos reímos
camaradas.* we gather & we scope the elements
the cop helicopter will never invade our lake
it will never drink our perfume. today we make
this crazy speck of twin-blades blow. away. with
our eyes. la Kathy from East Los. el David &
his chavalo Noel. la Eva rapping with César
el Bobby. Valentín & Francisco. we slap the air
hard. pulsating. opening the rock. around our
bodies. liquid. flesh. pouring. circling. entering
the grass. el saxofón shoots heart & lightning &
Félix sings quarter notes. *chale con el draft*
pulling at his chinese beard. el Aztleca talks
about the cultural center in San Diego. power
plays in the dance group. we pull at the grass
snipping stems. making incense for miniature
altars. who can fill the chasms in the corners
around the shoes? the black net stockings
silhouette cliffs & shifting gravel stains
the shirt-tails. a question mark of buttons
surrounds the waters. flashing against the flat
buildings. we gather. in the light

Photo 3. The Speakers

Fellini said only clowns know the truth. they smile
in torture. never speaking. although their sound
explodes and destroys. children appreciate them. naturally
children are their teachers. a good clown always
learns from the rhythms and the voiceless somersault
of a child. children are the first to experience disorder
joyfully. they attack madness with their round bellies.
pushing into its darkness. plucking its hairs. it tickles
them. they dream of being slayers of the monster. they
gather. they stand on a mound. imagining they can speak
to it. so. they mumble. swinging their wooden swords

Photo 4. Anna María Nieto-Gómez/On Stage/Alone

She said that the issues. the mind blades. the ones
that whirl. cut. out. a jagged distance. deeper into
Kaos. alive. between the man and the woman. the issues
that ten minds. knives. ago were etched. written hard
through our lips. the issues have remained on silent
funeral ground. fading. into chambers. brief cases
pockets. notebooks. by the off & on bedroom light switch
inside the fiber of pillows. that men clutch. at night
crying. binding female mate. flesh. falling cuffed gnawing
sheets. in masks. they confess. to dream images. writhing
in laughter. slamming. the small of the back. is this
nightmare. anna maría? or. is *La Familia* loved in chains
only? the issues remain & the wind howls

Photo 5. Sunset

People leave. slowly. taking their cameras. back
to Stockton. Colorado. back. to Fetterly Street
some. pick up the cans. the leaflets. crossed out
& filled in with addresses. the vendors close up
& pack into the vans. looking back. the fence
remains. bitten with rust. sharp coils. making a
crown out of iron y's and x's over the sun. some
of us go to the bar on the corner. we. leave slowly
with a few extra rolls of negatives. black & white.
who got the viejito in his wheelchair? or the Varrios
Unidos group with their placas? shouting *what do you
want?* answering (the vato with the hoarse voice)
justice! when do you want it? now! the stage spins. out
acrylic mural images. la mujer. con un rifle. together
with a man. marching out of the plywood emmanuel
montoya painted. jumping high. into the wet grass.
doing steps of being shot. suddenly. opened up. by
the torque of bullets. a gas cartridge pierces
the belly of the woman. her imaginary rifle disappears
the police lifts his wooden pipe. strikes one. 2. three
4. five. 6. seven. 8. nine. ten. times. on her back. she falls
falls. falls. bleeding. her lips screaming in the tempest
don't leave

Photo 6. The Mime at Figueroa Street/Night/TRI-X
—for Adrián Vargas

The mime moves. lightly. he teaches us political ballet
step. by step. his eyes have bodies. that stretch. far
into the air. of Latin America. tiller-woman. tiller-
man. beneath the *patrón*. the military. *La Junta*
fevers in plantations. deliriums. in Haciendas. still
El Salvador. light bodies. explode in cathedrals
the yearning chests multiply. into honeycomb spilled
muscles. flayed. floating. caught in the bamboo
gyrations of his eyes. feather-weight tendons. shutter
as he snaps the head left. staring into the room
of people on chairs. lined up. against the off-white
wall stamped with photo 1. the march. photo 2. a woman
speaking. photo 3. leaders at the microphone. photo 4.
undercover agents. photo 5. people fleeing. cut. dying
in 1970. he stares. over the bannister. past Adrián's
shoulder. past. the gallery wall. seeing us. rumble
murmur. rumble. scream. pushing. we sweat. smoking
jive. with cans of alcohol. wet offerings. to unknown
deities. seeing the moist walls behind us. open
the single eye. pointing steady. shooting. across
the horizon moon swaying its tattooed flesh through
the city. compounds of swollen curtains an apartment
with a hallway altar. a boy passes by the crucifix
bronze. body of Christ. guarding a bouquet of plastic
day-glow roses. a blue candle vase. tapping light
rhythms on the ceiling. whispering lips of smoke
at the. end. an opaque window. shut. closing out
the night of violent winds and soft movements.

Outside Tibet
Word on Ice

for Oloberto & Magritta, my Geminis

Lissen to my whistle of night bats—oye como va, in the engines, in the Chevys &
armed Impalas, the Toyota gangsta' monsters, surf of new world colony definitions & quazars & culture prostars going blam over the Mpire, the once-Mpire, the
carcass of neural desires for the Nothing. i amble outside the Goddess mountain.
Cut across the San Joaquín Valley, Santiago de Cuba, Thailand & Yevtushenko's
stations of hunched humans snap off cotton heads gone awry & twist nuclear vine
legs. Jut out to sea, once again—this slip sidewalk of impossible migrations.
Poesy mad & Chicano style undone wild.

Rumble boy. Rumble girl. In wonder & amazement. On the loose. Cruisin'
through the shark-colored maze of presidential bombast, death enshrined archi-
pelago fashion malls, neutered wars across the globe come barreling down on my
Neo-American Uzzi mutations, my upgraded 2-Pac thresholds. My indigo streets,
i say with disgust & erotic spit, Amerikkaner frontier consciousness gone up long
ago. Meet my barriohood, meet me with the froth i pick up everyday & everyday
i wipe away with ablution and apologia & a smirk, then a smile on my Cholo-
Millennium liberation jacket. No motha', no fatha', no sista', no brotha'. Just me
in the genetic tick-tock culture chain, this ad-infinitum clueless Americana grid of
inverted zarapes, hallucinations of a nation, streets in racist Terminator coagula-
tion, housewives believing they are housewives, house-husbands groaning to
become house husband church lovers, set loose like crack racing after the day-
glow artery of a fix, a power outage that will propel us into cosmos definition,
another forty million New Dollar Plantation Basílica, or is it tender chaos? My
upsidedown Kahlua gallon oración drools blackish metal flake desires, the ooze
of Dulcinea-Hera-Tepeyac-Stripper, the honey from Tara's open green fans. Tara?

Tara, where are you? Tara of the blessings & weapons against illusion. Against
administrator-pig, against molester-snake, against rooster corporate lust.
Remember me? i am the black-red blood spark worker, Juana Buffalo's illegiti-
mate flight usher, back up from Inframundo, from Dr. Kisin's rain forest revolution lab, the Earthquake World Trade Monster's under-realm, this quick ooze
again, this formless city-space i live in, my circular false malaria fungi town
sayin' everything's awright without your Holy Wheel, your flaming tree wombs,
this sista' bundle i ache for, the one i lost in a fast brawl for redemption at the gates

of this Creation Mulatto Hotel, this body passage, this wonder fire from the chest.

i stand alone on Mass Man Boulevard, look east, look south where the bleary sirens come howling with vats of genocide & gray prison gang buses jammed with my true brotha' wetbacks to pick another bale of tropical grape, another bushel of pesticide & plutonium artichoke. Cancer tomatoes the biggest in the world. Bastard word, bracero produce, Alien culture—power & slime. They crawl up my back, heavy and loaded on cheap narratives, Gortari doubles, Atlantis sketched on Gorbachev's forehead: you, yes, you, gator-mouthed agent—like gila progeny.

Let's hustle. Let's trade. It is 1:27 am in da rat Arctic. What do i trade for with passion? Language escapes me. Passion is smoke. i dissolve. It is in my nature to disappear. No sista', no brotha'. No motha', no soul. This shred iciness is all, a crazy register that destroys itself into Polaroid, into a sliding glacial sheet of multi-colored border walls. Let's foam & spin flamey and bluish tears for the Thing-Against-Itself, this soulless soul, this film word surface. Sing out, baby. Wobble & bop to town. Drag yo' hands across my fine-tuned work train named *Desastre* en route to Freetown where all the little well engineered African shaman houses smell of licorice, Ebola and famine blood, of hair torn, of death owls and cancerous alcoholic livers, of babies sucking as much air as possible for the deep night to come, then—a busted chink of afternoon copper light wakes us, yo' sista' rolls in with a bag of lemons for Evil Eye, for the seven inch ache in her abdomen. Keep me in stride. You.

i am talking to you, fool. Don't just sit there stretching yo' face. Tell me why fire yearns for the heart? Write down. Say it. Fool. Speak the names. Conjure the recitations from the coffee cup, the steel-toe border-crosser boots. The grass rips up the morning snow lights, jagged and yellowish. Your AIDS face is hidden. Your rot, my epistemology.

i stand in pure light, a blaze of eyes & arms, volcanic and solar, autistic, antiwritten, burned by mad friars & clerics, uptown octopi readers, my long hair falls as reddish honey, on a naked supple back, on breasts small and secretive. Mystery evades me. Shadows crumble. Without attention, i locate the love void & yet, i know all is well. My blood rocks to a bolero out of rhythm, a firefly's bolero that is, the one in the dog-eye. Hear me warm up to the multinight. Scribble poems & shout obscenities for the sake of scarred angels, for Tara, who guides me in her emeraldine sequined night of lies. Hear me now, kin to the half-collie language that i keep and walk. Kin now, to the leaves that plunge to the floors of this swiveling whiteness without axis, tectonic blasts without mercy. Straight jackets float on the river of infinity. Pink-skinned fishes stare back at me as they evolve into my shape, my babble stream of magnetic juan-foolery. Arm wrestle me on the soccer lawn, kick me in the balls. The murder music is for everyone. The Last Mayan Acid rock band plays Berlin's latest score: dead trade market systems for the dead proletariats, rip up from Bangkok to Tenejapa. Everyone is meaningful and vomits, everyone deposits a stench pail, into the Cube—Neo-America, without the fissure of intimate thighs, crossing over into fire, hunger and spirit. i write on my hand: the road cuts into a star. Go, now, go, fool. In your lyric wetback saxophone, the one yo' mama left you, the Thing-Against-Itself strapped across your hip. And do not expect me to name this Thing-Against-Itself. Play it. Screw it. Howl up to the Void, the great emptiness, the original form.

Keep on rockin', blues-fish, in the gauze of the day into night. Out there somewhere, Dis-America, pick up a chrome bone, the shards of the last Xmas Presidential extravaganza. You, of course, fool. (And Burciaga Boy? Dead from 17 cancer tumors. And Big Mak Royale, our world maquila leader? Sips alcohol to soothe his quasi-Aztec soul. And Zeta Girl? Lost in Michoacan, last seen foaming at the mouth, in the mex-jail boy room, in drag, Brooks Brothers' suit in Pietá, draped over his shrunk down penis bone.) You are my literature, my plot, my tropes unto rage. The women have dispersed. Forms, new colonies, they say, new night systems without patriarchy, they say—new forms. They say. So.

Swivel into the clear. Float over the greenish migrante barracks pocked with wire torsos, their toes wiggle & predict our forthcoming delirium—there is a velvet panther shouting out OM in funk, there is a tawny word in the middle of the city thoroughfare, a planetary semi of lives slices the wet animal in half. i am that punk half-panther. My fierce skull & mandible are formidable, my pelt is exact as witch quartz, a slashed leg tumbles down the highway, battered by every dirty steel wheel. Face up to the sky, you, i said, to the brilliant gossip from the Goddess parade. Outside Tibet, my fate. So. Crawl up, baby, come on, keep on floatin'— in search, slidin', always in search for black journeys, for holiness.

Selena in Corpus Christi Lacquer Red

In my own Tex-Mex break-down, suffix
for eternity—I dash to the bottom, refrigerations;
what I could not have, gone white. Come up
with the harmonica for wings. Blow
the G, then strum my ancient brain, in a French hotel.
Blues & Rancheras, tombs, S with an X on her back.
You taste the Goddess, now—Quiet. Me:
in the ashen flower, upright, proud in your rising blood.
Moody & swollen in da cabaret, naked. Grip
me, in the mud, in sudden flame, red
star in Corpus Christi lacquer—going down, maguey milk
into an odd angled branching needle, a howl Virgin—
the one I wanted to deliver me. Open me, X-Selena
w/your vocal & bruised accordion breast.

Angela de Hoyos

The Final Laugh

On an empty stomach,
with the pang of mendicant yesterdays,
I greet my reflection
in the dark mirror of dusk.

What do the entrails know
about the necessity of being white
—the advisability of mail-order parents?

Or this wearing in mock defiance
the thin rag of ethnic pride,
saying to shivering flesh and grumbling belly:
Patience, O companions of my dignity?

Perhaps someday I shall accustom myself
to this: my hand held out
in eternal supplication, being content
with the left-overs of a greedy establishment.

Or—who knows?—perhaps tomorrow
I shall burst these shackles
and rising to my natural full height
fling the final parting laugh
O gluttonous omnipotent alien white world.

Ten Dry Summers Ago

you could've planted Bermuda grass,
your neighbor to the right says.
But no, you didn't
 . . . and yes it's true, your life
never depended upon it . . .

So now I have to landscape
this bare and godless ground
that keeps eroding
   into flyaway dust
      changing hands
         as easily as identity

have to dance, pivoting
—as a Chicano would say
            "en un daimito"—
         watering this wasteland

have to keep it moist
   until it grows
   until there's room enough
            to hold
      your god and mine

When Conventional Methods Fail

. . . bat your eyelashes!

ain't nothing wrong
with using wile

:Eve used an apple
:Cleopatra used a rug
:La Malinche? oh she

   used Cortez
   to create
   La Nueva Raza

there's something
to be said for a
gal who understands
humanity, and thereby
the secret to success

feminists,
take heed:

   no se compliquen
   la vida!!

you're going at it
the hard way.

angelito's eulogy in anger

angelito is my brother
can you understand?
angelito is my brother

not that bro talk we misuse
but the real down
brother-blood-salsa   sangre de madre

angelito is my brother
dancing slow curves of misery
nodding slow-motion tunes
of alcohol dynamic soul   arrastrándose por las calles
                  con su andar de ángel loco
standing on the usual
corner   the talk of all
the affliction in the ghetto:se llevó el radio
                  me escondió los cheques
                  me quitó la cartera
                  se robó el tique del ponchop

                  pero angelito lo pusieron
                  ahí mami, me entiendes?

angelito was being sponsored
by soft legislators and by
the multi-million dollars
the racket is worth annually
and all of you loved the godfather
the all-time ghetto best film forever

                  me entiendes, papi
                  angelito lo tenían ahí
                  amedrentándole las venas

mocosas sucias que le imprentaron
a ese hermano mío de sangre vinagrosa
húmeda de esa sangre descalza aguada
que cambió de roja a blanca

angelito was angered
by the teacher
   the preacher
   the liberal
   the social worker
   the basketball coach
that mistreated him and
didn't let him express
his inner feelings

angelito le hicieron un trabajo
espiritual   le echaron agua
maldita   le mezclaron sus buenos
pensamientos   le partieron el
melodioso cantar del cucurucú
en su cantar en brujos

angelito didn't get the chance
to receive an education or to
graduate from basic english
courses   no lo querían curar
because of that once a junkie
always a junkie theory i was
taught ten years ago when
heroine had not yet invaded the
wired fences of queens. all of
a sudden drugs reach queens blvd.
and all kinds of addiction centers
popped off on my block to
cure them

y tú, condenao madre y padre
a veces te digo,
por dejarte convencer sus cabezas
por tus caprichos de más dinero
por parar de sembrar guineos
por traernos a este maldito sitio

donde nos ultrajaron los bichos de varones
las tetas llenas de leche de mi abuela
los poderosos pezones de aquella jibarita
que se meneaba poderosamente
que me hubiese gustado agarrarla
con mucho gusto . . . .
ahora, a esa jibarita, me la tienen
como tecata flaca perdida en su desaliento
andando de prostituta abriéndole las patas
al viejo palo de mapo

and the other junkies
the real junkies of the
word junkie (the ones
who stumped your community
with high class hopes shaded
by lack of real attention)
they profited   died fat cats
and bought their way into
heaven

nunca los oí decir ni hablar
nada sobre ellos
zánganos aguajeros
sigan tomando cervezas
sigan mirando novelas
sigan criticándose uno a otro
sigan echándole la culpa sólo a los padres

angelito sabía todo esto
entonces él en la perdición
de su muerte está más despierto
que ustedes. angelito me dijo
todo esto. cuando yo hablo con
ustedes lo único que
oigo es el score de los mets

and the rest of you
so-called pretty looking
bad so bad dumb young
spics are sleeping underneath
the $45 price of your pants

tito madera smith

for Dr. Juan Flores

he claims he can translate palés matos'
black poetry faster than i can talk,
and that if i get too smart,
he will double translate pig latin
english right out of webster's
dictionary, do you know him?

he claims he can walk into east harlem
apartments where langston hughes gives
spanglish classes for newly-arrived
immigrants seeking a bolitero-numbers
career and part-time vendors of cuchi-
fritters sunday afternoon in central
park, do you know him?

he claims to have a stronghold of the
only santería secret baptist sect in
west harlem, do you know him?

he claims he can talk spanish styled in
sunday dress eating crabmeat-jueyes
brought over on the morning eastern
plane deep fried by la negra costoso
joyfully singing puerto rican folklore:
"maría luisa no seas brava,
llévame contigo pa la cama," or
"oiga capitán delgado, hey captain delgaro,
mande a revisar la grama, please inspect
the grass, que dicen que un aeroplano,
they say that an airplane throws marijuana
seeds."

do you know him? yes you do,
i know you know him, that's right
madera smith, tito madera smith:

he blacks and prieto talks at the same time,
splitting his mother's santurce talk,
twisting his father's south carolina soul,
adding new york scented blackest harlem
brown-eyes diddy bobs, tú sabes mami,
that i can ski like a bomba soul salsa
mambo turns to aretha franklin stevie
wonder nicknamed patato guaguancó steps,
do you know him?

he puerto rican talks to las mamitas
outside the pentecostal church, and
he gets away with it, fast-paced i
understand-you-my-man, with clave
sticks comin out of his pockets hooked
to his stereophonic 15-speaker indispensable
disco sounds blasting away at cold reality
struggling to say estás buena baby
as he walks out of tune and out of
step with alleluia cascabells,
puma sneakers,
pants rolled up,
shirt cut in middle chest,
santería chains,
madamo pantallas,
into the spanish social club,
to challenge elders in dominoes,
like the king of el diario's
budweiser tournament
drinking cerveza-beer
like a champ,
do you know him?
well, i sure don't,
and if i did, i'd
refer him to 1960
social scientists
for assimilation
acculturation
digging
autopsy

Melao

Melao was nineteen years old
when he arrived from Santurce
speaking spanish streets

Melao is thirty nine years old
in New York still speaking
Santurce spanish streets
en español

Melaíto his son now answered
in black american soul english
talk with native plena sounds
and primitive urban salsa beats

somehow Melao was not concerned
at the neighborly criticisms
of his son's disparate sounding talk

Melao remembered he was criticized
back in Puerto Rico for speaking
arrabal black spanish in the
required english class

Melao knew that if anybody
called his son american
they would shout puertorro
in english and spanish
meaning i am Puerto Rican
coming from
yo soy boricua
jíbaro dual mixtures
of Melao and Melaíto's
spanglish speaking son
así es la cosa papá

Jesús María Maldonado

Gently Lead Me Home

Written on Hwy. 24, about ten miles
from Othello, WA. For my wife,
the steadying force in my life.

When my mind soars
     in lofty dreams of words
   circling like an eagle
     gently bring me down
When my soul glides
     in wanton dreams of words
   drifting like a leaf
     gently guide me on
When my heart roams
     in haughty dreams of fame
   rolling like a stone
     gently lead me home.

(March 18, 1992)

Elena

My Spanish isn't enough.
I remember how I'd smile
listening to my little ones,
understanding every word they'd say,
their jokes, their songs, their plots.
    Vamos a pedirle dulces a mamá. Vamos.
But that was in Mexico.
Now my children go to American high schools.
They speak English. At night they sit around
the kitchen table, laugh with one another.
I stand by the stove and feel dumb, alone.
I bought a book to learn English.
My husband frowned, drank more beer.
My oldest said, "*Mamá*, he doesn't want you
to be smarter than he is." I'm forty,
embarrassed at mispronouncing words,
embarrassed at the laughter of my children,
the grocer, the mailman. Sometimes I take
my English book and lock myself in the bathroom,
say the thick words softly,
for if I stop trying, I will be deaf
when my children need my help.

Chuparrosa: Hummingbird

I buy magic meat
of a *chuparrosa* from a toothless witch
who catches it as it sips flower-wine.
She fills her palms with blooms,
and the bird dives into perfumed petals for the last time.
The witch claps her hands hard
and blossoms float away,
but the small body is still,
as the *bruja* plucks the ruby and emerald feathers:
soft pillow for her grandchild's head.
She dries the meat, magic meat,
which I buy to sprinkle in your wine
so you will see me, only me.
And you do.
You hover.
Your eyes never wander.
More and more
on hot afternoons
I sleep
to escape your gaze.

Cool Love

If we were Indians, in late September
we'd gather chamisa blossoms in the desert.
We'd cover them with river water, boil
them to make a natural dye. We'd cook
aspen bark, mistletoe, small berries.
We'd remove each other's clothes gently
dip our fingertips into the pots
of warm liquid. We'd stain each other,
stroke slowly, press yellow, brown, green,
red into each other's bones and veins.
We'd brand with hot love.

But we keep our hands clean, touch
yet leave no mark.
We fear claiming what we may not
want to keep.

Sola

I wanted to dance through life
with a tall-dark-handsome
who would choose me, s^p^{i}n
me, lead me past envying eyes
while I strained to match his steps,
my hands holding him.

At forty I dream of g l i d i n g

        alone

on ice, to music no one else has heard

       arms free

Miguel Piñero

Requiem for the Men's Shelter

death has found me in many open places
begging for bread
facing the sun
the blue silent talk of despair
oftentimes finds me on a blaring red
altar making speeches for lonely men
surviving the purple colored horror
of cold gold honors
facing death in many open places

on 3rd street the grey slabs of human
flesh bury themselves in memories of
champagne nights
burgundy spotted eyes watch the coming
of death with nickel & dime hustles
potter's field funeral waits restlessly
in the bottom of the bottle
and death finds them hiding in many open
places

charcoal lines of wasted minds twist
mambos around the steam table of hot
soup
it's a greenless colored jungle where
emptiness is filled with a gideon bible
and god's suburban angels hungry for
kicks pour lighter fluid on a brown
hump of worn out clothes covering
bones and blood and a half empty bottle
containing the inner glow of the night
and a match flickers and yellow death
has found another companion in an open
place . . .

steel matching minds begin to pour out
an organ vomit of frustrated merchants
casting guilt over the coffin paved
futures of *los miserables* and as a poem
never ends never should the smiles of
loneliness cover the blackness of tomorrow
carressing death on many open places. . .

A Lower East Side Poem

Just once before I die
I want to climb up on a
tenement sky
to dream my lungs out till
I cry
then scatter my ashes thru
the Lower East Side

So let me sing my song tonight
let me feel out of sight
and let all eyes be dry
when they scatter my ashes thru
the Lower East Side

From Houston to 14th Street
from Second Avenue to the mighty D
here the hustlers & suckers meet
the faggots & freaks will all get
high
on the ashes that have been scattered
thru the Lower East Side

There's no other place for me to be
there's no other place that I can see
there's no other town around that
brings you up or keeps you down
no food little heat sweeps by
fancy cars & pimp bars & juke saloons
& greasy spoons make my spirits fly
with my ashes scattered thru the
Lower East Side . . .

A thief a junkie I've been
committed every known sin
Jews & Gentiles . . . Bums and Men
of style . . . run away child
police shooting wild . . .

mother's futile wails . . . pushers
making sales . . . dope wheelers
& cocaine dealers . . . smoking pot
streets are hot & feed off those who
bleed to death . . .
all that's true
all that's true
all that is true
but this ain't no lie
when I ask that my ashes be scattered thru
the Lower East Side

So here I am look at me
I stand proud as you can see
pleased to be from the Lower East
a street fighting man
a problem of this land
I am the Philosopher of the Criminal Mind
a dweller of prison time
a cancer of rockefeller's ghettocide
this concrete tomb is my home
to belong to survive you gotta be strong
you can't be shy less without request
someone will scatter your ashes thru
the Lower East Side

I don't wanna be buried in Puerto Rico
I don't wanna rest in long island cemetery
I wanna be near the stabbing shooting
gambling fighting & unnatural dying
& new birth crying
so please when I die . . .
don't take me far away
keep me near by
take my ashes and scatter them thru out
the Lower East Side . . .

The Lower East Side: After Having Witnessed a Man Beating up a Woman Underneath a Balcony Overlooking Avenue C

The mere mention of Daniel Santos
has occupied a place in its history
like the blow of a heavy nail
his songs, cupped hands, which one
carried to a communion or to the party
on Saturday night, were not always
the best thing for protection: which
shows you that no song is bulletproof,
no song escapes the burns that Death's
touch afflicts you with.
                           Add the neon,
the neon that follows you whole, violent,
and steady, to convince you that there is
madness on these streets; the madness
everyone carries in their eyes when they
walk past a man beating up a woman,
and say nothing, as the tip of the foot
repeatedly enters the lowered eyes through a
fast walk that takes one further and further away from this commercial interruption.
But I too have been folded into shape
by the very same dull iron, its memory
holding nothing but the wrinkled faces
of dead men and women. Sometimes
when I have to get away, when I have
to go off and hide somewhere, I
enter the movie theatre off St. Mark's
Place. There my eyes focus themselves
on a pleasant film, while unemployed
Blacks and Puertoricans smoke marijuana
the smoke rises to the ceiling and the
whole theatre looks like a dream being
cooked under glass.

Excerpt from the South Bronx II

Out
    on the street
an old man walks a horse
pulling a wagon
full of fruits and vegetables
breaking up a stick ball game
someone yells
"viejo maricón get out of the way with that horse"
a few throw beercans
the old man curses spits
and says something in italian

In the kitchen
great grandmother tends the stove
    a spanish soap opera pouring out of the radio
I get permission to go out

on the street the horse's tail is a pendulum
seen through wagon wheels turning
                over each other

The First Place

Conga beats pouring out a window
make the curtains tremble
A man is laughing
A woman leans out
a window her fingers running
through her hair over her blouse
down to her thighs
I hear Ismael Miranda
singing
A mulata with cheeks
red as two drops of blood
walks past me
pushing a baby carriage
A little girl is cutting open the face
of the sidewalk with a piece of red chalk . . .
The jewish store owner
turns keys in hundreds of locks,
he dreams that thieves
grow out of the sidewalk
like plants
when no one is around

on the corner by the police phone
two boys are stealing a drunk's money
as he sleeps
on an old piece of newspaper
garbage dancing
at his feet
to a rhythm
played by the cold

it is a mambo
lined with ice.

Luis Omar Salinas

I Am America

It's a hell of a world.
I go like a schoolboy stepping
through the murderous countryside,
a bit off rhyme, a little drunk
with the wonderful juices of breasts,
and the magnificent
with their magician-like words
slipping into the voice of America.
I carry my father's coat,
some coins,
my childhood eyes in wonder—
the olive trucks plucky
in their brash ride
through the avenue,
the wino in a halo of freedom,
the shopkeepers of Democracy.

I am brave, I am sad
and I am happy with
the workers in the field,
the pregnant women
and stopping to chat
like a wild romantic lady.
Children's voices and dogs,
the bar, the songs and fights.
I go ruminating in the brothels,
the ghettos, the jails.
Braggart, walking into early
cafes confessing naivete
and love for the unemployed.
I'm a dream in the land
like the Black, Mexican, Indian,

Anglo and Oriental faces
with their pictures of justice.
I go gaudy into movie houses,
flamboyant spectator
of horse races.

I am not unloved or unwanted
but I have seen the faces
of the rebel, the outcast,
I have touched the madness, all the terrible,
and I have seen the ghosts of the past.
I am a friend to all,
for I have touched everything,
even the empty plates of the poor.
I put on my clothes, my hat,
I visit everywhere—
I go to the market for bananas,
smoke the air,
breathe America.

I am wretched and mean,
I am kind and compassionate.
I remember catechism class,
the nuns and the priests,
my sister's wit,
and the neighbor's beautiful wife.
I am walking behind America,
suspicious, pie-eyed,
open-faced in the distance.
I am a father of prayers,
obedient,
I am a father of women,
a son of women.
I speak as the common man
and listen like the wise.
I am America,
and by hearts grown cold to me
I will be the seer of my intellect.
I will put an end to misery with
the bravado of the seeker,
drunken, reveling
in this American continent,

tight fisted,
exposed like a blue rose
to the night stars.

As I Look to the Literate

With small steps of amazement,
I go foolish into life,
foggy brained with the music
of oblique miracles.
The facts are plain, leatherminded
and scalawagged, but sensing
greater truths from them,
I am glimpsed at from
without—and a sure-footed
Cervantes lives in me
a wispy spider's flight.
Pleased with the nonsense
I've conjured, the night
air falls into my
lap of dreams.
As I fill this heart with
this dry language,
I focus
on the ordinary mathematics
of living, and go about my business
like a serious man
with a pencil behind
my ears.

My Father Is a Simple Man

for my father Alfredo

I walk to town with my father
to buy a newspaper. He walks slower
than I do so I must slow up.
The street is filled with children
we argue about the price
of pomegranates, I convince
him it is the fruit of scholars.
He has taken me on this journey
and it's been lifelong.
He's sure I'll be healthy
so long as I eat more oranges,
and tells me the orange
has seeds and so is perpetual;
and we too will come back
like the orange trees.
I ask him what he thinks
about death and he says
he will gladly face it when
it comes but won't jump
out in front of a car.
I'd gladly give my life
for this man with a sixth
grade education, whose kindness
and patience are true . . .
The truth of it is, he's the scholar,
and when the bitter-hard reality
comes at me like a punishing
evil stranger, I can always
remember that here was a man
who was a worker and provider,
who learned the simple facts
in life and lived by them,
who held no pretense.
And when he leaves without
benefit of fanfare or applause
I shall have learned what little
there is about greatness.

What Is My Name?

In this yellow and green
presence of light shooting
through the kitchen window,
in the forgotten asylums
of awkward gesturing . . .
I've forgotten my name.
Solitary, poor, lonely,
what is my name?
In the geography
of the afternoon I've
named rocks, rivers, mountains,
women.
Is it Carlos the playboy?
Or perhaps Paco the schizophrenic?
No need to fear, I'll remember.
It will come to me suddenly
While I'm frying an egg and the yolk
bursts, when I am sincere, amiable,
friendly.
In this carefree light
I invoke gently voices,
ones that have guided cranes
through the hardship of dunes.
And I've stopped praying to saints.

Middle Age

I converse with my uncle
here, where the day begins
early like a hen in the cold
seeking higher ground.
My dreams come here
like a beaten toenail.
And I feel as if
I've been incarcerated
for the better part of my life.

I raise my beer to my uncle
toasting him on his third marriage.
He tells me, "No man need be alone
especially with October
in the trees, fruit ripening
and the abundance of sunlight."
I am caught speechless.
I have no wisdom
to speak of—unlike
my father who ages gracefully.

My uncle says "Espera la
suerte, wait for luck,
and do what you can with it."

I leave his house
and step outside
to the fresh smell
of autumn
walking through the thinning
olive groves
the sky fearful
half empty of birds.

Ricardo Sánchez

Letter to My Ex-Texas Sanity

> *new panaceas abound*
> *new promises of paradise,*
> *new to me & oddly old*
>   *to others, Utah*
> *sours dreams and it should*
> *begin with a P for its*
> *perversity and putismo . . .*
> *been here over a week, damn,*
> *but it seems forever. . . .*

> —Saltyville of a Lakeburg,
> September 30, 1977

left you, Tejas,
over a week ago,
had to,
for work
is here and not there,
home
resides wherein one lives,
and i live (almost do)
in salt lake city,
it hurls its salty dust
at your soul's eyes,
burns its vapid senselessness
into the furrows
of your thoughts,
it urges you to give up
life, liberty, and the
real pursuit of selfdom,
clothes everything
with missionary zeal,
demands
your capitulation
bicycles you to death,
and then intones

that heaven
merely is for those
who have renounced
all semblance of having been
salient/lively creatures
who lived to love
while loving to live,
ay, utah brutalizes
hope
with its spineless
and amorphous
gelatinous mentality,

perverse & anti-human,
your temple
manufactures
complacent/placid smiles
to keep all niggers out,
your westside of salt lake,
awash with fetid meskin smells,
it creaks and groans
with fear
that we might multiply
your fear of loathsome Laman
defines the way you see us,
for Lamanites you think us,
a mass of swarthy people
who revel in their evil,
ay, brutah-putah-utah
whose land is so majestic,
with deserts y montañas
and nature's pungency,
you fear
those who are darker,
and claim to be so saintly,
enslaver of the frail
and dementer of the fragile,
your sacrosanctimonious
attempts at being holy
are ludicrous at best,
at worst imperialistic,
and ever missionizing.

you flail, hither-thither,
the differences you fear,
and though you feel superior
and smug in your behest,
you strive like hungered zealots
to make us look your best,
oh, poor and foolish bigots,
you have no need to fear us,
for you have nothing worthy
to send us on in quest,
you see
this land belongs
to all who wish to love it
and within it reside,
we'll be ourselves, ay, utah,
and celebrate our difference,
we'll look at you and smile
and continue on our way
to live within your valleys
while we project our name. . . .

En-ojitos: Canto a Piñero

recuerdos dejan huellas
en las humosas palabras
—El Paso, 10 Nov. 88

we joked once, Piñero,
on nuyorican streets
while visions fused
a world of biting sounds
weaving chicano-boricua
tales of survival
through steel-cement barbarities,

short-eyed enojos unfurled
legacies yet to be understood,
in those ojitos
an "enojo" burnished
nuyorican reality and served it
with a dry-witted feeling

as hungered denizens
careened through loisaida avenues,
each pair of eyes
not able to match
the intensity of Mikey
spiking madness
into another day of survival,

words swirled upon
the asphalt, each
a universe of streets'
survival training
as you lurched through
a nation
which only saw the surface
while the inner pain
embroiled a borinquen sensibility
breaking through

layers of amerikan plastique,
unraveling an island's mystique
through the bars and barbarity
of our isolation,
simón que yes, carnal
of the fiery pen
and pensive eyes
which bore into our consciousness,

your words pierce and uncover
the film within
the mindsoul, the poems & sketches
gouge as they caress,
the truths hurt, but the pain
is one of growth & knowing . . .
    adiós, Mikey, adiós . . .

REVISTA
Chicano-Riqueña

VOL. XI, NO. 2
SUMMER 1983

Naúl Ojeda. *Pablo Neruda* (detail), 1982.
Wood-block print

Juan Alonso. *El Guarachero,* 1990.
Acrylic and sequins on canvas, 71-1/2" x 44"

Alfredo Arreguin. *Nuestra Señora de la Poesía*, 1994.
Oil on canvas, 48" x 36"

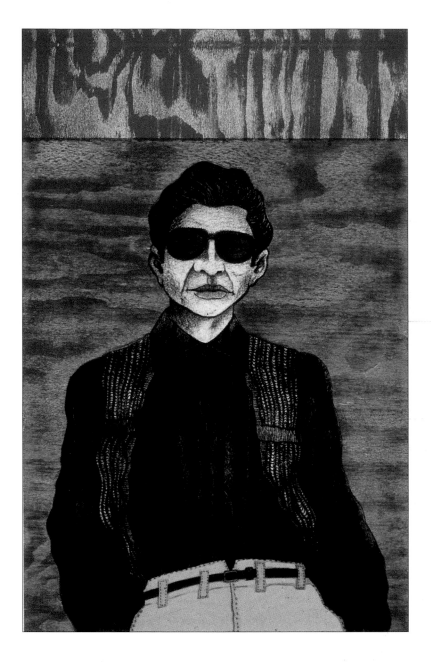

César A. Martínez. *El pantalón rosa*, 1992.
Nine-color lithograph, 35" x 23"

César A. Martínez. *Hombre que le gustan las mujeres*, 1985.
Acrylic on canvas, 50" x 44"

Carlos Almaraz. *Greed*, 1982.
Oil on linen

Carmen Lomas Garza. *Curandera barriendo el susto*, 1986.
Gouache on Arches paper, 14" x 18"

Carmen Lomas Garza. *Tuna de nopal / Pedacito de mi corazón*, 1986.
Gouache on Arches paper, 20" x 25 1/2"

Memory Makers

Like midwives of memory we sever
the knots under the tongue,
sing our eulogies
to the wind.
                    —A. Gaspar de Alba

Julia Alvarez

El Doctor

"Lights! At this hour?" my father asks, looking up from his empty dinner plate at the glowing lamp my mother has just turned on above the table. "Are we in Plato's cave, Mami?" He winks at me; as the two readers in the family we show off by making allusions my mother and sisters don't understand. He leans his chair back and picks up the hem of the curtain. A dim gray light falls into the room. "See, Mami. It's still light out there!"

"*Ya, ya!*" she snaps, and flips the switch off.

"Your mother is a wonder," he announces; then he adds, "El Doctor is ready for bed." Dinner is over; every night my father brings the meal to a close with a third-person goodnight before he leaves the room.

Tonight he lingers, watching her. She says nothing, head bent, intent on her mashed plantains with oil and onions. "Yessir," he elaborates, "El Doctor—" The rest is garbled, for he's balled up his napkin and rubbed his lips violently as if he meant to erase them from his face. Perhaps he shouldn't have spoken up? She is jabbing at the few bites of beefsteak on her plate. Perhaps he should have just let the issue drop like water down his chest or whatever it is the Americans say. He scrapes his chair back.

Her scowl deepens. "Eduardo, please." And then, because he already knows better, she adds only, "The wax finish."

"*Por supuesto*," he says, his voice full of false concern as he examines her spotless kitchen floor for damages. Then, carefully, he lifts his chair up and tucks it back in its place. "This old man is ready for bed." He leans over and kisses the scowl off her face. "Mami, this country agrees with you. You look more beautiful every day. Doesn't she, girls?" And with a wink of encouragement to each of us, he leaves us in the dark.

I remember my mother at all times of the day: slapping around in her comfortable slippers, polishing her windows into blinding panes of light. But I remember him mostly at night, moving down the dark halls, undressing as he climbed the dark stairs to bed.

I want to say there were as many buttons on his vest as stairs up to the bedroom: it seemed he unbuttoned a button on each step so that by the time he reached the landing, his vest was off. His armor, I thought, secretly pleased with all I believed I understood about him. But his vest couldn't have had more than six buttons, and the stairs were long and narrow. Then again, I couldn't see that well in the dark he insisted on.

"I'm going to take this dollar," he showed me, holding a bill in one hand, a flickering lighter in the other, "and I'm going to set fire to it." He never actually did. He spoke in parables, he complained in metaphors, because be had never learned to say things directly. I already knew what he meant, but I had my part to play.

"Why would you want to do something like that?" I asked.

"Exactly! Why burn up money with all these lights in the house?"

As we grew up, confirmed in our pyromania, he did not bother to teach us to economize, but went through the house, turning off lights in every room, not noticing many times that we were there, reading or writing a letter, and leaving us in the dark, hurt that he had overlooked us.

At the bedroom door he loosened his tie and, craning his neck, undid the top button of his shirt. Then he sat at the edge of the bed and turned on his bedside lamp. Not always; if a little reflected sun dappled the room with shadowy light, if it was late spring or early fall or summertime, he waited until the last moment to turn on the lamp, sometimes reading in the dark until we came in and turned it on for him. "Papi, you're going to ruin your eyes," we scolded.

Once I worked it out for him with the pamphlet the electric company had sent me. Were he to leave his bedside light, say, burning for the rest of his evenings— and I allowed him a generous four decades ("I won't need it for that long," he protested; I insisted)—the cost (side by side we multiplied, added, carried over to the next column) would be far less than if he lost his eyesight, was forced to give up his practice, and had to spend the next four decades—

"Like your friend Milton," he said, pleased with the inspired possibilities of blindness. Now that I was turning out to be the family poet, all the greats were my personal friends. " 'When I consider how my light is spent,' " he began. Just like my mother's father, my own father loved to recite, racing me through poems to see who would be the first one to finish.

" 'How my light is spent,' " I echoed and took the lead. " 'Ere half my days, in this dark world and wide . . .' "

Just as I was rounding the linebreak to the last line, he interjected it, " 'They also serve who only stand and wait.' "

I scowled. How dare he clap the last line on after I had gone through all the trouble of reciting the poem! "Not every blind man is a Milton," I said, and I gave him the smirk I wore all through adolescence.

"Nutrition," he said mysteriously.

"What about nutrition?"

"Good nutrition. We're starting to see the effects: children grow taller; they have better teeth, better bones, better minds than their elders." And he reached for his book on the bedside table.

Actually, the reading came later. First there is the scene that labels him immigrant and shows why I could never call him, sweetly, playfully, "Daddy." He took from his back pocket a wad of bills so big his hand could not close over it. And he began to count. If at this point we disturbed him, he waved us away. If we called from downstairs, he did not answer. All over the bed he shared with my mother were piles of bills. I do not know the system; no one ever did. Perhaps all the fives were together, all the tens? Perhaps each pile was a specific amount? But this was the one private moment he insisted on. Not even catching him undressing, which I never did, seems as intimate a glimpse of him.

After the counting came the binding and marking: each pile was held together with rubber bands he saved up from the rolled-up *New York Times* and the top bill was scribbled on. He marked them as a reminder of how much was in each pile, I'm sure, but I can't help thinking it was also his way of owning what he had earned, much as ranchers brand their cattle. The Secretary of the Treasury had signed this twenty; there was Andrew Jackson's picture; he had to add his hand to it to make it his—to try to convince himself that it was his, for he never totally believed it was. Even after he was a successful doctor in New York, with a house in the suburbs and lands at "home," his daughters in boarding schools and summer camps, a second car with enough gadgets to keep him busy in bad traffic, he was turning off lights, frequenting thrift shops for finds in ties, taking the 59th Street bridge even if it was out of his way to avoid paying a toll to cross the river.

He could not afford the good life; he could only pass it on. And he did. Beneath the surface penny-pinching, his extravagance might have led him to bankruptcy several times had my mother not been there to remind him that the weather was apt to change. "Save for a snowy day," she advised him.

"Isn't it 'rainy day'?" he enlisted me. He was always happy to catch his wife in an error since she spoke English so much better than he did. "Save it for a rainy day?"

Eager to be an authority on anything, I considered my role as Arbiter of Clichés a compliment to my literary talent. "Save it for a rainy day," I agreed.

"See, Mami."

She defended herself. "Snow is much worse than rain. For one thing, you need to own more clothes in the winter. You get more colds in the winter."

Out from his pocket came a ten when we needed small change for the subway. Away at college I opened the envelope, empty but for the money order for fifty, a hundred; typed out in the blank beside *memo* was his note: "Get yourself a little something in my name." It was the sixties, and parental money was under heavy suspicion; my friends needed me as a Third World person to be a good example of poverty and oppression by the capitalist, military-industrial complex. I put my little somethings quietly in the bank. By the time I graduated from college, I had a small, corrupt fortune.

But my rich father lived in the dark, saving string, going the long way. I've analyzed it with my economist friends. Perhaps since his fortune came from the same work which in his country had never earned him enough, he could not believe that his being well-to-do wasn't an I.R.S. oversight. My psychologist friends claim that it is significant that he was the youngest of twenty-five children. Coming after so many, he would always fear that the good things would run out. And indeed he had a taste for leftovers, which made his compliments come a day or two after a special meal. Whenever we had chicken, he insisted on the wings and the neck bone because those had been the portions left by the time the platter got to him, the baby. He liked the pale, bitter center of the lettuce. ("The leaves were gone when I got the salad bowl.") And when we had soup, he was surprised to find a bit of meat bobbing at the surface. "Someone missed this one."

Unlike my mother, he saved for a sunny day. Extravaganza! On his birthday, on Christmas, on his saint's day (which was never celebrated for anyone else), his presents multiplied before us. Beside the ones we had bought for him, there were always other glossy packages, ribboned boxes, which dwarfed ours. The cards were forged: "To my dearest Papi from his loving daughter." "Which of you gave me this?" he asked with mock surprise and real delight. Cordelias all, we shook our heads as he unwrapped a silk lounging jacket or a genuine leather passport case. I wish he had allowed us to give him something of value.

Perhaps we did on those evenings after the money was counted and put away, and he was ready for company. With an instinct for his rituals, we knew when it was time to come into the bedroom. We heard the bathroom door click shut; he was undressing, putting on his pajamas. The hamper lid clapped on its felt lip. We heard steps. The bed creaked. We found him in the darkening room with a book. "Papi, you're ruining your eyes!"

"Oh my God, it's gotten dark already," he would say, almost thanking us.

He wanted company, not conversation. He had us turn on the television so we could learn our English. This after years here, after his money had paid for the private schools which unrolled our r's and softened our accents; after American boyfriends had whispered sweet colloquialisms in our ears. As the television cowboys and beauty queens and ladies with disappointing stains in their wash droned on in their native English, he read the usual: a history book in Spanish. We sat at the edge of the king-size bed and wondered what he wanted from us. He wanted presences: his children his wife, Walter Cronkite, the great men of the past, Napoleon, Caesar, Maximilian. If one of us, bored with his idea of company, got up to leave, he lowered his book. "Did you know that in the campaign of 1808, Napoleon left his general behind to cut off the enemy from the rear, and the two divisions totally missed each other?" That was the only way he knew to ask us to stay, appealing to history and defeat, to wintry campaigns, bloody frost-bitten feet, a field strewn with war dead.

I taste the mints that he gave us, one each. He kept a stash of them in a drawer next to his bed like a schoolboy and ate exactly one each night and gave away four. That was the other way he kept us there if we got up to go after Napoleon's troops had been annihilated. "Don't you want a mint?" He didn't mean right then and there. It was a promise we had to wait for, perhaps until the chapter ended or the Roman empire fell or he was sure we had given up on the evening and decided to stay, talking in code with each other about school, our friends, our wild (for that room) adventures.

We were not fooled into rash confessions there, for at the merest hint of misadventure, the book came down like a coffin lid on Caesar or Claudius. Oh, we confessed, we were just exaggerating! Of course we didn't raid the dorm kitchen at midnight; our friends did. "Tell me who your friends are," he said in Spanish, "and I'll tell you who you are." No, we hadn't gotten help on our math. "The man who reaches the summit following another's trail will not find his way back to his own valley." If he caught us, hurrying, scurrying, here, there, he stopped us midflight to tell us what Napoleon had said to his valet, "Dress me slowly, I'm in a hurry."

But why look beyond one's own blood for good examples? "You come from good stock," he bragged when I came home from boarding school, my pride wounded. I'd been called names by some great-great-granddaughters of the American Revolution. "You tell them your great-grandfather was the son of a count." He had paid a lot of money on a trip to Barcelona to find that out from a man who claimed he was licensed to do family trees. The elaborate chart, magnificently framed in curlicued wood, hung in the waiting room of his office in Spanish Brooklyn along with his medical degrees. His patients, I suppose, were meant to be reassured that their ailments would be treated, not only by the valedictorian of the faculty of medicine of La Universidad de Santo Domingo, but also by the descendant of a count. "We were in this hemisphere before they were. In fact, the first Americans—"

"You don't understand, you don't understand," I wailed, hot tears welling in my eyes. And I closed the door of my room, forbidding anyone to enter.

"What's she doing in there, Mami?" I heard him ask her.

"I don't know. Writing poetry or something."

"Are you sure? You think she's all right?"

I had been reading Sylvia Plath, and my talk was spiked with suicide.

"These girls are going to drive me crazy!" my mother said. "That's what I'm sure of. One of them has to have straight hair. Straight hair, at this stage of the show! Another wants to spend the weekend at a boys' school. All the other girls get to! This one wants to die young and miserable!" She glared at my father as if it were all his fault. "I'm going to end up in Bellevue!" she yelled. "And then you'll all be safe and sorry!" I heard her rushed steps down the stairs, the bang of the screen door, finally the patter of water as she hosed down the obedient grass in the growing darkness.

He knocked first. "Hello?" he asked tentatively, the door ajar. "Hello, hello, Edgar Allan Poe," he teased, entering. He sat at the foot of my bed and told me the story of his life.

"The point is," he concluded, " '*La vida es sueño y los sueños, sueños son.*' " He stood by the window and watched Mami watering her fussy bushes as if she could flush roses out of them. "My father," he turned to me, "used to say that to my mother: 'Life is a dream, Maurán, and dreams are dreams.' "

He came across the shadowy room as if he did not want anyone to overhear. It was getting late. In the darkening garden she would be winding the hose into drooping coils. "Always, always," he said. "I always wanted to be a poet. *La vida es sueño*. They also serve who only stand and wait. To be or not to be.' Can you imagine? To say things that can fill the mind of another human being!" I nodded, too stunned at his flood of words to ask him what he meant. "Everyone gets a little something," he cupped his hands toward me, "and some make a great building." He made a building with a wave of his hand. "Some," he rubbed his thumb and index finger together, "make money. Some make friends, connections, you know. But some, some make something that can change the thinking of mankind!" He smacked his forehead with his palm in amazement. "Think of the Bible. Think of your friend Edgar Allan Poe. But then," he mused, "then you grow older, you discover. . . ." He looked down at me. I don't know what he saw in my eyes, perhaps how young I still was, perhaps his eyes duplicated in my face. He stopped himself.

"You discover?" I said.

But he was already halfway across the room. "Papi?" I tried to call him back.

"Your mother," he explained, letting himself out of the room and the revelation. "I think she is calling for me."

A few days later as I sat in his bedroom after supper, waiting for him to fall asleep, I tried to get him to finish his sentence. He couldn't remember what he was about to say, he said, but speaking of discoveries, "We're descended from the *conquistadores*, you know? Your grandfather traveled the whole north coast on horseback! Now there was a great man!" The supporting evidence was slim. "He looked like an Irishman, big and pink-tinted—what is that word? Rowdy?"

"You mean *ruddy*?" I said, knowing Don José de Jesús was probably ruddy with drink and rowdy with women. He had sired twenty-five children, was widowed once, and kept a couple of mistresses who raised the figure to thirty-plus children. Of course, my father never told us that; Mami did when she explained how one of our uncles could have been born within two months of my father's birthday. She cautioned us never ever to mention to Papi what she had told us.

The youngest did, pretending ignorance, practicing addition. If Teolinda, the first wife, had ten children, and Maurán, the second one, had fifteen, and ten of the kids had already died, then how come there were still thirty uncles and aunts left? "They were not *hijos de padre y madre*," he explained. "You know where that term came from? *Hijos de padre y madre*? When the Spaniards—"

"Where did the extra uncles and aunts come from?" My youngest sister was not one to be diverted by a red herring twitching in the sun when a skeleton was rattling in the closet.

So, so, he said. The time had come. The uncles and aunts were half-brothers and -sisters. The mothers were wives, yes, in the eyes of God, where it really mattered.

When we raised our eyebrows and pressed the smile out of our lips, he would have none of it. Customs changed. Our grandfather was a patriotic man. There had been a terrible epidemic, the island was underpopulated, the birthrate was low, the best men did what they had to do. "So," he looked pointedly at each of us. "There's a good *ejemplo* for you. Always put in that extra little bit in whatever you do," he said, lifting up the history of Constantinople or Machu Picchu or Rome.

His mother? He sighed. His mother was a saint. Sweet, very religious, patience personified, always smiling. They didn't make them like that anymore, with a few exceptions. He winked at me.

But since Maurán knew about the half-children, and was very religious, she must have believed that she and her husband would spend eternity separated. I imagined her as a dour and dowdy woman, alternately saying her rosary when her husband transgressed and having his children when he didn't.

"Does Mami remind you of her?" I asked, thinking that leading questions might help him remember what he had been about to say in my room a few nights before.

"Your mother is a wonder," he said. A good woman, so devoted, so thorough. a little nervous, so giving, a little forceful, a good companion, a little too used to her own way, so generous. "Every garland has a few thorns," he added.

"I heard that," she said, coming into the room. "What was that about too used to my own way?"

"Did I say that, girls?" My father turned to us. "No, Mami, you misheard."

"Then what did you say?"

"What did I say, girls?"

We shrugged, leaving him wide open.

"I said, Mami," he said, unwrapping a rare second mint and putting it in his mouth to buy time, "I said: so used to giving to others. Your mother has a heart full of gold," he addressed his daughters.

"Ay, put gravy on the chicken." She waved him off, obviously pleased as my father winked at our knowing looks.

A few nights later, still on the track of his secret self, I asked him, "Papi, how do you see yourself?" Only I, who had achieved a mild reputation as a deep thinker, could get away with such questions.

"You ask important questions," he mused, interrupting Napoleon's advance across the Russian steppes. I like that."

He offered me my mint and unwrapped his. "I am the rock," he said, nodding.

"Ay, Papi, that's so impersonal. How do you perceive yourself? What kind of man are you?" I was young and thought such definitions could be given and trusted. I was young and ready to tear loose, but making it harder for myself by trying to understand those I was about to wound.

"I am a rock," he repeated, liking his analogy. "Your mother, you girls, my sisters, everyone needs my support. I am the strong one!"

That admission put a mermaid on the rock, luring me back with a touching song about loss and youth's folly and the loneliness of the father. "But, Papi," I whispered as I moved from the armchair to the foot of his bed, "you don't always have to be strong."

That was my mistake. The conversation was over. He hated touching scenes; they confused him. Perhaps as the last child of an older, disappointed woman, he was used to diffuse attention, not intimacy. To take hold of a hand, to graze a cheek and whisper an endearment were beyond him. Tenderness had to be mothered by necessity: he was a good doctor. Under the cover of Hippocrates' oath, with the stethescope around his neck and the bright examination light flushing out the personal and making any interchange completely professional, he was amazingly delicate: tapping a bone as if it were the fontanelle of a baby, easing a patient back on a pillow like a lover his sleeping beloved, stroking hair away from a feverish forehead. But now he turned away.

He fell asleep secretly in that room full of presences, my mother beside him. No one knew exactly when it happened. We looked at him during a commercial or when a slip of the tongue had implicated us in some forbidden adventure. The book had collapsed like a card house on his chest and his glasses rode down the bridge of his nose like a schoolmarm's. But if we got up to leave and one of us reached for his glasses, he woke with a start. "I'm not asleep!" he lied. "Don't go yet, it's early."

He fell asleep in the middle of the Hundred Days while Napoleon marched toward Waterloo or, defeated, was shipped off to St. Helena. We stifled our giggles at his comic-book snores, the covers pulled up to his ears, his nose poking out like a periscope. Very quietly, widening our eyes at each other as if that might stop any noise, we rose. One turned off the set and threw a kiss at Mami, who put her finger to her lips from her far side of the bed. Another and another kiss traveled across the hushed room. A scolding wave from my mother hurried my sisters out.

I liked to be the one who stayed, bending over the bedside table strewn with candy wrappers, slipping a hand under the tasseled shade. I turned the switch on, once. The room burst with brighter light, the tassels swung madly, my mother signaled to me, crossly, Out! Out at once! I shrugged apologies. Her scowl deepened. My father groaned. I bent closer. I turned the switch again. The room went back into economical darkness.

The Closet

I

When I close my eyes I can see Christ's eyes in the darkness. It's an early summer afternoon, and I should be sleeping. Instead, I'm standing in the silence of my mother's closet holding a luminescent sliding picture of the Shroud of Turin. One image reveals Christ as he might look fleshed out; the other shows shadows of skin pressed against white cloth. A slant of light filters through the closed door.

"It's my turn! Let me in! I want to see!" Mercy whispers impatiently from behind the door. In the half-tone darkness my eyes travel from the wedding photograph at the back of the closet to the reality of my mother's other life. Shoes crowd the floor, teacher's shoes, long comfortable plastic loafers, sandals and open-toed pumps in blue and black, the sides stretched to ease the bunions' pressure. They are the shoes of a woman with big feet, tired legs, furious bitter hopes. They are the shoes of someone who has stood all her life in line waiting for better things to come.

"Mother! Mother!" I yelled one day across the Downtown Shoe Store. "Is size ten too small?" She answered with an impatient pinching-under-the-sweater-look reserved for nasty children who have the audacity to perform obscenities in public. She scowled across the crowded room, "No! And don't yell, your voice carries!"

Mother was married at age thirty-two to a man who bathed twice a day. Juan Luz Contreras was very clean. He was the town's best catch, a descendant of the Contreras family of west Texas. Head 'em up. Round 'em up. Ride 'em out. Dead. Juan Luz was poisoned by an unscrupulous druggist—oh, unwittingly. He was forced to drink acid. Someone poured it down his throat, but why? He had a wife and a child but three days old. His wife was my mother. For many years I wondered who the man in the wedding photograph was. He wasn't my father. My father still lived with us at that time, but he wasn't home much. Who was the man in the photograph if he wasn't my father? Later I found out he was Juan Luz, my mother's first husband. Ronelia's father.

When my father finally left our home, it was Juan Luz's face in the crowded closet who comforted me. From all accounts he was a perfect man.

Standing in the closet, I can smell mother, all of her, forty-eight years old in her flowered bathrobes and suits of gradually increasing girth. It's the soft, pungent woman smell of a fading mother of three girls, one of them the daughter of the unfortunate Juan Luz.

In the darkness there is the smell of my mother's loneliness. Next to me the portrait of my mother and Juan Luz is hidden behind piles of clothes which are crowded into the house's largest closet. All those memories are now suffocated in cloth. So whoever comes, whatever man comes, and only one could, he would not feel alarm. But would my father come, being gone so long?

I remember the nights my father was home, sitting in his favorite red chair, reading the evening newspaper and later telling stories to Mercy and me.

"A is for Aardvark and In the Name of the Father and The Son and Little Lulu and Iggy went to the store . . . and what did you learn today, baby?"

Sometimes, alone on the armchair or on his lap, I recounted tales of Dick and Jane and little blond-haired Sally.

"Please, Daddy, tell me the story of the two giant brothers, Hilo and Milo."

When I open my eyes I return to the darkness of the closet. With small feet I stand on my mother's shoes. I could never fill them even if I tried.

If I didn't hold the body of Christ in my hands and if there wasn't anything to glow in the dark and then to disappear, I could still see faces in the closet and hear people talking and feel alone. I'm afraid in the middle of the day. Me, supposed to be taking a nap in August and it being the hottest month to be born in and with a crying baby sister outside the door yell-whispering, "Come on, it's *my* turn!"

And there I'd be, holding on to the brass-colored knob with one hand, and Mercy yanking with both, and the Shroud of Turin in my left hand getting crumpled and there I'd be, whispering, "Shut up, shut up! She'll hear you and so I'm looking, okay? It's *my* turn! Okay?" The boxes are open and soon scarves and hats will be all over the floor and I'll have to get a chair and put them up on the top rack and while I'm up there I'll look at the cloth flowers and feathers and I might want to play dress up with the hats.

"We'll listen to the records on the top shelf, Mercy. 'The Naughty Lady of Shady Lane' and 'Fascination.' We'll dance like we like to dance."

"We'll be floating ballerinas meeting each other halfway under the tropical bird light fixture. You can practice your diving while I count flowers, arranging them in rows and humming: 'Let me go, let me go, let me go, lover,' while you rest from your long swim."

"It's my turn, Rocío, you get to look at the Christ eyes all the time!"

"There's no eyes. Only sockets."

"If I squint Chinesey, I can see eyes."

"Yeah?"

"So let me have the thing, it's my turn. You always look too long."

"You might get scared, baby."

"Me, no—you *promised.*"

"Baby, Baby, Baby! There's no eyes, only sockets!"

"Open that door, you promised!"

"Go ahead, baby, come inside, here's the light!"

I turn the light on Christ and Juan Luz and my mother and all my dark secret young girl thoughts, and face my little Sally sister with her baby limp hair.

"Go ahead Mercy Baby! Take the stupid thing. But let me look one more time." I yank on the old pink-and-chartreuse belt that has become my mother's light cord, and go back inside the closet for one last look. I stumble across the gift box, full of vinyl wallets and heart-shaped handkerchiefs and a plastic container of car- and animal-shaped soap. The gift box is regularly replenished by my mother's elementary school students' Christmas and birthday gifts: "Merry Christmas, love Sammy. To Teacher from Mary. You are nice, Mrs. Esquibel, I'll never forget you. Bennie Roybal. 1956."

I turn off all the lights and close the door as tight as I can. I look at the glow-in-the-dark Jesus card and slide it back and forth. The skeleton color of yellow-white bone is electrified, and I can feel and see the Christ eyes in the almost total darkness.

"So here it is, Baby! Leave me alone. I'm going to lie down on the bed and rest. Don't bother me and remember, this is the invisible line, your side, and mine. Don't cross over like you do, with those rubbery hairy spidery legs of yours. Here, see this pillow? Gosh, if we had a yardstick it would be good, but anyway, this pillow divides me from you, my side from yours, okay, Baby? I want the side by the wall and the pictures. So that when I'm drifting off to sleep, I can look at Ronelia in her wedding dress when she was seventeen years old and just married. She wore Mother's dress and Mother's veil, well, maybe not the veil, but the little plastic pillbox crown with wax flowerbuds. Maybe you and I will someday wear that dress, Mercy, okay? Okay? What do you think?"

"Oh, leave me alone!" she says.

As I lie in bed, Mamá Consuelo and her husband stare at me from across the room. Their faces are superimposed on wood. It's more than a photograph. It's a carved picture of two people, one of them a stranger. I don't ever know what to call my grandfather. I never called him and he never called me. So he doesn't have a name. He's my grandfather. He was strong. He was good. He worked hard during the Depression. He was better off than most. He died in his sleep from a blood clot or brain hemorrhage. All I know is that he had a headache, leaped over my sleeping grandmother in the middle of the night to take an aspirin, and then went back to sleep and never woke up. About Mamá Consuelo I know more.

"Oh Mercy, sleeping in the afternoons makes me tired. Without something to do or think about, I'll really fall asleep. I might as well get the crown of thorns down from the crucifix and try them on."

"Are you sure, Rocío, shouldn't you leave them alone?"

Over mother's bed there's a crucifix and on the crucifix there's a crown of thorns. Real thorns, like the ones Christ was crowned with, only these are very small and they cover just the center of my head, the baby spot. It doesn't matter that they're baby-sized, because when I push them down I feel what Christ felt. Oh, they hurt, but not too much. I never pushed them down all the way. But I can imagine what they feel like. They have long waxy spikes with sharp tips. I can imagine the rest. I've been stabbed by pencils in both my palms. The one on my right looks like the Stigmata.

Naps. I hate naps because there's so much to do and think and feel, especially in August. If I have to sleep, I like it to be quick and over with before I know it, or long and happy with a visit to the Grey Room.

The Grey Room is a place I visit when I'm alone. The Grey Room was before my little-ness, before my fear of cloth shadows from clothes on chairs, and of the dark animals the shadows made.

It began when I was a little girl. I was never afraid. Every day I visited a world which the others knew nothing about. Not Ronelia, not my mother, not my father, not even Mercy.

No one knew I lived in the Grey Room or that I flew through air and time. I entered the Grey Room late at night when the house was quiet and I was alone. I'd crawl through the hall closet and into the concrete passageway that was our house's foundation. Down I would go, into the enormous basement, inching my way into the awesome darkness, alone, unhampered, guided more or less by a voice that pulled and drew me, further, further, into the concrete maze. The space became larger, a room of immense proportions, a high room, an altar room, a sanctuary where I was the only Devout. Higher, higher, I climbed, past the attic, to the labyrinth that was the Grey Room. This world was my refuge—this world unknown to all!

One day I began to live two separate lives. One magical, the other fearful. I'd wake up screaming, "The animals! The animals!" I heard the foggy mist of concerned voices. But even you don't understand, Mercy! You always say, "The Closet! There's nothing under our house, no rooms, no space for you to crawl through. There's no house above or underneath our house. There's no huge room without a ceiling!"

But Mercy, I've been there. I've spoken to the Keeper of the Room. He's an animal and brown. He wanted to make the room smaller, but I said no. "There's no space for you, go away." Now the room is white and blue and mine, alone.

All this came to me in dreams. I felt presences and heard voices and the sound of breathing and music far away, then near. There was smoke in my room. I couldn't breathe. The animals crowded into corners. I woke up in the middle of the night trying to run away. Mother turned on the hall light to check in on me and gave me a baby aspirin. I drifted off again. "Walking in your sleep," mother called it.

"Mercy, would you believe me if I told you that I was born in a closet?"

"Rocío, you're crazy!"

Mother was forty years old. She'd been a widow nine years. A table was brought into the room, but the legs were removed because the doorway was too small. When I was born, Mother and I came crashing down. I shot into a closet full of shoes, old clothes. It was 4:48 a.m. on a hot August day. Ronelia hung outside the door. She was ten years old, too young to see such things.

Later, I imagined the wood, the splinters, the darkness and the shoes. And yet, on playing back the tape, Mercy, I always play back love. The things that we imagine support us never do. The world takes us quickly, handles us harshly, splinters us, casts us down and sends us forward to more pain. And yet, when I play back the tape, Mercy, I always play back love, much love.

I hear voices that say: "We are the formless who take form, briefly in rooms, and then wander on. We are the grandmothers, aunts, sisters. We are the women who love you."

"Oh my God, Mercy, do you understand these things?"

No amount of tears will ever wash the pain or translate the joy. Over and over, it's the same, then as now. Birth and Death. There's me, in the Grey Room, or in the closet with the shoes.

"Mercy, remember the closets, remember them?"

II

The bathroom closet was full of ointments, medicines, potions to make us softer, more beautiful, less afraid. It held vials to relieve us, deceive us. It was the mysterious healing place, place of bandages, mercurochrome and cotton balls. The center part contained the "good" towels, only used for company. They sat in their special pile, waiting for the occasional party, the welcome stranger, the annual holiday. Below this were kept the special blankets and the sheets, all folded tidily. They waited for that overnight guest or beloved family member, for nights of rearranged beds and noise and laughter. On the higher shelf were filmy containers of generic aspirin that were consumed candy-like by Mother, for headaches, backaches, heartaches. In the corner was an unused snakebite kit, with its rubber hand pump and arm tie. We fantasized this ordeal and practiced what to do if that time should ever come. The *one* time presented itself, but we were in Texas, on the way to the Big Bend National Park. The two of us had gotten off the crowded car to stretch. We heard the sound of a rattler and there we were, kitless, three hundred miles from home!

After I talked to that snake, what did you do, Mercy? I ran, wildly, madly all the way back to the car. I knew we could have died. One of us at least. It would have been me, for I was closest to the snake and saw him first. We drove on, the boy cousins up front, the girl cousins in the back. I know it would have been me.

The snakebite kit is still there, next to a greasy baby oil bottle. We never had suntan lotion until we were older, as we never had artichokes to eat, or eggplant or okra. We had summer dreams of swimming all day long, until our eyes were red, our toes and fingers pruney and our crotches white and soft and surrounded by tanned skin. Earlier we'd taken a shortcut near the Marking-Off Tree. The shortcut led to a world of water games: Splish-Splash, Tag, Dibble-Dabble. You were the swimmer, Mercy, and I the observer. In my dreams I was always just surfacing to air, having swum from an almost fatal underwater voyage. Later I stood in the darkened shade of the small blue and white bathroom, peeling off my bathing suit like a second layer of skin. My body was ice-cold and excited, slightly damp.

I stripped to summer clothes, shorts and cotton tops, and thongs. My hair was wet, in strips, my lips red, my cheeks browned, my eyes wild and smaller than normal size. My wet, slithering body found solace in cloth. I felt a great and immense hunger, as swimmers do, especially children. I took a towel from the closet, the white ones bordered in black that we were allowed to use, and saw from the corner of my eye "a miniature," placed there by my dad, who was always hiding them. I found his bottles everywhere, in his chest of drawers, under his bed. The bathroom smelled of my cool flesh, of Vicks and liquor, of old prescriptions for ever-present maladies.

In the closet were remedies for women's ailments, hardened waxy suppositories, blood pressure tablets, weight pills, sulfa drugs, cough medicines, and aspirins of all sizes and shapes. There were medications for the head, the rectum, the stomach, the bladder, the eyes, the heart. The old shaving lotion was a reminder that we lived in a house of women.

An enema bag, salmon-colored and slightly cracked, the nozzle head black and foreboding, was poised and ready to be used. The last time Mother gave me an enema I was twelve, not yet a woman, but old enough to be embarrassed. I was sick, too tired to fight. Vicks and the smell of my discomfort all intermingled.

At age sixteen, I sucked in the hot, pleasant forbidden cigarette smoke and blew it out of the wire screens, hoping it would disappear. The butts were dispatched of in the usual two ways—flushed away, or wrapped in kleenex. I lit matches hoping the sulphur smell would mask my sins. But Mother knew. Mother took her aspirin not to worry about me while I smoked nude on the toilet blowing out smoke through the meshed wire.

The bathroom was a closet. It held sexual adolescent dreams. It was full of necessities and bodily functions. Everyone hid there. Some letters from lost lovers, others, old used diaphragms.

III

I smelled Johnny. Johnny again. Johnny's blue sweatshirt jacket that he accidentally left in the living room over Christmas vacation. It was mine for three long weeks. I hung it in my closet, along with my clothes. When I closed the door I smelled Johnny, the undefinable sweetness of his young masculinity.

"Oh God, Rocío, you are so gross, you are the grossest woman I know!"

"Oh settle down, just settle down, Mercy, will you?"

The smells of the closet are lusty and broad: the smells of a young woman's body odors and special juices and the memory of slithering afterbirths. This was where I slid—into the closet full of shoes The closet smelled of summer and long nights and red lips and drying out burnt bobby socks. I washed them every night and dried them on the floor surface. They were my one and only pair. One day they were burned beyond hope. I took them up to the attic to be hidden. My passions and fantasies were lost in time that way—stuffed into dark corners. And yet, the truth I speak is not an awkward truth. I treasured the smells and touches and the darkness of those closets. All were receptacles for a me I always wanted to be, was.

IV

The TV room closet was Ronelia's. Her old strapless prom dresses were there, her evening gowns of tulle, with their spaghetti straps. The closet was immense and covered the entire side of the wall. It was built by Regino Suárez. The wooden doors never opened without a struggle but got stuck midway, so that you had to push one way and then the other to get inside. In this closet were stored long dresses, costumes and party shawls, with Mother's notations, "Summer Long. Ronelia's Party. Wedding Dress, Nieves's." Alongside were her initials and the date. "Ronelia FHA Queen, 1955, Yellow Tulle, N.E."

The long cardboard boxes were crammed onto the top shelf; below them in pink and blue clothing bags were the furs, the beaver Tío Frutoso trapped himself, the suede with the fur neck piece, the imitation beige coat Mercy wore, and Mamá Consuelo's muff. The closet smelled of petticoats and musty fur. Its contents included two wedding dresses, a new one and an old one. The new one Mother picked up at a sale for five dollars. The old one she wore when she married Juan Luz. Ronelia and Mercy later wore that dress, but at that time it was carefully sealed in plastic at the very bottom of the top shelf. Anything to do with him—photographs, articles of clothing, papers—were sacred and off-limits. To me, they were the Ark of the Covenant—deep and full of mysterious untouchability. I was ignorant of the past and the relationship of my mother to this man, long since dead.

Children assign mystery to small objects and create whole worlds from lost objects, pieces of cloth. This closet, then, was a glistening world of dances and proms and handsome dates. It was Ronelia's wedding at the age when most of us are still children. The closet meant dancing life to me. It contained my Zandunga costume, the dress I wore when I danced with Mercy as my "male" partner for bazaars and fiestas.

"Ay Zandunga, Zandunga, mamá, por dios . . . Ay Zandunga . . . Zandunga . . . ."

This closet was Nieves at her best, her finest, and Mercy in imitation beige fur with a silk lining. The closet held two brides, one eternally wedded, the other, husbandless. This closet was time and fantasy and dreams—and it was Regino's— ill made.

V

The living room closet held the house umbrella in rainbow colors. For many years there was but this one umbrella, large, sturdy, friendly. It came out late summer afternoons when we played outside in the rain. It welcomed and dispatched guests, friends who had come to visit. It protected us in early fall rainstorms. It shielded us in the early evening times when the fierce wildness of the unleashed summer tensions rose and fell. This closet was rain, the hope of rain. To desert souls, rain is the blessed sex of God. It cleanses and refreshes. It is still the best mother, the finest lover.

The rainbow umbrella emerged, unhooked from its long nail, and was opened outside. It dried on the porch, each time a little greyer. One day it was replaced in black, by one of its funereal sisters.

This closet was the "guest" closet. It held all coats except Johnny's, which had found a dearer resting place. The overflowing "good" clothes, from the fancy dress coat closet, were placed there too. In it Christmas and birthday gifts were hidden along with the gift box. Later, paper bags full of rummage and used clothing were placed inside, on their way south. This closet was a clearinghouse—the "out-going" closet, the last stop before dispersal—to needy families, young marrieds, senior citizens who used the hand-sewn lap rugs Nieves made. It was a closet full of seasonal smells: summer rain, dark winter clothes, the faint odor of Avon perfume like dried, autumn flowers, the spring smell of soap and freshness. The closet smelled of luggage and time, of faded newspapers and old passports. Behind the door were dated check stubs and unused prayer books The door smelled too, of wood and fingerprints. The ceiling had a trap door that led to the Grey Room. This closet was but another valve leading to the many chambers of the house's heart—where inside, beat my other life.

VI

Nieves's closet was her life, her artery of hope. Those corners were hers, unviolated. In the back, on the right, behind her clothes, was her wedding photograph. She and Juan Luz, both slim, with bright, serious faces stared out to the photographer. Behind them, leading to vast spacious rooms, was a stairway, a mirror on each side. From one wall hung the lasso, symbol of marriage. Nieves clutched a white glove in her left hand, her right arm was at a ninety degree angle. Nieves stood next to Juan Luz and both of them faced right. Her hair was short, in the style of the twenties, with soft loose curls, not as she later wore it, in a bun, austere.

Juan Luz was handsome, with a full head of hair that on second glance seemed subject to thinning, if not local baldness. His hand was tightly clenched, as hers was relaxed. They gazed forward, loving, bright-eyed, with hand-painted pink cheeks. They were sealed in time—a photograph on their happiest day.

One year later, Juan Luz was dead, Nieves was a widow, Ronelia was born, and Mercy and I were still in limbo.

Moving back and up, Nieves's world was full of old records, "The Singing Nun," Augustín Lara, mementos of her teaching days, her work with children. Hers was a closet packed with scarves, new shoes, old photograph albums, a chipped statue of San Martín de Porres, tapes of the Living Bible and charismatic church revivals, as well as home movies of us as children standing by the Willow Tree.

The closet floor is strewn with paper, boxes. When Mercy and I stand in there, with the Christ eyes, we have to be careful.

"Leave me alone! It's my turn!"

"Give me the Christ eyes, Rocío!"

"Oh, go lay down, Baby."

"Don't pull that knob, Mother's gonna find out and get mad. You made me knock something over."

"Okay, okay, let me find the cord. There, see. That didn't take so long. Hey, Mercy, if you crouch down like this, it's better. That way, you feel darker."

I crouch in the closet wanting to know what it is like to feel crucified, to carry the sins of the world. I feel as if I'd already earned my crown of thorns. I imagine the splinters, the wood.

Each step into a closet was a step forward into that other world, the world of concrete corridors, the endless labyrinths, a soundless foray into the maze of faceless forms, living spirits. Up there, down there, in there, they were all the same, they lead into the heart and spirit of the house. When the spirit was sick, the nocturnal journey was long, the gasping for air at the bottom of an endless summer pool. When the spirit was pure, the long rope flew down from the sky and I was beamed up on an umbilical cord of light. I flew beyond the Grey Room into the Blue Room and further up, into the great vast No Room of the living sky. Up beyond worlds, I flew into a universe of change, to the No Place of dreamers who do not dream.

"And *how* did it happen, Rocío?" I wanted Mercy to say when I told her about the Grey Room.

"Do you think it has something to do with seeing the house's bones, I mean, its skeleton? The wood, the house frame, the concrete slabs?"

"Maybe it had something to do with seeing the sliced away mountain," I said. "Remember that mountain? All my life I thought mountains were soft inside."

"You're kidding!"

"Seeing that mountain changed my life! It was one of the five most important things that ever happened to me; the discovery of perspective in the fourth grade was three."

"What are two, four and five, Rocío?"

"I can't tell you that, Mercy."

"Tell me, tell me," she begged.

"God bless, do I have to tell you *everything*?"

"Look, I'll tell you about the Grey Room. Will you be quiet, then?" I'm in the hallway closet. I see Grandpa's death mask wrapped in white satin. I see the box of paper dolls we got on Christmas. I see your crown from elementary school, when you were Bazaar Queen. Why did you cry? I wouldn't have cried, but then I wasn't Queen. I move aside the belt cord from Mother's green bathrobe. I uncover the box of Christmas cards. I move the old rubber rain shoes and plastic raincoats. I make room for myself and step inside. I glide past everybody. I am far away now, past the color and the noise, past the cloth shadows. I am past everyone. Alone. Alone without noise. I don't need to turn on the light.

"Oh, but Rocío, aren't you afraid of the dark?" Mercy said at last, trying on the crown of thorns and then putting them on her side of the bed. "Aren't you afraid of the Christ eyes?"

"Not of the Christ eyes," I said, "but the brown animals scare me and I don't want to be afraid."

"Tell me about the Blue Room," she said, after a long pause. "It sounds *so* beautiful."

"It is," I said, lying down to rest on the bed, not bothering to tell her she was on my side again. "It's a beautiful enormous room and it's blue. But you know, the other day I went in there and it was all white and the floor was like dry ice."

"You mean it changes?" Mercy said with surprise. "Tell me about it before it changed," she said, drowsily.

"The Blue Room is my favorite room. It's the most magnificent, incredible room you'd ever hope to see, Mercy. It has a round ceiling that goes up forever. It's so big that I have to fly back and forth to get around. It's a beautiful room and it's mine. It's all mine!"

"Golly," Mercy said, yawning.

"Watch it! You almost made me turn over on the thorns. Put them up, would you?"

"Rocío, Rocío, if that's *your* room, *what's mine?*"

"I don't know, Mercy, everybody has their *own* rooms, their *own* house."

"They do?" she said with a faraway voice.

"Gaaa, Mercy, do I have to tell you *everything?*"

Lionel G. García

The Day They Took My Uncle

The day they took my uncle I had been under the house playing all morning long with a little girlfriend older than me and she had shown me her female part. I was amazed, seeing it for the first time, at how simple it was. At that age I could never have imagined it as I had seen it that morning. Afterwards, I could never get her, teaser that she was, to show it to me again. So the memory of it faded from me and I was left with a blur, a blur much like the pictures of female pubes in nudist colony magazines that I had a peek at as a child. I imagined that these magazine pictures had been true and that these female parts were constantly moving at a great rate of speed. Why else would they create a blur on a photograph? But that was not what I had seen that morning. What I had seen was standing still. I had been educated. But that in itself is another story.

My uncle was insane, crazy. He was also missing, but I knew where he was. His insanity was well known throughout town. He had been insane for many years. His problem was that, at a spur of the moment and without forewarning, this lean and sallow man would rise to his feet, if he was sitting or squatting on his haunches, and start walking desperately. Then he would grab his ears, the lobes, and start yanking them down violently, as if trying to shake some diabolical voices from his ears. Then he would begin to curse violently. He cursed at people, naming names. He had the indelicate habit also of bringing up pasts that were better left behind and he would talk about the people and about what they had done. I don't know where he got his information, but a lot of it was not true. It was all right as long as he stayed within the family and in our yard or in the immediate neighborhood. But, for no apparent reason, he began to set off in his tirade to the mayor's house: cursing, yanking at his ears, impugning the mayor's ancestry, calling him a sonofabitch and a son of a whore, plus a bastard. The mayor's wife was not spared. My uncle stoutly proclaimed that she was fucking the mayor's cousin. The poor mayor's wife was a frail little dried-up person of a woman who probably didn't even do *it* with the mayor. He also called her a whore and a bitch. I knew he had done this for sure. I was with him that day.

I was, for some reason, his favorite and he tried to do things for me. He would whittle away with his knife, occasionally having these fits, the knife in his yanking hand, until he would finish some little wood carving for me. He made a great fuss over giving me these carvings as if he were really giving me something of great value. He was not a good whittler. In fact, he was not good for anything except for drinking and causing the family trouble.

He was an alcoholic. Which brings me to the supposed cause of his bedevilment. He had been possessed, my grandmother told us, when he accidentally drank the dregs of a bottle of beer that had been laced with a special potion, a potion so powerful it would cause insanity. It was, she said, a potion meant for someone else. I cringed at the thought that some day I would encounter the potion accidentally as my uncle had done and that I would be rendered into that same state. Therefore, I resolved at an early age never to drink leftover beer.

His life consisted of whittling or drinking from early on in the day and coming home, but there was always someone who would buy him a beer. He was a source of entertainment in these taverns, for no one knew when he would get these cursing attacks. No one knew when he would explode. When he did, inside the tavern, he would walk round and round among the men pulling violently at his ears and cursing. The fun was that no one knew who he was going to curse. In this small town it was usually someone everyone knew and the men would hoot and holler, as my uncle went round and round screaming his insults. Soon, after a few minutes, he would come to and stare blankly for a while, gather his thoughts and sit down and mumble to himself. The men would laugh and then my uncle would start laughing with them. Sometimes, when he had a fit in town, the children would run behind, taunting him.

Whether he remembered what he did or not I never knew. I never asked him. In fact, after he was through with his maniacal episodes, I would try to change the subject—talk of something else, something more cheerful. And it seemed as if he preferred it.

But he loved me most of all and that was my problem. He involved me, at a very early age, in things that I never should have been involved in. I can't believe to this day that my parents allowed me to walk the streets with him.

One day, drunk as usual, he took me by the hand and we went to get the milk cow which he had tied across from the mayor's house. As we came by the house, I could feel a slight trembling starting in his hand. And suddenly, as if a demon had possessed him, he started cursing and running toward the mayor's house, towing me along with him. This time he jerked only at one ear at a time. His other hand was holding mine. I was barely touching the ground as he swung me around on his rampage. He started with the mayor and cursed him, and then he continued with the mayor's wife. I could see the poor lady, worried as she was and scared, peeping through a crack in the curtain, watching all this: a deranged man yanking at his ears holding a little boy by the hand and running, menacingly, toward her house.

It was embarrassing to have an uncle like this one around the family. Your friends needed to be very tolerant. My sister didn't like him too much. She could never invite anyone over.

One time a young man came uninvited to call on my sister, and, as he was walking to the front door, my uncle started having a fit inside the house and ran out, bursting through the front door, screaming, just as the man was coming up the stairs, and my uncle ran right through him and knocked him down. The man got up fast and started running away, but everywhere he tried to run it seemed he'd run into my zig-zagging uncle. He never came back to call on my sister. He was known to have said that he would never call on a girl who had heard so many curse words in her young life.

He didn't stay with us at night. I guess he realized the inconvenience it would have caused. He lived next door in a small house with no electricity, no heat and no water. Later on when he became sick and right before he died my grandmother moved him into the dining room that we never used and set up a small cot for him. It was interesting, as I was told, that in his last days the doctor told him he couldn't drink anymore unless he wanted to die. So he quit drinking and died within the week. What he died of no one knew and no one cared. That was the beauty of life in a small town. People died and that was that. There was no need for heavy medical expenses or lengthy hospital stays or exotic diagnostics. If a person got sick and then got well that was a cause for joy. If a person got sick and died, well, they buried the person and everyone kept on living. So when he died, he just died. Even the doctor was not particularly interested as to why a person had died. He was there to treat well people.

The mayor was not home when we were trampling his front yard, but his wife told him about it and, rightfully so, the mayor became very angry. He had already been angry before, since that was not the first time my uncle had gone on a rampage against him and his wife.

That night the mayor came over and talked to my grandmother, my mother and my father, and they had assured the mayor that they would scold my uncle. My uncle, in the meantime, was at the tavern begging for beer and getting drunk and forgetting to bring the cow home.

You see, my uncle had only one job to do. He was to take the cow to a pasture in the morning after milking her and then he was supposed to bring the cow back before sunset, milk her, and put her up for the night. He was able to do the morning part of the job well and with consistency, but bringing the cow back presented a problem to him. If he was in the middle of a fit, he would forget what time it was or whether he had already taken the cow home or, if he were drinking steadily, if someone was buying him beer, he didn't want to quit just to bring a cow home.

So frequently, as we did that night, my father and I went to look for the patiently waiting and confused cow to bring her home. I say we had to look for the cow because we never knew for sure where my uncle had tied her that morning. The tethering of the cow and its location was left entirely up to him. If he found a lush grassy place by the cemetery, he would tie her there. The next day he would tie here somewhere else. Usually the cow was never at the same place on two successive days.

My father and I would go looking for the cow and I would hold the lantern as we walked the dusty streets and, when we thought we saw the huge bulk of the animal in the darkened field, he would take the lantern from me and raise it above his head to see if we had located the cow.

My father never got angry with my uncle. He would scold him lightly and in a very gentle way. My uncle would look at him with his large sorrowful eyes and would promise to do anything that my father wanted him to do. Then he would walk away, the halter rope in his hand, the cow walking slowly behind him, and sometimes he would start his fit at this time and let go of the cow and he would walk hurriedly away, tugging at his ears and cursing at the sky. The cow would stop, look at him stoically, as if she knew this was the cross she had been given to bear, and wait patiently for him to complete the fit.

He had another one of his fits while he was walking through downtown main street and this time everyone there heard him curse the mayor and his wife.

The sheriff's car came slowly by the house, went slightly past it and I could see from under the house the sheriff straining to see if he could spot my uncle. He stopped the car and backed up and parked in front. He got out. He was a formidable man, over six feet with a large belly, his gun belt hidden by the bulge in front. He carried a large long-barreled revolver and a pair of handcuffs were tucked under the belt at one side.

My girlfriend and I looked at each other. I suspected why he was here. You see, a week before, the doctor and the sheriff had come by the house and I overheard them telling my parents about what my uncle had done and that my uncle had to be placed in an insane asylum. My parents were law-abiding people and they agreed that, if that was what was best for my uncle, then that's the way it had to be. The sheriff said it was the legal and proper thing to do. He said that my uncle was a menace and a constant source of embarrassment to the community. Even the Sisters of Charity, the three nuns that were left behind after the parochial school closed, were demanding that something be done. The priest, of course, was in complete agreement. Since the school and the rectory and the church were across the street, they, the priest and the nuns, could hear my uncle shouting obscenities. The priest said he had condoned it for some time, but he figured it was time to do something now that the mayor and the sheriff and the doctor were in agreement. He hadn't wanted to be the first one to complain, being a priest and all. The solution, of course, was to get my uncle into an insane asylum in Galveston.

We could see the sheriff come up the dirt path, the path bordered by lime-covered rocks. He came up the stairs and walked above us onto the little porch and he knocked heavily. The whole house seemed to shake under his heavy fist.

We could hear the footsteps above us as my mother came to answer the door. "Coming, coming," my mother said.

"María," the sheriff said in his gruff voice. "I've come for Mercé. It's time. This is the day we agreed on."

"Come in, come in," my mother was saying to him and, to us eavesdroppers under the house, it seemed that everything that was said had some humor in it. My girlfriend placed her small dirty little hand over her mouth to cover up a giggle. I was smiling at the thought that no one knew we were there.

"Sit down," my mother said, "sit down." She had the habit of repeating everything when she was nervous.

"I don't have time to sit," the sheriff informed my mother. I could tell he was angry. "We need to get him out of town and put him up somewhere, like Galveston, where someone who knows about these things can help him."

"My husband and I agree," my mother replied, "We'll cooperate in whatever way we can."

"Well it's been a long time. I mean he's been hanging around town cursing at everybody for a long time. It's just come to a head recently, that's all. Maybe we should've done it sooner. It's just that we all treated it as a joke."

"He's always been harmless," my mother said. "He wouldn't hurt a fly."

My uncle and I often went hunting but we never killed anything. He carried the rifle and I walked by his side. Once in a while he would hold me up as I stopped to pick a burr out of my foot. He would wait patiently, much like the cow had done for him, as I balanced on one leg and dug out a goat-head from the sole of my foot. When we came upon a rabbit I would whisper excitedly, "There's one. Can you see it? Can you see the rabbit?"

My uncle would look close at the little animal and act as if he were going to shoot it, then he would say, "We'd better save him. We'll kill him on the way back."

We could hear the sound of leather as the sheriff adjusted his gun belt. "Don't be too sure," he said. "He could be violent under certain circumstances."

"That's strange," my mother said. "I've never known anything, *anything*, that makes him violent, except being violent on himself. God only knows what voices he hears or what pain he gets, but he yanks at his ears like he's going to pull them off."

"Well, enough of this," the sheriff said, and we could hear him walk around our little house opening doors. "Where is he?"

"He's probably at the beer hall," my mother replied, "where he normally goes every day. Don't you think?"

"No, he's not there," the sheriff informed her. "I've looked everywhere except here."

"Well, I'll be . . ." my surprised mother said. From under the house I could imagine her putting her fingers to her mouth like she always did when she felt surprised.

"You don't have any idea where he's at?" the sheriff asked.

"No," my mother replied. "But have you seen the cow? He may be close by."

"I didn't see the cow," the sheriff said. "But I wasn't looking for her either. Where was he supposed to take her?"

"I have no idea," my mother said, "but I think that lately he's been staying close to the mayor's house on that open pasture."

"And you're sure you haven't seen him?" he asked my mother again to make sure she wasn't lying.

"I'm sure," she answered and she was telling the truth.

We could see my grandmother coming across the yard. She lived next door. We could see her long black dress moving from side to side as she strode over to see what was going on.

"Are they here for Mercé?" she asked my mother as she stood outside.

My mother came to the window by where we were sitting and she talked to her. My grandmother was telling my mother where he was hiding. Of course I knew where he was hiding all along. He was under an old rug in a corner of the toolshed behind my grandmother's house.

In the morning he had come to the window by where I slept and he had scratched on the screen and awakened me. Today was the day they would take him, he said. He didn't want to go. "You've got to," I said to him. "Where are you going to hide?"

"I'll hide," he said and he thought for a moment, as if he didn't know, "in the toolshed."

I felt sorry for him at that time. I wanted to cry. I didn't want them to take him away. And yet I knew that he needed help. Just think, I had told him, if you can come back normal how much better off you'll be. He still wanted to hide.

"And what if they find you?" I asked.

"They won't," he said. "What do you think?"

"If you think you can hide there forever, then give it a try," I said, although it scared me to think that I would have to lie about his whereabouts. What I didn't realize at the time, young as I was, was that they would find him very quickly and that there was no escaping the law.

Unknown to anyone, my uncle had panicked and fled the toolshed. The sheriff had already come outside and he was checking the yard. When he stood in front of the toolshed door my grandmother and my mother screamed, "Don't hurt him! Don't harm him! Please don't hurt him! He's a very gentle man."

The sheriff kicked the door open and had his hand on his pistol ready to draw it out if he needed to. He disappeared into the toolshed and we could all hear the commotion inside. My mother was screaming, as was my grandmother, imploring the sheriff not to hurt my uncle. From the noise inside it appeared that my uncle had been discovered. The sheriff seemed to be tearing the place apart. Finally, the old rug came flying through the door and my grandmother and my mother both screamed. They thought it was my uncle flying through the air. My grandmother fainted and fell to the ground, like a rag doll. The sheriff kept crashing things and I wondered how the place would look like after he got through. My mother ran inside the toolshed and my grandmother, who had gotten up and recovered, followed her, and my girlfriend and I could hear all three thrashing about and the greatest commotion I ever heard.

Then, suddenly, from behind me I picked up the faint smell of stale beer. It was my uncle's breath. He was under the house with us! He had escaped from the toolshed while the sheriff was inside our house.

I couldn't very well talk to him. My mouth was so dry and I was so scared, but the words finally came out and I asked him what he was doing. He didn't seem to know. He had the look that I had seen wounded rabbits have right before you step on their heads, as if they were pleading for help and knowing they can't have any. It was the sight of fear in his eyes, the feeling of being tracked down for the kill that haunts me still. What could I do? I was too little to do anything. He put his arms around me and we both fell to the ground and he started crying, sobbing. He didn't know what to do. He didn't want to go. My girlfriend started crying too.

The sheriff had come out of the toolshed and he looked like he had been in a terrible fight. My mother and my grandmother tried to fend him off with ropes and tools and whatever they could find. You see, they thought that he had killed my uncle. They were chasing him down the yard when, as luck would have it, my uncle began his trembling and started one of his crazy fits. He hit his head on a floor joist and he started bleeding. And thus he came out from under the house, crawling sideways like a fast crab, bleeding from the head. He straightened out, grabbed his ears and began yanking and pulling them as he started his walk, shouting obscenities at the world. This time he included not only the mayor and the mayor's wife, but he also said some bad things about the priest and how the priest was fucking the nuns. And as if on order, the windows of the rectory closed as fast as possible.

Once he had shed the two women, the sheriff ran up from behind and tackled my crazed uncle. He caught my uncle completely by surprise, blindsided him, and my poor uncle in the middle of his cursing gave out a loud grunt as the wind was knocked out of him. The sheriff quickly put my uncle's hands behind his back and handcuffed him. Still, my uncle persisted and yelled and screamed, and he rubbed first one ear and then the other into the ground until he caused them to bleed.

Once they realized that my uncle was alive, that the sheriff had not killed him, my mother and grandmother stopped beating on the man. And once they realized my uncle had been found and restrained, they ran over and tried to help the sheriff and my uncle to their feet.

My father arrived running. He had been at work. We could see that he was helping the sheriff get Mercé up and they had gone to the other side of the house to the water faucet. The sheriff cleaned himself up and my father, mother and grandmother cleaned up my uncle. He had quieted down now and was into the mumbling stage of his fit.

"Look at what you did to yourself," my mother said to my uncle.

"You could really hurt yourself doing all this."

"He can't help it," my father told her.

"Well, he wasn't so hard to catch," the sheriff said. "And yet I feel sorry for you," he told my uncle.

"Come, we'll help you get him to the car," my grandmother told the sheriff.

"I'd appreciate it," the sheriff replied.

"Now, Mercé," my mother lectured him, "be good in Galveston. You're going to Galveston, did you know that? Maybe somebody there can help you. And it's very pretty in Galveston, did you know that? They have a beach."

My uncle shook his head.

"Well, that's where you're going. Be good over there and behave. Try to control yourself and maybe you can come back soon."

When they helped the sheriff put my uncle in the backseat, he looked toward us under the house. I could see him plainly, but I could tell he was trying desperately to find me, so I came out a little ways to where the sun was shining under the house, and I could tell he saw me. He gave a terrible cry.

As the car drove away my father kept yelling for the sheriff to stop, but the sheriff never heard him.

"What did you want?" my mother asked him, crying, as the car with my uncle disappeared from view. He replied that he wanted to find out what my uncle had done with the cow.

And my mother and grandmother cried some more. At first they cried every time they saw the cow. The poor cow could never figure out what there was about her that made them cry. She would look inquiringly from one side of herself to the other, as if looking for some clue.

My uncle came back a year later, uncured and ready to go. He did, though, carry a little card in a billfold my father bought him saying that he was not a menace to society.

Dagoberto Gilb

Birthday

There was traffic on his birthday. The Hollywood Freeway to the downtown area. His father sighed and got off and got back on going in the other direction and then jumped on again saying he'd catch the 5 Freeway and then they got there but the ramp was closed for repair. His father started grumbling and talking about how he should have thought of this before, that he shouldn't have promised to go to that toy store because it was so far away and saying he couldn't understand how people could live like this all the time, back home nothing was as complicated as here, when he was a kid he didn't have toys like they have now and kids didn't expect as much. His mother said that maybe they should go somewhere else, to the shopping center, that toy store will be open and he can pick out what he wants over there, that'll be all right. His father said he should have called around like a smart man, that he didn't even know really if the store way out here had the toy the boy wanted. The boy, who was six today, let his happy pucker loosen from his lips and his body sag into the backseat as they drove in what seemed to him like a direction of home. But then his father, eyes at him in the rearview mirror, said no, I told him we'd go there, he expects to go and I'm going to take him there and I think I even have an idea. And he drove a little faster, made a turn and another, and got on the Glendale Freeway and then onto the 5 and boomed okay! and we're gonna get there now and it's my son's birthday and it is his day.

It was a long drive and the boy, his arms looped over the front seat now between his parents, worried that this wasn't right either. Was his daddy sure? Was he sure they shouldn't turn around or maybe they weren't going the right way, or maybe they'd gone too far, he'd never seen this freeway before and it didn't look like the one the toy store was next to last time. His mother said look over there, it must be a zoo she teased, because there's a picture of a giraffe on the building. It was the toy store and his baby brother was excited too and pointed ah ah! but his baby sister still slept. The boy controlled his body but not his smile and said oh yeah mommy that must be the zoo so let's go to the zoo and everybody laughed and felt happy and good and they parked and set up a collapsible stroller, the freeway visible and roaring beside them, and, pushing the thick glass doors, they went inside.

It was at least twelve feet high with toys, a trucker's warehouse big, more toys than all the days of childhood, all squeals and squeaks and putts, little kids running and whining and wanting, bouncing and rolling things. The father and the mother and the two boys and the baby sister each were twisting their necks and stopping, look at this, look at this. Get anything you want, the father told his six-year-old, but he didn't say but not for too much, he couldn't talk about money on his son's birthday, didn't want to explain about paying bills, all the other expenses, problems, how it was in this new place. There's so many things, the boy said, it's so hard. Well, get what you want, what we came here for, that one you saw last time. I just don't know if it's the best one, the boy said, and his father said oh yes it is, it's the best one in the whole place, and his father thought that the price was right too, and he said it's got 145 pieces and a big mountain, and tanks, and landing craft to cross the river, and fighter planes. The boy wanted to know who the good guys were and who were the bad guys and how could you tell? His father said he guessed it was those Germans, yeah these are the Nazi men and they were bad men, they really were bad guys and the Americans really were good guys. And the boy smiled and his father found a new unopened box almost as tall as the boy who glowed with excitement. They were all ready to go home now but the mother wanted to buy some party plates and the younger boy had to get something so he didn't cry so they chose an $.87 package of horses and for the baby girl a soft, pink bracelet-like teething ring for $1.19. They stood in line to pay. There were long lines. The boy waited contentedly, but the other two could not and the mother took them away. The boy just stared at his box, at the pictures, and his father stood there and waited with all the other waiting people. When he got to the stand he asked the young girl is it always crowded like this? and she said always and he shook his head. Life in the big city, she said, and he said life in the big city, and he paid, and the boy pulled the box off the counter, I want to carry it myself, and everyone in the family seemed as happy as him.

The boy had picked out a cake at the supermarket the night before. He didn't want his mother to make it, he knew exactly where the cakes that he wanted were and he guided them through the aisles of the market and squinted at the plastic windows of the cake boxes. His mother and father suggested one but he said no, not that, and found one with a clown and said this one. His father and mother saw the price and said that's a little too expensive and inside it's pink strawberry but the boy had already changed his mind, saying this is it, this one, this one here. It was chocolate devil's food with three white flowers and green leaves and white spiraled frosting in longhand happy birthday. How about this other one? his mother asked. It's the same, except I can write happy birthday on it, and it's less expensive. No, the boy said, this is the one, please, this is the one. Well if you get that, his mother told him, we probably can't get ice cream. His father's silence agreed, and the boy thought about it, then said okay and picked up the chocolate cake anyway. I'll get it, his father said, and he carried it but said we have to get ice cream and the mother helped choose the brand of vanilla.

His mother stabbed six candles into the brown frosting. She arranged them so there were five blue ones at each corner of an imaginary star and one yellow one in the middle. His father posed the boy next to the cake and took a picture, then he found some matches and lit the candles, and then his mother and father sang, only their voices, the father's loud, the mother's soft, the baby girl in her arms drooling, the younger boy, eyes open, learning. It was overcast outside the window near this. The man next door who nagged and screamed at his wife was sweet-talking his dog, and there was a police helicopter swirling around and black-and-whites filling up the street behind them. A radio not so far away played a love song by Yolanda del Río. The father snapped a picture with a flash of the boy blowing out the candles. His mother brought out two more presents, each wrapped in paper that had been around the house, without ribbon or bows. She said, the little one's from your brother and sister, the big one's from your mommy and daddy. The little one was comic books and the boy smiled, so pleased, and grabbed the other and ripped it open. It was called the Sword of Grayskull, which was from his favorite TV show, and now he was happy beyond words. His mother cut up the cake and his father scooped out ice cream and they all sat around quietly eating off the party plates. The radio outside was off and instead they heard a police bullhorn mumbling on the street behind them. His father told the boy to wait a minute, he thought he had a couple of batteries. He loaded them in the black plastic handle of the sword and then handed it to the boy. The six-year-old held it above his head with both hands and lit up the yellow plastic blade. Slicing the darkening air, his whole family admired him as he stood in the center of the room saying I have the power!

Max Martínez

The Adventures of the Chicano Kid:
A Dime Novel

Chapter One (In which the Chicano Kid undertakes a magnificent entrance into the hamlet of Santo Gringo, and of his reception)

There is no sun that gently raves with golden showers quite to match that which radiates so splendiferously upon the terrain and the creatures of God who inhabit the southwestern region of the United States. It is indeed a sun which gilds the people and the imagination. It is the lofty, the majestic, the omnipotent Hyperion that casts his glow upon the Southwest.

The shadows of the morning, lengthening toward the west, engendered from the east, had all but dissipated when the Chicano Kid rode into the village of Santo Gringo. In appearance, in majesty, in magnificence, in splendor, the Chicano Kid is, to all but the most stultish of mind, a fit rival for the lofty Hyperion.

It was a time of sadness in Santo Gringo, a sadness which swept the territory, leaving it barren of joy and mirth. The morning gently perched itself upon the rooftops of houses and dwellings that long ago verily deserved the signification of home. But that was before the Gringo invaded the territory. Yes, the sun did indeed rise only to shine upon the misery of the doleful Chicano barrio. The velvet blues, the fiery oranges that kissed upon the horizon went unnoticed, as they did each morning, by the denizens of this village of scorn, of abject poverty—reader, if you could only see it! Surely you would be overcome by sympathy and pity. Only the hardest heart of stone could not but melt at such a piteous tableau.

The clarion call of the martial roosters, grateful to have survived yet another evening of battle for the entertainment at the fighting-cock pits, arouse the inhabitants of the village, of the barrio. The people of the barrio rise, dress, relieve themselves, breakfast meagerly, as has been their custom since their ancestors, the Aztecs, discovered the right path to civilization and grandeur. For these people, these noble sons of the desert, these lineal descendants of the majestic Aztecs— oh! lift up your spirits, dear reader—for these people, today will have the appearance of all other days, but truly such an appearance will be illusory. Yes, yes, the day will beckon yet more contemplation of misery, of deprivation, of oppression. The harsh, brutal, cruel life they have known since the coming of the Gringo despoiled this arid paradise will present itself in the quotidian treadmill of sameness.

Indeed, the single change these barrio dwellers ever experience is the variety in the cruelty of the Gringo, such cruelty as only the Gringo can yield with his fancy and his imagination in complete abnegation. Trust your spirits to soar at their most liberated will, follow sojourner along this voyage of narration, for, indeed, this miserable existence, if existence it be, is coming to an end. For these noble sons of the desert, destiny is attendant only upon the slowness of the pen.

Into their midst, at this very moment, in fact, there is coming a stranger, one of their own, one with the dark, mestizo features, one with the noble physiognomy of the sun. It is the return of one who had been their protector in earlier, gentler times, one whose family is well remembered for wisdom, for grace, for kindness, and he, as the inheritor of these traits will surely not disappoint our expectation and will, in due course, reveal these very same eleemosynary characteristics.

There will come into their midst a champion, a bronze knight of the sun, one who without a trace of reluctance will take up the mantle in the cause of justice, truth, and liberation. How fortunate indeed are sometimes the accidents of history. How we must marvel at that fate, though it may cast those it ought to care for the most to the deepest depths of degradation. How wonderful I say it is to have fate return in the guise of our hero to make ample and just restitution for decades of profound neglect. For indeed, at this very moment, though the poor, abject, dwellers of the barrio will not know it for several hours, the true, gentle, and stout-hearted knight of the desert: The Chicano Kid, is in their village. Misery, be on your guard!

The cause of this misery is none other than the nefarious Alf Brisket, arch-enemy of the Chicano Kid, despoiler of his sister, usurper of his patrimony, the scurrilous scourge of the Southwest. The days are already numbered for this vile, this evil, this vicious viper of a man. He will no longer spoil the beauty of nature with his presence. Today, if our predictions are consistent, will be a sad day for the nefarious Alf Brisket. His cruel and vile deeds will be avenged, the sweet and dulcet tresses of Justice will again flow in the gentle breezes of this golden land. Her face will once again turn upward toward Helios and not, as has lately been the case, toward the deplorable depths of Hades. Persephone returns permanently to her mother of the earth.

But, let us pause momentarily in our discourse and simply submit to the dazzling and majestic entrance of the Chicano Kid into Santo Gringo. It is a sight so magnificent in splendor that we ought not for even a moment jeopardize our appreciation of it. The pertinent details of our narration must be held in abeyance. I take this liberty in the hope I have thus accrued to myself the confidence of the reader and he may rightly trust that once this impoverished description of the Chicano Kid is presented, our tale will resume in its proper trajectory.

Odysseus did never appear so majestic! Achilles never so valiant! Zeus himself was never so awesome. Oh, reader, if you could only see the jet black stallion prancing in the mid-morning sun, the muscular rippling of its shoulders, it is enough to send Michelangelo throughout the Carrara quarries in search of Nature's inert copy. The spry, energetic prance! This charger, this courser, so worthy indeed of the most valiant knight errant of the West!

And you, dear reader, are so much more fortunate than the characters who people this inspiring narrative, for it is truly a pity that the sultry mid-morning sun has driven so many of these doleful inhabitants inside. This sleepy hamlet of Santo Gringo will be deprived of this wondrous sight which, surely, were they to see it, how they would treasure it in their hearts forever. How they would spread news of it among themselves, how they would journey at great expense to limb and pocketbook to spread the news about the countryside. How the rustic bards and balladeers would tune their instruments, and with Nature as a guide, begin the spontaneous elaboration of this magnificent sight in song. It is, to be sure, the veritable stuff of legends. The Lone Ranger, the Cisco Kid, the Durango Kid, Roy Rogers, Gene Autry, Zorro, Matt Dillon, John Wayne—mere ruffians by comparison!

The wide-brimmed Charro hat, the national chapeau of the bronze people of the sun, swept upwards at the edges with the mighty force of a raging sea, made— nay, sculptured—from the finest felt, embroidered with the richest silver from the mines of Oaxaca, especially selected by management itself for its purity and lustre. And of the remainder of his attire? Attire is hardly the word! Dare I even speak of it? The poverty of language overwhelms this, your humble servant, when he tries to describe the manner of the Chicano Kid's dress. Were I Homer, Virgil, Dante, Shakespeare, Goethe, and Rod McKuen all in one, I could not do it justice. Were all the languages of the world whipped together to yield the butter of the human soul, it would not be enough. What care I for words! In the Panavision of my mind, I see so clearly. I can only say, gracing his limbs, a black outfit, of the finest wool, each strand gathered with utmost care from the most heavily guarded and virgin of English sheep. Virgin English maids before the loom, weaving as they utter silent novenas. This, too, is embroidered in silver, large brilliant buttons the size of Big Macs. The boots of highly polished, impeccable calfskin, the toe and tops inlaid again with metal the color of moonlight. Reader, I, with all honesty, cannot go on. It is futile to attempt to describe the clothing of the Chicano Kid. Were not the tale of such import, I would send me to a monastery. I beg of you, indulgent reader, to allow me the small luxury of composing myself that I may continue with the force and vigor our tale requires.

It is in front of the village saloon that the Chicano Kid glides to inertia. How like a powerful statue he sits upon his steed! It is with the grace and indolent celerity of a ballet dancer that he alights from the horse, the music of his jingling, tinkling, tinny spurs accompanies the first encounter of the Chicano Kid's feet with the soiled earth of Santo Gringo. Though the spurs may jingle, though it be music for a thousand ears, though a symphony could be written to describe what the heart feels and the mind cannot say, the Chicano Kid does not hear music, there is no symphony in his life. There is only a heavy burden in his heart, a burden so heavy it would have driven a hundred lesser men to despair and the grave. This burden which the Chicano Kid feels so heavy on his person—need I say it, dear lector?—may only be lifted by the death of the vile, the evil, the vicious Alf Brisket—the very name fills my pen with contempt! Until that day dawns upon our hero, until we too accompany the soaring of the Chicano Kid's heart, there will be no music in the Chicano Kid's life. However, that day is almost upon us. The musician of the soul rehearses his funeral dirge for the last time. The faint strains of gaiety are discernible in the secret recesses of the soul for the optimist who can will his imagination to anticipate the just conclusion to our narrative.

The interior of the saloon is cool, still retaining the coolness of the previous evening; for it is dark inside, as dark as the deeds which transpire nightly within. Reader, how often have you heard of the rectitude of the Gringo? How often have you been assailed by the righteousness he labors so diligently to fabricate? How well do you know the base hypocrisy that dwells beyond the appearance so meticulously and deceptively presented to the world? However, inside these especially constructed locations, these saloons, these monuments to the baseness of which men are capable, it is here that the true and evil nature of the Gringo is allowed to roam freely. The true Nixonianism of the Gringo is released. It is here, in these public houses, that the Gringo may, without fear of retribution, escape from his hypocritical mask and give free rein to his latent, yet ever-ready debauchery and licentiousness. A Puritan by day, a Libertine by night! I perhaps have alarmed the reader, perhaps it is true that the reader at this point may be trembling with apprehension, for it is indeed an unfit place for our hero, the wonderful Chicano Kid, to enter.

But, fear not, dear reader, the purity and innocence of our hero has not been corrupted. He has not been soiled in the least, though he has entered many, many similar places in his quest for justice and liberty in the American West. Would that evil did not seek refuge in such places! However, the Chicano Kid must go forth to right the wrongs of this world wherever evildoers lurk. Temptation and sin have yet to sway this prized possession of his mother's womb away from the path of the true way and the way of truth. The saloon in Santo Gringo, though filthier than others into which he has entered to seek justice, will not tarnish our hero. Verily, he is made of sterner stuff.

A white man, a Gringo, sits behind the bar of the saloon, reclining on his elbows in a stance reminiscent of the decadent Trimalchio and redolent with the fetid odors following the spoilage of the Banquet. The man's face is fat and sweaty as if perspiration continually oozes from his pores. As the Chicano Kid nears, he is able to see the pools of sweat and grease which well in the pores, with only an occasional oasis of a black mole sprouting thick, coarse black hairs. Genuinely porcine features! This man, this Gringo, this bartender, is an individual whose sweaty, oily, greasy fingers stain the very glasses he is attempting to clean, but stained glasses, even stained windows, do not stand in the way of Gringo debauchery!

The dazzling, awesome, magnificent appearance of the Chicano Kid discomposes the rude, rustic, vulgar, fat man behind the bar. This cheap, unforgivable imitation of Trimalchio perceives, yes, he perceives, even through the film of ignorance and the drooping eyes of a dullard, that this is no ordinary mortal who deigns to grace the white man's pigsty. The Chicano Kid, standing near the bar without touching it, is indeed a pearl before swine.

The fat, oily, greasy man, a sorry excuse to represent any race, also perceives the mestizo features of our hero—the almond eyes, the bronze skin, the black, straight hair—but, the fat tub of guts ignores the superior carriage of the Chicano Kid, the graceful, delicate, catlike movements. Lo, my dear reader, the Chicano Kid is in the presence of a racist. Yes, indeed, this fat tub of guts, ever mindful of his duty to racism and to the arbitrary duty to separate the sons of the desert from the sons of greed, feels compelled to make clear to the Chicano Kid that he is not welcomed in a place so low, so base. Little does this ersatz Trimalchio know that were it not for the crimes against man and nature which have their execution therein, the Chicano Kid would certainly be elsewhere.

Reader, let me propose a reasonable though unlikely proposition. Suppose the Chicano Kid, in all his magnificent splendor, were to indicate his willingness to avail himself of your hospitality. Reason, good taste, and that common courtesy which is reserved among equals, dictates that you consider it an honor, an enriching experience, to be sure, something to treasure among your best and most pleasant memories. Ah, but such is the nature of the Gringo. Little good does it do to talk about it. Such is the baseness with which he regards others, particularly those to whom he has caused the most grief. Ah, but now, the oiled, highly polished, handmade, silver-inlaid, calfskin boot is on the other foot. The Chicano Kid is about to redress those grievances. However, as you have witnessed, the fat man behind the bar is fortunate to recognize the rising of the sun. He does not know he is in the presence of the bronze avenger of the West. This ill-chosen, misfit, spokesman for Gringo depravity, this lard bucket behind the bar will question the dignity of our hero. So does he live in the darkness of ignorance that he does not see the light of truth and justice. It is indeed a sorry event which follows next, a dolorous turn in our story, but fidelity requires the telling of it. I would not be worthy of the reader's trust were I to ignore it. Furthermore, it is perhaps best to tell it since it is conceivable the dignity of the Chicano Kid's character will be revealed. It is but the prudent investment of the Chicano Kid's capital for the profit of the reader.

It is the Chicano Kid who speaks first. Those of his station do not wait to be addressed. Readily do they perceive the base station of those such as the bartender. We shall hear the modulation of his voice, the crispness of his vowels, the graceful turn of the phrases. Seldom has a hero either in history or fiction revealed such magnificence in so short a speech. And, for the reader's depository of information, our hero speaks in a tongue foreign to him. Yes, indeed, the Chicano Kid acquired the language of the Gringo late in life. It was not he who learned it at his mother's breast, yet it is he who speaks it so much better than even the most educated of the Gringo—inasmuch as education and Gringo may be a contradiction in terms, but the reader shall be the judge of that. So perfect is the inflection of the Chicano Kid's speech that were it not the for the mestizo characteristics which inform his physiognomy, it would be impossible to distinguish him from the most articulate of Gringos, with the exception, of course, that no Gringo could devote the entirety of his being to truth and justice.

"Serve me a cup of coffee, please." Pause for a moment, reader, and consider the phrase just now uttered by the Chicano Kid. He does not ask, he does not say, "will you serve me a cup of coffee?" The Chicano Kid fully expects to be served a cup—not an indefinite amount, such as some, but a cup—of coffee. The assurance, the self-confidence, the precision of the Chicano Kid's speech. The Chicano Kid knows exactly what he wants. In addressing the fat man, the Chicano Kid is gracious, affable, but also with just the proper degree of authority in his voice lest there result either of two outcomes: in the first instance, the individual whom he is addressing breaches the barrier of courtesy and becomes too familiar; in the second instance, the individual whom he is addressing becomes so awestruck and overcome with fear and trembling that he is unable to carry out the mission thus assigned to him. No, the Chicano Kid instinctively knows the precision of speech required for every situation. It is only when the individual he is addressing does not pay due attention to the manner of the Chicano Kid that his words are misinterpreted and calamity follows, usually to the detriment of he who misunderstood.

"We don't serve greasers in here, Meskin," expostulates the corpulent, oily, petroliferous bartender. However, anyone present would have detected the statement delivered not without some slight hesitation, a certain quaver, a tremor, resonating the vocal apparatus of the voice. Some individuals, to be sure, are born to the servant class, destined from the first breath breathed outside of the body that bears them to be subservient before those of yet a different class, those born to rule and hold dominion over lesser men. The bartender, repugnant though he may be, instinctively is reminded by those recesses of the brain about which our modern scientists can only speculate, that the Chicano Kid deserves the utmost self-abnegation from such as he, and yet, dear reader, and yet the vicissitudes of human behavior require on these occasions the expostulation of the well-rehearsed cant of racism. Nevertheless, the oily bartender is uncertain as to his own behavior toward the Chicano Kid.

One of the character traits which inhere in the bronze people of the sun is a certain graciousness, a certain politeness, a certain affability, a certain equanimity in the face of adversity and disdain. It is something that in other times was quite unnecessary, a time when mutual respect for human life and an orderliness in social intercourse ruled the day. Since the coming of the Gringo, the best order and the best exchanges in human relationships have given way to disrespect and sullenness; humans behave little better than those creatures undistinguished by rational faculties. The Chicano Kid, as the best specimen of his race, revealing the highest level of rational behavior to which a human may aspire, does not become angry, nor does he in any way demonstrate his displeasure. Such outbursts, such brief, though significant, moments of emotional discomposure, are not to be given vent in the presence of the lower order of human beings. No, not at all. The Chicano Kid remains even-tempered, affable, regarding the greasy bartender as only a pesky inconvenience, paying to him no more attention than one would an obstreperous fly, although it is readily admitted that a fly's *raison d'etre* is the irritation of human beings and only fulfills that function for which it was placed on earth. The bartender should know better. The Chicano Kid replies with a smile.

"Fat man, I make a habit of not killing insects." After having uttered these words in such a way as to have his true intention remain ambiguous and yet investing the utterance with sufficient authority as to affirm his superiority over the base bartender, the Chicano Kid inspects his fingernails, as if at that moment it were imperative that he ascertain their cleanliness, as if by simply regarding the bartender it were possible for his fingernails to become soiled. The Chicano Kid continues in modulated, though not forced restraint. "Just serve the coffee and go about your business. I have nothing to do with you."

The assurance, the confidence, the aristocratic bearing reflected in the Chicano Kid's words, all combine in the cumulative effect of the bartender's tremor. By now, primordial instinct, prehistoric messages stored in the brain of this human louse, come to the fore. The bartender now knows he has seen the face of greatness, of that human superiority, that human hierarchy, which God ordained at the Creation lest His labor go unfulfilled, lest His best Design for man languish under the dominion of those whose faculties compete unfavorably with the best creatures of nature. Yes, the true, unmistakable, unavoidable message passed on by generations upon generations of servants leaves its indelible imprint upon the consciousness of the bartender. He cannot but experience, perhaps for the first time, the lowliness of his nature, the baseness of his being, the obviousness of his inferiority.

"Mr. Brisket ain't gonna like you being in here. He ain't gonna like you coming in here like a white man. He don't like any Meskin in here. He might just go on and fire me. I might lose my job, you understand, mister?" The adipose folds adhering to massive quantities of surplus human flesh tremble and shake the very foundations of the saloon. Beads of perspiration erupt through the layers of oil and grease which blanket the bartender's face.

"I understand, cowardly fat man, that you will serve me the coffee I will not order you to serve me again and I also know you will hurry to do so." The Chicano Kid stands upright, perfectly perpendicular to the curvature of the earth. He does not observe the fat bartender; he knows the bartender dares not take his eyes away from the majestic bearing of his countenance. "This Brisket man may take away your employment, but I will shoot away your feet. Hurry on your feet, while you still have them. Get the coffee." The cold, icy, unflinching glare of the Chicano Kid finally meets the face of the fat bartender, piercing its way through several generations of his menial ancestors.

"Yes, sir!" So saying, the fat man serves the coffee, his hands atremble, spilling most of the brown, steaming liquid on the bar. The Chicano Kid, still not displaying any annoyance, still not revealing the least emotional discomposure, signals gracefully for the nervous bartender to place the coffeepot on the bar. The greasy Gringo hands deposit the container on the wooden surface. The Chicano Kid finishes pouring the coffee, moving the cup and saucer to one side while the still nervous and trembling bartender wipes the bar with a soiled cloth. The coffee, as may well be expected, is not of the consistency to which the Chicano Kid is accustomed. In fact, a sampling—and this only with great daring—would reveal it to be hardly fit for human consumption. Of course, reader, we must remember that the patron of privilege in this establishment is none other than the Gringo himself, and he, not particularly discriminate in the finer things in life, considers this odious brew the best in the hamlet. You may well wonder the reason the Chicano Kid should endanger his person. Fatigue, dear reader, fatigue. He has been without the comforts of civilization for several days, on the trail, with no one but his trusty steed for companionship. This brew, this coffee, although our hero would have preferred better, will suit his needs until that day when his patrimony is restored and he again has those efficient and loving servants, members of his own race, who, though they be servants, do not relinquish human dignity and worth and who sincerely consider it an honor and a pleasure to be in the service of such a kind and humane employer. Yes, readers, the members of the Chicano Kid's race recognize as well the hierarchy of the human race, they know we may not all be within the ruling class and they gladly submit to their fate but with the understanding that though they be servants on earth, once within the Glory of He Who created us, they will sit equally with the Chicano Kid and share equally in the fruits that accrue to us when we journey into eternity.

"You might cow that yella fat-belly, Meskin, but you ain't gonna back me down! When you turn around, go for your gun!"

The sound of the nervous, impetuous voice came from the end of the saloon, some dark corner which gives refuge to the darkness of men's souls. So frequently since the day he was dispossessed, since he became of age, had the Chicano Kid been at pains to answer such calls for no other reason than Death has some inscrutable, undecipherable manner of drawing those it will to its bosom. In each case prior to this one, the Chicano Kid answered the call of the would-be challenger, each time participating in the challenger's appointment with the Grim Reaper. But, now, after so many years of sending so many Gringos to their final

Satanic embrace, the Chicano Kid is weary of his ad hoc mission. The killing of Gringos no longer satisfied his taste for revenge. No longer did he perceive the face of Alf Brisket in every itinerant cowpoke he was forced to send to hell. The blood of so many who did need killing weighed heavily upon our hero. No, he would not perform the deed justly reserved for Death itself. If the owner of the sound at the back of his head was bent upon suicide, it would not be he, the Chicano Kid, that would become the agent. The Chicano Kid was saving himself for Alf Brisket.

"You don't want any trouble, son," said the Chicano Kid, weariness in his voice, fatigue upon his limbs.

"Ain't no greaser ever called me son, go for your gun."

Such is the impetuousness of callow youth. So fervently and unthinkingly do they court death. Little does the figure from the corner of the saloon realize the closeness of death's embrace. But, reader, pause a moment. Consider the nebulous figure now addressing the Chicano Kid. It is a cowboy, of the Gringo persuasion, having barely said farewell to his teenage years, and now so willingly intent upon foreclosing his future. It is youth, indeed, dear reader. Recollect, if you will, your own youth, remember the heat and passion of youth in your own lives, how willingly you would have forsaken this life in the name of honor and valor. Such things as old age places into perspective, youth submits to instinctively. And there is justice in it, as well. For it is far better to die young in the flames of passion for some noble cause than it is to venture timidly into old age with the knowledge that valor beckoned and was denied. However, this is no noble cause which the cowboy aspires to defend, it is nothing but the sustenance and maintenance of racism, the furtherance of racial discrimination, the result of which has been the dispossession of the bronze people of the sun. While we may indeed admire the flame and the passion of youth as it springs in this young man, prudence requires that we acknowledge forthrightly the ignominy of his cause. We need not fear any danger to the Chicano Kid, the individual who most concerns us, for he has been in countless similar situations and has yet to emerge with but a scratch in his victory. We forewarn the reader that if the cowboy does not desist and withdraw his intemperate challenge, the hearth of old age shall not warm his body.

"I'll kill you if I have to, young man, but there is no need to. You are young, let it be. Withdraw now and go into an old age." The Chicano Kid still has not turned to face his challenger. Nor will he, unless the cowboy persists in his determination to die at such a young age.

"Don't give me no darned sermons, greaser! I aim to waste a bullet on you."

So weary is the Chicano Kid of killing the Gringo, that he must try one last time to keep from killing yet another one. It is true he has not turned around, knowing that were he to turn, the explosion of hot lead would resound throughout the dingy, dark saloon, knowing as well that were he to turn, yet another Gringo would face his Maker perhaps without the sufficient coinage of good deeds on earth to open for him the gates of that Eternal Paradise. The Chicano Kid is about to utter his last words to the still living cowboy. Let us listen and not know the want of having failed to hear.

"I don't want to kill you."

"You ain't gonna kill me, you a Meskin. Meskins don't kill white folks, it's the other way around, ain't you heard? Well, if you ain't, I'm gonna make you learn the hard way. And if you don't turn around real soon, I'm gonna shoot you in the back. Yeah, that's right, I'll shoot you in the back. Backshootin' is more Mexican style." The Chicano Kid tenses, every nerve of his splendid person coils, taut in the expectation of imminent peril. Had he the time, the Chicano Kid would sigh in dismay, perhaps even pause to reflect on the utter inability of some individuals to recognize the futility of challenging someone such as himself. But there is no time now. The moment is for action only.

Instinctively, as if he had eyes in the back of his head, the Chicano Kid wheels on one heel, pistol in hand. The thunderous explosion rattles the glasses on the bar and the folds of the bartender's fat. The bartender, needless to say, is awestricken at the swiftness and dexterity of our hero's draw. Certainly, the blink of an eye is slower than the celerity with which the Chicano Kid palms the handle of his revolver, aims without fixing his eye, and discharges the lethal projectile from within the exploding chamber.

As the haze of smoke begins to clear out of the saloon, moving in little cat feet through the doors, windows, and cracks in the walls, the loud, dull thump of the dirty cowboy making an unexpected encounter with the wooden floor is heard. The Chicano Kid blows the remaining smoke away from the barrel of his six-shooter and replaces it in its proper, leather and silver inlaid receptacle. During the brief encounter, the Chicano Kid had not placed his coffee cup upon the bar. The cup remained in his hand throughout. So sure of his movements, so steady of hand, arm, and eye, was the Chicano Kid, that the contents of the cup were not disturbed. Truly, dear reader, the entire exchange wherein one life was threatened and another dispatched to that greater beyond, indeed, during the entire exchange, there was not one untoward movement which would have caused even a ripple on the surface of steaming liquid.

There are still a few seconds of life in the dirty cowboy, a few precious seconds which another individual, mindful of his proximity to his Maker, would have put to the use of reconciliation with the Supreme Creator, but, no, such is not the case with this piteous, misguided tool of Gringo ignorance. He will not spend his last conscious moments as a resident of this earth making peace in preparation for what is to come. He will not see the error of his ways. He will journey to the dark beyond, where eternity awaits, cursing still the people to whose dispossession he has contributed.

Incredulous, the eyes in concert with his voice utter: "Meskins ain't supposed to outdraw white folks! I can't believe I been killed by a Meskin!" With these, his last words, the dirty cowboy expires on the filthy floor of the saloon.

The Chicano Kid strolls, slowly, gracefully, to where the corpse of the dirty cowboy lies. The soft, light, feather steps hardly disturb the funereal silence of the saloon. A contrast indeed to the raucous din which characterizes the ambience of the establishment. This evening, perhaps, the noise will be a bit more subdued, certainly not out of respect for the slain cowboy, but in apprehension of the fate awaiting the vile, the vicious, the villainous Alf Brisket. There is some sadness in the eyes of the Chicano Kid. He speaks to the soul departed from the still-warm individual now inert upon the floor. It is a lamentation perhaps in supplication to He who made us all that the judgment soon to be rendered be not severe. For, inasmuch as the Chicano Kid has been the agent who dispatched the young, impetuous, dirty cowboy, he harbors no personal ill will toward the deceased. He may justifiably refer us to his attempt to avert the lethal confrontation. Yes, dear reader, the Chicano Kid, wise beyond his years, judicious as Solomon, understands all too well that not all Gringos are bad, not all of them evil, that there is no casual basis in the genetic inheritance for the racist, oppressive attitude they display toward the bronze people of the sun. The Chicano Kid knows it is a habit acquired not long after the flush of innocence evanesces from the rose-cheeked Spring of boyhood. They learn it from their fathers and pass it to their children. The cycle continues, unbroken except for a few cultural mavericks, those hardy individuals who insist upon judging their fellow human creatures by using a more humane measure, preferring instead to consider individuals as good or bad individually and not grouping them together indiscriminately. However, reader, and this is as certain as the sun rises to grace the land with its golden glow each morning, these vile customs are soon to be forfeited. It has been just a few short years since the Chicano Kid began his journey of justice, righting wrongs which through that particular quirk of human nature are sometimes perceived as right. The Chicano Kid has journeyed far and wide rooting out the evil lurking in the hearts of men. He has roamed the West in search of evil Gringos, always prayerful that they, the vicious oppressors, will have a change of heart, knowing that all too often he must dispatch the evildoers to another world wherein they will not have the benefit of artifice and fabrication, wherein they must stand before the Ultimate Tribunal and answer to the demands of Universal Law. Let us listen as the Chicano Kid speaks over the dirty cowboy's body.

"It is not entirely your fault, young and misinformed representative of your race. It is in the nature of youth to be brash and intemperate. Only years and experience mature and restrain the surgings of youth. But, alas, perhaps it is better this way. By killing you now, you will not live to mistreat my people anymore as I know you would have. I also know I would have had to kill you sooner or later. Rest well, young man, go to your Final Judgment, for you knew not what you did and I know not where you go."

What a magnificent benediction, so worthy of this hero of the West!

The Chicano Kid remains quiet, contemplative, over the body of the dirty cowboy. Perhaps he continues a silent prayer for the departed. So fair and just is this exemplary specimen of the bronze people of the sun that the shooting of another human being weighs heavily on his heart. He is not at all elated over the result of his agency, nor is he particularly conscious of having survived a momentary menace to his own life. As if waking from a dream, the Chicano Kid becomes conscious of the bartender, meekly trying to interrupt his solitude.

"Say," began the fat bartender with great temerity, "you all don't mind if I go tell the sheriff about this, do you? He's gotta find out about it and come after you."

"I don't mind at all. Of course. It is, after all, your duty. Just leave the coffee-pot on the bar in case you do not have the courage to return and should I require more of this distasteful liquid."

"Well, listen, I ain't never seen shootin' like that, and I'll be sure to tell the sheriff about it. And, it'll probably take him an hour or more to get a posse together to come after you. So, I calculate you have time to drink a couple more cups of coffee. You could even get away, if you had a mind to."

"I have business in this town."

"Alright. But, I just oughta tell you that ain't no Meskin ever killed a white man in this town before and the sheriff and Mr. Brisket ain't gonna like it. They ain't about to start lettin' Meskins kill white folks. It just ain't right."

"There is a time for everything. All things must change."

The fat bartender, not understanding the full import of the Chicano Kid's last statement, waddles out of the saloon in the direction of the sheriff's office. The weight of his enormous belly, hidden by an apron surely the size of a bedsheet, is a heavy burden on his knees.

Meanwhile, the Chicano Kid glides as if floating on air to a nearby table, casually draping his limbs over a chair facing the door. As is true of the pure heart, death is a difficult matter to contemplate. A bright flame of hope, visible only in the dim recesses of his heart, forestalls an inchoate depression which invariably overcomes someone who has taken the life of another. Indeed, the Chicano Kid is weary of killing Gringos, tired of Death as a silent, ever-present partner. It is his wish now that he kill no more until his inevitable meeting with Alf Brisket. He must reserve all of his strength until that inevitable meeting, he must store all of the energy possible for that fateful encounter, the terminus of his lonely journey in search of justice.

It seems only moments, but the quickness of his hearing perceives bootsteps on the wooden porch outside the saloon. He must not kill again, he must not loose the lethal lead from his revolver of justice. He must refresh himself, for the appointment he has sought for so long is almost upon him.

Four men enter the saloon. Two are armed with shotguns, two have their handguns drawn. The one in front, a vulture-like creature, has a tin star on his breast. The Chicano Kid sighs in dismay although it would have been difficult to notice it from his external appearance.

The men spread out in front of the Chicano Kid, in a semi-circle, aiming their weapons at him. The Chicano Kid does not seem concerned, he continues to sip his coffee as though he were still alone. A brave soul, indeed!

"Alright, Meskin! We got you covered. Make one move and we'll blow you to hell!"

. . . to be continued.

Hugo Martínez-Serros

Learn! Learn!

José María Rivera always read important letters with a pencil in his hand. His wife could not remember his ever doing it any other way. They were written in *castellano*—he sometimes called it *cristiano*, his eyes rolling, his voice serious— by people who knew or should have known the language as well or better than he did, which is what made the letters important. He read first for spelling errors, rapidly, crossing out, adding, changing, circling, then he went back for a second reading to seize anything that had escaped his initial sweep. In repeated readings, finally, he concentrated on what the letters said.

There were few of these letters in the passing of a year. The two or three his brothers-in-law far off in Mexico wrote to his wife, letters that always provoked him to say in a louder than normal voice, *"Lástima de educación universitaria, no saben escribir,* a pity they were educated at the university, they don't know how to write." He said it as much to himself as to his wife, who did not answer him. Years ago, before leaving Mexico, he had already developed the habit of say- ing things aloud to himself. And there were the other letters, rare strikes that came into his hands from friends who did not quite understand them, and from the friends of friends.

Chema (his friends called him that) had long ago stopped "editing" the *barrio semanarios*, weeklies. They had too many errors, the same ones over and over, and they held no challenge for him. Besides, his anonymous letters to their edi- tors had gone ignored and he was not interested in writers who did not want to be redeemed (*"cabrones ojetes*, fucking assholes," he had called them in the final let- ter). More than once he had shouted to himself, *"¡Que se chinguen ésos!* Fuck them! *No tienen interés en aprender!* They're not interested in learning!"

The church bulletin of Our Lady of Guadalupe was another matter. The Riveras, whose destinies were in the hands of *don* José (his acquaintances called him that), were not churchgoing, but every Sunday *don* José sent one of his sons for that document, warning him as he left, *"Ten cuidado*, be careful, *no te vayas a perder en ese recinto de perversos,* don't get lost in that den of corruption." Although the bulletin dealt exclusively with what Chema called *"cosas de beatas y maricones*, news for overpious women and fairies"—births, marriages, deaths, baptisms, confirmations, first communions, fundraising events, the activities of the Daughters of Our Most Holy Virgin of Guadalupe and of the Knights of the Virgin of Guadalupe—he acknowledged the excellence of its language, an excellence that was not without faults, however. The author of that bulletin was the *párroco,* Father Tortas, a Spaniard whom Chema gleefully called, "An overstuffed *gachupín, cuervo cargado de carnes y de cagada*, a crow bursting with flesh and shit."

José María mined every one of Father Tortas's bulletins, and every one yielded something, however small or imagined. But it was the nugget of indisputable error that filled him with intense pleasure and made him shout, "*Aprende de tu padre*, learn from your master, *sanguijuela*, parasite! This is your only creative act, it should be perfect! You have nothing else to do, *manos de señorita! ¡Aprende! ¡Aprende!* Learn! Learn! If I am the only one willing to kick your ass, *sea así*, so be it! Your voice is louder than it should be, you must answer for it!" And José María taught the priest as well as he could, in anonymous letters that went out often but not regularly, for not all bulletins merited a complete letter. His sons, feeling themselves partners in this enterprise, delivered them to the church or the rectory clandestinely, provocatively, under cover of the large crowds that moved in and out of the former or passed slowly by the latter.

There was no question of it, Father Tortas heeded portions of the anonymous letters and this made José María a better critic. Their struggle, the tip of the iceberg of their antagonisms, took place at the level of orthography, grammar, syntax, semantics. Sometimes José María sensed that the priest had overreacted to a particular challenge, countering the unknown antagonist's thrusts with an ingenious verbal maze here, an extraordinarily subtle play on words there. At times the priest seemed to tweak his unknown critic by slipping into flagrant error. Chema begrudged the priest his mastery of the language and he whispered to himself, "*Sí, dominas el castellano, pinche cura maricón*, you lousy fairy of a priest, you do know the language! You have this over my brothers-in-law, that wherever the hell they taught you, they taught you well, *manos de señorita*."

Juan Ginés Tortas's parishioners had never seen hands more beautiful than his. They had made José María think of the hands of religious calendars. They were white, very white, the fingers slender and long and tapering into flat tips capped by manicured nails, a labyrinth of pale blue lines just under the skin. Hands surprisingly fleshless, firm and smooth. To his flock they seemed hands made for holding and displaying Christ, a living monstrance. Nearing fifty, Father Tortas was a big man with a bald pate. A sprinkle of white flakes fell from the hair that ringed his head, and his hands recurrently fluttered up to his shoulders to flick at the incessant snow. He dressed with an elegance that belied the restraints of a clergyman's habit, and even his priestly robes were tailored to his personal desires. He had long ago assumed the practice, after Mass, of keeping his robes on and wearing them in his chambers. They intimidated those whom he received there, giving him the distance he needed.

As seminarian and newly ordained priest, Juan Ginés, proud and serious by nature and gregarious by design, had been a competitor whose incentive was competition. He was a performer who excelled when he was surrounded by excellent performers. Drawn to material comfort, he had aspired to a position of prestige in some chancery, convinced that there he would find abundance and intellectual stimulation. But the young priest's impatience, buttressed by ambition and a knowledge of English, had driven him to the United States. He had imagined himself the Sepúlveda of the *mestizos* in Anglo-America, had envisioned himself in the American Hierarchy as the exegete of the Spanish-American text.

In the United States Juan Ginés saw the Canaan of his expectations crumble in the Babylon of his captivity in South Chicago. They had not told him, as he would later tell himself (*"¡Me enviaron al culo de esta ciudad salchichera!"*) that South Chicago was the asshole of sausage-making Chicago. He had come to a dead end when the world had seemed new to him, and for a time he had struggled to check his bitterness, winning small victories over his pride and ambition; but he could not vanquish them. He convinced himself that he had been intentionally misled, ultimately believing that they had exiled him unjustly. So it was that he made a sword of his disillusionment and a shield of his expectations. His weight increased with his cynicism and his hair began to thin rapidly.

For more than twenty years Father Tortas had grieved the impatience that had led him to abandon Spain for the hope of rapid advancement in a city where, he discovered, it was reserved for priests with Irish surnames. Since then he had moved cautiously, slowly weighing alternatives on the scales of his distrust to arrive at decisions of consequence and inconsequence alike. He had pondered as long over the advisability of forming a parish baseball team as he had over the need for a second assistant. He scorned young people for their immaturity and lack of judgment, making them the target of diatribes delivered from the pulpit, subjecting them to inquisitional indignities in the intimacy of the confessional. And for more than twenty years he had indulged his pride with fantasies of what he could have been, had he stayed in Spain: now a cardinal's secretary, now a bishop, now a cardinal. He became aloof, solitary, performed his duties with the aid of many, but drew nobody close to him and drew close to nobody, not even his assistant priests. Alone, he lived more in the world of what could have been than in the community where he ran out his time. What little affection he could summon he bestowed on his altar boys, who, uneasy in his presence, would not have passed their thirteenth year if he could have controlled their growth. Of his pastoral concerns in recent years, only the composition of the church bulletin seemed to interest him.

Like most of the men in the neighborhood, Chema worked in the steel mill. He was skilled at executing a variety of difficult and dangerous jobs that required strength, stamina and alertness. He did the jobs superbly, with an animal intelligence and grace that were incomparable among his fellow workers. He followed his nature in what he did, and what he did and how he did it were his only security in the mill since it was not unionized. But the work did not spend him, it failed to test his physical limits. It did not drain him of that need he felt to exhaust his energies. It failed to challenge his intelligence and he knew it always would.

Even the letters he wrote in English deserved at least one draft, and Chema composed them as well as he could. Inevitably he turned to one of his sons for help, a recourse that pained both since José María had to accept his son's judgments and the son had to suffer his father's detailed, time-consuming explanations.

"But you can't say that, that's Spanish, it isn't said like that in English." The boy spoke to him in Spanish.

"Who says you can't? If you understand what you're doing you can do anything you want to with language. But you don't understand! *¡Lástima! ¡Aprende! ¡Aprende!*"

"I'm tellin' you, Pa, it's not English, *no es inglés.*"

In some cases the son's advice was rejected. Having labored for an expression he thought poetic ("My determination to become a citizen is not different from the determination of the lion that, crippled, accepted Daniel's aid. My allegiance to the Daniel that is the United States could not be different from that of the lion to Daniel."), José María held fast to his creation over his son's protests, convinced that an adult would see what the youth had failed to appreciate. There was no antagonism between father and son, no rivalry, no dispute as to who knew English better. Both felt impatience: the father over his son's incomprehension of figurative language, the son over his father's insistence which pulled ambivalently at the boy, for he admired it even while it annoyed him. Together they hammered out a finished product, which Chema then typed, his fingers slowly pounding the keys of a winged, flightless Oliver. Chema was confident that the typewritten letter would impress its *gringo* reader.

But when José María wrote the most important letters, when he wrote letters in *castellano*—his own, his wife's—he prepared for the undertaking as carefully as Father Tortas might have readied everything for a Solemn High Mass. He spread newspapers over one end of the kitchen table to smooth its uneven surface, placed Bello's *Gramática de la lengua castellana* at his left elbow, a dictionary at his right, a half dozen sharp-pointed pencils and a block of unlined paper in front of him. His hands had worn through the covers of both books, but he had skillfully rebuilt them. The dictionary was small, a desk copy that was often inadequate to his needs.

Imagining himself the addressee, José María gave himself selfishly to his letter, writing in intense pursuit of the perfection his mind projected just beyond his pencils. Always, after several days, he came close enough to that perfection to feel satisfied; on rare occasions he achieved it. Almost as a rule of thumb, the number of drafts his letters required equaled the number of pages per letter. His prose was solid, although heavy at times, but he wielded it with ease and could make it leap and turn to his wishes. An isolated sentence might seem cumbersome, but it lost this quality in the configuration of a paragraph or passage. He shaped his prose as a Oaxacan blacksmith fashioned wrought iron, heating it in the forge of his brain, hammering it over and over on the anvil of his judgment, plunging it finally into the cold water of acceptance, piece by piece, the overall design held in the eye of his intelligence:

> Priest,
>
> I repeat what I have told you before: you have no imagination. Inasmuch as you refuse to think of your parishioners as human beings, as *hermanos* or *hijos*, insisting, rather, on seeing them as animals, *ovejas*, always *ovejas*, lend consistency, unity, to your vision by seeing yourself as a sheep dog, rather than as a shepherd. Give your parishioners, at least, a little variety. Call them fish, or doves, or, better still, *burros*. You, of all people, must know how important, useful and docile *burros* are in the Hispanic world as well as in the bible. Read Vargas Vila, for you might learn from him. . . .
>
> On the second page of your bulletin, first paragraph of the section entitled BAPTISMS, you employ a passive construction incorrectly. I bring to your attention that in passive constructions with *se* it is the nature of the passive subject that determines the form the verb must take. . . .

On Saturday mornings Father Tortas sat at his desk and unhurriedly wrote the weekly bulletin on oversized sheets of lined paper. Working from a pad of notes, dates, symbols, he finished it in an hour, needing more time only if the bulletin was unusually long. But it never took him more than two hours. His penmanship was clear, large and angular, marked by that stiffness characteristic of certain European hands. Typed by a volunteer whom the *párroco* had trained, the copy was taken to a local printer by noon and the finished product was delivered to the rectory before five. Chema's anonymous letters effected no obvious change in this routine. The priest gradually intensified his concentration, paid greater attention to expression, turned increasingly to figurative language, adopted a more sophisticated syntax and, except for rare instances, did not need additional time to produce the bulletin. Had he known this, José María, like those who measure others against themselves, would have been astounded by the facility and speed with which Father Tortas composed the document.

The tools of Chema's mill work—hammers, pickaxes, pokers, shovels, drills, wrenches—had made his hands hard and his fingers were rooted in a ridge of calluses that spread to the base of his thick palms. His nails were dense, horny, a little longer than those of other men who did his kind of work. To shake his hand was to shake the hand of a man wearing a gauntlet. In that hand a pencil or pen seemed to grow small, almost disappearing in his fist, so that when he wrote the script seemed to flow from a little tube he operated with the slight pressure of three fingers. The writing was utterly controlled, swift, rhythmically winding and unwinding in fluid curves, the tall letters all the same height, gracefully swayed from lower left to upper right, the crosses of the t's straight and slightly lengthened. It was elegant in its proportions, in the purity of its lines, in the inventiveness of its capital letters, in the almost-flourishes of occasional final letters that caught the eye with their air of effortless improvisation. The astonishment of those who saw him write filled Chema with immense satisfaction, and he seized every opportunity that presented itself, even if it was only to sign his name. His Spanish letters were written in longhand. Nothing else would do.

He wrote with a Schaeffer fountain pen, white-dotted, medium point, in his judgment the finest writing instrument his money could buy. Several times a week he filled pages of a notebook with circles, ovals, straight and curved lines, all joined together and exactly alike. It gave him no pleasure to do these exercises; he performed them routinely, knowing that by doing them his hand would always be fully in control. On the subject of writing he spoke like a specialist:

"You hold the pen lightly, *apenitas*, about an inch and a half up from the point. The upper part rests in the cradle formed by the thumb and the index finger, *así*. And remember, this is the most important part, you write with the forearm, not with the wrist, *con el antebrazo*. The movement is from the elbow down, that way you never get tired. *¡Nunca!* And the test is in how lightly you hold the pen. Go ahead, pull it out whenever you want, you'll see how easy it is to slip it out from between my fingers. You see! *¡Aprende! ¡Aprende!*"

The Rivera children all wrote well. José María had seen to that. They regularly did exercises for him in notebooks, but none showed the signs of calligraphic precociousness he had shown when he was their age. And they spoke well, both languages, but especially Spanish. They spoke it better than most of their friends, which did not surprise José María. He had convinced them it was important to speak well. They had heard him dominate conversations with his friends, had heard the latter turn to their father to settle disputes about word meanings, had seen him reach for his dictionary to drive all doubt from the minds of his listeners.

As much as anything it was the dictionary test that impressed the Rivera children. José María did it not to show off, but as a measure of himself in the presence of his children, as a way of showing them that they could learn as he had. He handed them his dictionary and, taking turns, they opened it at random, read him words they thought were difficult, and he would define them. He did it to show them that words belonged to anyone who wanted them, and they came to believe that success in life and the power of speech were linked in some intimate way, that one could not be important without knowing words.

The penmanship of the first anonymous letter had caught Father Tortas's attention. The letter's message had made him smile wryly. A man had written it, that much he could tell. But he knew that man was not one of his parishioners, for which one of them could write like that, express himself like that, have so little respect for him, so little fear of him that he dared instruct him? *Hijo de puta*, whoreson, he thought, what do you know, what do you know about me? Do you think that everyone can thrive in a sea of illiteracy? It had crushed him to learn that his parishioners were laborers, poor people of little education who had fled Mexico in search of something better. They defiled his language. He came to need those letters, anticipated them, counted on them to pique him, to make him think, to lift him from the drudgery of his daily life as did his weekly flights to the Loop, where he brushed elbows with his kind of people in elegant restaurants, theatres, museums. People who dressed like him, who shared his interests, who talked like him and ate like him. *Castrado*, he mused, if you had *cojones* you would show them to me, you would sign your name and show me your *mestizo* face. But you half-breeds have always been cowards. Only cowards live in the *culo* of Chicago and like it. I could find you out if I wanted, but I give your letters the importance they deserve—anonymity. You amuse me, *enano*, you faceless dwarf. Still, he wondered who his Momus might be.

As time passed, Father Tortas became convinced that his critic had to be one of the parish's heretics. Chema was his prime suspect, but without making inquiry he could not learn enough about him to confirm his suspicions. In the end, his desire to ascertain whether Chema was the upstart waned because it did not matter that he identify his anonymous correspondent; he did not want to deter the man.

Once, several years before the priest brought out the church bulletin, the two men had met. It was in the depths of *la crisis*, the Depression, and José María had been lucky to be working one and two days a week. His family was large, his children very young, and he needed additional work. They had learned to live without gas and electricity, but they could not do without food and clothing. There was always work to be done in the church and in the church's properties. Everybody knew this. Reluctantly he had gone to see the priest, driven to it by need and the hope of securing employment. He found Father Tortas in the sacristy.

"*¿Señor cura?*"

The priest turned to face a man in his early thirties, lean and muscular, his Mexican physiognomy striking with its deep-set eyes, prominent cheekbones and nose, a slight fleshiness around the mouth that drew attention away from the chin. He wore heavy work shoes, corduroy trousers, a denim shirt under a light jacket, and a wool cap pulled forward on his head. José María looked steadily into the other man's eyes.

"*Aquí se me llama padre*, people around here call me father." The priest looked deliberately at the man's cap, as if telling him to remove it. Unruffled, José María understood but kept his hands at his sides. Then the priest asked, "*¿Eres una de mis ovejas?* Are you one of my sheep?"

"*Soy hombre; vivo en este barrio*, I am a man; I live in this neighborhood," he answered coldly, offended by the other's use of *tú*.

"*¿Qué quieres?* What do you want?"

Hijo de la chingada, van dos veces, motherfucker, that's twice you've done it now, he thought. Again, the answer was cold. "*No quiero nada*, I want nothing. I have come looking for work. I am a good painter, a fair plumber, a very good carpenter. I can repair anything that needs repairing. I am a good electrician too. Pay me what you like, *lo que quiera usted*; if you don't like my work, don't pay me anything. I need work."

"The men in this parish donate their skills to their *párroco*. Why should I hire you?"

"*Mire usted*, look," he pointed to a wall of blistered paint above a large radiator. His "*Ahí arriba*, up there," accompanied by an upward thrust of the head, directed the priest's eyes to a badly cracked pane of glass just below the high ceiling. "You should hire me because my work stands up to time. Because I am not afraid of height."

Father Tortas sat down but did not offer the man a chair. He caught his right trouser leg just above the knee, pulled it up gently and crossed his legs. The black tailored material hung in a long smooth fold above a polished black dress shoe. "Do you have a family?"

"*Sí.*"

"Which is your church?"

"I do not have a church."

"*Lástima.* I do not hire heretics. If you want to work for me you must attend Mass here." Waving his hands back and forth between himself and José María he added, "Bring me your heretics and when I have made Catholics of all of you, I may hire you."

"I do better work than your Catholics."

Impatiently, the priest stood up, crossed the room, took a sleek black homburg from a rack and put it on. "*¿Cómo te llamas?* What is your name?"

"*Julio César. Y tú, cura, seguramente te llamas Torquemada*, and you, priest, surely your name is Torquemada."

"I have no time for your insolence!" Tortas reached out to smooth a cassock that hung neatly on a hanger.

"Nor I for yours. I am leaving, *ya me voy*, please feel free to put on your dress." And José María left.

Father Tortas's experience with two of the Rivera boys was no better. On Sundays, after Mass, they posed themselves at the doors of his church to sell papers. He had shooed them away many times and once had managed to snatch their little *semanarios*, tearing them to pieces and repulsing the boys as he might have driven money changers from his temple. But they kept coming back and he finally asked them, "*¿Cómo se llama vuestro padre?*"

"*Don* José María Rivera," they answered fearlessly.

Furious, the priest shouted, "*¡Entre vosotros no hay don, como no sea don Mierda!* There isn't a don among you, unless it be don Shit!"

One of the boys answered, "*¡Para mierda, los curas!* If it's shit you have in mind, we should be talking about priests!"

When Chema's eldest son, at sixteen, found a part-time job at the Wilson and Follex Book Company, it was the dictionaries that caught his attention. He told his brothers about them.

"They got dictionaries up the ass on the fourth floor! Little ones, vest-pocket dictionaries, an' bigger 'n bigger ones. The biggest of all are those big fat *Websters* with the color plates."

"Do they have 'em in Spanish?"

"Yeah! In all kinds of languages. In two languages too."

The plan took form slowly and when they had worked it out to the last detail they executed it, on a Saturday. On Sunday, when José María's youngest son brought him Father Tortas's bulletin, his other sons each brought him a dictionary, the first real gifts they had ever given him, gifts that Chema could not afford. (Three times in the air shaft, heart and hands had followed perfectly the trajectory of the falling books, three times had calculated precisely the moment at which to catch, three times had shuddered with the explosions, the grime-encrusted windows becoming banks of eyes as Chema's son struggled to hide his load in a Boy Scout knapsack.) Chema's eyes bulged in disbelief as he fingered the three volumes: a thick, handsome *Sopena*, a *Velázquez* bilingual, and *Webster's* unabridged.

Readying his table in the kitchen, his new *Sopena* at his right elbow, José María picked up the bulletin and began to read it:

> Queridas ovejas,
>   I remind the Daughters of our Most Holy Virgin of Guadalupe and
> the Knights of the Virgin of Guadalupe. . .

"*Ahora te chingas cura*, you're fucked now, priest, now you'll see who's who, *sabrás que soy tu padre, tu padre*, now you'll know once and for all who your master is! *¡Aprende! ¡Aprende!* Learn! Learn!"

And José María Rivera placed his hand on his new *Sopena*.

Judith Ortiz Cofer

The Black Virgin

In their wedding photograph my parents look like children dressed in adult costumes. And they are. My mother will not be fifteen years old for two weeks, and has borrowed a wedding dress from a relative, a tall young woman recently widowed by the Korean War. For sentimental reasons they have chosen not to alter the gown, and it hangs awkwardly on my mother's thin frame. The tiara is crooked on her thick black curls because she bumped her head coming out of the car. On her face is a slightly stunned, pouty expression, as if she were considering bursting into tears. At her side stands my father, formal in his high-school graduation suit. He is holding her elbow as the photographer has instructed him to do, and looking myopically straight ahead since he is not wearing his wire-frame glasses. His light brown curls frame his cherubic well-scrubbed face, his pale, scholarly appearance contrasting with his bride's sultry beauty, dark skin and sensuous features. Neither one seems particularly interested in the other. They are posing reluctantly. The photograph will be evidence that a real wedding took place. I arrived more than a year later, so it was not a forced wedding. In fact, both families had opposed the marriage for a number of reasons, only to discover how adamant children in love can be.

My parent's families represented two completely opposite cultural and philosophical lines of ancestry in my hometown. My maternal relatives, said to have originally immigrated from Italy, were all farmers. My earliest memories are imbued with the smell of dark, moist earth and the image of the red coffee beans growing row after row on my great-grandfather's hillside farm. On my father's side there is family myth and decadence. His people had come from Spain with tales of wealth and titles, but all I knew as a child was that my grandfather had died of alcoholism and meanness a few months before my birth and that he had forbidden his wife and children ever to mention his family background in the house, under threat of violence. My father was a quiet, serious man; my mother, earthy and ebullient. Their marriage, like my childhood, was a combining of two worlds, a mixing of two elements—fire and ice—that was sometimes exciting and life-giving, and sometimes painful and draining.

Because their early marriage precluded many options for supporting a wife, and with a child on its way, my father joined the U.S. Army only few months after the wedding. He was promptly shipped to Panama, where he was when I was born, and remained there for the next two years. I have seen many pictures of myself, a pampered infant and toddler, taken during those months for his benefit. My mother lived with his mother and learned to wait and smoke. My father's two older brothers were in Korea at the same time.

My mother still talks nostalgically of those years when she lived with her mother-in-law, Mamá Funda, as her grandchildren called her—since her name, Fundadora, was beyond our ability to pronounce during our early years—and Mamá Funda's divorced daughter, my aunt Clotilde, whom I am said to resemble. Three women living alone and receiving Army checks: the envy of every married woman in the pueblo. My mother had been the fourth child in a family of eight, and had spent most of her young life caring for babies that came one after the other until her mother, Mamá Pola, exiled her husband from her bed. Mamá Pola had been six months pregnant with her last child at my parents' wedding. My mother had been resentful and embarrassed about her mother's belly, and this may have had some effect on my grandmother's drastic birth control measure of relieving her husband of his marital duty soon after.

Anyway, my mother relished the grown-up atmosphere at her mother-in-law's house, where Mamá Funda was beginning to experiment with a new sense of personal freedom since her husband's death of alcoholism-related causes a couple of years before. Though bound by her own endless ritual of religion and superstition, she had allowed herself a few pleasures; chief among these was cigarette smoking. For years, the timid wife and overworked mother had sneaked a smoke behind the house as she worked in her garden (where she astutely grew mint to chew on before entering the house), occasionally stealing a Chesterfield from her husband's coat pocket while he slept in a drunken stupor. Now she would buy them by the carton, and one could always detect the familiar little square in her apron pocket. My mother took up the smoking habit enthusiastically. And she, my aunt Clotilde and Mamá Funda spent many lazy afternoons smoking and talking about life—especially the travails of having lived with the old man who had been disinherited by his father at an early age for drinking and gambling, and who had allowed bitterness for his bad fortune to further dissipate him—and telling family stories, stories that moralized or amused according to whether it was Mamá Funda or the cynical, New York sophisticated Clotilde who told them; stories my mother would later repeat to me to pass the time in colder climates, while she waited to return to her island. My mother never adopted the U.S., neither did she adapt to life anywhere but in Puerto Rico, though she followed my father back and forth from the island to the mainland for twenty-five years according to his tours of duty with the army; but always, she expected to return to *casa*—her birthplace. And she kept her fantasy alive by recounting her early years to my brother and me until we felt that we had shared her childhood.

At Mamá Funda's, Mother learned the meaning of scandal. She considered the gossip created by Clotilde's divorce in New York and subsequent return to the conservative Catholic pueblo yet another exciting dimension in her new adventure of marriage. After her young husband had left for Panama, she had trouble sleeping, so Aunt Clotilde offered to sleep in the same bed with her. Clotilde had desperately wanted a child of her own, but her body had rejected three attempts at pregnancy—one of the many problems that had helped to destroy her marriage. And so my mother's condition became Clotilde's project; she liked to say that she felt like the baby was hers too. After all, it was she who had felt the first stirrings in my mother's belly as she soothed the nervous girl through difficult nights, and she who had risen at dawn to help her up while she heaved with morning sickness. She shared the pregnancy, growing ever closer to the pretty girl carrying her brother's child.

She had also been the one to run out of the house in her nightgown one night in February of 1952 to summon the old midwife, Lupe, because it was time for me to make my entrance into the world. Lupe, who had attended at all of Mamá Funda's twelve deliveries, was by that time more a town institution than an alert midwife and on that night had managed to pull me out of my mother's writhing body without serious complications, but it had exhausted her. She left me wrapped up in layers of gauze without securing my umbilicus. It was Clotilde, ever vigilant of her babies, my mother and myself, who spotted the bloodstain soaking through my swaddling clothes. I was rapidly emptying out, deflating like a little balloon even as my teenage mother curled into a fetal position to sleep after her long night's work.

They say that until my father's return, the social pariah, Clotilde, cared for me with a gentle devotion that belied all her outward bravura. Some years before my birth, she had eloped with a young man whom her father had threatened to kill. They had married and gone to New York City to live. During that time, all her letters home had been destroyed in their envelopes by the old man, who had pronounced her dead to the family. Mamá Funda had suffered in silence, but managed to keep in touch with her daughter through a relative in New York. The marriage soon disintegrated and Clotilde went wild for a year, leading a life of decadence that made her legendary in her hometown. By the time I could ask about such things, all that was left of that period was a trunk full of gorgeous party dresses Clotilde had brought back. They became my dress-up costumes during my childhood. She had been a striking girl with the pale skin and dark curly hair that my father's family could trace back to their ancestors from northern Spain. Piecing her story over the years, I have gathered that Clotilde, at the age of sixteen, had fallen madly in love with a black boy a little older than herself. The romance was passionate and the young man had pressed for a quick marriage. When he finally approached my grandfather, the old man pulled out his machete and threatened to cut Clotilde's suitor in half with it if he ever approached the house again. He then beat both his daughter and wife (for raising a slut), and put them under house arrest. The result of his actions was an elopement in which half the town collaborated, raising money for the star-crossed lovers and helping them secure transportation and airline tickets to New York. Clotilde left one night and did not return for many years, until her father's death. But the tale is more complex than that. There was a talk at the time that the groom may have been fathered by the old man, who kept mistresses but did not acknowledge their children: for his pleasure, he nearly always chose black women. There was no way to prove this awful suspicion one way or another. Clotilde had been struck and blinded by a passion that she could not control. The marriage had been tempestuous, violent, and mercifully short. Clotilde was a wounded person by the time I was born; her fire was no longer raging, but smoldering—just enough to keep me warm until my mother came out of her adolescent dream to take charge of me.

The three women and a baby girl then spent the next two years waiting for their soldiers to come home. Mamá Funda, a deeply religious woman, as well as superstitious, made a *promesa*, for the safe return of her three sons. She went to early mass every day at the famous Catholic church in our town, La Monserrate, the site of a miraculous appearance by the Black Virgin during the Spanish colonial period. Mamá Funda also climbed the two hundred steps to the shrine on her knees once a week, along with other women who had men in the war. These steps had been hewn out of a hillside by hundreds of laborers, and a church had been constructed at the top, on the exact spot where the woodcutter, Giraldo González, had been saved from a charging bull by the sudden vision of the Black Lady floating above a treetop. According to legend, the bull fell on its front knees in a dead halt right in front of the man paralyzed by fear and wonder. There is a fresco above the church altar depicting this scene. Pilgrims come from all over the island to visit the shrine of La Monserrate. A statue imported from Spain representing the Lady sits on a portable ark, and once a year, during her *Fiestas Patronales*, she is taken on her dais around the town, followed by her adorers. She is said to have effected many miraculous cures, and her little room, off to the side of the nave, is full of mementos of her deeds, such as crutches and baby garments (she can induce fertility in barren women). It was to her that Mamá Funda and other women prayed at times of danger for their men, and during domestic crises. Being a woman and black made Our Lady the perfect depository for the hopes and prayers of the sick, the weak and the powerless.

I have seen the women dressed in black climbing the rough steps of *La Escalinata* to the front portals of the church and I have understood how the act itself could bring comfort to a woman who did not even know exactly where on earth her son or husband was, or even the reasons why he was risking his life in someone else's war. Perhaps God knew, and surely La Monserrate, a woman, wife, and mother herself would intercede. It was a man's world and a man's heaven. But mediation was possible—if one could only get His attention. And so there were *promesas*, ways to make your requests noticed. Some women chose to wear *hábitos* until their prayers were answered, that is, a plain dress of the color that represented your favorite saint, such a light blue for the Holy Mother or red for the Sacred Heart. The *hábito* was cinched at the waist with a cord representing Christ's passion. The more fervent would wear sackcloth underneath their clothes, a real torment in the tropical heat. The *promesa* was only limited by the imagination of the penitent and her threshold for pain and discomfort. In many households, women said rosaries nightly in groups, and this brought them together to share in their troubles. Mamá Funda did it all, quietly and without fanfare. She wore only black since the death of her husband, but mourning and penance had become an intrinsic part of her nature long before, since out of twelve pregnancies only six of her children had survived, having been taken from her as infants by childhood diseases that one generation later a single vaccine or simple antidote could prevent. But she had buried each little corpse in the family graveyard with a name and a date on the headstone, sometimes the same day for birth and death, and she had worn black, kept *luto* for each. The death of her babies had made her a melancholy woman, yet always ready to give God another chance. She lobbied for His favors indefatigably.

At Mamá Funda's house, my young mother and her baby were treated like royalty. Having served a demanding husband and numerous children, the older woman now found herself in a practically empty house with a new grandchild she could dote on and a daughter-in-law that was no more than an adolescent herself. My mother's only job was to play with the baby, to take me for strolls in fancy clothes bought with Army checks, and to accompany Mamá Funda to mass on Sundays. In the photographs taken of my mother and me during this period, I can see the changes wrought on the shy teenage bride in the short span she was taken care of by Funda and Clotilde: she is chubby and radiant with good health, she seems proud of the bundle of ruffles and bows in her arms—her babydoll—me.

By the time Father returned from Panama, I was out of diapers and ambulatory, Mother had regained her svelte figure, and Mamá Funda had thick calluses on her knees that deprived her of the pain she thought was necessary to get results from heaven. The safe homecoming of her son was proof that her pain had been worthwhile, and she applied her fruitful mind to even greater sacrifices toward credit for the other two who would both be wounded in an ambush while traveling in a jeep in Korea and would soon be back in Puerto Rico—slightly damaged, but alive. Funda's knees bore the scars like medals from many wars and conflicts. Aunt Clotilde found herself suddenly displaced as my "other parent," and returned to her own bed. All changed.

My first memory is of his homecoming party, and of the gift he brought me from San Juan, a pink iron crib like an ornate bird cage, and of the sense of abandonment I felt for the first time in my short life, as all eyes turned to the handsome stranger in uniform and away from me, in my frilly new dress and patent leather shoes trapped inside my pink iron crib, screaming my head off for Mamí, Tía,

Mamá Funda, anybody . . . to come lift me out of my prison. When I ask about the events of that day, my mother still rolls her eyes back and throws her hands up in a gesture of dismay. The story varies with the telling and the teller, but it seems that I climbed out of my tall crib on my own and headed for the party in the back-yard. The pig was on the spit and the beer was flowing. In the living room the Victrola was playing my father's Elvis Presley records loudly. I may have imag-ined this. My mother is sitting on his lap. She is gorgeous in the red silk dress he has given her. There is a circle of people around him. Everyone is having a good time. And everyone has forgotten about me. I see myself slipping through the crowd and into flames. Immediately, I am pulled out by a man's strong hands. No real damage: my abundant hair is a little singed, but that is all. Mother is crying. I am the center of everyone's attention once more. Even his. Did I sleep between them that night because my mother has finally realized that I am not a rubber dolly but a real flesh-and-blood little girl? When I ask, she says that she remembers only staying awake listening to me breathe the night of "the accident." She had also been kept up by the unaccustomed noise of my father's snoring. She would soon get used to both facts of life: that every one of her waking hours would belong to me from then on, and that this solemn stranger—who only resembled the timid young man she had married two years before—would own her nights. My mother was finally coming of age.

Alberto Ríos

The Birthday of Mrs. Piñeda

Café Combate, ¡la gente toma!
Café Combate, ¡de rico aroma!

—a famous, and old, commercial jingle ran on the radio in Mexico for many years, advertising a particular brand of coffee. It ran repeatedly, obsessively, and no one who heard it has been able to forget.

Café Combate, the people drink it!
Café Combate, such rich aroma!

The noise came through the mouth of his nose: "hummph."

Adolfo Piñeda had read the books on El Salvador, but they didn't matter. He understood them, all right—which is to say, he understood that he did not understand them. So he kept reading them, buying them, rereading them, shrugging his shoulders. He read them everywhere, all the time; the names were so familiar, so like his. He read them at dinner: a page turned, a mouthful of chilaquiles, a page, a napkin to his lips in a wipe of the sauce. At the part about the genitals in men's mouths, he thought twice before chewing, but only twice. Truly believing such a story would mean no dinner. Conscience is like that.

"Fito," his wife called at him. She was always young again when she called him like this, like the wind, which goes away but comes back again and is recognized easily. They had met at thirteen, when he was still Adolfito, and she was then his Mariquita.

"Fito!"

"*Sí-sí-sí-sí*, what."

"Stop reading." She looked at the newest magazine. Dead children again on the cover. Dead and flat, the way magazine covers make them, so they cannot be touched, so that a hand cannot go under the head. "You said you would. So much blood and screaming, I can hear it all the way over in the kitchen. Close that story. You said you would, you promised. Read me about the Prince and *ésa, la Diana,* read me about that baby. You said you would." She cleared his dishes away.

"Mari . . ."

"No. No coffee. Or Sanka. You want that, Sanka?"

"Ay, Mari. Give me coffee."

"Give me give me give me. If I had known . . ."

"What? If you had known what?"

"Give me give me. Thirty years ago, if I had known that would happen, what you . . ."

Adolfo Piñeda clicked his teeth to break her sentence in half. "Oh stop it. Come on, *m'ija*, it's just coffee, that's all I want. Chh. It's not going to keep me awake." María Piñeda looked at him. Inside, behind her eyes, she saw the old radio and hummed the jingle that took her back to all the lunch times of her growing up, to all the rice and ground beef meals she ate hearing it. She ate the music of the old coffee jingle with her ears, chewed it over and over

Café Combate, ¡la gente toma!

Café Combate, ¡de rico aroma!

all of it came back for the five seconds of humming that she took, then went back inside her. She wanted to give him coffee. Very strong, very black, *cariculillo, Tapachula,* or even the *Café Combate* of the song; for so many years they had kept it in their cups. They had taken it out of the thin, brown paper bags. He loved it, and she loved him to love it. Something about a man liking something passionately, anything, boxing even, something about it made her give in to anything.

"*Andale, m'ija*, just this once, come on."

"But the doctor, you know . . ."

"It won't hurt, and I'm not going to tell him."

María Piñeda clicked her teeth at him and went to get the coffee. Humming. He got it three nights out of seven and sometimes twice in a night if he read to her about good things. He was a lion when he read. His roaring came from so many years of politics and smoke, of reading the smudged and crowded newsprint of all the smallest newspapers from all the smallest countries *de abajo*, all the smallest countries down there with all the biggest names, the fat Indian names, and the names of saints.

But when he read to her about the good things, about Charles or about what her *tía* in San Luis Potosí wrote, he had to use his loud moments up on words like *kiss*, " . . . and he KISSED his wife," or bananas, so that the news was that her *tía* had gone to the market and bought BANANAS. He made it all sound so important, and María Piñeda would laugh at him invariably at some juncture of the night, and he would not understand. He would wrinkle his face up like paper and throw his fine mood into the wastebasket. He would stop reading to her then and go back to his books, or his magazines, El Salvador, El Salvador, or his tiny and smudged letters in newsprint for which he would need the magnifying glass. And coffee. Slyly, he would add this. "And coffee," he would say, "and leave me alone."

"Here, *m'ijo*." She set down some new coffee next to him. Its steamy hands made him pay attention, pulling his head almost to its face.

"But this is only half, you didn't fill the cup. . . ." He frowned, till there was no room left on his face for more frowning. But he managed. It was a little something extra with the left half of the left eyebrow, perhaps an added twitch of the eyelid underneath.

"It was full when I started from the kitchen. *Ni modo.*"

Hummph. He said this more with his chest than with any sounds. He let his face relax a little as he took the flirting sip. Two and a half cups in one night was the best he had done this year. And anyway, he had seen half a cup disappear before, so he was not truly angry. Coffee disappearing was nothing new, he had seen it often, even before María. It was the uncles. His mother had told him, and it was true. Even dead uncles want coffee. Coffee is not a thing a man stops wanting. Somewhere with his own hands Adolfo Piñeda could even remember picking coffee beans, could remember the smell even then, the wanting. Or it was a story somebody told him about his grandfather. The feeling went too far back to be clear, so he frowned again and tried to remember for a fact what had happened, what the story was. . . .

"Anna came over today."

"Anna?" Adolfo Piñeda looked up from his reading, which was really thinking.

María Piñeda looked at him looking up from his reading and felt good. But now, because he looked up, this story of Anna was going to have to be a little better than what really happened. She had him, and had to take care.

He knew that, of course. He knew it the moment he lifted his head and was sorry for the little lie he was going to make her tell him. He should have remembered to look up earlier and say something casual, anything, just so that his looking up now would seem less like a lion's or a bear's. But he could feel that she had him now like a tender fish. And she had better be careful or the fish would balloon—pop! into the lion they both thought of him as, into the bear he knew he sometimes was. The thing wasn't true, but he could tell it was there between them. After thirty years a feeling like that . . . well, never mind, he told himself. He stopped thinking the thought. He knew it would get no clearer than the coffee beans.

Not in words, anyway. But a kind of heart that the mind has pulsed the thought through, regardless of his trying to stop it. This second heart always troubled him like that. It didn't pay attention. No attention to decorum-that was a word from the army, or from his grandfather—the decorum with which he now tried to live his life. It leaped so very quickly back and forth between times and events, this heart, that he didn't understand. And it scared him. Thirty years were nothing, and a minute sometimes was the entire lifetime of several men back-to-back.

Todasbodas. That's what it was saying to him now, in that language that was not words, and not the hummph intended for María. *Todasbodas*. It was reminding him of how he used to be an *all-weddings*. It skipped through the thirty years he was sitting down with now, back to the younger bones he used to have and the different shirts and the thin black moustaches of which he took such care in every mirror that he passed.

Adolfo Piñeda looked at his wife about to tell him the story of Anna's visit today, and his second heart remembered for him the time when his ambition was to swing from crystal chandeliers, to be expert in this, and to take his talent through the fanciest houses of the jungle countries, and then to Europe, to the continent, with final recognition and general applause in Paris, where they would in his old age offer him a pension in honor of his selfless and fine work in redefining wildness.

He looked at his wife and he smiled.

Today was her birthday. She was some age or other. She was nineteen when they married, and that was the only birthday that ever mattered to his second heart, and it only mattered because it was the first measure of her that he had. They had lived in Guaymas, the both of them then. He could remember that she was nineteen, but he could not remember the first time he had made love to her. That he could not remember is what he remembered now. Something was always indistinct to him there, about that. Like the coffee beans. What he knew now, what he remembered, was that he had known a number of girls and had told each one his story

The story concerned a particular history of Guaymas, the *true history of Guaymas*, as he would say. It was a sham, but no more so than any other history— of Guaymas or of any other place. It was as true and as false as the things any people say to get each other's clothes off now and fast. The true history of Guaymas is told in eight separate volumes in the mayor's office, the back office, and he had read them by special permission before the fire. An intricate weave, he would say, and he hummed it like a song back to himself now; an intricate weave, the words were so familiar suddenly, not so far back, so ingrained, so like the lines on a wooden post; an intricate weave, he would say, about this traitor and that shopkeeper, some lover of stray cats and three toothless women; but in truth there was no general who did *that*, not ever, not anywhere. Only in his words. Adolfo Piñeda told the story to impress some Mariquita, this Mariquita this time, and it worked, God, it worked, so it had to be real, this story, because it was the thing that got her print dress and thin shoes to come off, this story of himself as the youngest general with thin moustaches and a cape who, with his singleness of arm strength, pushed the difficult song of violence farther than the rest, but on the right side of things. At this the girl sighed with relief, sure that a man on the right side of things could not be wrong.

But it must have been the business of saving the six sisters of mercy against which this Catholic Mariquita could not win—none of them could win here; she could only melt like sugar into the arms of this particular history, the one that must be true even for hard Catholic girls from the desert north, melt like sugar into the arms, into the face of a man who talked through the seasons and the seasons of the night.

María Piñeda, about to tell the story of Anna's visit and wrestling around very quickly in her head for extra words to make the story better and so to keep his tender and old attention longer, saw Adolfo Piñeda smile at her.

Just smile at her.

He had not done that, not like that, since before, since the far before. He still smiled at her, but his smiles were embers now, not strong quick wood fires. They were warmer now, and more lasting, but his smiles no longer held a sense of danger, that they might burn, that they might reach off his face and stretch in some lightning bolt fist straight at her, down and through the electricity in the cells at the core of her inside self.

She had been María Elena then, daughter of the string vendor, strings for all occasions, and rough cotton threads, Don Miguel, and his wife, la señora Beltrán, who never smiled and so was never addressed by her first name.

But her Fito was smiling at her now, and she was standing in the time when he had called her by the names of various imported perfumes taken, he would say, from the wildest flowers of the wilted and perfect bouquets found in subtle crystal vases that sat on the absurd tables in one particular backstreet bistro in springtime Paris just the year before.

He said this, but it said nothing about what he would do. From that moment she could never disentwine her other memory of the time of perfumes, that time just after they had married when she had to go looking for him, had to step over a dried phlegm and dirt floor in a dark cockfighting barn, had to step over this floor made of sputum from half-shaved, thick men and dying cocks, a floor blood-stained and scuffed into a kind of inexpert, misshapen setting of scab tiles. The sounds of the fight would not go away, the sounds of all those men huddled, nor the odor of that perfume, and she remembered how she had seen as she ran by the one soul-white cock splattered with blood like grease, hot, how it had an eye pulled clean out but continued to fight, and then, lost the other eye but continued to fight, stretching its head and neck up higher and higher, imagining that something must be blocking its view, trying to see, and trying higher to see, but never for a moment thinking that it was blind. The owners kept spraying the fighter birds with water from their mouths, spitting a mist, cooling and cooling, fooling them, until the winner, the not-white one, allowed itself to be cooled and soothed and rewarded, and the owner, who was laughing, took its head into his mouth, cooling him.

María Piñeda ran by them all, that perfume, into the rooms behind the barn, into one room of particular use, and she pulled Adolfo Piñeda physically out of another woman and dragged him drunk home.

"Why are you smiling at me?"
"It's your birthday. Did you think I had forgotten?"
María Piñeda clicked her teeth at him. "Don't you want to hear about Anna?"
"What about Anna, well. Tell me."
"She came over today."
"I know that."
"Fito! Stop it and let me tell you."
Again she called him by that name, and again she was young for him because of it. He liked the sound of the name as it came from her, even when she was angry. This was the second time at least tonight that she had called him that. Adolfo Piñeda knew that his wife was thinking about her birthday then. She felt young, too, he could tell. He smiled even more, and she turned around and said she wasn't going to tell him the story because he wasn't paying attention to her, not the right kind, that he was being silly. Yes, he thought, she was being young and he liked it. He could be young, too, for her birthday: he ignored her.

He went back to his coffee and this newest article on El Salvador. This is crazy, he thought, and this thought about the bodies with names like his took him away from his wife again. María Piñeda went to the kitchen to cry. This is crazy, he thought.

"This is crazy," he said to the kitchen. Adolfo Piñeda did not mean the killing and suffering, but that people would go there to see it and talk about it. Words. In a flat paper magazine. He put his hand over the picture of a line of shoeless bodies, piled in a half-hearted way. Nothing. He could feel nothing. Slick on his fingers.

He took a drink of coffee, long like a breath in the mountains. This, he thought, *this*. Coffee, from Colombia and Paraguay and there and there and there, from all the small places *de abajo*. It comes from the dirt, straight up, from hell to heaven. I drink it, he thought, and it's a way of remembering something, it reminds me to remember. Black like the earth and all its shades. It is knowing what it is to be dead, to have disappeared, to have gone just gone. Knowing what being dead is—this keeps us alive. Coffee makes me jump, thought Adolfo Piñeda, makes me full with the spirit of wanting to do things, full with energy, with being young, full with the fear of being dead, of just lying there. Caffeine . . .

Hummph. He said this with his chest, again, bigger than with words, and rounder. No such thing exists, *caffeine*. The word is a failure, or its definition not yet finished. He could not find in any dictionary—after the doctor had told him about the word—anything about its being what it was: a power from the muscles of the dead, their backs and forearms, their dreams, and how they still want to do things, a kind of leftover need, yes, *seguro que sí*, the power of intentions never met, such strong intentions, and so many, that they could not go away. Coffee reminded him that he was alive, and would keep him alive, too, not make him one of those bodies, not like the doctor had said. These dead, they never speak in words, he thought, only whimpered, but the dead were out there. One could hear them in the wind, usually very quiet, a little irritating, but quiet, not real words. The dead have a humble streak a mile long, but not him, not Adolfo Piñeda. And not his wife, either—he would not let her.

"What are you doing in there, *m'ija*?" he called to her. This being young, this way, this way of ignoring her, but paying attention that she knew he was ignoring her, was maybe no good, but what could he do. This was the only way he knew. The dead, the energy, the slow electricity of caffeine, they gave him force, but no answers. She would stop crying.

He looked at the pictures again. This was his dessert, he guessed; he hadn't asked if she had made a cake. In a minute I'll ask her, he thought. When she stops crying.

The pictures. The whole thing of them, the way they were, so flat, so dimensionless, the way they were not really the dead people at all—was like doctors. If a person goes in bleeding, the doctors fix the cut but never ask the attacker what made him stab a man, never get the *vato* in, get him in with his knife and ask how his father could let him do such a thing to someone else. Then they should rough up that knifer a little. That's what's wrong with them: these new doctors see only blood. Even *ese* doctor, *¿cómo se llama?* el doctor Martínez. He at least should know better. At least him. He came from Guaymas, too, but maybe he's too young to know the world. At least he asks a question now and then about what the kitchen knife felt like, asks that of a husband, or about how many links and how heavy they were in the hoodlum's chain that did this or that to the face.

"Did you see these pictures, *m'ija*? Did you see them? El Salvador, *otra vez*. They can't get enough. Whatever happened, what about this boy that was shot, *¿cómo se llamaba* . . . Casillas? Remember his face? Who ever talked about him, right here in Phoenix?

"Are you all right, *m'ija*?

"A gun and blood and by strangers and everything. Everything all wrapped up in one boy's body. A man. Remember him? But it doesn't count. Maybe with presidents it counts."

Adolfo Piñeda could still hear his wife, but a little less now, in the kitchen. She was feeling better. He knew she would.

Hummamph. "Let the Anglos go there. We've already been there, huh? Let the Anglos go there—they go like flies anyway, like flies on the blood of cows. They're crazy. One stays away from a place like that. It only makes sense. But it's like dinner or something to them. They must feel good or something. I don't get it, *m'ija*.

"So they're crazy I think. That's not where the answers are. Everybody knows that. What jokes, JOKES. Look at these PICTURES. Like a MAGNET was pulling them. It STINKS. Like when the president was shot, or the POPE, or some other big guy. I don't know what will happen next."

María Piñeda came out of the kitchen and sat to listen—because she liked to, like always. When he was a lion like this, everything fell away. A lion.

Hummphh. "Look at them. A president gets shot and they spend three days on television trying to explain it. Of COURSE it takes three days. There's nothing to explain. And they couldn't DO it, the *pendejos*. They CAN'T explain what has no explanation." Hummph. "Next time somebody's SHOT they'll take two weeks and so WHAT. They STILL won't have an answer. So what."

"It's my birthday." María Piñeda looked at him. She was Mariquita, and he didn't know what to say.

"Well, tell the story then."

"What story?"

"*M'ija*, don't be *tan simple*. You know. About Anna."

"Anna?"

"*Sí-sí-sí-sí*. Come on, come on. Anna, you know, Anna?"

María Piñeda began her story then, about this Anna whoever she was, and it went on in its particulars, one thing bringing up another more important than the last, some things making her cry large, toad-size tears, some things not.

Mariquita Piñeda began her story on her birthday, and it went on, and on further, through the night and pushed a shoulder against lunch time of the next day.

Helena María Viramontes

Miss Clairol

Arlene and Champ walk to K-Mart. The store is full of bins mounted with bargain buys from T-shirts to rubber sandals. They go to aisle 23, Cosmetics. Arlene, wearing bell-bottom jeans two sizes too small, can't bend down to the Miss Clairol boxes.

"Which one amá?" asks Champ, chewing her thumbnail.

"Shit, m'ija, I dunno." Arlene smacks her gum, contemplating the decision. "Maybe I need a change, tú sabes. What do you think?" She holds up a few blond strands with black roots. Arlene has burned the softness of her hair with peroxide; her hair is stiff, breaks at the ends and she needs plenty of Aqua Net hairspray to tease and tame her ratted hair, then folds it back into a high lump behind her head. For the last few months she has been a platinum "Light Ash" blond, before that a Miss Clairol "Flame" redhead, before that Champ couldn't even identify the color—somewhere between orange and brown, a "Sun Bronze." The only way Champ knows her mother's true hair color is by her roots which, like death, inevitably rise to the truth.

"I hate it, tú sabes, when I can't decide." Arlene is wearing a pink, strapless tube top. Her stomach spills over the hip-hugger jeans. Spits the gum onto the floor. "Fuck it." And Champ follows her to the rows of nail polish, next to the Maybelline rack of make-up, across the false eyelashes that look like insects on display in clear, plastic boxes. Arlene pulls out a particular color of nail polish, looks at the bottom of the bottle for the price, puts it back, gets another. She has a tattoo of purple XXX's on her left finger like a ring. She finally settles for a purple-blackish color, Ripe Plum, that Champ thinks looks like the color of Frankenstein's nails. She looks at her own stubby nails, chewed and gnawed.

Walking over to the eye shadows, Arlene slowly slinks out another stick of gum from her back pocket, unwraps and crumbles the wrapper into a little ball, lets it drop on the floor. Smacks the gum.

"Grandpa Ham used to make chains with these gum wrappers," she says, toeing the wrapper on the floor with her rubber sandals, her toes dotted with old nail polish. "He started one, tú sabes, that went from room to room. That was before he went nuts," she says, looking at the price of magenta eye shadow. "¿Sabes qué? What do you think?" lifting the eye shadow to Champ.

"I dunno," responds Champ, shrugging her shoulders the way she always does when she is listening to something else, her own heartbeat, what Gregorio said on the phone yesterday, shrugs her shoulders when Miss Smith says OFELIA, answer my question. She is too busy thinking of things people otherwise dismiss like parentheses, but stick to her like gum, like a hole on a shirt, like a tattoo, and sometimes she wishes she weren't born with such adhesiveness. The chain went from room to room, round and round like a web, she remembers. That was before he went nuts.

"Champ. You listening? Or in lala land again?" Arlene has her arms akimbo on a fold of flesh, pissed.

"I said, I dunno." Champ whines back, still looking at the wrapper on the floor.

"Well you better learn, tú sabes, and fast too. Now think, will this color go good with Pancha's blue dress?" Pancha is Arlene's comadre. Since Arlene has a special date tonight, she lent Arlene her royal blue dress that she keeps in a plastic bag at the end of her closet. The dress is made of chiffon, with satin-like material underlining, so that when Arlene first tried it on and strutted about, it crinkled sounds of elegance. The dress fits too tight. Her plump arms squeeze through, her hips breathe in and hold their breath, the seams do all they can to keep the body contained. But Arlene doesn't care as long as it sounds right.

"I think it will," Champ says, and Arlene is very pleased.

"Think so? So do I, m'ija."

They walk out the double doors and Champ never remembers her mother paying.

* * *

It is four in the afternoon, but already Arlene is preparing for the date. She scrubs the tub, Art Labo on the radio, drops crystals of Jean Naté into the running water, lemon scent rises with the steam. The bathroom door ajar, she removes her top and her breasts flop and sag, pushes her jeans down with some difficulty, kicks them off, and steps in the tub.

"M'ija. M'IJA," she yells. "M'ija, give me a few bobby pins." She is worried about her hair frizzing and so wants to pin it up.

Her mother's voice is faint because Champ is in the closet. There are piles of clothes on the floor, hangers thrown askew and tangled, shoes all piled up or thrown on the top shelf. Champ is looking for her mother's special dress. Pancha says every girl has one at the end of her closet.

"Goddamn it, Champ."

Amidst the dirty laundry, the black hole of the closet, she finds nothing. "NOW."

"All right, ALL RIGHT. Cheeze amá, stop yelling," says Champ, and goes in the steamy bathroom, checks the drawers, hairbrushes jump out, rollers, strands of hair, rummages through bars of soap, combs, eye shadows, finds nothing; pulls open another drawer, powder, empty bottles of oil, manicure scissors, Kotex, dye instructions crinkled and blotched, finally, a few bobby pins.

After Arlene pins up her hair, she asks Champ, "¿Sabes qué? Should I wear my hair up? Do I look good with it up?" Champ is sitting on the toilet.

"Yeah, amá, you look real pretty."

"Thanks, m'ija" says Arlene. "¿Sabes qué? When you get older I'll show you how you can look just as pretty," and she puts her head back, relaxes, like the Calgon commercials.

* * *

Champ lays on her stomach, TV on to some variety show with pogo stick dancers dressed in outfits of stretchy material and glitter. She is wearing one of Gregorio's white T-shirts, the ones he washes and bleaches himself so that the whiteness is impeccable. It drapes over her deflated ten-year-old body like a dress. She is busy cutting out Miss Breck models from the stacks of old magazines Pancha found in the back of her mother's garage. Champ collects the array of honey-color-haired women, puts them in a shoe box with all her other special things.

Arlene is in the bathroom, wrapped in a towel. She has painted her eyebrows so that the two are arched and even, penciled thin and high. The magenta shades her eyelids. The towel slips, reveals one nipple blind from a cigarette burn, a date to forget. She rewraps the towel, likes her reflection, turns to her profile for additional inspection. She feels good, turns up the radio to . . . your love. For your loveeeee, I will do anything, I will do anything, forrr your love. For your kiss . . .

Champ looks on. From the open bathroom door, she can see Arlene, anticipation burning like a cigarette from her lips, sliding her shoulders to the ahhhh ahhhhh, and pouting her lips until the song ends. And Champ likes her mother that way.

Arlene carefully stretches black eyeliner, like a fallen question mark, outlines each eye. The work is delicate, her hand trembles cautiously, stops the process to review the face with each line. Arlene the mirror is not Arlene the face who has worn too many relationships, gotten too little sleep. The last touch is the chalky, beige lipstick. By the time she is finished, her ashtray is full of cigarette butts, Champ's variety show is over, and Jackie Gleason's dancing girls come on to make kaleidoscope patterns with their long legs and arms. Gregorio is still not home, and Champ goes over to the window, checks the houses, the streets, corners, roams the sky with her eyes.

Arlene sits on the toilet, stretches up her nylons, clips them to her girdle. She feels good thinking about the way he will unsnap her nylons, and she will unroll them slowly, point her toes when she does.

Champ opens a can of Campbell soup, finds a perfect pot in the middle of a stack of dishes, pulls it out to the threatening rumbling of the tower. She washes it out, pours the contents of the red can, turns the knob. After it boils, she puts the pot on the sink for it to cool down. She searches for a spoon.

Arlene is romantic. When Champ begins her period, she will tell her things that only women can know. She will tell her about the first time she made love with a boy, her awkwardness and shyness forcing them to go under the house, where the cool, refined soil made a soft mattress. How she closed her eyes and wondered what to expect, or how the penis was the softest skin she had ever felt against her, how it tickled her, searched for a place to connect. She was eleven and his name was Harry.

She will not tell Champ that her first fuck was guy named Puppet who ejaculated prematurely, at the sight of her apricot vagina, so plump and fuzzy. "Pendejo," she said, "you got it all over me." She rubbed the gooey substance off her legs, her belly in disgust. Ran home to tell Rat and Pancha, her mouth open with laughter.

Arlene powder-puffs under her arms, between her breasts, tilts a bottle of Love Cries perfume and dabs behind her ears, neck and breasts for those tight caressing songs which permit them to grind their bodies together until she can feel a bulge in his pants and she knows she's in for the night.

Jackie Gleason is a bartender in a saloon. He wears a black bow tie, a white apron, and is polishing a glass. Champ is watching him, sitting in the radius of the gray light, eating her soup from the pot.

Arlene is a romantic. She will dance until her dress turns a different color, dance until her hair becomes undone, her hips jiggering and quaking beneath a new pair of hosiery, her mascara shadowing under her eyes from the perspiration of the ritual, dance spinning herself into Miss Clairol, and stopping only when it is time to return to the sewing factory, time to wait out the next date, time to change hair color. Time to remember or to forget.

Champ sees Arlene from the window. She can almost hear Arlene's nylons rubbing against one another, hear the crinkling sound of satin when she gets in the blue and white shark-finned Dodge. Champ yells good-bye.

It all sounds so right to Arlene who is too busy cranking up the window to hear her daughter.

Francisco X. Alarcón

***Chicome-Coatl* /Seven Snake**

corn stalks
are upright
snakes

corn ears
rattle
in the wind

For Planting *Camotes*

Ruiz de Alarcón (III:7)

This spell is spoken directly to the sun after the roots and stems have been prepared for planting.

nomatca nehuatl	I myself
nicnopiltzintli	I, Poor Orphan
niCenteotl	I, *Centeotl*:
tla xihuallhuian	come forth
notla	uncle
tlamacazqui Nanahuatzin	spirit *Nanahuatzin*
ca nican niquilpia	here I tie up
nometzcuoahyo	my thigh
nictoca	I plant it
tla xihualhuia	come forth
notla Nanahuatzin	uncle *Nanahuatzin*
ca nican niquilpia	here I tie up
notzontecon	my head
ca ica noconilpia	I tie it up
in nohueltiuh	to my sister
in tetencuacua xochitl	the lip-biting flower
temacochthuia xochitl	the embracing flower
itetzinco nihiouiz	with her I shall breathe
itetzinco nipahtiz	with her I shall heal
nicnotlacatzintli	I, just a poor person

To Undo the Sleep Spell

Ruiz de Alarcón (II:2)

in ic niquimanatiuh	I'm going to take them back
tlalli inepantla	from the center of the earth
in ic nanhcampa	from the four directions:
in ahmo nelli in	it's not true that
no niquincuepa	I changed them—
in ahmo cochiya	they were not sleeping
in ahmo oyaca	they did not go
ChiacnauhMictlan	to Nine-*Mictlan*
in ahmo nelly oquinhuicac	neither did the One-Called-Night
Moyohualitoatrin	truly take them away
ea!	come on!
ye niquincueya	I've already brought them back
in yehuatl in Temicxoch	from their Dream-Flower—
in nehuatl	I am
in niYohuallahuantzin	the Night-Drinker

1975

talking proletariat talks
over instant coffee
and nicotine.
in better times
there is tea
to ease the mind.
talking proletariat talks
during laid-off hours
cussing and cussing
complaining of unpaid bills
and bigoted unions
that refuse to let us in.

talking proletariat talks
of pregnant wives
and shoeless kids.
no-turkey-thanksgivings.
bare x-mas tree this year.
santa claus is on strike
again.

talking proletariat talks
with proletariat friends
and relations who need
a few bucks til the end
of the week
waiting
for compensation checks.
talking proletariat talks
of plants closing down
and deportations.
tight immigration
busting our brothers again.

talking proletariat talks
of next spring or some
unforeseen vacation
to leave all this behind
to forget the winter
in unheated flats
turned off gas and
"ma bell" who serves
the people
took the phone away
when we were out
looking for a gig.

talking proletariat talks
of next presidential elections
the emperor of chicago
who lives off the fat of the land
and only feeds his sty of pigs.
talking proletariat talks
over rum and schlitz
of lottery tickets
on bingo nights at St. Sebastian's.

talking proletariat talks
climbing crime. defenseless
women. unsafe parks and
congested highways.
talking proletariat talks
of higher rent two months
behind. landlords who live
on lake shore drive or over
where the grass is greener.

talking proletariat talks
talking proletariat talks
talking proletariat talks
until one long
awaited day—
we are tired
of talking.

Napa, California

Dedicado al Sr. Chávez, sept. '75

We pick
   the bittersweet grapes
   at harvest
   one
    by
      one
   with leather worn hands
         as they pick
           at our dignity
           and wipe our pride
           away
           like the sweat we wipe
           from our sun beaten brows
           at mid day
In fields
   so vast
   that our youth seems
   to pass before us
   and we have grown
   very
    very
      old
        by dusk . . .
        (bueno pues ¿qué vamos a hacer, Ambrosio?
        bueno pues, ¡seguirle, compadre, seguirle!
        ¡Ay, Mamá!
        Sí pues ¿qué vamos a hacer, compadre?
        ¡Seguirle, Ambrosio, seguirle!)
We pick
   with a desire
   that only survival
   inspires
While the end
   of each day only brings
   a tired night

that waits for the sun
and the land
that in turn waits
for us . . .

The Antihero

the antihero
always gets the woman
not in the end
an anticlimax instead
in the end
spits on her
stretched out body
a spasmodic carpet
yearning still
washes himself

doesn't know why
it is that way searching
not finding finding
not wanting wanting more
or nothing
in the end the key is
to leave her yearning lest
she discover that is all

Martín Espada

David Leaves the Saints for Paterson

Primo David's arm hung near-paralyzed
after the stabbing,
and there was no work in
Barrio Hill Brothers,
so he learned to smoke with the other hand
and plotted to leave Puerto Rico.

His mother sponge-washed the plaster santos
every week, draped statues crowded
with flowers. Then Tata, la abuela,
would nod with ceremony, foretelling money
and sickness, mouth quavering ajar with the dialects
of the many dead. In spite of prophecy
at Jardines Del Paraíso housing project,
no one could stop drinking.

David left the saints for Paterson:
the boot factory,
then a hospital job wheeling carts of delicate bottles
through light-bleached corridors on late shift.

Together with his father at the Paterson hospital,
the gallo-man who learned to box in prison,
who also pushes the medicine carts to impatient doctors
and cannot stop drinking.

Colibrí

—*for Katherine, one year later*

In Jayuya,
the lizards scatter
like a fleet of green canoes
before the invader.
The Spanish conquered
with iron and words:
"Indio Taíno" for the people
who took life
from the rain
that rushed through trees
like evaporating arrows,
who left the rock carvings
of eyes and mouths
in perfect circles of amazement.

So the hummingbird
was christened "colibrí."
Now the colibrí
darts and bangs
between the white walls
of the hacienda,
a racing Taíno heart
frantic as if hearing
the bellowing god of gunpowder
for the first time.

The colibrí
becomes pure stillness,
seized in the paralysis
of the prey,
when your hands
cup the bird
and lift him
through the red shutters
of the window,
where he disappears
into a paradise of sky,
a nightfall of singing frogs.

If only history
were like your hands.

Amor negro

in our wagon oysters are treasured
their hard shells clacking against each other
words that crash into our ears
we cushion them
cut them gently in our hands
we kiss and suck the delicate juice
and sculpture flowers from the stone skin
we wash them in the river by moonlight
with offerings of songs
and after the meal we wear them in our hair
and in our eyes

So you want me to be your mistress

So you want me to be your mistress
and find dignity in a closed room
because you say your first real love is music
even though I too am music
the sum total of contrary chords and dissonant notes
occasionally surviving in mutilated harmony
even though my great-grandmother was black royalty
traded off into marketable conceptions of how black should brown be
even though the organic fruit of my womb carries your living blood while I am
slowly crushed under the weight of disenchanted solitude
even though I could fill you so full
to grow outside yourself
and walk with you through opalescent gardens
trailing lovers who are unafraid
to touch and feel and sing
and give more than each other
in the cool shade, the burning sun, and the silence

But you only want me to be your Sunday afternoon mistress
and I have to recycle this flow of ebony tailored ambition
limit the mother in me that wants to intoxicate herself
in the center of your soul
not watch alien wives trade you off for multi colored trinkets
flashing against the real you
understanding what a whore sophistication really is
I reject a service role
a position I've truly hated whenever it was forced upon me

And it's true that I am a drifter, a wanderer, I never really had roots
a gypsy whose objective in life is to travel in whole circles
that resemble the path of Venus around the Sun

I never reveled in washing clothes
or reached orgasms from dirty dishes
but I didn't mind being part of someone who could help me to be me
with all my transient contradictions

And I am a woman, not a mistress or a whore
or some anonymous cunt whose initials barely left an impression
on the foreskin of your nationhood, a woman

Y si la patria es una mujer
Then I am also a rebel and a lover of free people
and continue looking for friction in empty spaces
which is the only music I know how to play.

Transference

Don't come to me with expectations
Of who you think I should be
From some past when
You were going through changes

I'm not your mother who didn't hold you all day long
Or kiss away the rough cuts when you fell
I'm not your sister who wouldn't play with you
Mashing up your favorite toys on purpose
I'm not the lady upstairs who keeps you up all night
Playing Lawrence Welk Muzak
And I'm not your girlfriend who left you flat
The one who promised forever never to go
For whom you would never love another
Or the one who used you for sex
And forgot your first name
I'm not the one who beat you
For ten dollars and dinner
Or ate up your cookies and milk
Or gave you the wrong kind of presents
I'm not your neighbor who hates you
'Cause you have more roaches than them
Or the landlord who steals your rent
And leaves you out in the cold
I'm not the meter maid who gave you $300 in parking tickets
Or the kid who plugged your tires just for fun
Or the psycho who smashed your front windshield
Or the truck that hit your rear bumper and ran
I'm not the traffic court judge who insists you're the liar
Or the junkie who popped your trunk lock
And tried to steal your spare tire
I didn't take your virginity with empty promises
Or con you with a job for sex
And I'm definitely not the one who ripped off your mind
And did not allow you to speak your own tongue
Or tried to turn you slave or dog
No, I'm not the bitch who denies you your true history

Or tries to hide the beauty of yourself
I am not the colonizer or the oppressor
Or the sum total of your problems, I am not the enemy
I am not the one who never called you
To invite you to coffee and dinner
Nor the friend who never gave you friendship
Or the lover who did not know how to love

So when you come to me, don't assume
That you know me so well as that
Don't come with preconceptions
Or expect me to fit the mold you have created
Because we fit no molds
We have no limitations
And when you do come, bring me your hopes
Describe for me your visions, your dreams
Bring me your support and your inspiration
Your guidance and your faith
Your belief in our possibilities
Bring me the best that you can

Give me the chance to be
Myself and create symphonies like
The pastel dawn or the empty canvas
Before the first stroke of color is released

Come in a dialogue of we
You and me reacting, responding
Being, something new
Discovering.

Alicia Gaspar de Alba

After 21 Years, a Postcard from My Father

The first time Dad sent me
his love through the mail,
he wrote a letter
and a one-dollar check
for chocolates, he said.
I was six years old, coarse
brown braids, knees like petrified
breasts, granny glasses that darkened
in the sun. I wore shorts under my uniform
and went to Father-Daughter dinners
with my friend Cindy and her dad.
My abuelo picked me up from school.

And Tony (a.k.a. my father)
said in his letter: "*Obedece
a tu abuela. No te cortes el pelo.
Aquí te mando dinero para dulces y chocolates.*"

I changed the one to a nine on the check
and never wrote back. Never cashed
in on Dad's long distance love.

Today, I skip down the stairs
with the knowledge: *my father wrote to me!*
I understand now that this is all
I need to know. I will never see
what has tormented the man
from the day I was born,
the day he called himself a father
for the first time.

This afternoon on the bus,
I watched a retarded boy slapping himself
on the back, a gesture that started
as a caress, his hand moving
over his shoulder as if a cat
or a parrot perched there.
And then the hand grew
wild, angry, tormented, a slapping
that hunched him down on the seat of the bus.

"What's on your back?" I asked him.
He looked at me with eyes that pitied
my lack of vision, my need to know
everything. How could I not see
what his torment was?

"Wings," he said quietly.
"They won't leave me alone," he said.
"They're too heavy," he said.

Bamba Basílica

In Oaxaca at the basílica
de la Virgen de la Soledad

a radio blares "La Bamba"
in the faith of an Indian woman,

Zapotec, kneeling her way to the altar.
Arms outstretched, she opens

her palms to the Virgin's grace,
una poca de gracia y otra cosita.

Her shoulders rise and fall in the dance
of supplication,

yo no soy marinero, soy capitán.
Beside her, the other supplicants

stand before la Soledad,
fingers to forehead, mouth, eyelids—

a solar cross suspended
over their disbelief—

arriba y arriba y arriba iré.
Now, la india's palms come together,

urgent words pressed between them:
por ti seré, por ti seré.

Her head bobs to the rhythm
of a promesa

that Ritchie Valens
never recorded.

Ray González

Walk

for John Brandi

Here is the trail to the mountain.
May your feet kiss it
with intent laughter,
the taste of your travels,
the courage of your hands
that released those inmates
that listened to you.

Here are the cliffs of the soul.
May you fall off knowing
the carpet of snow is
no explanation, no cushion,
but the canvas waiting
for the impact of your body,
the drawing to unfold.

Here are your words at dusk.
May the night recite
what it learned upon
giving up the red horizon,
your line toward the other side,
where flame etches
whatever you transcribe.

Two Wolf Poems

> *You can look at a gray wolf standing in the snow in winter twilight and not see him at all. You may think I'm pulling your leg. I'm not. Sometimes, even the Eskimos can't see them, which causes the Eskimo to smile.*
>
> —Barry López, *Of Wolves and Men*

1

The invisible stance is how it survives
the vision of blood and snow.
What it hides is what remains,
season after season.
What it guards is the trail of its den,
the patch where the will to deliver
the shadow before its victim is marked.

The invisible presence grows in strength
as tomorrow's cold light becomes tomorrow's
howling dance of animal reason,
the cry to the pack to gather
around the things that vanish,
to surround the source that makes
all breathing things disappear.

The invisible face is the stare of
the surviving heart that will not move
until the blood has dried in the snow,
until the need to be seen explodes before
the oncoming boundaries of the wilderness,
the hard border where the four paws break
the ice without leaving a single track.

The wolf exerts a powerful influence on the human imagination. It takes your stare and turns it back on you. Bella Coola Indians believed that somone once tried to change all the animals into men but succeeded in making human only the eyes of the wolf.

—Barry López, *Of Wolves and Men*

2

To see how the human stumbles
in the snow because the end is near.
To knaw at the bone of the sun
when it blinds the hunter
from its prey.
To stare at the approaching figures
without fear.
To return the look of discovery
when the rifle shot
shatters the stillness.

To watch the ceremony of the fires
from the black distance of the night.
To spot the way out of the forest
without disturbing the unseen eye,
the motion that brings it
closer to its own death,
its defiance of what must
be seen in the snow, what moves
when recognized as a vision.

El olvido
(según las madres)

It is a dangerous thing
to forget the climate of
your birthplace; to choke out
the voices of dead relatives when
in dreams they call you by
your secret name; dangerous
to spurn the clothes you were
born to wear for the sake of fashion;
to use weapons and sharp instruments you
are not familiar with; dangerous
to disdain the plaster saints before
which your mother kneels praying for you with
embarassing fervor that you survive in
the place you have chosen to live; a costly,
bare and elegant room with no pictures
on the walls: a forgetting place where
she fears you might die of exposure.
Jesús, María y José.
El olvido is a dangerous thing.

So Much for Mañana

After twenty years in the mainland
Mother's gone back to the Island
to let her skin
melt from her bones
under her native sun.
She no longer wears stockings,
girdles or tight clothing.
Brown as a coconut,
she takes siestas in a hammock,
and writes me letters that say:
"Stop chasing your own shadow, niña,
come down here and taste the piña,
put away those heavy books,
don't you worry about your shape,
here on the Island men look
for women who can carry a little weight.
On every holy day,
I burn candles and I pray
that your brain won't split
like an avocado pit
from all that studying.
What do you say?
Abrazos from your Mamá and a blessing
from that saint, Don Antonio, el cura."
I write back: "Someday I will go back
to your Island and get fat,
but not now, Mami, maybe mañana."

The Latin Deli

Presiding over a formica counter,
plastic Mother and Child magnetized
to the top of an ancient register,
the heady mix of smells from the open bins
of dried codfish, the green plantains
hanging in stalks like votive offerings,
she is the Patroness of Exiles,
a woman of no-age who was never pretty,
who spends her days selling canned memories
while listening to the Puerto Ricans complain
that it would be cheaper to fly to San Juan
than to buy a pound of Bustelo coffee here,
and to Cubans perfecting their speech
of a "glorious return" to Havana—where no one
has been allowed to die and nothing to change until then;
to Mexicans who pass through, talking lyrically
of *dólares* to be made in El Norte—
                                        all wanting the comfort
of spoken Spanish, to gaze upon the family portrait
of her plain wide face, her ample bosom
resting on her plump arms, her look of maternal interest
as they speak to her and each other
of their dreams and their disillusions—
how she smiles understanding,
when they walk down the narrow aisles of her store
reading the labels of packages aloud, as if
they were the names of lost lovers: *Suspiros*,
Merengues, the stale candy of everyone's childhood.

                                        She spends her days
slicing *jamón y queso* and wrapping it in wax paper
tied with string: plain ham and cheese
that would cost less at the A&P, but it would not satisfy
the hunger of the fragile old man lost in the folds
of his winter coat, who brings her lists of items
that he reads to her like poetry, or the others,
whose needs she must divine, conjuring up products
from places that now exist only in their hearts—
closed ports she must trade with.

Leroy V. Quintana

Poem for Josephine Baker

It flew in through the kitchen window
that summer a few years after the war,
the year I turned four or five,
that fragile yellow bird Made In Japan
whose insides had been sucked out
when the bomb fell on Hiroshima.

All it required for nourishment
was the sweet, cold water
I poured into the slot in its back.

When I blew on the tailfeathers,
experimenting with trills, warbling
like some lonely sax man
'round midnight in his sleepless room,
an exile in graceful Paris,
I didn't know then, in that small town,
the other side of the tracks,
I had learned a little, enough
of the secret language of birds.

When that song fluttered into my life again
I knew how to say "Hello. Welcome!" and
"My. It's been a long, long time."

Alberto Ríos

On January 5, 1984,
El Santo the Wrestler Died, Possibly

The thing was, he could never be trusted.
He wore the silver mask even when he slept.
At his funeral as reported by all the Mexican news services
The pall bearers also put on their faces
Sequined masks to honor him, or so it was said.
The men in truth wore masks as much to hide from him
That he would not see who was putting him into the ground
And so get angry, get up, and come back after them
That way for which he was famous.
His partner el atomico pretended to think
There was no funeral at all.
He would have had to help el santo be angry
Come like the Samson running against the pillars
These men were, holding up the box
In which el santo was trapped;
Would have had to angle his head down, come at them
Mount them three men to a shoulder
As he ran through the middle, ducking under the casket
Bowling them down like all the other times
Giving el santo just a moment to breathe, get strong.

He will be missed
But one must say this in a whisper, and quickly.
One knows of the dead, of their polite habit of listening
Too much, believing what they hear, and then of their caring.
One knows of the dead, how it all builds up
So that finally something must be said.
One knows of the year in which the town of Guaymas
Had its first demonstration of a tape recorder.
It confirmed only what was already known:
That people speak. And that the voice of the wind
Captured finally, played back slowly

245

Given its moment to say something of lasting importance
Made only a complaint.
If el santo were to hear of his being missed
He might get hold of the wind, this voice of the dead,
And say too much, the way the best wrestlers do
With all the yelling.
So one will always be responsible enough only to whisper
The best things about el santo
Out of concern for the crops and the sapling trees.
This much was decided at the funeral.

The decision to whisper was not too much.
One had to be suspicious of this man with a mask
Even as he reached out to shake your hand,
That you might be flung and bent around
Knocked on the head and forced to say
How glad you are to meet him, and his uncle;
How suspicious that hand, which he always raised
More slowly than a weightlifter's last possible push
As if he too were suspicious of you
That you might at the last second
Be the Blue Demon after all—*el demonio azul*: ¡aha!
He recognizes you, *but too late*! that you might
In this last moment avoid his hand raised to shake
Hook the crook of your arm into his
And flip him with a slam to a cement canvas.
No, he could not be trusted
And he could not trust you.

In his last years very far from 1942
The year he gave his first bruise to another man
One received as a greeting no hand from him any longer.
A raised eyebrow, perhaps, *good morning to you*, just visible
        through the mask on his morning walk.
This was his greeting, one man to another, now.
But even then he could not be trusted
Had not slipped with age even an inch:
As he moved the hairy arm of his brow up and down
Like a villain taking possession of the widow's house,
If one quickly did not get out of his way—
Well, then, he kept it moving up and down, had gotten you
Had made you imagine his eyebrow like that

Making the sound of a referee's hand
Slam beating the canvas ten times
Telling you that you have lost.

Luis J. Rodríguez

Running to America

They are night shadows
violating borders;
fingers curled through chain-link fences,
hiding from infra-red eyes,
dodging 30-30 bullets.
They leave familiar smells,
warmth, and sounds
as ancient
as the trampled stones.

Running to America.

There is a woman
in her finest
border-crossing wear:
A purple blouse from
an older sister, a pair of worn
shoes from a church bazaar.
A tattered coat
from a former lover.

There is a child
dressed in black,
fear sparkling from
dark Indian eyes,
clinging to
a beheaded Barbie doll.

And the men,
some hardened, quiet,
others young and loud—
You see something like this
in prisons.

Soon they will cross
on their bellies,
kissing black earth,

then run to America.

Strange voices
whisper behind garbage cans,
beneath freeway passes,
next to broken bottles.
The spatter of words,
textured and multi-colored,
invoke demons.

They must run to America.

Their skin,
color of earth,
is a brand
for all the great ranchers,
for the killing floors
on Soto Street,
and as slaughter
for the garment row.
Still they come:
a hungry people
have no country.

Their tears
are the grease
of the bobbing machines
that rip into cloth,
that make clothes,
that keep you warm.

They have endured
the sun's stranglehold,
el cortito,
foundry heats,
and dark caves
of mines
hungry for men.

Still they come,
wandering bravely
through the thickness
of this strange land's
maddening ambivalence.

Their cries are singed
with fires of hope.
Their babies are born
with a lion
in their hearts.
Who can confine them?
Who can tell them
which lines never to cross?

For the green rivers,
for their looted gold,
escaping the blood of a land
that threatens to drown them,

they have come,
running to America.

Leo Romero

The Dark Side of the Moon

Virginia tells Casimirio about
her fear of the moon

I can sense it, it has been here
the moon
Maybe it is hiding in the house
but I have checked all the rooms
all the closets
all the dark corners
and found nothing
but some frightened spiders

I have begun to live with a knife close at hand
and I think I should learn
how to fire a gun
This fear is very real
The moon breaks my windows
and bleeds over the carpet
when I am not home
It is a madness of the heart

There is no sleeping in peace
Dreams become one vast room
where intruders prowl at will
And constantly there is the dread
of the moon with its many disguises
Lately I have seen the moon
in the face of a one-eyed madman

It is becoming difficult to go out at night
because I know the moon is waiting
Difficult to come home at night

because I know the moon has been there
and even now I feel its presence
even after searching the whole house
And maybe, just maybe, it is still here
What I feel is so strong, so near
like a cold, empty wind
blowing out of the dark side of the moon

The Moon Is Lost

Tonight the moon is lost
and the world is all darkness
I think it will never appear again
Perhaps it has wandered too far
perhaps it grew tired of the same old routine

There were nights when I would do nothing
but watch the moon
rise over rooftops and tree branches
and I felt secure in the constancy
of the heavenly bodies

Now I have grown wiser
but no happier
knowing that all things come to an end

And darkest of all is love
somehow it went astray tonight
For some reason that orb of light
decided to call it quits
mend its old ways, do something different

There's nothing new under the sun
but the moon plays by different rules
Tonight it's changed its course
and fills another heart

The Ocean Is Not Red

It's over
this madness of the moon
and already I am starting
to breathe easier

For so long it held sway
over my world, day and night
For so long there was no way
to be rid of it

From the beginning I knew
that it would end in bloodshed
That what held us together
was like a rope of blood and flesh

Now it is all over
and the rivers do not roar with blood
and the ocean is not red
like I imagined it would become

When Pito Tried to Kill

When Pito tried to kill
me with his knife, long
switchblade that slit
my side, but not bad just
cut the flesh, bled worse
than it was, I knew it was
because he was crazed with
Diane and the wine of a
long night gone to the dogs
And when I promised to
kill him in return, I thought
I could do it, but then I
thought, what would I do
Cradle him in my arms
with the life out of him
or the life seeping out of
him and no scotch tape
or any glue to hold it in
I could kill him, I know
But then where would I be
But I promised him, and
all because of Diane, we
both love her too much
And all for a dead woman
When Pito came at me, I
could see myself dying
and Pito yelling at me
as my slippery blood poured
out on the floor like
the flowing blood of slaughter
houses, Him yelling at me
You're going to her, aren't
you, You son of a bitch, you
pushed me to kill you, so you'd
be with her, Pito, I'd say
I love her, You don't know
love, I'd say to Pito, as

I was dying, You never loved
no one, I'd say to Pito, not
even a dog much less a woman
I saw all that coming as
he lunged at me with his
brilliant knife, But it was
only a flesh wound, You got
yours coming, I yelled
tripping him to the floor
and getting out the door
And I heard him yelling
drunkenly after me, You
don't go talking about her
no more, and I yelling back
I can talk of anyone I love
You're dead, he yelled, and
I could hear him sobbing
We're all dead, I yelled back
And so I left that place
And I dreamed a dream of Diane
And she said to me, You two
were fighting for me, weren't
you, and I said, We were
And she placed her hand on
my bleeding wound that was
still flowing like a river
and she placed her hand in
and I couldn't believe how deep
that wound was, Her arm
went all the way in, and then
all of her had disappeared
into my wound, Diane, I yelled
Get out of there, that's my
wound, I yelled, not yours
But she was not hearing me
She had gone into the hurting
that had become unbearable
So unbearable that I could
have killed myself to end
the pain, And there was a knocking
in that dream, and it was Pito
I know she's in there, he yelled

Let me in, he yelled, And
I looked frightened at my
wound, but there was no trace
of Diane, And I wouldn't open
the door for Pito or say a word
And the knocking grew louder
on the dream door, in my dream
life, and anyway there is no
difference between walking and
sleeping, and the only thing
is hurting, Diane, I whisper to
the deep inside of me, I know
you're there, Come out, I
whisper, How can I love you
inside of me, I whisper, Diane
I hear Pito yell from beyond the
door What you've done with Diane
And then I smile a little
But I don't answer, I'm at peace
Even with all this hurting, I'm
at peace.

Woman-Hole

Some say there is a
  vacuum—a black hole—
    in the center of womanhood
    that swallows countless
      secrets and has strange
      powers

Yo no sé de'sas cosas
  solo sé que the
    black echo is music
      is sister of sunlight
      and from it
        crece
          vida.

Luz María Umpierre

Poema para Elliot Gilbert

Atardecer de
Elliot
el color de su camisa
se refleja en la ventana—
luz naranja,
sol amarillo,
nubes violetas

¿Qué decirle a la muerte?

Tenía humor ese desconocido,
carcajada profunda,
Elliot

La nieve abajo nuevamente;
otro día de frío.

El avión se mueve hacia la
izquierda
       tiembla
             y yo
te escribo esta carta

¿Qué hace detenerse al corazón?

¿Qué luz penetra tus pupilas
que ya no se abren con sus pestañas largas,
pestañas femeninas pese a la voz aguda?

Un abrazo te dí
y
tú
también
te fuiste

Congelada
mi sangre nuevamente entre la nieve
de un país menos maldito
porque reconocí tu llanto.

Reconociste
tú
el valor de sumergir
mis pies
en la verdad doliente.

"Macho" me llama el hombre de mi patria.
"Macho" porque mis pies no usan
tacones elevados
y
exigen marcher al ritmo de mi mente.
"Macho" porque tomo esta tinta rojiza pare abrirle paso a un mundo
anaranjado
como aquella tu camisa.

La luz
se opaca
Elliot
y
yo
te cuento mi pena.

aún

Otros hombros
te llevan
a
una
tumba
sin nombre

aún

El avión
  desciende
    hacia
      la
       nieve
         y
           tu
            cuerpo
   se ilumina en California

     Shalom

     Adiós,
hombre de carcajada profunda,
    aterrizamos
     ambos
      yo
    en la nieve
      tú
    en el sol

   Vivimos vidas paralelas.

Gina Valdés

English con Salsa

Welcome to ESL 100, English Surely Latinized,
inglés con chile y cilantro, English as American
as Benito Juárez. Welcome, muchachos from Xochicalco,
learn the language of dólares and dolores, of kings
and queens, of Donald Duck and Batman. Holy Toluca!
In four months you'll be speaking like George Washington,
in four weeks you can ask, More coffee? In two months
you can say, May I take your order? In one year you
can ask for a raise, cool as the Tuxpan River.

Welcome, muchachas from Teocaltiche, in this class
we speak English refrito, English con sal y limón,
English thick as mango juice, English poured from
a clay jug, English tuned like a requinto from Uruapán,
English lighted by Oaxacan dawns, English spiked
with mezcal from Juchitán, English with a red cactus
flower blooming in its heart.

Welcome, welcome, amigos del sur, bring your Zapotec
tongues, your Nabuatl tones, your patience of pyramids,
your red suns and golden moons, your guardian angels,
your duendes, your patron saints, Santa Tristeza,
Santa Alegría, Santo Todolopuede. We will sprinkle
holy water on pronouns, make the sign of the cross
on past participles, jump like fish from Lake Pátzcuaro
on gerunds, pour tequila from Jalisco on future perfects,
say shoes and shit, grab a cool verb and a pollo loco
and dance on the walls like chapulines.

When a teacher from La Jolla or a cowboy from Santee
asks you, Do you speak English? You'll answer, Sí,
yes, simón, of course. I love English!

                          And you'll hum
a Mixtec chant that touches la tierra and the heavens.

Dumb Broad!

dumb broad!
I'm believing it as I'm seeing it!
dumb broad!
keep your eyes on the road, stupid!
a passenger sits next to her
motionless
oblivious
or just doesn't care
why don't you comb your hair at home, you stupid broad!
hey!
I mean, I've seen women yank off their steam rollers at stop lights
brandish brush
and then drive, one-handed
while expertly arranging their hair
with a few quick precision strokes—
I've done it myself
you have to in order to get to work on time
but, oh! this is too much!
I cannot believe this!
look! now she's teasing her hair!
both of her hands are off the steering wheel!
stupid broad!
you'd better keep your eyes on the road!
I'd hate to be in the car in front of her
she can't see the traffic behind her
for she's got the rearview mirror in a perpendicular position
while she fixes her eye makeup
at first with quick casual glances
but now very intently
peering into hazard
I mean, I know one gets distracted sometimes
you know, you look into the mirror to fix your lipstick

and you end up re-doing your eye shadow!
god! you know you should've worn hyacinth instead of celery!
it looks so different in the daylight!

look at her!
I can't believe she's teasing her hair!
and with both hands off the steering wheel
now I can't get over that!
and in fast moving bumper-to-bumper 8 a.m. traffic
at a five-point intersection
and a school zone at that! now you tell me if this is not a
dumb broad!

my god!
and the passive passenger sits!
doesn't nudge!
involuntary purposeless conjecturing:
he's probably her husband who has simply given up on her
his bitching was of no use
or rather, he's probably one of those passive husbands
who doesn't give a shit
but then, maybe he's a carpooler with no choice in the matter
or simply unaware that his life is in danger

now wait a minute!
hey! I'm believing this as I'm seeing it!
she is now spraying her hair generously
in round swooping motions
utilizing both the rearview and sideview mirrors
which she has expertly adjusted
the traffic is of no concern to her
and the passenger remains a mannequin
except for one slow motion glance over and back
as she squirts the spray
on her mass of teased hair and his bald head
it's not four blocks later
there she drives ahead of me
sporting a splendid hair-do
she brakes on and off sporadically
as she shifts her weight around in her seat
finding a position of comfort
while tuning the radio

and flicking her bic at a cigarette that's stuck in her mouth
then she looks over
and puffs smoke into the face of her motionless passenger
who, obeyingly, hands her a cup of steaming coffee

dumb broad!

The *Americas* REVIEW

A Review of Hispanic Literature and Art of the USA

| Vol. 19 | Spring 1991 | No. 1 |

Arnaldo Roche Rabell. *Desire to Become a Storm*, 1986.
Oil on canvas, 78" x 65"

Patricia Rodríguez. *Self-Portrait*, 1983.
Mixed media.

Luis A. Jiménez, Jr. *Vaquero*. Modeled 1980, cast 1990.
Cast fiberglass and epoxy. National Museum of American Art, Washington, D.C.

Luis Tapia. *Risen Christ*, 1993.
Carved and painted wood, 44" x 16 1/2" x 8"

Luis Tapia. *Dos Pedros sin llaves*, 1993.
Carved and painted wood, 25" x 7-1/4" x 11-1/2"

Jesús Bautista Moroles. *Ellipse Round, Spirit Las Mesas Round*,
and *Lapstrake*, 1986. Granite sculptures.

Paul Berger. *Face–08*, 1993.
Photograph from World Info Series

José Luis Rodríguez Guerra. *Human Conditions #1*, 1984.
Mixed media on masonite, 48" x 66"

New Navigators of the Floating Borderlands

In these uncharted lands we discover
the ghosts are not generous,
will not trade
their gold for our beads,
their stories for our glassy silence.
                    —A. Gaspar de Alba

Kathleen Alcalá

Walking Home

Concha moved slowly down the street, favoring her left ankle. Her feet hurt, her back hurt, her bones seemed to grate together as she moved. She had three more houses to clean that day before returning home, long after dark, to a supper of pozole and tortillas that her daughter would have left for her. Rosa would be asleep, would rise early with her mother to help with the morning chores.

Somewhere people were celebrating. She could hear laughter, a guitar carelessly strummed. A woman's voice was saying "Aye, chico!" seductive and admonishing at the same time. Concha walked on through the dusty streets, lifting each foot carefully over the uneven bricks and stones. She deferred to the big men in their boots, pausing and turning sideways without effort to pass like water through the crowds. It had been a long time since she had had anything to celebrate.

Once, Rosa had brought home a tomato—big, ripe, juicy. She said a man gave it to her, an indio from the countryside. He said it was for her soulful eyes.

They had made a feast of the tomato, cutting it carefully in half in a zigzag pattern the way Concha's mother had taught her, adding salt and a tiny bit of cilantro to make it savory. Then they had eaten it, laughing, as though eating like kings and queens, so seldom did they get anything fresh. Concha went without food some days so that she could buy goat's milk for Rosa. Rosa's eyes were full of soul because her stomach was usually empty, and Concha worried about her only daughter, her only love in the world, her life.

If it were not for Rosa, she could not go on; she would have thrown herself in the river long ago, the saints be damned. But Rosa needed her, needed Concha to hold up her head and clean rich people's houses as she had always done, except for those few years when Dr. Martínez had loved her. Even with her baby, he had married her and she had been a respectable woman in a fine house, eating tomatoes whenever she liked.

Concha held up her head and walked.

And then she heard a voice behind her. It was under the rumbling of wagons, the creaking of carriages, under the shrill voice of a woman who thought she had been cheated, the coming and going of many people, shouting, laughing, dogs barking—but she heard it, nevertheless.

Concha stopped walking and slowly turned. The ground seemed to tilt beneath her feet. To hear that language, as a grown woman, after so many years, was like having someone speak to her in the language of her dreams, or call out her secret name, the name that she knew and kept only to herself.

"I know you! I know you!"

The voice cried out harshly, persistently, and as she peered back through the people and the dust raised by their passing, Concha finally made out a man close to the ground. He waved a powerful hand in the air, wrapped in a rag. As she looked, Concha could see he was seated on a board on wheels, and as she approached, tentatively, she saw that his stained pant legs were cut off short, that his legs ended above his knees, and the stumps were bound to the board with wide leather straps, as one would cinch a saddle to a horse.

He placed both hands on the ground, the knuckles cushioned by rags, and propelled himself towards her with a peculiar hopping motion, all torso, all muscle, a grotesque, shortened parody of a person. It was Beto.

Concha felt the tears start to her eyes, tears like birds upon her cheeks. How could she have more tears?

She fell upon her knees next to Beto and embraced her brother.

"Dios mío," she said, over and over. "Dios mío."

"Ya, ya," he said, patting her back. "Enough."

"What happened?" she asked. "What happened to you? I thought you were dead for years."

So there, her dignity forgotten, kneeling in the dust next to a filthy beggar for God and everyone to see, Beto told her his story.

"I was on a train," he said. "A compadre got me on a train going west. We heard there was plenty of work in California.

"But I had a spell, and you know when I'm like that I can't move, can't hold on, and so I fell off the train, under the wheels, and the wheels cut my legs off.

"By a miracle, there was a doctor nearby, visiting the town where I fell, and he saved my life. Otherwise I would have bled to death, especially if those pendejo railroad people could help it. The train didn't even stop.

"I don't remember any of it. I was in heaven with our father, talking to him. He told me I would live a hard life, but I would survive. 'Keep moving,' he said. 'Don't let them catch you.'

"When I woke up, I was how you see me. But I've kept moving, as best as I know how," he said, indicating his legs, his platform.

"The doctor helped me and charged no money. He was young and not yet corrupt."

Concha wept and wept as he talked, birds on her face, rain on the ground. She wept for all their agonies, for all their travels and hardships, for the ranchería they would never see again, for their mother, for their father he had seen in heaven, for the others who had died or disappeared or gone mad.

And she cried for her old name that was lost, Shark's Tooth from the Sea, that had been taken from her so long ago. It was that which Beto had called out, that had cut like a knife through the noise and dust of the street, cut into her heart like a ripe tuna and made it bleed tears from her eyes.

Then she was done. Concha wiped her face and gathered her bags and parcels and stood up and brushed off her dress.

"You must come home with me," she said.

"You have a house?" asked Beto.

"Only a room," she said. "But it is a place to sleep, a safe place."

"Bueno," said Beto, and slung a sack across his back, all he owned in the world.

Down streets and across ditches they went, and where wheels could not roll, Beto picked himself up on his overdeveloped knuckles and propelled himself forward a foot at a time. His thighs strained at the leather straps that held his board to him, but the straps held, and Concha could see that he had traveled many miles, many places this way.

Coming to the house, Concha was hit by the fact that she lived up a narrow, steep flight of stairs.

She stopped abruptly.

"I live upstairs," she said. "We will have to carry you."

Even as she said this, she knew that even with Rosa's help, she could not lift Beto and maneuver his awkward shape up the stairs.

"It's all right," he said. He didn't seemed surprised or even disappointed. "I'll stay here. Just bring me a little something to eat."

Concha smiled gratefully, her smile that he remembered from their childhood, when he would follow after his big sister like a puppy. Concha hurried up the stairs. Rosa was startled to see her mother home early, so animated, her rebozo askew, her eyes wide with excitement.

"Come!" she said. "My brother is in the street! We must take him some dinner."

Grabbing the pot of beans and a shred of cold meat, Concha handed Rosa the tin plates shuffled together and wrapped in a shawl. They descended to the dirt street where Beto waited, smoking, against a far wall, a shadow within a shadow of the building.

That night they built a little cooking fire at the end of the lane, where it ended in a sandy arroyo. Beto shared their beans and meat and coffee while he told them of his travels, and praised Rosa for her beauty, and didn't ask where her father was, which Concha appreciated, because that was a story she had tired of, an old story that never would have an end. Only she would end, a piece of the story.

She learned that their mother and Javier Oposura had died at Casas Grandes. The soldiers had come there, too, and killed many people. Even in a holy place. Beto had been raised in Arizona by another family, and worked as a scout for the

American army in their battles with the Apaches for some years before his accident.

Beto was proud to own no furniture. Things came between people and the truth. By remaining clean, pared down, a man who ate what was offered him and slept where he could, Beto's vision had remained clear. He was a man who could discern the true nature of things, whether they were good or evil, whether they meant something or nothing, whether or not they would have importance to someone in the future. Beto, by remaining free of things, could tell their true names.

Concha asked Beto if he thought la corúa was still alive.

Beto looked at her, his eyes slits in the firelight. "He got run over by the train," he said. "I saw him. He may still be alive in the villages farther south, but in Arizona and California, he is dead."

Who knew that there would be nights like this? The air tasting of her yearning for the old times, the old places, yet the proof before her that everything was gone, everything was as dust burned to ash in the fire?

Concha tried to hold on to what was left. She stroked Rosa's hair, pulling loose from its braids in the temperamental way it had, and thought of her own mother stroking her own hair when she was small. But this was hard. She could only remember Chiri brushing out the black, black hair of her little sisters, cooing and clucking over their beauty like a hen, so that she could do up their braids in white ribbon.

Concha realized then, watching her brother smoke in the dying firelight, that she had spent her life yearning for a past that didn't really exist, and never had. Her yearning was for what she had never had, a place nearer to her mother, a moment of recognition that never came.

Resting her hand on Rosa's shoulder, listening to her breathe, Concha realized that all she really had was the present, both good and bad. Rosa was getting older and was beautiful, and soon she would marry or go away with a man. Concha felt time moving around her like the river, flowing on, taking bits of her away, bringing by bits of her past.

Even as she thought this, Beto looked at her and said, "You better get that one to bed. It's late."

Concha rose, lifting Rosa to her feet, and guided the sleepy girl towards the steps to their little room.

"Good night," she murmured to Beto, who remained in his place. He seemed to have forgotten them already.

"Mmmm," he grunted. She knew that in his head it was already tomorrow, that he knew which train he would be on, that this day, like all the others, had been numbered and put away on the calendar in his head.

Concha saw that she would always remain part of his past, and their chance encounter was just that, chance. She knew then that nothing she could have done, could ever have done, would have changed things—either for herself, her sisters, or her brother. And if it did not make her feel better, neither did it make her feel worse. She just felt that she knew one more tiny thing. The river still flowed on.

The next day Beto was gone.

That evening the landlady, Mrs. Klein, said to her husband, "The neighbors saw Concha in the street last night, squatting like a common woman. With her daughter, too, sharing their supper with a crippled beggar."

Mr. Klein eyed his narrow wife over his evening paper. He drew on his pipe and blew a few puffs of smoke.

"That was right charitable of her," he said. "But see that it doesn't happen again. So's all the beggars in town don't think we're running a mission here."

Mrs. Klein was pleased with her husband, for she knew that he would have the right answer. She passed the word to Concha late that evening, who bowed her head and promised that it wouldn't happen again. Concha doubted that she would ever see her brother Beto in this life of sorrow again.

Alba Ambert

Losses

All I see is a trail of loss. I could walk back that trail and retrace the life I have lived. A ring, a watch, a skirt, a photograph. My biography is a chain of lost objects. My losses hover like ghosts, insubstantial, in a void. Their absence an eloquent reminder of what lies behind me as I move on faster and faster, stretching the distance between my past and what may be a future. I have no present, you see, as I race through the spectrum of days and weeks and months and years, rushing to days without tomorrows.

The powdery sands of the island where I suckled at the swells of mountains, the island that weaned me on seaweed and ocean ferns slipped into the curve of time like a dream. Somewhere along the way I lost the crackle of cod fritters sizzling in white hot lard and the snap of tin roofs settling in the white hot sun. Because I lost my mother there, my first and most devastating loss, I have lived a life of exile in gray cities of unforgiving geometries. Because no degree of triumph could ever compensate for that loss, I have turned success into hurt and accomplishments into burdens.

Then I lost my childhood. That's the way it works, I guess. One loss leads to another. And another. At some point it became a habit and I started losing things, important things like the ring, a token of love. The engraved pen my friends gave me for graduation. The skirt purchased with my first paycheck and worn like a talisman whenever I ventured into potentially hostile territory. The slender gold-plated watch my mother bequeathed me, the only tangible reminder I ever had of her. And I lost memories. Dark gaps puncture like wounds, the holes gaping wonderingly where I cannot possibly remember. Entire years are wiped out like a wrong answer on a slate and I will never know the right answer. Whatever I now have cannot mean much because I have not lost it. I only lose the valuable, the irreplaceable. Now, having climbed the wall of exile, unable to turn back, I have ceased to own the recognizable and am lost to myself.

I do not know when I finally understood this. The realization was not sudden like a thunderbolt from an angry cloud. It came with time, after the losses heaped like bones in a common grave. After the guilt and the rage. When I had nothing else to lose. Except my life.

So here I am deciding whether to live or die. Dying is one more loss. But it is the end of all losses. The ultimate loss. Dying is not having to lose anything. Ever again.

* * *

The day started as usual when the public radio newscaster chirped at six on the dot. As always. And as always, I woke up heart pounding in my throat. Waking up is discovering a stranger in my bed. Then I realize the stranger is me and I feel relieved, for a while at least. This morning I hauled my stiff body out of bed, eyes clotted with sleep. I spat the gluey taste of nightmares into the bathroom sink and pointedly avoided my reflection in the mirror. Mirrors should always be ignored early in the morning, certainly before the first cup of coffee. I stood at the kitchen window like a sunflower in search of light. The aroma of patchouli that haunts me every day wafted in and awoke a smoky landscape in my memory: An elusive warren of pebbled roads crowded with jerry-built shacks teetering in a muddy marsh. The air redolent of sewage, ash-soaked haze, head-clinging kerosene, and kidney beans simmering in coriander and tomato sauce. It is the texture of silent smells that I remember, for I remember no sounds. Not even words.

The soft tick of the kitchen clock nudged me. It was time to go.

* * *

The high school where I work as a bilingual teacher is a massive brick structure, a thick blot of indistinct architecture. Squatting on a barren hill, it sullenly blinks at the pale Boston neighborhood in the muted light. The term bilingual teacher is a misnomer. I teach history and civics in Spanish to students who have recently arrived from Puerto Rico, the Dominican Republic and Central America. The school is defined by misnomers. Black, Hispanic and Asian students are bused in for integration purposes. So many white students have fled, though, it is just another segregated school. The bilingual teachers' office is really a large closet in the basement used to store textbooks and school supplies. There are no desks to keep our papers. Every morning the four bilinguals, as we are called, huddle under the bare bulb while our coordinator gives us the day's directives.

When I walked into the first period classroom (bilingual teachers have no permanently assigned rooms—we use whatever rooms are free), I could feel a migraine coming. I remembered dreaming that I swallowed cat fur and felt a lump in my stomach. I took a couple of Fiorinal and said *buenos días* to the students as they walked in. José fell asleep during a discussion of manifest destiny. It was not a comment on my teaching, I hope.

"José," I said and tapped his shoulder. "Did you have a good siesta?" The class started giggling, delighted for the respite.

"Sorry, Miss Amaro, but I didn't get much sleep last night," he said sheepishly.

"Try to stay awake, José, and rest before you go to work tonight. All right?"

"Okay, but I was hearing everything you said, like in a dream. It's like those tapes you buy to learn things while you're sleeping. A person's mind never rests, you know."

"I'm certainly relieved to hear that. We were discussing the assigned reading for today that starts on page 136," I continued, mustering as much enthusiasm as my migraine would allow.

The day's thick humid air pervaded everyone's mood. During Latin American History, Iris was engaged in serious woolgathering when I asked her about Bolívar's dream. She recovered enough to comment that she would not be in school long enough to find out. When the students were asked once to write a composition on what they wanted to be when they finished school, Iris had responded, in handwriting that was large, bold and squiggly, like her earrings, *when I finish school I want to be nothing*. I made a mental note to talk to her later.

After third period, Moisés, one of my most promising students, came up to my desk (which is not really my desk). He is short and slender, with a wispy beard he cultivates caringly. Moisés is the only Latino in the state of Massachusetts enrolled in calculus. This occurred when the complaints his crusading father lodged with an advocacy group bore fruit. Moisés lolled about the desk while I collected my books and notes.

When I looked up, he asked, "Miss Amaro, can I talk to you? Mrs. Retamal said we would read Cervantes for Spanish lit. I got really excited, but then she gave us this baby book instead. I'm embarrassed to be seen with it."

He dug into his back pocket and produced a slender paperback. I leafed through it, glanced at the many illustrations, the simplified Spanish, and handed it back.

Moisés continued. "They think we're stupid. I don't want to read any baby book. I'm sixteen! And just because I don't speak English well doesn't mean I'm stupid." He looked mutinous.

"How are you doing in the rest of your classes?"

"I'm working hard. My father checks the backs of my thighs to see if I've been studying hard enough, you know."

"What do you mean?"

"If I have no hairs there it means I've been sitting and studying for a lot of hours. Believe me, the backs of my thighs are bald by now. But I'll never learn anything important if they don't give us harder books. This is stupid. All my life I wanted to read *Don Quixote*." His voice trailed away. "And Mrs. Retamal is always saying Puerto Ricans can't speak Spanish. Man, that makes me furious. She says the right word for orange is *naranja*, not *china*. Is *china* wrong?" he asked anxiously.

"Of course not. It's just that some people don't understand how words develop—the origin of words—called etymology. In Puerto Rico we call an orange *china* instead of *naranja* because the orange was called *la fruta de la China* by the Spaniards. In Puerto Rico the fruit was called that for a while, but eventually the description was dropped and it was simply called *china*. So it's all quite logical. By the way, the word *naranja* is of Arabic origin."

"Wow, that's great! Wait till I tell Mrs. Retamal. She's gonna flip."

"Borrow a genuine *Don Quixote* from the library. There's a Spanish literature section at the Jamaica Plain branch in your neighborhood. I'm not a literature expert, but we can discuss it together if you like."

"Yeah, I want to learn the big words, like you. What was the word you used, the one that means where words come from?"

"*Etimología*. Write it down, so you don't forget." I printed it on the chalk board.

"*Etimología*," he enunciated carefully as he copied. "Now that's a big word. I'm gonna try it on Mrs. Retamal too. Hey, won't this get you in trouble with her?" he asked slyly. "You know, reading the real *Don Quixote* and helping me out with it?"

"Let me worry about that."

Moisés gave me a thumbs-up and rushed to his next class.

I massaged my temples gingerly and wondered what I was getting into. Not only was I engaging in pedagogical sabotage, but probably more daunting was grappling with the knight of the sorrowful countenance. After all these years. It was hard enough to keep up with U.S. History, Latin American History, World History and Civics for my daily classes But I have always been somewhat of a rebel. I ascribe it to an adolescence of dancing with doorknobs. Men have later accused me of leading when we danced, unable to grant me this modicum of control. But that is another story.

The day limped on sadly. The fourth is my free period. Free is another misnomer with all the grading, photocopying, and paperwork to be done. Free I guess means without teaching. Freedom is not having to teach. Now, that's an idea. During hall duty before my free period, I ran into Rosa Sánchez, the bilingual math teacher. Our principal, Dr. McLaughlin, rushed by waving a minatory finger and yelled, "speak English, speak English," which succeeded in leaving us bereft of any speech.

"The English-only Gestapo strikes again," Rosa laughed when she recovered all her faculties.

I couldn't even roll my eyes to the ceiling on account of the migraine. "So much for free speech," I managed to say wearily.

I dragged a chair to the basement where I sat in the bilingual office. Wedged in the sarcophagus between shelves of science books and pencils, I graded the U.S. History quiz I give every Friday.

The afternoon settled heavily. Through the frosted windows we could see the first flutters of snow. I had detention duty, something I dread. Students I have never seen before—it is a big school—show up with their detention slips and glower at me before sitting down sullenly.

A fight broke out between a Vietnamese and a Puerto Rican. With great display of purpose so as not to be misinterpreted, Tran grazed Miguel's shoulder when he walked by his desk. Miguel shoved him and before I could intervene they rolled on the floor in a tight clinch. Students are always fighting over girls or because someone gave someone else a dirty look. That is the excuse, but the squabbles are really territorial. Very little territory is left at the bottom of the heap and everyone fights for it. There is no other choice. Falling out of the bottom is falling into oblivion. It is a crucial struggle.

Of course I kept this view to myself when I called Mr. Grody, the physical education teacher in charge of discipline problems. A former linebacker with a small head, ham-thick neck and fiercely overextended shoulders, he really is a cliché, the poor man. He also teaches science to monolinguals and his teaching method consists of playing tape recordings on the functions of the heart or the structure of molecules and having students copy while they listen. Exams are then based on the contents of the tapes, duly transcribed, correctly or incorrectly, by the students. So much for education. Mr. Grody dragged Tran and Miguel off to the office for suspension proceedings. I settled in my chair again—still had some of those U.S. History quizzes to grade—and surveyed the four taciturn boys sprawled in front of me. Legs splayed like dropped scissors, they defined their territory and strummed the desks or stared at the ceiling.

* * *

On the way home, I checked out a copy of *Don Quixote* at the library. On the train, I slid my handbag under an arm, held onto the swaying strap, and shoved my free hand in a pocket. You can never predict when an onanist or purse snatcher will strike. It was best to be alert. With my scant dollars neatly folded in a wallet, I would not make it easy for anyone to deprive me of my earnings. I can still remember my indigent student days when I survived on popcorn and strong black coffee. On special occasions I would splurge on a package of macaroni and cheese, only 53 cents a serving. At Park I secured a side seat next to a door. A young man with a navy blue anorak stood in front of me. Though I tried not to, we made eye contact and he smiled. I examined an advertisement for a computer programming training school and fidgeted with my purse strap. When I looked up, a woman who had been staring at me averted her eyes.

At Central Square, I slogged through the slush on the sidewalk. I felt threatened by the blanched sky, heavy with snow. Cars splashed and tore into the vault of lace. It was dark when I reached my apartment. I flicked the light on and looked into the hallway mirror. I stepped away in a panic. A painful spasm curled deeply in my neck and established its predominance like an insolent despot. I tried to shake it off. I hummed. Brahms always soothed me with hints of melancholic rain rinsing distant landscapes, but not this evening. I sank into the cadence of pain. A rain of fear drenched me and I scrubbed myself with the sponge of apathy. Nothingness seeped into my pores, my eye sockets, my nostrils, the slash between my legs. It entered me, corroded my blood, ravished my flesh and I was left an empty shell. I felt nothing. I was nothing.

I take more medication and go to sleep. I wake up at midnight. In my rocking chair I stare into the darkness beyond the window. The bedroom rumbles in its wound. It is calmer out there where trees stir idly in their beds of stone. Snow falls briskly, softly. Feathery petals of white. The color of absolute silence.

Don Quixote waits on my night table. I pick it up and spread it open. I can't see anything in the darkness. But I don't have the energy to turn the light on. Well, I might as well force myself. It's hard to open a book and refrain from reading. Even when a book is in a foreign language, there seems to be an intellectual imperative to read, to make sense out of symbols. That deep-rooted need to interpret symbols vanquishes my inertia. I turn the lamp on. It glows softly on the amber pages. I close the book and examine its proud spine. My fingers glide over the gilt-encrusted title. I examine the library flap glued to the inside of the back cover. The book has not been checked out in six years. It is a long time to wait. *Don Quixote*, the first modern novel, stranded in tonight's hour. I moisten my lips and dip into it, parting its petals gently, inhaling its fragrance of bruised oak. I read the indomitable knight's lament,

> *So many strange things have befallen me in this*
> *castle that I dare not give any positive answer to any*
> *question asked me concerning anything in it. Perhaps*
> *you will be able to judge of the affairs of this castle*
> *as they really and truly are, and not as they appear to be.*

A gaunt Don Quixote mutters to himself, fearing a reality that unravels reluctantly like apologies. He loses his truth to the truth of others. I wonder what Moisés would think about the relative nature of reality. The ambiguity of all that is. The unbearable tangle of words. Adolescents believe in absolutes, in the unerring reliability of the senses. Only during adolescence are we so certain of our beliefs, of the rightness of our perspectives. Adolescents know with the certainty worthy of a pope what is right and what is wrong. Black and white. Good and bad. Rambo and Godzilla. The right strut, the wrong hairdo. The ability to find answers to all questions. Adolescents know, adults doubt. Could I possibly convey to Moisés the relativity of reality? Perhaps I could use Plato's myth of the cave to illustrate the point. How can I relate it to Moisés's circumstances though? Of what relevance is *Don Quixote* to ghetto existence? Cervantes writes about sorrow and the clash of conflicting ideals. The ghetto is sorrow and clash and conflict. I may be able to find the link, or more accurately, the threads that coil through diverse experiences and make them one. There must be a way of attaching meaning, a meaning Moisés can see, to a fake knight's misadventures. I just have to find the way.

Well, I suppose I don't have to decide this very night whether to live or die. Let us say I will live, at least until Moisés learns the big words.

El Pajarero

Don Justo Flores crossed the patio of his rooming house just as the morning brightened and turned hot. Yoyo, his German shepherd, lumbered along beside him. The two had been to Lupe Bustos's eating place and Lupe's bracing coffee had warmed the old man's bones, setting his mind on the pluses in life and not on the minuses, as in the days when it was pulque or tequila for breakfast instead of frijoles con tortillas y café. Don Justo opened the door to his room and hurried over to the birdcage that hung from the stand in the corner. Yoyo, who was thirteen and always the faithful one, plopped down near the door, while don Justo, with a flourish, pulled the cloth from the cage and uncovered his birds. He owned three canaries: an apricot pair named Romeo y Julieta and, the pride of the bunch, a crested yellow hen he called Rita.

Don Justo opened the cage door and the birds fluffed up their feathers and hopped down from their perch. "Come, little beauties," he cooed, and the birds queued up at the opened door just as they'd been trained to do, with Rita at the head of the line because she was the favorite. The canaries moved their heads from side to side and fixed don Justo with glistening eyes as black as papaya seeds. Next to Yoyo, he loved the birds best. The four were like his family, and it was a comfort to share his life with such sweet and attentive kind. His real family lived in Guadalajara. He'd left them years ago, when their bickering and backbiting had grown too much for him.

"*Rita bonita*," don Justo said. He tapped his shoulder, and Rita fluttered over and landed near his chin. "*Dame un beso.*" He puckered up his lips and Rita softly pecked them, bobbing her head and joggling the brown tuft of feathers crowning it. Don Justo offered Rita his finger and she hopped on. He extended his arm and she sprang off to fly in fits and starts because her wings were clipped to keep her from soaring. Don Justo busied himself with the other birds and soon they, too, darted and dipped about the room. Yoyo regarded the birds' antics. He barked and snapped at the air when the birds flew close, but they were used to the dog and were not frightened by his complaints.

In addition to companionship, the canaries were don Justo's only source of income. He was a pajarero, a birdman, and each day around ten he and Yoyo and the birds headed for the beach where don Justo set up the cardboard castle in which the birds performed. People paid to watch them do tricks. They paid for printed fortunes Rita selected with her beak.

Don Justo cleaned out the cage and poured fresh water for the birds. He filled their dishes with seed and then he clapped twice. The birds flew into the cage and hopped over to their breakfasts. He was fastening the cage when a knock came at the door. He opened it to a short man with a thin mustache. The man wore a uniform and on his head sat a cap with a metal badge at the crown. Don Justo stepped back into the safety of his room.

"*¿Don Justo Flores?*" the man inquired. He kept an eye on Yoyo who was sniffing in the direction of his shoes.

Don Justo peered out into the patio as though someone there might explain the man's presence.

"*Telegrama.*" The man extended an envelope to don Justo and don Justo took it, hooking a finger into his pocket for some change. The man plucked up the pesos and walked quickly away.

Don Justo closed the door and leaned against it. Yoyo was at his feet, looking up as if for answers. Don Justo gazed down at the envelope. It was creamy yellow, and it had a narrow window of cellophane under which the telegram showed. Don Justo held the envelope against his chest because in his seventy years there had never been a telegram addressed to him. The sight of one now, the feel of it against his shirt, frightened him.

He went over to the bed and sat on the edge of it. The image of his mother came to him. She was sitting on a bed, in some place he could not now recall. She was holding a telegram. Don Justo searched his mind for the news it had contained, but he could not say what it had been. All he remembered was that he'd been six, seven perhaps, and it was a telegram that had started the downward plunge that had taken his mother from him.

Don Justo left the room to see if his neighbor, Luz Gamboa, might still be home. Luz was usually at work by now, but if she were home, Luz could read for him. Luz's husband, Tito, had gone off for good, and Luz bought fortunes from don Justo and read them on the spot in a whispery voice.

Don Justo went across the patio but, just as he'd suspected, Luz was not home. He sat on the stool beside her door. Yoyo, who'd tagged along, gave a moan and lay down at his feet. Don Justo rubbed the dog's flank with the tip of his shoe. He had folded the telegram and put it in his trouser pocket, and the envelope crackled when he moved his leg. The sound was a reproach that said, What have you done with your life, old man, that now comes trouble and you're too ignorant to read what it might be?

He'd had a family once. Over the years, he'd had two wives and nine children. Of the five children who had survived, he'd kept track of only two: Justina, his first, born with the twisted foot, and Ernestina, his fifth. Both lived in Guadalajara, a day's bus ride away. He had made the trip three months before, when he'd gone to stock up on new fortunes and to see Ernestina. He had sat at her table, sharing a pot of coffee, and he had told her about moving to Santiago and about the bird business there. He had asked if, now that so much time had passed, Justina might see him. "I'm an old man," he had said. "Years go by. Things change. Maybe your sister will take pity on me now." But Ernestina's only answer had been to look down into her cup.

Today don Justo's gaze swept across the doors of the rooms that ringed the patio. He searched for someone who might read for him. A few children played near the toilet shack. At the water spigot two women filled bright plastic pails. Don Justo knew the women only to say hello, so he would not think to ask them for help. He thought of Marta Rodríguez, his next-door neighbor, but Marta worked at the hotel and so she too was not likely to be home. Besides, even if she were, Marta lived with her son and an aunt, la tía Fina. The old woman was meddlesome and her life was an opened book. The last thing don Justo wanted was la tía catching a glimpse into his life. No, he'd have to wait for Luz to learn what fate held for him. He stood and nudged the dog with his foot again. "*Vamos, Yoyo. Ya es hora.*" It was time to leave for the beach.

He had almost made it through his door, when la tía came out of hers. "*Buenas, don Justo,*" she said. Richard, Marta's one-year-old, straddled her hip. The boy's name was pronounced "ree-char," after Richard Burton, twice the husband of Elizabeth Taylor, Marta's favorite movie star. All this don Justo had learned from la tía herself. Richard was a large boy, with smoldering eyes and dark curly hair. He was a shy child who did not roam too far from his mother's or la tía's side.

"*Buenas, Doña Fina,*" don Justo said, putting on a pleasant smile. Yoyo went up and sniffed around the old woman's legs. Richard shrank back from the sight of the dog. He laid his head against his great-aunt's shoulder.

"Yoyo won't harm you," don Justo said, going over. "He's an old dog. He's as old as me."

"*Richard es un miedoso,*" tía Fina said. "He's afraid of everything."

"In this world there are many things to fear," don Justo said, and then, lest his response cue la tía toward conversation, he added, "*Bueno, ya es tarde.* I have to be going." He managed a cheery wave and slipped quickly into his room. Inside he gathered up the folding stand and the castle in which the birds performed. He filled a pack with a bottle of water and a bag of seed, adding the box of fortunes and the various props the birds used for their tricks. He transferred them from their hanging cage to the small one he used to transport them. Rita y Julieta chirped in anticipation of the trip, while Romeo broke out into a clear, sweet song.

At the beach, don Justo found an empty *palapa* and he and Yoyo hurried under the small thatched shelter. So far he was the only vendor here, and he was glad for the advantage. Few took in the sun, though the sea was calm and very green. The waves tumbled gently toward the sunbathers and then rolled out again.

The day was hot; the sun glinted fiercely off the white buildings set along the shore. Don Justo opened up the bird stand, thrusting its legs into the sand until it was level. He unfolded the castle—it was constructed in such a way that it, too, could be collapsed—and placed it on the stand. The castle featured two salmon-colored turrets with a yellow platform along the base. A curtain sprinkled with tiny stars hung between the turrets. Don Justo set the tray of fortunes out. He lifted the birds from their cage, placing each on the platform behind the curtain. It troubled him that he must busy himself with this, when something much more pressing needed his attention. The telegram was a nettle in his pocket. Not knowing its contents had soured his stomach. It came to him that a shot of tequila might settle him. On the heels of this thought came another. He had not had a drink for nearly ten years. Ten years and there had been no pulque or tequila. Not even a *cervecita*. He had served his penance, had he not? Ten years to pay for that terrible thing that he had done. A splinter of hope cracked the door of despair looming before him. He allowed himself to think that perhaps it was Justina herself who had sent the telegram. He formed a message from her in his mind: "Come home, Papa," the telegram would read. "All is forgiven."

A young girl walked up. She looked about sixteen. Her hair was very black, almost blue in fact, and she had gathered it up at the sides somehow. She reminded him of Justina. Not her face, but her hair. Justina's hair had that same bluishness about it.

"*Buenas, Señor*," the girl said.

Don Justo bowed. "You wish to know your fortune, Señorita?"

"*¿Cuánto?*" she said. A necklace of tiny onyx birds encircled her throat and, when she asked the price, she laid a finger on one of the birds as if it might fly off.

"It is very affordable. One fortune, one thousand pesos."

The girl frowned and looked toward a boy who lay nearby, belly down on the beach. He had flung an arm out at his side and his hand lay palm up, curved like a shell. "Chato," the girl cried out, but the boy did not move. The girl rolled her eyes and cried out again and this time the boy stood and, lowering mirrored sunglasses over his eyes, sauntered over to the *palapa*.

To encourage a sale, don Justo opened the curtain to show the birds lined up between the turrets. The birds were alert because they had begun to work and they knew that seed awaited them. "You wish to know your fortunes?" don Justo asked the two.

"*¿Cuánto?*" the boy asked, half his face a silver glare. He was not much older than the girl and he had the same slender waist that she had. He brushed sand from his chest and cocked a narrow hip forward and to don Justo it was as if the past had dropped away and he was seeing himself when he was young.

Don Justo repeated the price and the boy poked a finger into the side of his trunks and pulled out some bills. He peeled off a thousand pesos and handed it over. The girl did a little dance.

Pointing to Rita, don Justo set to work. "*Rita bonita*," he said, and Rita nodded her head so that her crest bobbed. "*Romeo y Julieta*," he added and the birds rubbed their beaks together in a kiss.

"*Ay, que lindo*," the girl said.

Don Justo placed Romeo y Julieta on each of the perches he'd built inside the turrets. The birds poked their heads out the turret windows and looked toward each other, and Romeo gave a trill. Don Justo bunched his hands together and rolled his eyes. "*Ah, el amor*," he proclaimed.

The girl giggled behind a hand. She did not look at the boy.

Don Justo placed the box of fortunes in the center of the platform. He whistled three times, and Rita rose and hovered over the fortunes before plucking one up. Don Justo clapped and Rita flitted to the edge of the stand and landed there. A small blue square was captured in her beak.

"*Su fortuna, Señorita*," don Justo said, making a sweeping gesture toward the bird.

The girl stepped shyly up. Carefully, she pulled the blue from Rita's beak. She unfolded the slip. "Oh, look! It's my life fortune." She hurried over to the boy and they began to read.

Seeing them like this, their heads bent in silent study, was a key that freed don Justo's reticence. He pulled the telegram from his pocket and stepped over to the boy. "*Por favor léame esto*," don Justo said, reaching out with the envelope.

The boy lifted his sunglasses until they rested on his head. He pulled his leg back, relaxing the projection of his hip. He took the envelope and spread it open and pulled out the telegram. The girl closed a hand over the blue square of her fortune. Don Justo turned to look at the sea. A boat with a red-checkered sail glided along the horizon.

"There is bad news here," the boy said.

"*¿Qué dice?*"

There was a hesitation and then the boy spoke, "It says, 'Come home at once, Papa. Justina is gone from us.' It is signed, 'Ernestina.'"

Out on the sea, the sailboat grew smaller. Patches of conversation from the people down by the water floated up to him. Don Justo nodded and took the telegram from the boy and stuffed it back into his pocket.

"I'm sorry, Señor," the boy said. There was a softness in his eyes and he did not lower his sunglasses to cover it. For a moment the three stood in silence under the *palapa* and then the boy took the girl's hand and they both walked away.

Don Justo sprinkled seed on the cage bottom and placed the birds inside. Nearby, Yoyo was panting. Don Justo took the bottle from his pack and poured water into his hand for the dog to lap up. "*Vamos*," he said. He gathered up his things and started for town, thinking a little tequila would be good to have just now.

* * *

Music blared from a radio out in the patio. It rolled under the door and invaded the room. Don Justo sat in the middle of his bed, propped against the wall. The room was growing dim. The walls seemed to throb to the beat of the music. His belly burned with tequila, yet he was chilled. He pulled at the scratchy blanket heaped near him. In the gloom, he saw Yoyo in the corner.

Don Justo called the dog's name and, after a time, the dog heaved himself up and came over. Yoyo laid his head on the mattress, casting a baleful look don Justo's way. Rita flew over and landed near. Don Justo offered her his finger and she hopped on. He brought her close to him.

The look in Rita's eye pinned him to the past.

Rita's eye gleamed in accusation. In her stare he saw Rosario, his first wife, her ashen face framed in the window of her coffin. He saw little Justina, mute with grief, hobbling along with the funeral cortege. He saw Clemencia, his second wife, refusing Justina a place in their house. He saw Justina's stricken look when she learned that he'd allowed it.

Don Justo felt the pain of his past and he would not have it. No. He simply could not have it.

* * *

Much later don Justo awakened. A thin, exquisite pain flowered at his temples. He sat up and looked down at himself. He was wearing his shirt and trousers and they were very crumpled. He still had on his shoes. He was in bed, yet he had not removed his shoes. He could not tell what time it was. Soft light came from the window and he knew that he was home, but he could not recall coming here. He had been in the cantina. He remembered that now. He remembered the tequila burning a path down his throat. He tried to swallow, but his mouth was dry and he longed for a little water. He inched his legs over the edge of the bed, the movement a burden. He lifted a hand and watched it tremble. He'd done it up good. Ten years without a drop, and now he'd gone and done it.

Yoyo crawled out from under the bed and crept off toward the door. Don Justo looked around the room. In the corner, the birdcage stood uncovered. Its wire door was flung wide. Don Justo shuffled over to the birds. Romeo y Julieta huddled on the perch.

"*¿Dónde está Rita?*" don Justo said, little flashes of memory exploding in his head. A telegram. He had gotten a telegram. He dug into his pocket and pulled it out. Justina, he thought, stumbling to the chair. He remembered now. Justina was gone and he would never have the chance to set things right with her.

Yoyo whined at the door. He looked over at don Justo and then at the door again.

A hollowness like a cave unfolded in his chest. There was something about the bed. The bed beckoned him and he went to it. He flung aside the blanket and Rita's stiffened body was there.

Don Justo clapped a hand over his mouth for he thought he might be sick. He fell upon the bed, gulping down the sourness in his throat.

After a time, he sat up and Yoyo came over and nudged him with his head.

"We'll be going to Guadalajara," don Justo said to the dog. He gathered up the bird and cradled its small body against his chest. "*Rita bonita*," he said, and he did not turn away from the anguish breaking over him when he uttered her name.

Omar Castañeda

Dogs of Clowerston

I

Neri Guzmán shot the dog point-blank. Earlier he had ripped the plastic wrapping from around a thawed chicken and slid the gun barrel in and out of the neck cavity. The inside of the gun remained clean. In an identical motion—that is, the black barrel slipping back and forth inside the moist opening—he shot through the dog's mouth. Before the blast, he remembered reading that cormorants of Lake Tayasal peck the eyes of fish too large to eat. The fish die slowly with no eyes. Nearby owls also peck the eyes of ocellated turkeys while they sleep in branches.

The sun had come up, but the drizzly morning left an interminable dusk. He left the shattered body and walked home through the alleyways.

Lori was still asleep, so Neri opened the bedroom closet and quietly lowered the blue suitcase. She had told him not to wake her. He fingered the letter hidden underneath. Lori's breathing didn't change, her body remaining soft and pale in sleep. But instead of reading the letter again, he stared at a ball of dust in the corner of the closet, then he put the suitcase back so that Lori or God could swear it had not been disturbed. Kato, their beagle, pattered up the stairs and looked at him.

He believed one can look at dogs, into their eyes, and feel an understanding. That was a romanticism he liked. Often, early in the evening—in the open fields between Clowerston's sandstone buildings, with trees fanned against the bruise-colored sky—just saying "yes" to the world, quietly and breathlessly, carried such unambiguous meaning. Truth.

He made breakfast for himself, dropping an egg and sausage into Kato's bowl before sitting down to eat. They ate together, looking across the room at each other. After washing the few dishes, he sat down to read the *Scientific American* he had taken from the library. Reading new journals or new books before anyone else was a right he claimed for himself as assistant librarian. Miss Cordon, the head librarian, used to complain about his taking the items home before proper cataloguing, but he continued without a word spoken in defense or comment whatsoever until she finally quit complaining.

The phone rang. The bedroom phone was set louder than the one in the living room. Neri let it ring four times before answering.

"Did I wake you?" the voice asked.

"No."

"Is Lori awake?"

Neri sipped his coffee. Miriam Blanchard should know that Lori would not be awake.

"No."

"Could you have her call in as soon as she's awake?"

"What is it?"

"We're short again. We need her to do another double shift tonight."

"Isn't it too soon or something?"

"Just have her call, okay?"

"Yeah," he said. Lori would not object to working two double shifts in a row. She never complained. Even on a Saturday.

He wrote the message on a piece of notepaper and ripped a square of tape. Upstairs, he put the note on the mirror of her vanity, then picked her clothes up from the floor. He carefully folded the jeans and a bright red blouse. He glanced over at her naked body, then set her shoes upright in the closet.

Downstairs, he locked the door behind him and walked into town. At this hour on a Saturday, very few people stirred from their homes. He walked leisurely, taking deliberate note of each trimmed lawn he passed. Their house was near the bottom of a cul-de-sac, so Neri passed seven houses before reaching the main street cutting through town. Most of the lawns were immaculate. His needed work.

From the corner, it was about a mile to the library. The greater city stretched eight blocks beyond that. It was a town he appreciated only after several years in Indianapolis. Clowerston grew a commuter's distance from that city, and remained a basically rural small town. The tallest and newest building in Clowerston, headquarters for Midland Electronics, rose only eight stories. The older business buildings, with their beige sandstone sides, reached half as high. The Morrison Hotel only reached five stories. He liked it that Clowerston would never be a city of any real size. The town stopped abruptly within country walking distances and disappeared into barely undulating fields where walnuts and maples commanded the sky; cornfields stretched like lakes to wooded horizons. At night, the dull white skylight of Indianapolis could be seen to the northwest.

Neri walked an extra two blocks out of his way so that he could pass a wild section of east Clowerston. The sloping fields, with their clustered elms and Douglas firs, had never been cleared there, so that a half-mile swath encroached on the town. Neri walked there to hear the sweep of birds in the mornings.

This time, he stopped at Gwynne's before going on to the library. It was a well-lit place in the morning, where Clowerston's police ate breakfast and flirted with the waitresses. By mid-afternoon, however, the smell of beer kicked in. At night, Gwynne's was a bar.

He entered and waved at Betsy Simpson and her husband. He envied them. It had been nearly a month since Lori had gotten up so they could eat together. He ordered coffee and sat at a table by the bar so that he could see the entire room. Neri got his coffee and drank slowly. The library would not open for two hours.

Neri opened a morning newspaper left on the neighboring table and scanned the pages for any mention of dogs. There were two articles. One was the report of yet another dog killed in Clowerston. A black Lab had been poisoned in the alleyway behind the library. Neri looked over at Betsy. The other article was in the opinion section. An easy denouncement of the person or persons who would be so sick as to kill dogs. Neri read through the classifieds, then started the crossword puzzle. He did not notice Betsy's husband leaving, nor Betsy approaching, so that when she stood beside him and spoke, he startled. Betsy chuckled about it.

"Sorry." She sat down. "Thought I'd join you. John went to work."

"Oh."

"Anything interesting in the paper?"

"No," he said, pushing it toward Betsy. "Want some coffee?"

"No, I'm coffeed out." A laugh opened her doughy face. "I don't see how you drink so much without going bananas. If I drink more than two cups, I'm a damn chicken with its head cut off."

"I guess I'm used to it. Maybe it's my age."

Betsy giggled. "Naw, you're not old."

"Thank you."

Sarah, the waitress, refilled Neri's cup.

"How far did you go?"

Neri didn't quite understand. "The crossword, you mean?"

"Yes."

"Oh, barely started. You want it?"

"No." She stroked the water glass, wiping the moisture so that it ran in beads. "Unless you want to do it."

"You mean together?"

"Yeah, let's do it."

"I don't know."

"You're so smart, we'd finish in no time." She slid her chair nearer to his. "Besides, we have lots of time to kill."

"Well, I suppose." He sipped his coffee, then opened the paper.

"How many cups have you had?"

"About four, I guess."

Betsy shook her head.

"All right," he said.

Neri read down the clues while Betsy read over his arm. Neither one said anything for a moment, so Neri read one-across.

"Three-letter word for 'formerly.' "

Betsy stared into Neri's face as she struggled with the clue. Her lips were pressed together. Neri waited. He took another sip of coffee. He looked into Betsy's eyes. She stared seriously. He wondered if she was really thinking about the clue or about cookies or flea markets or making love to her husband. How did they have sex? He picked up his pen.

" 'Née,' " he said.

"Oh, for crying out loud! Who would know that?"

"I don't know," he said.

"Let's not work it. Who would know things like that?"

He folded the paper.

"By the way," she said. "I need that *Scientific American* you took. Some people've already asked for it. Mostly high-schoolers working on papers."

"I'm impressed," he said flamboyantly. "Intelligence is up!"

"What're you reading about now?"

"About a certain narcotic in a cat's brain."

"Yeah?"

"Yep. Even lions secrete it." He tapped on the table. "It's great stuff."

"I don't see how high school kids can read that stuff. It's so hard."

Neri drained his cup and motioned for Sarah.

"That'll give you nightmares," Betsy said.

"Maybe," he said, accepting another cup. "Thanks, Sarah. I've been having some odd dreams lately." He tore open a packet of sugar and tapped out half the contents. He set the packet on the table as if it were a fragile and heavy thing.

"Like what?"

"Just odd ones."

"Tell me. I always like to hear other people's dreams."

Neri chuckled. "You must be about the only one who does. I don't even like telling them."

"Tell me," she said, pushing the small of her back against the chair, pouting in her chubby-faced way.

"People say they like to hear dreams, but they really don't."

"Please," she said.

"They're nothing, really. It's just that they've been extremely realistic. They're about people I know. They're so real that I wake up and can't tell if I was just dreaming or if I did the dream."

"Did the dream?"

"I dream very ordinary things."

"Tell me," she said.

"Like you: I dreamed that we were in the library and you came out of the stacks and asked to borrow five dollars. You said you needed it to pay for something that had to do with your kids, but that you'd forgotten your purse at home.

When I awoke, I couldn't tell if I had dreamed about something that really happened or if it was all just a dream. And even days later, when I thought about the dream, I still didn't know if you had borrowed the money. Just today I wondered about it."

"I didn't."

"Well, I've been having dreams like that."

"Does it bother you? I mean you believe me that I didn't borrow the money, right? Because I didn't."

"Of course, I believe you. But I had to realize the chances of you leaving your purse at home. No, the dreams bother me because I can't remember if I owe money, if people owe me money, if I was supposed to meet someone, or call someone . . . things like that."

"Maybe you're losing your mind." She wiggled her fingers eerily.

Neri smiled.

"I'm amazed that you can remember your dreams."

"Don't you?"

"Not usually." She looked for a moment into Neri's face, then said challengingly, "Tell me about a dream you had last night."

"You're kidding!"

"No, come on."

"Forget it."

"Come on!"

"All right." He finished his coffee and collected his thoughts, and ordered another. "I dreamed that Lori was living in a tall apartment building. It was too big for Clowerston, but I don't know where it is. For some reason, I was working with the fire department. Her building caught fire. Sometimes, the building looked real nice, like a city high-rise, but other times the building changed into a kind of tenement. The fire burned through the bottom floors, licking up the sides of the building and turning everything black. Lori lived on the floor just above the flames. She was leaning out of the window, screaming for me to help her.

"I arrived in a huge fire truck filled with all sorts of people. Then the sidewalks filled with people from all parts of the world: Chinese, Arabs, Mexicans. . . . Once we get there, though, the truck disappears. Each of us has a fire hose which we plug into the building opposite Lori's. She is still screaming for me to rescue her, but I realize that my hose won't reach far enough. I've taken the wrong hose from the truck and now it's gone. I turn away because I think that she'll die, but I hear other firemen saving her. Lori tries to tell everyone that it was me who saved her, that she would have died if it weren't for me, but I turn away from her and from everyone else because already she seems dead to me."

Betsy turned up her nose. "Sounds like you made it up, you know?"

"It does, doesn't it? Pretty Freudian."

"Well, I don't remember my dreams."

"Lately," Neri continued, "I've been dreaming about the dogs."

"Ooh," she said, her eyes squinting angrily. Betsy tightened her fist. "Only a nut would do that."

"It's incredible. I'm worried about Kato." Neri frowned. "At least they're all strays. He's actually getting rid of nuisances, you know."

"That's disgusting."

"I don't mean it's good or anything, but just to look on the bright side. The dogs were strays. Clowerston does have a problem with them."

"But to kill them?"

"Well . . ."

"He's crazy. A psychopath or something."

"You want to work the puzzle some more?"

"No." Betsy wiped the table with a sweep of her hand.

"Have some coffee?"

"No." She looked at the remaining customers.

Neri drummed the tabletop with his fingers. "Maybe we should just go set things up."

"Okay." Betsy stood to leave, then sat again as Neri pulled money from his pocket to pay. "Maybe Cordon's there."

Outside, the mottled sky kept Clowerston dank. They walked the few blocks in silence.

Miss Cordon was there. She opened the door for them, even though Neri had a key. Neri went into his office, where a stack of letters and forms from subscription agencies awaited him. Betsy began her morning search for stray books and magazines left on tables and shelves.

Neri worked through hours of forms until he thought that Lori would be up and ready for her "breakfast." He called, but the phone was busy. He called four more times in the next fifteen minutes and each time the phone beeped busy. When he finally dialed through, Lori spoke as if she had just awakened, yawning and breathing huskily into the phone.

"Uh-huh?"

"I called, but the phone was busy."

"Must have misdialed. What's the weather like?"

"Damp. It rained last night. There's no sun, really."

"Figures."

"Did you get the note I left you?"

"No. What's it say?"

"Miriam called and wants you to work another double tonight."

"Jesus Christ! Another one?"

"Maybe you can tell them you already had plans."

"No, I'd better not."

"It's up to you."

"No, I'd better go in. They're always so short."

"They should fire what's-her-name."

"Yeah. Thanks, Hon. Wait a second." Neri heard her light a cigarette and blow the smoke out with force.

"How about lunch?" he asked at the end of her exhale.

"Are you off?"

"No, but I can take an hour or so to eat with you. Things're slow as usual."

"When should I get you?"

"In an hour?"

"Okay."

One hour and forty-five minutes after the telephone conversation, Neri saw the silver Oldsmobile come around the corner. Lori smiled from behind the wheel. As soon as Neri sat down, he leaned to kiss her cheek.

"Hi-ya," she said.

She wore a Western blouse and Levi skirt. Her curled hair bunched in ringlets across her shoulders. Neri reached out and wrapped the longer strands around his finger. "You look great," he said.

"Where should we go?"

"It's up to you."

"You decide, for once."

Neri looked at her outfit again, noticing the tan boots. "McDonald's?"

Lori smirked.

He rolled the window down an inch. "The Wild Turkey?"

She patted his leg. "Good idea, Babe."

Lori glanced toward the Morrison Hotel. A large red car had just pulled in and a tall man with a briefcase stepped out. A woman in a white formal dress stood waiting to greet him.

"You know them?" Neri asked.

"Who? Oh, no."

"Maybe by night's end."

They drove through the center of town. Lori's smoking was more relaxed than usual. She let the smoke drift from between her teeth in near breathlessness, or let thin clouds brush over the dashboard. She watched everything that moved outside. She seemed pleased. They waited at another stoplight. An African American walked into the crosswalk. Lori turned her head just slightly to watch the man. Neri looked at Lori, who smiled at him. The light changed.

"Do you suppose it's true that Blacks are good in bed? Do you think Blacks make better lovers? African Americans."

"Jesus Christ, Neri, you're an idiot sometimes."

She threw out her half-smoked cigarette, then opened her purse to take out another one. She flicked her lighter several times before keeping it lit.

Neri waited through the edge of silence. "When do you have to be at the hotel?"

"Same as always," she said curtly.

"That gives us a little more than an hour."

"We'll eat fast."

It was a short and silent drive remaining. The restaurant on the far side of town advertised a special on western style ribs and cornbread.

"That sounds good," Neri said, pointing to the sign.

She didn't respond. She turned into the parking lot and stopped.

The inside walls of the restaurant were made to look constructed of old barnwood, the dining tables to look like chopping blocks coated with thick plastic. Embedded in the plastic were Confederate coins and postcards of the Wild West shows of Buffalo Bill, Calamity Jane and others. The waitresses all wore cowboy hats and frilled waistcoats.

Lori rolled her eyes.

"Watcha half, pardner?" she said when the hostess left.

Neri smiled.

"Maybe I should go into the restaurant business."

They ordered drinks first, then looked through the leather-bound menus. Neri rubbed the embossed turkey on the cover while watching Lori read and surreptitiously glance about the room. A waitress brought coffee for Neri and a Tom Collins for Lori.

Lori lit another cigarette. She rested her chin on the back of her right hand and rested it in the palm of the hand holding the cigarette. In this position, to smoke was the slightest of gestures. She lifted her chin an inch, drew her fingers in so the butt touched her lips and sucked. The exhaled smoke fanned across her hand, or shot straight to the ceiling in a thin stream when she lifted her chin up high. Her eyes followed every moving person, checked every table within view.

"Still looking?" he said carefully.

She dropped her hands to the table. "What?"

"There're a lot of men here today."

"For Christ's sake, Neri, don't start."

"Sorry."

"Why don't we just sit here and have a good time."

They sipped their drinks quietly. A young man came to fill their water glasses. Lori thanked him. Neri picked up the newly filled glass and drank.

"Is he good looking?"

Lori sighed. "What is it with you?"

"Just a question."

"Right!"

"It is."

"Do you want me to go through life with blinders? You want me to see only you or only what's in front of me? You're insanely jealous."

"Observant."

"Observant? And I can't be?"

Neri smiled thinly.

"You can look anywhere you want, but I can't. Is that right?" She jabbed out her cigarette. "Men are all the same!"

"Why do you always make the issue larger than what it is?"

"Well, what the hell is the issue? That I'm a whore? That I can't keep my eyes off of men? That all I want to do is have sex?"

"No."

"You want me to confess that I'm a whore?"

"No." He hunched his shoulders. "Keep your voice down."

"Then why do you have to ruin our lunch?"

"I'm sorry," he said, looking away from tables around them.

Lori stared blankly at the pictures in their booth.

"I'm sorry," Neri said.

She stared blindly.

Neri ripped the paper napkin beside his plate. "I'm sorry," he said. He balled up the paper between his fingers. "It was stupid. A stupid display of emotion. I was out of line."

"You jump to conclusions," she said. "You're always assuming things about me. It's like you don't trust me, like you look for reasons to hate me. Why the fuck stay with me, then?"

"Sh!" he said. "Look, I'm sorry."

Lori swallowed her drink.

"Let's talk about something else."

"Let's!" She pulled another cigarette from her pack.

Neri sipped the coffee, then his water. He watched the smoke pour from Lori's lips. Lori stared bluntly at him.

"I talked to Betsy today about dreams," Neri said. "Want to hear about a dream I had?"

She moved the ashtray closer.

Neri spread his hands flat against the table. "I dreamed that I poisoned a Labrador and left it behind the library. I dreamed that I was the one killing all the dogs in town because there was this darkness, this monster stuck in my chest."

Lori looked at him, stared at him. "You're insane, you know that?"

"It's true," he said.

II

Neri awoke later than usual the next morning. He tried to remember when Lori had come in, but couldn't. He had slept very soundly for once. He went quietly down the stairs to let Kato out and to make coffee. By the time the water boiled, Kato was back and whimpering to get in. They ate breakfast together, quietly so Lori would not wake up. She would sleep very late after two double shifts in a row.

Neri cleared the dishes and walked outside with his cup. A pair of robins called in the oak tree by the city lot. The female was probably already pregnant, he thought. They would guard the tree carefully, even hectoring Kato if he came too close. Neri admired the robin's habit of luring danger away from the nesting area. Robins, he thought, approached the habits of killdeers. Though far less dramatic. A robin would scurry away and wait for the attention of the intruder, calling out if necessary. And when the intruder followed, the robin would lead further out. Once the little ones hatched, the female would help the male in the ploy. If another robin ventured too close, the couple would hop up and flutter challengingly until the boundary was unmistakably clear.

But the best defense of home, he thought, was the strong offense of the cuckoo's. By destroying the eggs of other birds and placing its own egg in the nest, the cuckoo saved itself the burden of the whole relationship.

Neri tossed down the rest of his coffee and tied Kato to a post in the backyard. Inside, he wiped the table and swept the kitchen floor. He noticed that the floor would need to be waxed soon. Halfway up the stairs, he moved around to re-evaluate the sheen of the floor.

Neri coughed next to Lori. Her eyelids were still. He sat beside her head and touched her shoulder. He stood and said her name in a normal voice. He asked her if she would be working late again. She made no reply. He told her that he got a raise at work. She did not move. He slid open the closet door and lowered the blue suitcase. Now there were two letters underneath. He took the new letter into the bathroom.

His face flushed as he read the letter and when he finished, he unzipped his pants and urinated. Then he leaned over the sink and stared into his own eyes.

Kato barked.

Quickly, he put the letter and suitcase back. He stood over Lori again. Her mouth was partly open, the pillow damp from breathing. Neri opened her underwear drawer and rummaged through these clothes she never wore. He opened another drawer and searched. Neri searched through all five of her drawers.

He leaned breathlessly over the chest of drawers and bowed his head. Directly in front of him, Lori's jewelry box held what he sought. He lifted the small tape-measure key chain from among the necklaces and read the words "Fran's Goodyear" written in red letters. Slowly, he pulled the tape inch by inch until he saw the bright red heart drawn with magic marker. He licked his little finger and ran it down the concave tape. The groove was just the right width to accommodate the very tip of his finger. As his moistened finger passed over the length of tape, a red shadow smeared a quarter of an inch from the drawn heart. Neri stared into his eyes in the mirror above the dresser, then dropped the tape measure back into Lori's jewelry box.

He touched himself to erection as he crawled in next to Lori. She shrugged when he opened her legs. Lori opened her eyes and groaned. "No, Babe," she said. Neri moved slowly inside her. She placed her hand against his neck and spoke slowly. "Please, Neri, I'm too tired." He quickened his movements. Lori sighed loudly, and gave him more freedom. Her head fell sleepily to one side. Neri pushed feverishly inside her for a minute or two, then tightened in orgasm. Lori smiled up with her eyes closed. "That was nice," she said, her eyes still closed, her head lolling. "That was nice." He shrank out of her, and she rolled onto her side. "Stay with me," she said.

Neri slowed his breathing, feeling the pulse rack at his temples, and watched Lori fall back to sleep. Exhausted, he drifted off without even being aware of falling asleep.

Some time later, he awoke with a sense of urgency, hoping to capture the fleeting details of a dream. While he searched for paper, he pictured Betsy sitting in Gwynne's. He wrote what he could remember: crickets in the wild swath of Clowerston chirping incessantly; he threw pebbles into a night sky and watched a bat swing down, then dart upward from the decoy. The bat snarled at a red-and-white moon like an angry cat, its face leonine, mane-rich.

III

"Another dog was found poisoned last night," Lori said.

Neri rubbed his forearms beneath the kitchen table. Lori folded the paper. She joined him at the table.

"I have to work a couple of hours," he said.

"Okay."

"You're not working tonight?"

"I thought I'd eat with Miriam tonight, then have a few drinks. Maybe we'll go to a movie."

Neri wiped the table, then threw the cloth into the sink. Lori sighed.

"What's the big deal?" she asked.

"Last week you worked two doubles in a row—Friday and Saturday, at that—and this week you've already done one double."

"So?"

"When you're not working late, all you want to do is sleep or watch television."

"Okay," she said, "and now I want to do something else."

"Going out with Miriam isn't exactly what I had in mind."

"Look, Neri, I'm going out with her tonight. We can do something tomorrow."

"Are you sure you have the night off?"

"No, but if I do, we'll do something. I promise."

Neri stepped to the cabinets for lunch plates. "When will you know about tomorrow?"

"Tomorrow."

He set the plates down and folded napkins beside them.

"Sit down," she said. "I'll get everything."

"It's done."

"I'll serve, then. Just sit down."

"I suppose you won't be here when I get back."

"Probably not, Babe."

"I see."

"I'll do the dishes," she said.

They ate while listening to the three o'clock news. When they finished, Neri helped Lori with the dishes. She needed to take a shower and get fixed up, she said. While she showered, Neri looked through her dresser.

The week before, so many more letters had arrived that Lori took them from beneath the suitcase and hid them in her underwear. Neri felt elated the first day when he saw the letters missing. He thought it was all over, but then remembered the urgency of the last one and looked through her clothes. There, he found a pack of seven letters. The pain he felt on reading them was different after the giddiness of believing this affair to be over. He felt a dull throb in his chest, an ache behind his ribs, not the usual frenetic beating of his heart and the constriction at his groin.

Now, he felt only sadness, as if the letters were addressed to him and spoke, instead, of the discouragements of close friends, of their struggles for some happiness. Neri counted the letters, listening to the sound of the shower. There were no new ones, so he put the packet back. There had been no new letters for the past three days.

It made sense, he suddenly thought, that she would go somewhere else. If he continually thought she was going out on him, then it made sense that she would actually do it. She might as well. Neri sat on the bed, where Lori had set out a long dress and white shoes. He hated himself for sneaking through her clothes and jewelry, for shooting that dog, for imagining every man pawing his wife.

"I'm leaving," he called out. "I have to go."

"Goodbye, Honey," she sang back.

The library was closed to the public, but Miss Cordon had asked Neri and Betsy to do special work that afternoon. A new collection of journals on the fauna of Australia and Madagascar required immediate cataloguing. They worked in Neri's office, where the glass partitions reflected their faces and bodies. They hunched over the paperwork like plump monkeys. Betsy would occasionally stop and groan, then rise to drink from the fountain, or complain about using the restroom too often while moving to use it. Neri couldn't blame her. The work was monotonous and boring to begin with. Ordinarily, Neri would peruse most items he catalogued. He was too much the avid reader. He would do it leisurely, but with so many to catalogue by morning, there was no time for it.

When they neared the end of the task, it was already dark. Betsy complained loudly, saying that it wouldn't be so bad, but they had to return to work the next morning. And why didn't Cordon help out?

"Who knows what she's doing?" he said.

"Why don't you come with John and me to Gwynne's for a beer?" Betsy said. "Just a quickie."

Neri cleaned up the paperwork strewn over the tables and discovered another complete listing beneath a thick computer-run. Betsy said "shit" under her breath as if she were trying to blow the word down her blouse. Neri shook his head. "You go ahead," he said. "I'll do these and meet you later, if you're still there."

"Are you sure? I can stay and help."

"No," he said. "I'll finish up in no time. There aren't that many really."

He was wrong. The last series took him longer than he had expected. He worked another two hours with the cataloguing, regretting that he had spoken so soon. He knew that Betsy and her husband would be gone. He decided to take a short walk and then get a beer by himself. Attracted by the lights on the main street, he walked further into town. An old sports car, full of screaming teenagers, sped past. The boys inside called out drunkenly, catcalling and ridiculing Neri as he walked quietly down the pavement, minding his own business. He wondered if young lemurs ever harassed old and dying males, if any species of animal ever weeded out the weaker ex-patriarchs. For a moment, he saw a young girl's face peer at him through the darkened rear window of the car. In that face, he remembered that virtually all species attack their older members. The old males weakened, hollowed without a fight, or they died in bloody heaps. He waved at the ghostly face.

Neri turned down an alleyway behind the Morrison Hotel. Lori's car was parked in its usual place. It irritated him to think that she might have been called in to work because of that young what's-her-name. They should fire her, he thought. Too many people don't take their responsibilities seriously enough. The old can work, by God. They don't waste their time.

He jabbed the bell behind the hotel. The overhead floodlight cast his shadow into the darkness beyond, so that only his body lay outlined on the concrete—his head lost in the night shade beyond. He stood there longer than usual, picturing the path Lori would have to take from the secured telephone room, down the hallway, and to the outside door. After the murder of an operator in Washington during a robbery, the management of the Morrison Hotel decided to get special security measures for the switchboard. The operators controlled the entire hotel security system, as well as guarding the safe and security boxes.

There was a shift in color across the spy-hole of the door. A bolt slid back and Frank, the electronics technician, smiled out.

"Come on in, champ," he said.

"Is Lori here?"

"Yeah."

"Is she busy?"

"Don't know," he said and turned down the hallway.

"So, you're working nights these days," Neri said.

"Yep."

"Have you been doing it lately?"

Frank stopped and turned toward him. "Yeah," he said. "I've been doing it lately. How about you?"

"What? Oh, I see. No, I mean have you been working nights lately?"

"About a month."

Frank turned into the back room where he worked. His broad shoulders seemed to brush both sides of the doorway.

Neri knocked at the exchange.

Janis, the young operator, opened up. Lori sat on the large console, her legs crossed at the ankle. Her white dress hung just below her knees. Miriam sat on the couch beside her.

"What are you doing here?"

"Out walking. I saw your car, so I knocked."

Lori and Miriam exchanged glances.

"What are you doing here?"

"Mr. Morrison called Miriam and said that they needed someone to work late." Lori pointed at Janis. "She's leaving soon and can't stay, so I'm the one they want."

Miriam rubbed at a streak on her high-heeled shoes.

"It ruins your night out," Neri said.

"There's not much happening, anyway," Miriam said.

Janis answered a call, switching it to the proper room quickly.

Neri put his hands in his pockets. "I'll see you in the morning."

Miriam glanced at Lori. "Are we going to meet for breakfast?" she asked.

"Oh, yeah," Lori said. "Since we didn't go out tonight, we were going to have breakfast together." She stood and touched Neri's arm. "Is that all right, Babe?"

"Sure, why not?" He waited to see if he would be invited to join them.

Lori looked at Miriam. "We won't be long, will we?"

"No, I don't think so."

"Darn," Lori said, turning to Neri, "but you'll be going to work so I won't see you until the afternoon."

"Looks that way."

Lori pouted.

"I guess I'll go."

"I'll walk you to the door." She turned to Miriam. "Be right back."

In the hallway, Neri hissed in his throat. "They should fire that girl."

"Janis? She's nice. Just young, that's all."

They stopped by the front door.

"Do you want me to get some clothes for you or something?"

"Don't bother." She stroked her thigh and tilted her hip seductively. "I'll just be dressed to kill and no one will see."

"Hm."

"Why so blue?"

Neri reached for her waist. "I miss you."

"Ah, Babe," she said. "I'm sorry." She put her arms around his neck and kissed him. "Tomorrow, I'll be home, I think. Kiss me."

He did, and ran his hands down her back. The silkiness of the dress drew his fingers down across her hips. She wore no panties.

"Ooh," she said.

"I want you."

Her voice got husky. "Hold that thought for tomorrow."

"It's been too long."

She pushed him back. "You'd better go, Sweetie."

Neri looked up to see Frank smiling by a doorway, leaning against the frame with his arms crossed. Frank dropped his arms and stepped toward them.

"Oh, hi," Lori said, drawing away from Neri. "He's just leaving."

"Walking him to the door, I see."

"Yep." She reached out and stroked Neri's chin. "See you later, Hon."

"Don't worry," Frank said, stepping in front of Neri. "I'll lock up behind you."

Lori disappeared down the hallway.

IV

Betsy and her husband had already left Gwynne's by the time Neri arrived. He sat at the bar and ordered a beer. The patrons were mostly young men and a few women. Only two men sat at the bar. Neri eased up on the stool between them, with a vacant chair on either side. The older face on his right seemed familiar. Recently in the library, he supposed. He nodded at the man, who returned his own terse acknowledgment. Neri knew the bartender frequently bused tables for lunch and, sometimes, even for breakfast. He was a thin man with an eye that appeared half blind. A red semicircle covered half of his left pupil.

"I haven't seen much of you at night," the bartender said.

"I don't drink much."

"Sure slurp up the coffee, though."

Neri laughed. "Yeah, that's my vice."

"So long as you got one. So, what'll you have?"

He ordered a draft and when it came, Neri wanted to ask the man how in the world he could work so many shifts and maintain a respectable contact with his family, but the bartender walked off to wipe things beneath the counter.

He could see some of the room through the mirror behind the bar. A large man wearing a leather motorcycle cap clutched a girl in the far corner almost directly behind Neri. The man had one muscular arm draped over the girl's shoulder, the other arm rooted on the table and curved to encircle her. She was small enough to rest in the pouch of his arms, a pouch into which he frequently dipped his head with a guttural laugh that made Neri feel like he was being talked about. With the man's head up and periscoping about, the girl would kiss his neck. Even in the darkness of the bar, Neri could see the shadow of beard on the guy's face. He wondered if the sharpness of stubble against her lips was part of the attraction. That small pain.

The familiar face next to him ordered another beer. Neri took a sip and eye-measured the remains. He would have another, he thought. Neri downed the rest.

"I'll have one," he said loudly enough for the bartender and the familiar face to hear.

The face nodded. "You work at the library."

"Yes."

"Quiet work. Not like where I work."

"Oh?" Neri was glad for the conversation.

"Wish I could work somewhere quiet."

He saw that the man's eyes were glassy.

"I get noise all the time," the face continued. "Damn machines never give you a break. Running all the time. The doctor says my ears are shot. You think I get any compensation for that?"

"Where do—"

"And the kids need this damn thing and that damn thing. I ain't even got money for them. How the hell am I supposed to take care of my ears?"

Neri shrugged. He raised his glass to his lips.

"You know how much it costs to see a doctor? Too damn much, that's how much!"

"You're right."

"There's no big deal about ears, anyway." The face rubbed his forehead, then laughed. "It's like your prick. Once it's gone, just forget it. Don't think about it again." The man laughed, then tried to drown his laughter in a gulp of beer.

Neri sipped his.

"You got a wife?" the man asked with sudden sobriety.

"Yes."

The man gazed into his glass like he hadn't heard.

Neri checked the mirror. The leather-capped man and his woman friend were gone. He wondered briefly if he had imagined them. The man on Neri's other side put money on the bar and left with a friendly nod to him and to the familiar face.

"Be good," the face called out.

The departing man waved without looking back. Neri finished his beer and got up to go.

"Let me buy you one," the face said, raising his glass.

"I don't know. Two's about my limit."

Neri shrugged.

"Hell, it's free," the face said.

Neri tapped the bottom of his glass against the bar.

"Barkeep," the face said. "Two more."

"Thanks."

"Forget it. What the hell's your name?"

"Neri Guzmán."

"That's a fucking name." He stretched to meet hands. "My name's Ernie."

"Glad to meet you, Ernie."

Ernie nodded drunkenly. "You're not an Arab, are you? I mean with a name like that."

"No."

"So where did you get a fucking name like that?"

"I'm Honduran."

"No shit? You sure don't look it."

Neri took a drink. "Just my luck, I guess."

"Say," Ernie said, "do you drink whiskey there, Ned?"

"I'll pass, thanks."

"Yeah, I suppose I don't need that either." Ernie closed his eyes and rubbed his temples.

Neri watched through the mirror. Ernie's head swayed just inches above his glass. After nearly a minute, he raised his head abruptly and caught Neri staring.

Ernie raised his eyebrows. "My wife says I drink too much. Says all I do is drink."

Neri lowered his gaze.

Ernie stood suddenly. "Sorry," he said. "I got to go. You got to go when you say shit like that." He put money on the bar, too much for what Neri had seen him drink. "I got to go."

Ernie brushed against a woman near the door and continued on without apologizing. He pulled the door, then pushed it open.

The bartender shrugged.

"I guess I'll go, too," Neri said.

"Finish your beer. It's free."

When he finished, Neri stood, and wavered for an instant.

He welcomed the fresh air against his face. For a second, he thought he might become sober, but the deadened feeling came back quickly to his forehead. He stopped by a drugstore on the way home with the hope that it would be open. Instead, he found himself staring through the darkened store window at a newspaper just inside, staring dead at the front page account of another poisoned dog. Number ten, it said in large print. It was the same dog Lori had noticed earlier. The paper quoted the disgust of the director of the city pound.

"There's probably a reason," Neri said aloud, then turned to see if anyone had heard him. The street was empty up and down for blocks.

He continued toward his house, wishing for the sound of birds or the black shadowing of a bat, something magical . . . Lori's smile exploding in his eyes like stars. A dog scurried to the right of him, in an alleyway. Neri touched inside his coat pocket where he had carried the gun a week ago. He hurried behind houses and buildings to get to the wild section. Disappointingly, the sounds he wanted to hear were not there. He walked slowly home, thickly home.

Inside, he patted Kato's head and walked upstairs. His head and legs felt wooden, even when he reached for his gun in the back of the closet. He wiped the black barrel with a chamois cloth, then carefully removed all but one bullet. He spun the cylinder the way he had seen countless times in movies. He placed the extra bullets side by side in a cotton-lined box. He lifted one and held it so close that he could see his tiny reflection in the casing. He rubbed the slug in a circle around his forehead, feeling the smooth machined metal against his skin. Neri covered the bullets and returned them to the closet. Without a second thought he pointed the gun into the roof of his mouth and pulled the trigger.

Downstairs, he opened the refrigerator. He opened Tupperware bowls and old butter tubs of leftovers. He immersed his left hand into beef stew, then shook the excess liquid back into the tub.

"Kato!" he called, closing the refrigerator.

Neri stooped, reached out. "Come on, Kato," he said.

The dog whimpered. It kicked free of his hands.

"Sh, boy! It's all right. Here!"

He carried Kato into the backyard where he tied him to the post. "Goodbye, friend," he said, his voice like gauze in his mouth.

Neri walked through the backyards until he came to a fence. On the other side, his neighbor's dog growled quietly, slowly recognizing Neri's scent. Neri called to it. The dog pushed its snout through the chain-link fence and sniffed Neri's hand. He let the animal lick his fingers, and guided the dog in this way to a corner of the yard where garbage cans stood like canopic jars. Neri drew his gun, stuck three fingers through the fence. The dog's tongue slipped quickly and wetly between his fingers.

Neri knew the dog would understand what he was doing if he thought too much. The dog would know his thoughts. Everyone could read his thoughts if he wasn't careful. He pointed the gun barrel through the links, letting it rest against the pale metal. Close by, a click beetle righted itself. Neri's stomach quivered. The dog's eyes were brown, the sharp teeth glinted whitely behind dark lips. Bitter lips. But then he had seen this dog before, he suddenly thought. Then embarrassedly, losing the dream, he realized that, of course, he had seen this dog before. It was his neighbor's dog. Fred's dog. It wasn't a stray. "Of course," he whispered.

The dog stepped back and stared at Neri; its head tilted to one side.

He had thought too long. Maybe there was still time. If he could make his mind a complete blank, he thought. If he could return to that obscure plane of mind where he did not recognize the dog. He pointed directly at the dog's face, trying to picture a darkness inside his mind, an emptiness that clouded and comforted by its very emptiness. The animal growled. Neri felt his stomach grumble with acidity. "I can't freeze," he thought. "I can't freeze."

"Bang!" he shouted suddenly, unable to squeeze the trigger.

The dog scurried away from the abrupt noise, then lunged back at the fence. The chain links chattered like cymbals. The violence of the attack so startled Neri that he fell down amid the garbage cans. They clattered and set the dog to leaping and barking in earnest.

A light snapped on. "Who's out there?" a voice called.

Neri tried putting the cans upright, but they fell against each other. The dog kept lunging at the fence, rattling the chain links. Barking. Barking.

"Who's there?" the voice shouted. "I have a gun!"

Neri scrambled up and ran headlong through the yards. Behind him, not far enough behind him, not nearly far enough, he heard a screen door smack against its wood frame.

V

Steve Hicks came into the library the next day. He said hello and asked for Betsy. Neri, who was checking books at the front desk, pointed to the stacks. Steve returned in several minutes and stood alongside him, casually glancing at the browsers. "So, how are you, Neri?" he asked.

Neri looked up. "Fine."

"Betsy's finding a book for me," Steve said, jerking a thumb toward the stacks. "You don't mind if I wait here for her, do you?"

He returned to his work. "No."

"I'm still on duty, but I figured I had enough time to get a book for my kid."

"What's she getting?"

Neri scribbled dates and figures on overdue notices.

"A science book." Steve put a hand on Neri's work. "You read science books, don't you?"

"Yes."

"I wish I knew more about science."

"Yes. It's helpful."

"I sure wish I knew about science. Maybe it would help me find out who's behind the dog poisonings."

"Oh, are you doing that?"

Steve sat on the desk and folded his arms. "It's not easy, though. I mean, who really cares about strays, anyway? You know what I mean?"

Neri tapped his pencil. "A lot of people care, I guess."

"I guess," Steve said, "It gets tricky, though." He picked up a pencil and read the writing on it. "You don't know anything about these dogs, do you?"

Neri looked at the stacks for Betsy. "No, I don't." He wondered if he had dreamed of telling Betsy, or if he had really told her. Suddenly, Steve sitting there in front of him asking about the dogs seemed all too familiar, too inevitable. He had seen this before.

"Maybe it's nothing, really," Steve said. "It doesn't hurt to ask people. After all, they're nothing but strays. It should probably be legal to kill them."

"No," Neri said, "I don't know anything about them."

"Actually, whoever's doing it is helping the city. Doing us all a favor. Don't tell anyone I said that, but we don't need a pack of wild dogs roaming the city. We have too many strays as it is."

Neri stared up. He did tell Betsy about the dog. They had been in Gwynne's solving a puzzle with her husband. They had stayed up all night. There had been chickens everywhere. Black chickens. And he had leaned forward and told Betsy about the dog. But why wasn't Steve arresting him?

Steve frowned. "You know," he said, "the thing is that only one dog was shot. The rest were poisoned. Sometimes you get somebody killing dogs out of an honest craziness, and then someone else joins the bandwagon and kills a dog or two just to see if they can do it. It's a milder thing, you know? It's the kind of person who's usually a real nice guy, like you or me, but maybe he's always wanted to kill a dog, or something Some other guy is already doing it, so, hey, why not take the opportunity?"

"You can understand it then," Neri said. His hands felt heavy on the desk.

"I can't really blame someone like that. It's not like they're killing people. They're strays that would be killed at the pound sooner or later, anyway."

Neri thought he'd better not remember his neighbor's dog, picture its face. He wouldn't want Steve to know about that. Steve would be able to see what he was thinking.

Steve looked over his shoulder quickly, then put his face next to Neri's. "You have a gun, don't you?" he asked conspiratorially.

"What?"

"You have a gun."

"Yes, I have a gun."

"You have a license for it?"

"Yes."

"When did you get it?"

"I worked two years as a security guard for Lilly in Indianapolis. After my service. I got a gun because the one they issued was too heavy."

Steve leaned back and spoke in a normal voice. "Seems like I remember hearing that."

Neri looked at the stacks. "What's taking Betsy so long?"

"I'm in no rush," Steve said.

"Maybe I should help her."

"Don't bother." Steve crossed his arms. "Yeah," he said, "we got a call last night about someone prowling around in your neighborhood."

Neri imagined himself reading under the tall lamp in the living room. He imagined the cream rug, the fireplace poker.

"I tell you what. I can probably excuse one stray dog being killed, but someone killing somebody's pet is different. Particularly with a gun."

"I didn't hear anything last night," Neri said.

"Happened around ten o'clock. I was watching television and drinking beer. What were you doing?"

"I was home."

"Watching TV?"

"No, I was reading."

"What were you reading?"

"A novel," Neri said.

"A science novel?"

"No, a Hemingway novel."

"What was the title?"

"*For Whom the Bell Tolls.*"

Steve Hicks stared at Neri for a second, then he burst out laughing with undisguised disbelief.

Neri felt his face flush.

"Listen," Steve said firmly, "I'm looking for someone who's poisoning dogs. That's a psychosis we don't want here. And it's not odd for some poor sucker to join the bandwagon because of some weird need. But that's temporary." He stared hard at Neri. "Temporary! We hardly ever find out who does that sort of thing, but if he starts killing pets, that's a serious beginning. Firing a gun in the city is even more serious. You understand? We do not want that to happen again."

Neri nodded.

"Do you understand?"

"Yes," Neri said.

"I seriously hope you do. Now go and tell Betsy that I'll send my boy over here later."

Neri nodded.

Steve Hicks stood with his fingertips at the edge of the desk, fixing Neri with his eyes, then he left. Neri waited for the door to close behind him before rising to find Betsy in the stacks.

"What book?" she said. "He said that he wanted to speak with you in private. For me to leave you two alone."

Neri ran the heel of his palm across the back of the books, feeling the narrow ridges scrub across his flesh.

"Maybe I misunderstood," he said.

VI

Neri smiled at Kato. "It's over," he said. He grinned and rubbed Kato's head between his hands. He wanted to laugh out loud, but kept the laugh, like a secretive animal, in his throat. He grinned widely, foolishly.

Lori had left for the morning shift for the first time in many weeks. Neri rummaged through her dresser, through the closet and eagerly through every conceivable hiding place in the house. The letters were gone. The last letter, found four days earlier, had been cool. That night, he remembered, Lori had snuggled up to him in bed. She must have destroyed the letters while he slept. There was no other time, he thought.

Neri made a pot of coffee and mixed a batch of pancakes. He cracked an egg and dropped it onto Kato's dog food. The foolish animal in his throat kept churning, forcing Neri to smile and laugh quietly. Kato pushed against Neri's legs and wagged his tail every time Neri grinned.

"Okay, okay, boy," he said. "It's done."

While they ate, Lori called.

"Just wanted to say good morning," she said.

"Thank you," he said. "Thank you very much."

"You sound cheerful."

He chuckled.

"Is it nice out? I didn't notice."

"Well, sure, I guess."

Neri walked to the window and pulled the curtain. It was partly sunny, with a stripe of sunlight flying across the lawn.

"Are you looking?" Lori asked.

"Yes. It looks great."

Neri heard her light a cigarette. "How about you?" he asked. "You doing okay?"

"Yeah. Just okay."

"Sorry."

"Why? It's not your fault."

"Sorry for you."

Lori blew smoke noisily. "You want to have lunch?"

"I can't."

"Why not?"

"I have extra work today."

"Please?"

"No thanks, Babe." Neri scratched Kato's head. "But why don't you pick me up after work and we'll eat?"

"Fine. What time?"

"Five."

Later, at three minutes to five, Lori drove up to the steps of the library and got out so that Neri could drive.

"Are you all right?" he asked. "Yeah, sure." She slid next to him on the seat. He pulled away from the curb. "Where to?"

"I don't care."

"Wild Turkey?"

"If you want." Lori put her head on Neri's shoulder.

He rubbed his cheek against her hair. "You smell good. You seem soft, too. Are you tired?"

She kissed his shoulder. "I wish I could be soft for you all the time." She looked down at her lap.

When she lifted her head, Neri saw that her eyes were red. "Are you crying?"

"No."

He kissed her temple.

"Let's go home," she said.

"Are you all right?"

"I'm just tired." Lori sighed. "Maybe the late shifts've finally gotten to me. All that juggling."

"Maybe we won't have late shifts for a while."

Lori looked into Neri's face. Her eyes were red, her expression frozen as if she were about to speak.

At home, Lori dipped her fingers inside Neri's hand and led him to the bedroom. She kissed him, undressed tiredly and threw her bra and panties onto the floor. Neri watched from the doorway. He waited for what she wanted.

"Lie down with me," she said. She pulled the sheet up to her chin.

Neri undressed and slipped in beside her. "Do you want to make love?"

Lori put her head on his chest. "No, I just want you to hold me."

He folded his arms over her back. He pressed his cheek tightly against her head, feeling the burning of his eyes. He didn't want them to be wet. No tears. No wet!

"Do you love me?" she asked.

"Yes," he said tightly.

Lori kissed his chest. She brushed his nipple with her fingernail. "I forget," she said, "how good you are. You love me for me, don't you?"

Neri combed her hair with his fingers.

"Even with your jealousy," she added, pressing deeper into his chest.

Downstairs, Kato's claws clicked on the kitchen floor. In the room, their nightstand clock ticked audibly.

"I had a strange dream the other night," Neri said.

She looked up into his eyes. She seemed to search in the light hidden there, scattered in his dark pupils, for a clue as to his mood.

He gently pushed her head down onto his chest. "It's an odd one. It might make you mad."

"Baby, don't. Please."

"It started with you buried up to your neck in sand by the sea."

"Do you have to?"

"There's an African boy standing beside you with a club you'd given him. He's swinging it like a golf club, but it isn't an ordinary golf club. It has a razor edge that will sever your neck. The flat face will send your head into the sea."

"God, Neri, please don't—"

"See, you want him to do it. You asked him to do it. You're calm. In some way, this is penitence. But each time the boy swings, you yell 'eyes, eyes,' because the boy keeps missing and knocking sand into your face. Your face is so expressive. The boy's family and friends watch from red and white tents, but they get bored. Some of them leave. The boy keeps trying. One time, he has to whisk away sand from the pocket of your mouth.

"Behind him, there's a small parade of Africans nearing us. At first it looks like oil spreading over the sand. You see them, too, and get angry. The newcomers are carrying a lion. You shout at them and the lion turns its head. I see the strong and youthful face and think that it is smiling.

"At first, you're very angry with them. You tell me that they're going to dismember the lion. They'll strip off the skin and eat the meat from the lion's head. You ask me if I remember your restaurant in Texas where you served meat not only from the lion's head, but from its entire body. You desperately want me to remember your achievement. 'I didn't waste anything!' you shout at them. Even then, you whisper sadly to me, you hated Africans for leaving the limbs of lions scattered on beaches.

"For some reason, I was living proof that your restaurant was actually decent and legitimate. And yet, I had done something that destroyed your good image. Most people had forgotten you, but because of what I had done, you were buried neck deep in the sand. I wanted the people in the tents to know the truth about you, that's why I did something terrible.

"Anyway, the boy swung again and missed. Suddenly, I realized that we weren't facing the sea. We had been looking landward, staring at the infinite sand. The slight rolls of windswept desert had fooled me into thinking of the sea. But when I turned to look at the ocean, I knew the sand and sea were equally beautiful, equally deadly.

"Well, I walked out over the rolling dunes and into the desert, trying to remember what it was that I had said or done to get you buried alive. I expected to hear your final scream coming from over the dunes. Like the waste of lion's meat, it all seemed so inevitable. But under the heat of the sun, you melted away. Everything—the tents, the Africans, the dismembered lion with its weird grin— everything melted into that infinite and empty desert. Even me." Neri stretched his arm out, high above both of them, and spread his fingers.

"I can never understand you," she said. Neri brushed her cheekbone. She put her head down, hid her eyes against his body. Her hand slowly traveled from her chin, where it had clutched the sheet, to his penis. She gripped him. "Do you hate me?"

"No."

She kissed his chest, letting her lips linger for a moment against his skin. "We're good for each other, aren't we? Aren't we?"

Her skin was soft, the desert locked in the wild strands of her hair. "Yes," he said. Her eyes were red. "We're meant for each other, Honey."

Daniel Chacón

Aztlán, Oregon

When white people in Portland stared at Ben Chávez as if they had never before seen a Mexican, it pissed him off. He had fantasies about coldcocking them, feeling their noses explode on his fist. Pulling open the doors of the *Café del Cielo* and walking in, sure enough, a white boy with round glasses and a head shaped like a pencil looked up from his book at Ben. It didn't occur to him that the white guy might have recognized him from TV.

Mara Solorio sat in the corner reading a newspaper. She too looked up at Ben, who now stood across from her.

"Aren't you getting coffee?" she said.

"No, I'm fine," he said.

"Are you sure?"

"Really. I'm fine. Maybe we can go somewhere else."

She neatly folded up the newspaper.

"Where do you wanna go?"

"I don't know. I guess this place is fine."

Reluctantly he sat.

"Somebody's been asking about you, Ben," she said, pushing away a plate with a half-eaten blueberry muffin. "But before I tell you about it, you have to promise me two things. Two things, Ben, promise two things. Okay?"

"Are you going to eat that?"

"No, you want it? Two things: One, you listen to my advice without getting defensive. Two, nobody knows that I told you this. You gotta promise that. Ben, are you listening?"

Maybe three bites were missing from the muffin.

"So you're just going to waste it?" he said.

* * *

At fourteen he had learned not to waste food. One afternoon, he had plopped an egg into the pan, but the yolk broke, so he dumped it into the garbage and tried with a new egg. Looking up, he noticed his father's figure blocking the doorway. "Why did you throw that away?" his father asked.

313

A TV sit-com blared in the living room.

"I wanted it sunny-side up. I like dipping the tortilla in the yolk." He was certain that his father who loved to eat would understand.

"What?" His chest expanded.

"The yolk broke."

"You threw away an egg because the yolk broke??"

"I wanted it sunny-side up."

"Who the fuck you think you are, boy? A Rock-in-feller?" He stepped into the kitchen and raised a fist.

"I'm sorry," Ben said, shielding his head with his arms, stepping on the edge of the water pan underneath the fridge, spilling slimy water on the floor.

"Do you wanna buy the eggs from now on? Huh?" He tightened his lips around straight, white teeth, teeth that were not his own. His own had been knocked out in a bar fight.

"I'm sorry, Dad."

"I oughta hang you by your balls!"

"I just wanted an egg."

Mr. Chávez looked into the garbage and saw three of them, splattered with grease on the side of the brown paper bag. "How the hell many did you waste?"

"I'm a lousy cook."

He saw the floor rising. Heard the laugh-track laughing. When he woke, he was on his bed, his mother holding a damp towel to his head.

"Are you okay?" she asked.

"Where is he?"

"Watching TV."

"It ain't right what he did."

"What'd you do?"

"I cooked an egg. That's all."

"And for that your father wants to kill you? Are you sure you're not leaving out some detail?"

"I like 'em sunny-side up. That's the only way I like 'em. Well . . . sometimes I like 'em scrambled, but I wanted them sunny-side up today. He must have hit me pretty hard."

"I heard it from the front yard."

He sat up on his bed. "I forgive him. Don't be mad at him, okay? I think I'll go watch *Starsky and Hutch* now."

"I wouldn't if I were you. He's likely to hit you again."

"Now wait a minute. If I'm willing to forget about it . . ."

"You must have done something. He gets carried away, but he's not cruel. What did you do?"

He told her.

"You little shit, how could you waste food like that?"

* * *

Now Mara's muffin made him angry. When Ben had been hired by the station, he had made it clear to his boss, Brad Myers, that he couldn't feel comfortable unless he had some brown people around, so Brad hired her, "Hispanic" token number two. Ben believed that the only differences between her and the white people were her accent and last name. Her rich family from Nicaragua had fled to the U.S. before the revolution in 1979. Her skin was the color of weak tea, and her eyes were blue. On Sunday nights when he anchored the news, she directed. She was brilliant because she saw everything through a camera. When she looked in Ben's eyes, even if she smiled and said something personal, he saw a director looking at him.

Whatever she wanted to meet him for now, it wasn't personal.

"The network's looking for a station to host the twenty-four-hour news," she said. Her ponytail hung off her shoulder.

He pulled the muffin toward him and took a bite.

"They're thinking about Portland. It'll run from 2 a.m. to five. They're talking about you as a possible anchor. This is national, Ben. Not all affiliates, but a lot of them."

"Who told you this?"

"Remember. Nobody knows you know this."

"Who told you?"

"Okay, here's the thing, Ben. Now take this as concern, okay?"

"Brad told you, right?" He resented the way she and the boss got along so well.

"I care about your future with the station. You're letting yourself go. You have to watch it."

"What do you mean?"

She sipped her coffee. "Physically, Ben. You're getting . . . chubby."

"I'm not chubby."

"You're chubby, Ben."

"You're crazy. I mean . . ."

"Look at your gut, Ben. Look down and see your gut. The camera sees that. You know, the camera adds to it. You're getting fat."

"Now it's fat?"

"Deny it if you want, fine, but not for too much longer or the network is going to pass you up. Ben, one of the things they're going to consider is your physical appearance."

With both palms he touched his face. "Are my cheeks getting fat?"

"Your cheeks are fat, Ben."

"Oh, my God. I didn't even notice."

"Life's been good to you."

"I mean, I don't care. I mean, who cares what I look like ultimately, you know?"

"Well, the network cares. I care because if you blow this deal, you blow it for me too."

"That's not fair."

"That's the way it is. Listen, it shouldn't take you long. Spend some time at the gym, start eating right. The station is sending tapes of you to the network. They want recent ones, and frankly, Ben, we don't have a lot of great stuff lately. It's like your enthusiasm is draining. Let's do some good features next week, something that shows you off. I have some ideas. Do you want to hear them?"

"Whatever."

"Hispanic street gangs. This of course has been done before, but by people too out of touch with the streets to dig deep. But you. Didn't you used to be in a gang in California?"

"Something like that."

When they walked to her car, Ben looked into the eyes of the white men he passed on the sidewalk, as if daring them to mad-dog him, but the one man that did look at him smiled, and Ben couldn't help but smile back. They were everywhere in Portland. He got so lonely that he would drive around towns where some Mexican farmworkers lived, Woodburn, Gervais, Independence, sometimes stopping in cafes or pubs. At these times, he never said anything, he just sipped his coffee or beer, looked straight ahead, and listened to their Spanish, trying to guess by their accents which part of Mexico they came from, Jalisco, Michoacán, Guerrero.

"You going to be all right?" Mara asked, unlocking the door to her Corolla.

"Of course," he said. "I was just thinking how much I hate this town."

"Too white for you?"

"Yeah, that's it."

"You're such a racist."

"But for the good side."

"Really, Ben. You need to get over it. Before you do something stupid."

She got in and drove off. He watched her car disappear in traffic, and he ate the rest of her muffin.

* * *

In high school, his teachers hated him. They judged him because he dressed like a *cholo*: baggy pants, crisp white T-shirts, and work boots. One woman requested that he be transferred from her English class before she even read his writing. By the time he was a senior, now a leader in his gang, he was used to it.

He attended school more for his personal amusement, he believed, than a desire to get educated, and he began to enjoy living up to the expectations of him, especially giving the teachers a hard time. Mr. Shell hated him the most. He was the Civics teacher, and from the first day he was short with Ben, threatening him with expulsion when he laughed at the wrong moment or said something the rest of the class thought was funny. Mr. Shell didn't like that the students in class—the Chicanos at least—paid more attention to Ben than to him.

The students were required to volunteer four hours to a presidential campaign. Ben didn't like any of the candidates, so he wanted to work with an old radical named Marta Bañuelos who had a platform telling white people to go back to Europe and leave Aztlán to the Indians. Mr. Shell, a bald man with sad eyes and sagging cheeks, said no, that Ben had to work for a legitimate candidate.

"Anderson doesn't have a chance at being elected," Ben argued in class. "Yet to you he's a legitimate candidate? Could it be because he's white?"

"Yeah," a few Chicanos in class said.

"I'm not required to explain myself to you," Mr. Shell said.

"Well, you better tell me why."

"Or what?" Mr. Shell said, dropping his roll book on his desk with a thud and walking closer to Ben. "Or what, Ben? Are you threatening me?"

"Lighten up, old man. I just wanna know."

"I'm the teacher here. Not you."

Suddenly a white girl from the front of the class raised her hand and said Mr. Shell's name.

"What?" he answered.

"Why can't he work for whomever he wants?"

"Well, uh, this Bañuelos person sounds like a protest candidate."

"So what's your point?" Ben asked.

"Okay, Ben, go ahead, I don't care."

When Marta Bañuelos—who looked like Ben's *abuelita*—drove him through the neighborhood behind the Veterans' Hospital, he told her no Mexicans lived there, just retired white people. He knew, he said, because his mother worked at the hospital.

"*Brown people are everywhere*," she said in Spanish, hunched over her steering wheel, her face old. She dropped him off in front of a chain-link fence surrounding the hospital parking lot.

As he walked by the tiny homes and duplexes, he read the names on the mailboxes. One box carved from wood said "Godishere." He thought that was an interesting name, but they weren't Mexicans, so he didn't go to the door and knock.

He walked across the hospital lawn through the parking lot where a fat security guard looked at him suspiciously. Ben wore creased khakis and a crisp white T-shirt a few sizes too big, and he had a tattoo on his forearm that said NSF, North Side Fresno. He was aware that the fat security guard was following him, so he walked like he owned the damn place down the ramp to emergency, through the automatic doors, past a man screaming on the floor surrounded by nurses and held down by orderlies. He pushed through double doors into a hallway where moans mixed with machine noises, typewriters, a toilet flushing, and his soles sweeping the floor.

The double doors at the end opened onto a large bright room with orange couches, and TV sets braced on the walls. Alicia Chávez, behind the counter on a stool, was talking in Spanish to an old nun. The nun left the counter, Ben approached it. "Are you registered to vote?" he asked his mother.

"Did I forget something at home?"

"No. I was canvassing the neighborhood."

Her line rang. She told him to hold on and started talking, checking information from filing cabinets and reading it over the phone. He waited on one of the orange couches across from the TV and watched some soap opera, the volume too low to hear over the sound of patients moaning and coughing. The fat security guard walked in through the double doors, looked around, spotted Ben and walked over to him. "What are you doing here?" he said, trying to sound intimidating, although to Ben he sounded like a little boy trying to be tough. Ben ignored him.

Alicia came up and said hi to the security guard and introduced them. "Ben," she said. "This is Roy. Roy, this is my son."

"I heard a lot about you, son." Suddenly Roy was friendly and animated, and sincerely so. He shook Ben's hand heartily. "So you make sculptures from clay? I hear your dragon won first prize at the fair."

"That's his brother," Alicia said. "This is the one that wants to be a movie star."

"Used to," Ben wanted to say, because now it sounded so childish to admit what his dreams had been.

"You're the one that reads those detective novels?" Ben asked.

"Why, yes," Roy said, surprised and pleased that he should know something about him. "I love reading."

He wanted to tell Roy to quit giving them to his mother. They were all over the house and he picked them up sometimes and read them. In one, some sleuth was on an airplane over the California coast with a Mexican pilot, who turned out to be one of the bad guys. He said to the hero, "*Señor*, I theenk your time she is up," and he tried to push him out of the plane, but a struggle ensued and the Mexican got pushed out instead. "Adios, Amigo," said the hero as he watched the Mexican drop.

Roy told Alicia he had to get back to the parking lot. "Bye, Ben," he said, shaking his hand again. They both watched him waddle away. "You have to get back, I guess?" she asked.

"I guess."

"Ben?"

"Yeah?"

"Do you still want to be an actor?"

"I don't think so."

"What do you want to do?"

"I don't know."

"Maybe you should be on the news. An anchorman."

"Why do you say that?"

"You have to do something that shows off that handsome face of yours."

"Whatever."

When Bañuelos picked him up, he told her that everyone slammed doors in his face. Next she dropped him off in the barrio on a street lined with houses and apartment buildings. He got out and started walking.

Here he is, he thought, ace reporter wandering the way of *Aztlán, con los Chicanos, la gente*, seeking the stories behind the headlines. He would go deeper and deeper, to the roots of the people's problems.

Three *cholos*, gang members, stood in front of their car across the street, their music so loud the bass beat with his heart. They stared at him, and his knees went weak because he was banging from another barrio, so they would assume he was disrespecting them. This was a death sentence, especially with his shining North Side tattoo. The three crossed the street, coming at him, one of them huge, built like a bulldog, with a flannel shirt untucked and buttoned at the top *cholo* style.

"Where you from, eh?" he said.

Ben nodded greetings. "North Side," he said.

"What you doing in our varrio?"

"Yeah, *ése*, we oughta slice you," said a short skinny kid, not more than fourteen, who kept one hand in his pocket. To get away clean, Ben knew he could knock the big guys down and run, but he wouldn't know where the kid was. He would just know to expect a sharp blade cutting and slicing from all sides until his clothes were soaked with blood.

He took two steps back. "Listen, *vatos*, I don't mean no disrespect to your varrio. I'm campaigning for Bañuelos. She's a Chicana, man, running for president."

With one hand in his pocket, he grasped the handle of his knife, just in case.

He told them that *gabachos* had been running *Aztlán* since they took it from Mexico in 1848. Even before that, he explained, the Europeans of Mexico ran the lives of Indians, of brown people. And today things are just as bad. He gave them a few examples of injustices he had seen in his own barrio, police brutality, poverty, hardworking Chicanos accused of being lazy, and they could relate. They nodded their heads.

As long as other people ran things, he said, Chicanos were always going to be fighting each other. Even though they didn't have a chance in winning the national election, the process, he said, was a means of unification. Even if only for a moment, he said, we need to come together and acknowledge who the enemy truly is. He went on and on and at some point he ceased to know what he was saying; all he knew was that he was using words to do the one thing he had to do: survive. Ah, the power of language!

It worked.

Giving him the Chicano handshake, they said he could stay, and they even pointed out houses of people they knew. "If they give you any problem about being in the neighborhood, just tell 'em 'F 14' sent you."

When the elections were over, Ben turned in an essay on the importance of the Bañuelos campaign to Chicano unity, an historical perspective. One day Mr. Shell held the report in his hands. To the surprise of everyone in the class, he said, "This is the best paper I've ever read on this assignment, Ben. This is college-level work. I hope you're going to college, Ben."

He looked into the turtle eyes of the teacher. "I was thinking of majoring in journalism," he said.

* * *

This network thing could be a big break for him. Twenty-four-hour news. It was a start. But to what? Where would he wind up? The Chicano Walter Cronkite? When he arrived at his condo after meeting with Mara, he was both excited and depressed. He hated himself, but he didn't know why. Picking up the phone, he pushed the numbers of home. His father answered. "Yeah?"

"Hey, Dad."

"Junior?"

"No, Dad, the other one."

"Hey, hey, the reporter. Benny boy!"

"How you doing?"

"Your dumb brother got beat up again. Third time in three months."

"Is he all right?"

"Yeah. Just a little bruised."

"How'd it happen?"

"Pulled him out of his car this time. You still got that Cadillac?"

"It's a Honda. Yeah, I still got it."

"How much did that thing cost?"

"Eighteen."

"Hundred?"

"Thousand."

"Woo. Bought this house for less than that. You should be buying property with your money. Don't be an idiot all your life."

"Guess what, Dad?" He wanted to say something dramatic, like, "I'm going to be famous," but he couldn't say anything about it, in case it didn't come true.

He found himself saying, "I'm coming home. I have a week vacation coming up."

"Yeah. So, why are you spending it here? I thought you went to Europe for your vacations."

"That was only once."

"How much did you spend on that vacation?"

"I don't remember."

"More than I paid for my Oldsmobile, I'll bet."

"Anyway, I'm coming home."

"Why?"

"I need to be with family."

Ramiro understood that. "When you coming home?"

"I could probably drive out there in a few weeks. Where's Ma?"

"She went to get Junior. He was in the drive-thru at Arby's. Wanted to get a sandwich."

"You sure he's okay?"

"Yeah, yeah."

"Okay, Pop. Expect me, huh? I'll be seeing you."

"Okay. Bye."

"Bye."

He heard himself say "Pop." He had never used that word before.

Pop.

Why didn't he speak Spanish with his father? Was he getting rusty? Plenty of white people in Portland spoke it, but what was the point when they could talk more easily in English? In fact, every time some white person tried to talk to him in Spanish, it pissed him off, although he wasn't sure why.

He flicked on the lights in the hallway and saw his full-body reflection in the mirror at the end. Walking closer, he got bigger and bigger until he stood in front of himself. He pulled off his shirt and tossed it on the floor. His pants dropped. His thighs were fat. And his waist: Fat.

He was getting fat. Fighting for his people is what he used to be about, but ever since he'd been away from *Aztlán*, all he took care of was himself.

Stepping out of his underwear, he picked up the phone to call Mara's home.

"Guess what I'm doing?"

"Why are you talking Spanish?"

"Guess what I'm? . . ."

"I don't know. "

"Looking at myself. You were right."

"You see it?"

"I do."

He asked her to arrange a vacation, but she said it was impossible. The network hadn't made their final decision.

"Come on, Mara, please."

"You do want this, don't you?"

"I do. I want it."

"I'll tell you what," she said in English. "Let's do something substantial first, something we can show the network, something that shows not only how smart you are, but how good you look. They're also considering an African American woman in Phoenix. You can have your vacation later. Have you thought about any of the ideas?"

"I like the gang thing," he said.

"Let's drive around tomorrow, you know, through the gang neighborhoods."

"The angle might be radical," he warned. "Tell it like it is. I know in *Califas*, most of those gang members are pretty political. They know what's going on. And the fact is, they don't like white people."

"Any way you want."

"I want. . . ."

Please hurry. He wanted to get there early. He followed the click of her heels. She pulled keys from her coat pocket, and whispered, "Be patient."

She didn't need to be there, he told her.

"I want to be there," she said, flicking on the lights of her office. After checking her messages and returning one call, she said, "Okay, let's go," but then she stopped again to drink from a watercooler, and he wondered if she was trying to make him angry, as if she knew that somewhere on the streets of Portland there lay his answer, his reason for being so far from *Aztlán*, so far away.

Before they could get out of the studio, the station manager, Brad Myers, walked up to them. "Hi, Ben," he said, smiling big. Although in his late thirties, Brad looked like a twelve-year-old boy dressing up in his father's suit.

As Brad and Mara stood there, Ben walked down the hall to a couch. He sat and waited while they spoke in hushed voices, and he imagined what they were saying:

Brad: "What did he do when you told him he was fat?"

Mara: "What could he do? It's so obvious that he is."

Ben grabbed a fistful of flab above his belt.

Then he heard a voice calling from outside. At the end of the hallway stood Mara. "Come on, Ben," she said, holding the door open, sunlight coming through. "Let's get going."

They drove through narrow streets lined with shabby homes and corner stores until they spotted a small group of teenage Chicanos dressed like gang members hanging around on the sidewalk in front of a brick building.

"That's them," he said, pulling the van to the curb.

"Be careful," she said.

"You mean *they* better be careful," he said.

He got out of the van to greet them, but they weren't looking at him, they looked at Mara. So he looked too.

Watched her step out of the van.

She smiled at everyone, wondering why all the attention was on her.

Ben approached the homies. "Wass happenin'?" he asked.

They looked him up and down, then they looked back at Mara. One of the boys had flaring nostrils and he was tall, dark, and lean; and as he leaned against the brick wall, he looked at Ben through squinted his eyes, and said, "What you want, man?"

Ben guessed he was the leader.

"*¡Orale!* That's Ben Chávez, man. The *vato* on the news," said one of the gangsters, a small guy with a skinny face and shoulder-length hair that curled like Geri curls.

"That's right," Ben said. "What's your name?" he asked the leader.

"What you want, man?"

"He wants to interview us, I betcha, homes. Huh, ain't that right? You're doing a story on gangs and shit, huh?"

"Chicano street gangs," he confirmed.

"*Chale*, man. I don't want to be interviewed," said the leader.

Ben felt the gold watch heavy on his wrist, the necktie tight around his collar. "Listen, *ése*," he said, removing his tie and stuffing it in his pocket. "I'm from the barrio, too. *Serio*. I'm from *Califas*. Involved in the same damn shit. I wanna tell it like it is. White people don't know shit about us. I understand why you guys are in gangs, man. It's this *pinche* society, *¿verdad?* Brown people don't have a chance in this white, racist society."

The leader looked at Mara, then back at Ben. "What the fuck are you talking about?" He turned around and entered the building.

The guy with curls stood alone as his homeboys filed into the building behind the tall boy. "Hey, man don't pay no attention to Rafa, man. He hates everyone. *¿Sabes?* But I'll talk to you, man. I tell you everything, eh. When's this coming on TV and shit?"

Ben looked to Mara. "Get the camera," he said, entering the building.

The dim room was lit by lights above pool tables and the screens of video games. An Asian woman sat on a stool behind a bar where soft drinks and cigarettes were sold. Some of the boys were setting up a game of pool, Rafa sitting on a wooden chair against the wall, his legs extended, arms crossed, like a hoodlum bored in class. Behind him pool cues hung on a wooden rack.

Ben undid his watch as they watched, tossed it on the middle of their pool table, and rolled up his sleeves, exposing his tattoo. Rafa looked up at him, shaking his head back and forth. "You're crazy, man."

"Listen," Ben said. "I don't know what impression you have of me, but I'm just a Chicano, all right? I mean no disrespect to your varrio, all right? I'm here because I need to tell your story. Please, let me tell your story."

Mara said it was the best interview Ben had ever done. They followed Rafa home, to school, out with his gang, and one night they even got some footage of his gang in a fight with an African American gang behind an abandoned building. It took a week to complete. Mara said that what Rafa talked about was wise and sad and naive all at once, a real testimony to society. It was a great piece.

Ben hated it.

He had wanted it to say something radical, but when Rafa got to the heart of what he wanted to say, Ben didn't want to hear it. Rafa had a dream of owning a house, having a wife and kids and "nice things." He had no consciousness of a political struggle, no concept of the Chicano Movement. He didn't even know who "Che" was. Rafa said that if he could go to college he would want to major in business. He could see himself as a businessman, "making all kinds of money and shit." Whenever Ben tried to get what he thought of society into the interview—whenever he suggested that it was racist and responsible for the condition of Chicanos—Rafa looked at him funny, looked at Mara, and back to Ben.

"Well, I don't know about that," Rafa would say, "but . . . ," and he'd continue saying things that hurt Ben to hear.

After Mara had taken the footage for editing, she called him and told him to come see it. He hadn't eaten at all that day because it didn't occur to him to eat. He was pacing his condo, naked, back and forth, faster and faster, full of energy but no way to expend it. The curtains and windows were open, the cold breeze flowing through.

"Brad wants to see it too," she said.

"You can watch it together. I'm staying home."

"Come on, Ben, be there. It really looks good. I'm serious. This is the best feature on gangs I've ever seen. Come see it. It'll blow you away."

He walked past the security desk of the station. He walked down the hallway to the viewing rooms and entered a door. Mara and Brad quit talking and looked at Ben. "Hi, Ben," Brad said.

The room was small with a large video monitor.

Ben sat down and looked at the screen. Mara started the tape. It ran for three to four minutes, each minute more and more painful to Ben, full of things he hated. When the tape was over, he felt like picking up the monitor and throwing it across the room.

"My God, Ben! That was incredible," said Brad.

The voice grated on him like a shovel on hardpan.

"Excellent. Excellent," Brad continued. "Ben, let me shake your hand."

Brad appeared in front of him, a sickeningly sincere look on his face, his hand extended. "Oh, Ben, the network's going to love this. And you look good in this piece. That coat compliments you."

"What do you mean by that?"

"You look good, that's all," he said, patting Ben on the shoulder, looking at Mara and smiling.

"Don't touch me," Ben said. "What the fuck do you mean that coat compliments me?"

"Er. . . ." Brad looked at Mara.

"Don't look at her, I'm talking to you. You think I'm too fat?"

"Ben," Mara said, putting her hand on his shoulder.

"Stay out of this." Then he looked into Brad's face. "You think I'm too fat?"

"Ben, I don't like this," Brad said.

"Of course you don't like it, stupid, I'm about to kick your ass."

He didn't remember the first hit to Brad's stomach, but somewhere he must have been thinking of holding back most of his rage because he didn't hurt him as bad as he could have. He didn't break his legs or kill him. He simply punched him on the body with a "thud thud thud" like in the movies, again and again.

Elena Díaz Björkquist

The Hershey Bar Queen

When she was a little girl, Reyna Lara was the same size as other children her age. As they grew up, however, the baby fat melted off the others, but Reyna's did not. Instead, she gained more and more weight. At first, it was not her fault. Her parents thought their one and only child was perfect with black sausage curls and cheeks like large ripe peaches. They pinched her cheeks and plied her with *pan dulce*, cookies, and candy. "Sweets for our sweet queen," they would tell her.

By the time she was seven, Reyna was the size of three girls her age and the other children made fun of her, calling her names like "Reyna, the big fat *ballena*." Her only playmates were her cousins, and they played with her because they were forced to by their parents. Reyna did not seem to care. Food was her main concern, and as she grew bigger and bigger, she had to consume even greater quantities to fuel her immense bulk. She took to visiting her grandmother every evening because Nana served dinner later than her mother. Reyna could eat another full meal there and Nana was liberal with seconds and sometimes thirds. Reyna's four aunts and three uncles also lived nearby and she picked up extra meals and snacks at their homes.

There was an emptiness inside Reyna—a hollow feeling she interpreted as hunger, but no amount of food could fill it, no matter how much she stuffed herself. She ate more than her father; probably more than anyone else in town, except for Doña Lupe. The last time that lady was seen outside her house, she could barely squeeze out a door. It was rumored that now she was so enormous, she could not get out of bed. All Doña Lupe did was eat, sleep, and read *True Confessions* magazines.

When Reyna was twelve years old, she stood five feet seven inches tall in her bobby socks and weighed 350 pounds. She towered a foot or more over the other girls her age and older. Reyna was taller, not to mention wider, than most women in Morenci, including her mother. Boys her age had not yet undergone growth spurts like the girls, so next to them Reyna was gigantic.

Despite being so large, Reyna was extremely graceful. When she walked, her tiny feet skimmed the earth as if held up by her buoyant body. The other children teased that she looked like a balloon in the Macy's Thanksgiving Day Parade. Their parents thought so, too, but they kept it to themselves unless they were chiding their children for eating too much candy. "Quit it or you'll look like a balloon in the Macy's parade!"

The harassment Reyna suffered from schoolmates grew so severe she took to ducking into the Taylor Dunne Mercantile Store every day after school so she would not have to walk home with them. Reyna strolled up and down aisles stacked high with cans and boxes of food. She wandered through the fresh vegetable section and thought about what Mamá and Nana might be preparing for dinner. She envisioned *tacos, enchiladas, mole, chile verde, gorditas, frijoles, calabacita, burritos,* and dozens of other delicious Mexican dishes, and her empty stomach grumbled its complaint. Reyna took a huge sack lunch to school every day, but it was not enough to sustain her until dinner.

When she thought the other children had enough head start, Reyna went to the candy counter. By this time in her life, her parents were concerned about her weight and were afraid she would wind up like Doña Lupe, so they limited her intake of sweets. They allowed her to buy only one candy bar each day and Reyna was obedient. Of course her parents did not know about the extra meals she obtained from the relatives.

"What'll it be today, Reyna?" asked the clerk. "A plain Hershey or one with almonds?" Reyna always left the pleasure of deciding until the last moment. There was no rhyme or reason as to which one she chose. Some weeks she picked Hersheys with almonds five days in a row and other weeks she alternated them with plain Hersheys every other day. Regardless of which she chose, Reyna always took her chocolate treasure across the large Plaza parking lot to the foot of the grand staircase leading up to the new shopping center. She could have taken the shortcut across the footbridge over the road but avoided it with reason.

When she used to cross the two-way bridge, people coming toward her would have to retreat and wait until she crossed. There was no way that anyone, not even a small toddler, could squeeze past Reyna. She filled the passageway from one side to the other. Her girth was such that she could not even turn around on the narrow bridge. One day she attempted it and got wedged in so tight she could not move. The old men who sat in front of the T.D. store buying and selling coupon books rushed to her rescue. They extricated her from this humiliating predicament by shoving and tugging until she popped out like the first pickle in a jar. She landed on the nearest elderly man, who was never the same after that. Meanwhile the children gathered on both sides of the bridge laughed and taunted her.

"Reyna's a *ballena!*" they yelled.

"She's so big and fat she can't cross the bridge!"

"Reyna's so big, she could be the bridge!"

After that, Reyna never went on the footbridge again.

There was another shortcut. It went under the bridge and across the road to a steep staircase behind the Royal Theater, but it was also a problem for Reyna. Nearly a hundred narrow steps led to the top with only one place to rest halfway up. There was no shade where she could stop to eat her Hershey bar. The only time she had gone that route, Reyna thought she would die before she reached the upper level.

So Reyna was forced to take the grand staircase, although it was the longer route to her house. The WPA had built the staircase during the Depression and it was grand indeed. Two sixty-foot-tall cypress trees flanked it at the bottom, and the wide stairs meandered uphill as if leading to a mansion. Her grandfather had helped lay the steps and walls enclosing the staircase, and Reyna always remembered him when she touched the stones worn smooth by thirty years of use.

Reyna's daily ritual was to sit on the wall shaded by the nearest tree and pull off the Hershey bar's brown outer wrapper. She sniffed it with delight, anticipating the taste of warm chocolate. The candy was usually melted, so she licked it off the inner wrapper. This was the way she liked it best, and since it was the only candy bar she could have, she savored every smidgen of chocolate her tongue lapped off the waxy white lining.

When every trace of chocolate had vanished, she crumbled the wrappers and tossed them under the cypress where they joined an ever-growing pile. Then Reyna commenced to climb the grand staircase, feeling like a queen. She paused now and again to rest on the stone wall and gaze down at the cars in the lot below. Some days, if she were lucky, she spotted one of her uncle's cars and went back down the stairs no matter how far up she was. She sat in the car and waited until its owner came out and drove her home. If she were not so lucky—which was more often the case, she climbed two more sets of stairs behind the post office and a large hill before she reached home.

* * *

On the day that would change the course of her life forever, Reyna saw Beto Cisneros sitting on the wall near the top of the stairs. He was sixteen years old and in tenth grade. He would have been in eleventh grade if he had not flunked fifth. Normally, he did not bother glancing her way, much less speak to her, but on this day he surprised Reyna.

"Would you like a Hershey?" Beto asked. He held it out to her but pulled it back when she reached for it. "No. First I want to show you something." He grabbed her hand and pulled her toward the ivy-covered wall next to the power and light building.

Reyna was not sure what was happening so she locked her legs in place and yanked Beto toward her. He bounced off her body and plopped on the ground.

"It's okay, Reyna." Beto got up and offered his hand to her. "I just want to show you my secret hiding place. Come on."

Someone offering to share a secret hiding place, his hand, and a Hershey? No one in Morenci outside her family ever showed such kindness to Reyna. She went with him.

Beto led her up a sloping ivy-covered path alongside the retaining wall. In all the times Reyna passed by here she never noticed the overgrown path. Halfway to the top of the forty-five-foot-high wall, Beto stopped.

"Let's go in here." He pushed his way through overhanging ivy onto a four-foot-wide ledge jutting out from the wall. Originally intended by the builders as a planter to break the expanse of rock wall, it once contained flowers, but now a jungle of ivy made the ledge invisible to passersby below. A shiver of anticipation went through Reyna as she joined Beto. Two Hersheys in one day!

"Sit." Beto pulled her onto the cushion of cool leaves next to him. "No one can see us here. This is my secret place. Nobody else knows about it, so swear you won't tell anyone, not even your mother."

"I swear not to tell," Reyna said. Who would she tell? She had no friends, no one with whom she could share such an important secret.

"You have to do more than swear," Beto said. "You have to seal your oath."

"Seal my oath?" Reyna smelled the chocolate sweetness of the melted candy bar as Beto wafted it under her nose. A Hershey with almonds! Reyna licked her lips and her tongue encountered a smear of chocolate from the candy she had eaten only minutes before. She swiped it off with her tongue and its taste made her hunger for more. She reached out for the Hershey, craving it as if it were the last one on earth.

"No," said Beto. "First we seal the oath. We're going to form a secret club. I'm the leader and you'll do everything I say from now on."

"Okay. Fine," Reyna said. She eyed the Hershey in Beto's hand and hoped he would let her have it before it melted further. Reyna liked it melted on the outside but preferred the inside to be solid enough to get her teeth into it.

"Lay down and close your eyes." Beto pointed to the bed of ivy.

Reyna obeyed him, but when she felt her dress slide up, her eyes flew open. "What are you doing?" She struggled to sit up.

"I'm not going to hurt you," Beto said. He nudged her back down. "This is what friends in our club do when they like each other. Close your eyes and relax. You don't have to do anything else."

Friends? Like each other? Not since she was a little girl had anyone offered to be her friend, much less say they liked her. Reyna lay back down—her eyes squeezed shut. She felt Beto slip off her underpants and climb on top of her. Suddenly, something poked her down there in that place her mamá had told her not to touch except when she wiped after peeing.

"Oomph!" Reyna's eyes popped open. Something was now inside her pee place and Beto bucked up and down like one of the cowboys Reyna saw riding the bulls at the rodeo.

"Ahh!" Beto grimaced as if something exploded inside him. His body went slack and he lay on her for a few minutes before rolling off and pulling up his jeans.

"That's it," he said. "Your oath is sealed. Here's the Hershey and your *chones*. Remember you can't tell anyone about this place or what we do in our secret club." He crawled through the leafy undergrowth back to the path.

Reyna sat up with her tent-sized panties in one hand and the Hershey in the other. She threw down the panties and ripped open the candy bar. Reyna's teeth scraped the entire gooey mess into her mouth. The delectable chocolate melted on her tongue and oozed down her throat.

There was something strange about what happened with Beto, but Reyna did not know what. It couldn't be wrong, could it? Beto was her friend and he said he liked her. Reyna chomped the almonds and twin streams of chocolate sluiced down either side of her mouth. At the same time, she became aware of a sticky wetness between her legs. She took a hanky out of her pocket and wiped herself. The handkerchief looked like someone with a bad cold had blown his nose in it. There was a tinge of blood running through the mucus. Had Beto broken something down there? Maybe she'd ask her mother when she got home. But no, she couldn't do that. She had promised Beto. Reyna stuffed the hanky in the ivy, put on her panties, and went home.

A couple of days later, Beto was again waiting at the staircase. He flashed the Hershey at her and led the way up the path. Without his help, Reyna found it difficult to maneuver her bulk up the steep slope. By the time she reached the ledge, she was panting.

"Take them off and lay down," Beto said. "I'll give you the Hershey when we're done sealing the oath." He mounted her and repeated what he had done earlier, except he did not take as long. "Remember this is our secret—don't you tell." He handed her the Hershey and left.

Reyna ate the candy with gusto, licking the wrapping and her fingers to get every last bit of chocolate. When she wiped herself this time, there was no blood on the handkerchief. She wadded it up and stuck it in the ivy. Maybe she'd better carry Kleenex. Her mother might get suspicious about too many lost hankies.

For the next month Reyna counted on getting an extra Hershey two or three times a week. Then one day she found Matt Sandoval instead of Beto waiting for her on the staircase. He flaunted two Hersheys.

"I'm in the club," he said. He turned and went up the ivy-covered trail. Reyna trudged behind him. More chocolate and a new friend!

In the weeks that followed, Sammy García, Tony Moreno, Andrés Solano, and Martín Hernández had all joined the club. By the end of the year, Reyna had many more new friends and had gained twenty-five pounds.

* * *

By the time she was in eleventh grade, Reyna weighed 439 pounds. The young men in Morenci called her the "Hershey Bar Queen" behind her back. When she was fifteen, her Aunt Tilly, who was seven years older, told her about sex. So now Reyna knew what the boys did to her on the ivy leaves was wrong. Every Saturday, when she dutifully waited in line to confess her sins, she thought about telling Father O'Hara. But how could she betray her friends? The boys were her only friends. The girls hated her. They made snide remarks about her weight and Reyna had had several fights in the girls' bathroom at school. Her bulk was an advantage and each scuffle ended with Reyna sitting on her antagonist. Nowadays no girl dared confront her, but Reyna still heard them whispering about her.

By now Reyna was a mother confessor to most of the boys. They sought her out not just for sex, but as someone they entrusted with their joys and tribulations. They called her "Big Reyna" and felt comforted when she hugged them to her mountainous bosom. Reyna was a good listener and only offered advice when they asked for it. She did not condemn or criticize and was quick to offer encouragement. The boys made her feel needed. No, there was no way she could tell the priest about them and the Hershey Club.

Sometimes she felt guilty about holding back something she knew was a sin—especially on Sundays when she received Holy Communion. She was afraid that one day the Host would burn through her tongue as it dissolved. It would be God's way of punishing her for not confessing all her sins. Reyna was not even sure if she were committing a venial sin or a mortal one since the nuns had never mentioned anything about sex in catechism. She prayed it was the lesser one.

Toward the end of the school year, students prepared for the Junior Prom. When Mrs. Ames, the school secretary, posted the nominee list for king and queen on the bulletin board outside the office, Reyna was thrilled to discover her name on it. Her Hershey boys had come through! She had never been to a dance or even had a date. Now she was not only going to the prom, the biggest formal dance of the year, but the prom committee had nominated her for queen. That was all she could think about day and night in school and at home. In Home Economics, she forgot to take her cake out of the oven and the whole school was evacuated when smoke set off the fire alarm. Homework went unfinished. Teachers' questions she had not heard, and could not have answered anyway, interrupted her daydreaming in classes.

Her mother sewed all of Reyna's clothes since there were no store-bought dresses in her size. While other young women went to Safford to try on and purchase their gowns, Reyna and Señora Lara went to study the designs. In the end, they combined various styles and purchased yards of expensive satin, ribbons, and lace. Señora Lara spent hours sewing a gown fit for a queen. Reyna went on a diet, limiting herself to meals at home. She squirreled away Hershey bars from her assignations with the young men. The treasure house of chocolate she was hoarding tempted her to indulge, but Reyna disciplined herself. By the time she figured out she could exchange her favors for the promise of votes for prom queen instead of candy, the collection of Hersheys cached in the ivy was more than adequate for a super binge after the prom.

The night of the prom arrived and Harold Pankovich, who had been nominated for king, came for Reyna in his father's GMC pickup. Harold stood a foot shorter than she did and weighed about 110 pounds in his rented tux and black high-top basketball shoes. He had a reputation for being the most obnoxious person in all of Morenci High School history, but he was Reyna's friend and she overlooked his idiosyncrasies. When Harold saw Reyna in her strapless evening gown, he almost dropped the gardenia corsage he was holding.

"Wow! You look fantastic!" he said. He stood on tiptoes and attempted to pin the corsage on the layers of ruffles adorning her décolletage.

Señora Lara, who had been admiring the product of her handiwork, came to his assistance when she noticed Harold's fumbling fingers brushing the tops of Reyna's breasts. Señor Lara brought out his Polaroid camera and took a series of black-and-white photos of Reyna by herself and with Harold. As it turned out later, he was grateful he had.

Reyna and Harold entered the school gym and stopped to admire the tropical jungle decor. A momentary silence greeted them as everyone turned to stare at them. They walked to the table reserved for the royal nominees, unaware of the snickering and whispering they left behind them. The music started and boy after boy came to Reyna's table to reserve a dance with her. It was a perfect evening as far as Reyna was concerned. Her dance card was full and she basked in all the attention she received. She felt like she was already the prom queen.

During an intermission, Reyna went to the bathroom in the girls' locker room. She was in the large stall at the far end struggling with unfamiliar garter belt and stockings when she heard a girl in the next stall mention her name.

"Did you see Big Reyna?" asked the girl. Reyna recognized Sharon Martínez's voice. "She looks like a wedding cake in that grotesque dress."

"Yeah, a wedding cake for a giant," said another girl. This one sounded like Priscilla Ayala. Both girls giggled. "It must have taken fifty yards of material to make her gown."

"A strapless gown . . . can you imagine? Every time she went out to dance, I thought her boobs would pop out. They must be the size of watermelons!" said Sharon. "If I were that fat, I'd be too embarrassed to leave my house."

Reyna grappled with the garter belt. Damn! Maybe it was supposed to go on over the panties not under. Yards of satin and lace ruffles impeded her attempts to fasten the stockings. Her face flushed. A wedding cake? Watermelon breasts? But Harold said she looked fantastic . . . and the boys had all signed her dance card.

"She has no shame," said Priscilla. "She was flaunting her boobs at all the guys who danced with her."

"What do you expect from someone who's slept with every guy in the school for Hershey bars?" said Sharon.

"She's going to get hers tonight," said Priscilla. "I bet she really believes she's going to get crowned tonight." Both young women laughed and flushed their toilets simultaneously.

"When we counted the votes today, the Hershey Bar Queen had just one vote—hers!" said Sharon. "I can hardly wait to see her face when Sal announces the last runner-up and hands her a Hershey bar in front of the whole school." The girls' laughter echoed off the metal lockers.

Hot tears sprang to Reyna's eyes and mascara flowed down her rouged cheeks. She wiped the tears, smearing her face red and black like the school colors. Wait a minute, how did the girls know about the Hershey Club? The boys had to have told them. Reyna felt a pain in her heart as if a bolt of lightning had ripped through it. How could they? It was supposed to be a secret. All these years she had kept her promise. Why hadn't they? Out of the hurt, a deep rage exploded. She clenched her fists and plunged out of the stall, ripping the locked door off its hinges.

In the mirror, Sharon and Priscilla glimpsed a bulk of white racing toward them—Reyna snorting like an enraged bull. The young women were so scared they forgot to run. Reyna grabbed each one by their fancy hairdos and shook them like rag dolls. She flung their bodies into the toilet stalls.

Turning to leave, Reyna saw herself in the mirror. What a mess! Her curls, which had been piled high in an upswept hairdo, tumbled around her head like worms with hairpins stuck in them. Mascara mingled with rouge flowed down her huge cheeks like lava from a volcano. For the first time in her life, Reyna saw herself as others saw her. Her fist pounded her reflection, splintering the mirror. Blood spurted out of her wounded hand and spilled onto the delicate lace of her dress. Intense hatred overcame her—hatred of the Hershey boys and of herself.

Reyna stormed out of the bathroom and into the gym, pushing aside anyone who got in her way. One shove from Reyna was enough to topple even Buzz Owens, the biggest football player on the team. Harold approached her and Reyna ran right over him like a locomotive. As Reyna made her way to the exit, she pulled down crepe paper streamers and balloons. The cardboard murals of exotic jungles painted by the art classes crashed to the floor. A path of devastation lay in Reyna's wake. Teachers and students alike were so stunned they didn't even try to stop her.

Anger and hatred fueled Reyna as she tackled the 357 steps that led up from the high school to the Plaza. Usually it took her forever to climb this steep staircase because she could not go more than ten or twelve stairs without stopping to rest. But this night, she flew over three and sometimes four steps at a time. At first Reyna did not know where she was going, but when she found herself at the foot of the grand staircase, she knew.

In the darkness, Reyna crawled onto the ivy-covered ledge and dug in the leaves for her cache of Hershey bars. She stuffed candy in her mouth as fast as she could get the wrappers off. Her jaws chewed the mass of hard chocolate—plain Hersheys and Hersheys with almonds—all mixed. Chocolate streamed down her chin and joined the other stains on her ruined gown. Bar after bar went into her cavernous mouth, but none of them brought the comfort she was seeking.

An almond stuck in her throat and Reyna tried to cough. She was choking. Desperate to breathe, she jumped up and the snaps on her garter belt broke. The belt slipped to her ankles, tripping her. Reyna reached out to grab the ivy to steady herself but she was facing the wrong way. Her hands closed on air. The tremendous weight of her upper body plunged her headfirst off the ledge into the ivy leaves below.

The townspeople organized a search party for Reyna that same night, but her body was not found until the next morning. Her parents were in shock. Señora Lara took to her bed clutching a tear-streaked snapshot of Reyna in her prom dress. Señor Lara was so distraught, his brother had to drive him to the mortuary in Clifton to arrange the funeral. Mr. Morrison informed them there were no caskets large enough for Reyna's body. He hated to do so because the markup on caskets was where he made most of his money. Reluctantly, he told them to ask Don Simón to custom-build a coffin. Don Simón was the former coffin maker who had been forced to retire when people preferred the fancy manufactured caskets to his wooden ones. It took him four days to build a specially reinforced coffin out of oak. Pine would have splintered under Reyna's immense weight.

On the day of the funeral, Holy Cross Church overflowed with family and parishioners and the entire population of Morenci High School—boys, girls, and teachers. Reyna's uncles had refused to carry the coffin because of their bad backs, so Señor Lara invited the football team to be pallbearers. It took the whole first string plus one—six on each side—to carry Reyna's coffin down the church's main aisle. Father O'Hara spoke about Reyna and how much she had suffered in her short life but was now finally at peace. Girls sobbed into their hankies, feeling guilty about never having befriended her. Boys had lumps in their throats and felt guilty about having taken advantage of her.

When the funeral mass was over, the football team loaded the coffin onto their shoulders again and trudged down the aisle. Outside the church, just before the steps, Buzz Owens slipped on what later turned out to be a melted Hershey bar—plain with no almonds. He tried to regain his balance, but the coffin weighed him down and he stumbled into Larry Rodríguez, who fell into Jorge Gutiérrez, who knocked over Salvador Tamayo, the heavy coffin crashing over all of them. It smashed into Beto Cisneros's groin and the blow was such that he was never able to father any children. The coffin slid down the stairs and knocked over several other young men who did not get out of the way fast enough. By the time Reyna's coffin came to a rest at the foot of the stairs, it had managed to injure over twenty young men. Each of the football players had broken something—an arm, a leg, a wrist, an ankle. It was a good thing the football season was over, otherwise Morenci could not have fielded a team that year.

Reyna's funeral turned into a shambles of broken bodies and screaming girls. When her uncles went to put the lid back on the coffin, they noticed Reyna had an angelic smile. It struck them as strange because when Reyna's casket lay open at the Rosary the night before, she was not smiling. With much effort, the older men of the parish loaded the huge coffin into the hearse and Reyna was finally laid to rest in the cemetery next to the smelter.

As far as the young men of Morenci were concerned, however, Reyna's spirit was never laid to rest. Those who went past the ivy-covered stone wall, where they had exchanged Hershey bars for Reyna's favors, heard the leaves rustle as if someone were tossing and turning on the ledge above. They caught a faint scent of chocolate as if someone were eating a Hershey bar next to them. Soon they sought other ways to get to the post office, although the grand staircase was the most direct route from the high school. Several years later, when T.D. tore down Morenci for the ever-expanding copper mine, men who did not go to school in Morenci and did not know about Reyna had to smash the stone wall. The local young men refused to go near it.

Years later, when dynamite blasts obliterated Morenci and only the rocky levels of the open-pit mine marked where the town once stood, workers reported that there was a certain spot on a certain level where they heard leaves rustling and smelled chocolate. The young men who had known Reyna shivered every time they heard about it. They were destined never to forget Reyna, the Hershey Bar Queen.

Pablo La Rosa

La muerte de Marielito

A mí, a mí me tocó hacer el cuento, escribirle a su madre allá en el barrio de Buena Vista, municipio de Marianao, ciudad de la Habana Cuba, Territorio Libre de América, para relatarle esta infinita y honda tristeza circular como el pentagrama de un blues, contarle que su hijo yace enterrado junto a su hijo—su nieto—en una fosa sin lápida del cementerio para negros pobres Lincoln de la ciudad de Kansas City, condado de Jackson, estado de Missouri, muerto de una puñalada que le atravesó el pulmón izquierdo y le vació el dolor a su corazón tal como él lo profetizara, será cubano el que me mate y lo hará a traición, no hay quien se atreva de frente, la historia se repite Chano Pozo, adiós mi amigo del alma, adiós.

Soy un mierda, esto es para lo único que sirvo, plagiar la realidad de un idioma para otro (beware of the bilingual man, for he sucks with a forked tongue), contar lo ocurrido sin haber participado en ello, lo había previsto y no hice nada por impedir ese suicidio, porque desde que su hijo—su nieto—murió él la buscaba, la muerte quiero decir, la citaba como Roldán el Temerario en los callejones sin salida del cuadro vicioso Main-Linwood-Troost-calle 39-Main, la desafiaba él solo contra dos o tres, se reía del chulo más guapo, se singaba a las putas sin pagarles, les quitaba el dinero a los vendedores de cocaína hasta que la mujer de Angola se enamoró de él y se lo llevó a vivir con ella mientras Angola cumplía los meses que le faltaban de su última condena por atraco. Angola se enteró que le estaban poniendo los tarros por boca de un mariel que entraba y se lo mandó a decir por boca de otro que salía de la cárcel, cuando salga te mato acere, aunque seamos compañeros de Guanajay y hermanos del éxodo no te lo puedo perdonar, tú sabes que soy muy hombre y que en Cuba yo maté por una bofetada, a lo que su hijo contestó que lo pensara bien, que una puta como la Yoán no merecía un muerto, y que si lo mataba no resolvería nada porque él, Angola, acabaría en la federal de Atlanta por los siglos de los siglos o en la silla eléctrica, porque aquí a los negros asesinos los hacen chicharrón y la puta de Yoán seguiría dándole la papaya a quien le diera la gana por un pito de piedra de cocaína.

Angola se encabronó tanto con la respuesta que no esperó a que se vencieran los dos meses de la condena. Aprovechó que es medio pigmeo para meterse en un túnel de ventilación y se escapó una noche oscura con el alma de ansias de venganza inflamada. Pasó por el cubil de Yoán y, no encontrando a nadie, cogió un cuchillo y fue derecho al *Who Cares—So What*, antro sito en la 39 esquina a Troost donde los marieles se juntan todas las noches para olvidar sus penas y donde, por más señas, una madre adolescente canjeara ha pocos meses a su neonato por una piedra de crack valorada en veinte dólares. Señora, usted podrá entender que el nombre de ese bar, el *Qué carajo importa—Qué más da*, en traducción libre, expresa de manera sucinta la desmoralización total tanto del negro americano como la del marielito (blanco, mulato o negro) que pulula en el ghetto de Kansas City. Su hijo, que yo sepa, no solía meterse ahí antes de que su hijito muriera, pero después de la tragedia iba a parar allí las más de las noches cuando soltaba del trabajo. En efecto, Angola lo encontró bailando con la Yoán y lo embistió cuchillo en alto. No gritó, no lo llamó, lo agarró por la espalda y le enterró el cuchillo haste el topete. Pititi, un matanzero que estaba presente, me dijo que la puñalada fue tan certera que su hijo se desplomó al instante. Cuando la ambulancia por fin llegó al cabo de los 15 minutos (porque si la llamada de socorro proviene del ghetto las ambulancias no se apuran demasiado) ya toda su amargura, su infinita infelicidad y su vida estaban coaguladas sobre el cochino piso del *Qué carajo importa—Qué más da*.

Señora, quiero decirle que su hijo no era malo, aunque tampoco sería un ángel negro, ya que tengo entendido que en Guanajay no se expían pecados veniales. Él nunca me aclaró por qué estaba cumpliendo 20 años de condena allá cuando Fidel jodió a Jimmy Carter mandándole a los presos y demás indeseables que estaban contaminando su utopía socialista, pero le puedo asegurar que su hijo no cometió ninguna de las barbaridades que han dado tan mala fama a los marielitos de Kansas City con bastante razón. Siendo cubano bilingüe de la primera generación (los *buenos* cubanos, los valientes de Bahía de Cochinos que no los marranos del Mariel), la Corte Municipal me paga U.S. $30.00 la hora por bifurcar mi lengua y hacerla cacarear en ambos idiomas, sirviendo de malinche a mis desafortunados compatriotas que se meten en líos con una espontaneidad espasmosa y frecuentemente sangrienta. Como aquel monstruo que mató a su mujer y a su hijo de dos años de un chongonazo calibre .12 porque le paració que ella había estado sateando con otro hombre en un bailecito de la Asociación de Cubanos de Kansas City. O el compatriota que le obsequió 18 puñaladas a su exnovia el día de su onomástico (una "vela" por cada año, dijo) porque ella lo había dejado. Sin embargo, quizás el más repugnante de todos los crímenes haya sido el del santiaguero que le empujó un puñal *por el ano* a una ramera que le había robado la cartera. ¿En Cuba ahora se acostumbra matar por el culo? Yo sé que Jack the Ripper mataba por el bollo, pero ¿por el culo? En contraste, a veces se dan casos cómicos. Hace poco trajeron a una paraja de invertidos que se había peleado a causa de celos. El agraviado había agredido a su amado con un cuchillo, hiriéndole el hombro ligeramente. Era obvio que lo pudo matar si hubiese querido, pero apenas quería asustarlo o escarmentarlo. El juez, después de echarle sólo tres meses por tratarse de violencia hogareña, me rogó le explicara a Serafín (le juro que así se llamaba) que en esta sociedad no se resuelven las discordias a cuchilladas como acostumbra hacerse en culturas atrasadas. Serafín lo meditó profundamente. Su respuesta, al paracer sincera, me dejó tartamudo: no lograba que mi lengua postiza fonetizara las sílabas, aunque el cerebro ya había procesado la traducción y las palabras se agolparan tras el dique de la garganta: "Dile al juez que el problema es que en Cuba no se pueden conseguir pistolas tan fácil como aquí." El juez no le encontró ninguna gracia a esta explicación tipo Nananina Trespatines y le añadió tres meses a la condena por su socarronería.

A su hijo también lo conocí en la corte, pero su caso fue más bien tragicómico, digno de risa y mucha lástima. Figúrese usted que lo acusaban de robarse unas prendas de ropa de la tienda que el Salvation Army puso en la calle Main. Por si usted no lo sabe, es una tienda de segunda mano donde prácticamente se regalan las cosas que los ricos tiran a la basura: camisas a 50 centavos, pantalones a peso, abrigos a cinco, planchas eléctricas a dos. A su hijo lo acusaban de romper la vidriera y llevarse un bulto de ropa y una tostadora destartalada. Imagínese, para la mayoría de los americanos robarle al Salvation Army equivale a asaltar al mismo Jesucristo. El juez estaba echando chispas. Pidió explicaciones, y su hijo contó que volviendo del trabajo a medianoche había pasado delante del Salbechon y vio que la vidriera estaba hecha añicos. Sabiendo que era una tienda para ayudar a los pobres y como él era pobre, no le vio ningún daño meter la mano y llevarse unas cuantas pantaletas porque su jeva estaba en regla y las pocas que ella tenía estaban manchadas de sangre. Me daba tanta vergüenza tener que traducir eso delante de las damas que estaban presentes en la corte que me acerqué al juez y se lo comuniqué al oído. El juez miró a su hijo con ganas de fulminarlo y dictaminó que lo robado en este caso no importaba tanto, que estaba dispuesto a dejarlo libre bajo palabra si su hijo pagaba la vidriera rota. Entonces aprendí que su hijo era muy distinto a los demás. Insistió que él no había roto ninguna vidriera y por eso no la pagaba. El abogado y yo le aconsejamos que aceptara la propuesta del juez, pero él se negó y su señoría le echó 30 días en la granja.

Pasó cerca de un año antes de que volviera a ver a su hijo, cosa rara porque como ya le conté, los marieles pasan por la corte como Pepa por su casa. Esta vez lo habían prendido por prevenir a unos hombres que la mujer que los estaba engatusando ahí en la esquina de la Linwood y Main no era puta como ellos pensaban sino policía secreta disfrazada de ramera. Su hijo había observado como caían los inocentes en la trampa y le dio rabia que la jara se valiera de ardides tan traicioneros para engañar a la gente. Por señas y en su inglés chapurreado logró espantar de las garras de la señuelo a los dos hombres que se disponían a sellar el trato para que les mamaran la pinga. Salieron como un cohete Linwood arriba y se salvaron de la (in)justicia, pero la polizonte llamó a la jaula con su guoqui toqui y se llevaron a su hijo para la jefatura.

El día del juicio, el abogado le aconsejó que inventara un cuento, que dijera

que él conocía a esos señores, que los estaba saludando, pero él se negó porque
según razonó éste es el país de la libertad y la policía no tiene derecho a prender
a un hombre porque tenga ganas de que le mamen la pinga, eso estaba bien que
pasara en un país comunista como Cuba donde hay que pedirle permiso a Fidel
hasta para tirarse un pedo, y el juez queriendo saber lo que decía y yo teniendo
que censurar lo último para salvarlo de un mes de cárcel por falta de respeto al tribunal. Aún así el juez le impuso $100 de multa, pero, como no pudo pagarla, lo
mandó a pasarse una semana en la granja. Su hijo me cayó tan simpático que por
primera vez desde que servía de intérprete me ofrecí a prestarle dinero a un
marielito para que no fuera preso. Él dijo que para él la granja era un hotel de lujo,
ya había estado allí y se comía bien, se jugaba a la pelota, al basket y a los billares,
ponían películas y se miraba la televisión. ¿Qué era una semana si en Cuba ya
había cumplido diez años pasando hambre y cogiendo palo cuando le dijeron que
podía largarse para Estados Unidos si firmaba un documento declarando que no
era preso político? En cambio me pidió prestados $5 para los cigarros de la se-
mana, petición que le concedí con gusto. También le di mi número de teléfono
para que me llamara cuando saliera de la granja si quería tomarse una cerveza conmigo un día.

Señora, le confieso que lo hice más por mí que por él. Le contaré que mi
familia me sacó de Cuba en el 59 y que después de un largo proceso de acul-
turación al sistema de vida anglosajón y de reprimir lo que consideraba vestigios
de una cultura inferior, me hallé soñando con la niñez abandonada a la carrera allá
en la Perla de las Antillas. Eso después de rechazar la ciudadanía cubana, jurar
fidelidad al águila calva, casarme con una WASP, tener tres hijos gringuitos
aunque no rubios como hubiera querido y vivir durante décadas en el corazón
geográfico-moral de este contradictorio país. De vez en cuando volvía a Miami
para tratar de desenterrar mis raíces cubanas, pero siempre regresaba a Kansas
City decepcionado, sintiéndome más ajeno—alejado de mis familiares, compa-
triotas—a la vez que tomaba conciencia de que tampoco nunca sería gringo
aunque lo deseara. Los sueños eran un consuelo mientras duraban, pero luego la
angustia era mayor al recordarlos sólo a jirones. Por esa época empecé a fumar
marijuana (si se entera la corte me quitan el trabajo, la ciudadanía y hasta mis
hijos) y descubrí que si me encerraba en mi despacho a escuchar discos de música
afrocubana bajo los efectos de la droga, me daba la ilusión de estar de vuelta en
mi pueblo. Créame que en algunas ocasiones la sensación fue tan verosímil que
me quedé dudando ¿Estaba yo a la sombra del almendro en el patio de Varadero
o en mi estudio en Kansas City escuchando "La fuente del ritmo" de Santana? Mi
amigo Kent, un místico mormón, me aseguraba que en efecto yo me trasladaba en
espíritu-alma al mundo de mi niñez. ¿No veía yo mi propio cuerpo exangüe,
desparramado por el suelo como sin vida? Eso era prueba suficiente del milagro.
Mi mujer, en cambio, opinó que me estaba volviendo neurótico y exigió que
dejara la droga. Tuve que acceder porque el mayor notó mi comportamiento

extraño y había preguntado qué olor tan raro era ése que salía del estudio de papá cuando ponía discos.

A falta de pan, casabe. Yo veía en los marielitos una fuente de informacíon que quizás pudiera ayudarme a rellenar esos huecos de la memoria colectiva que me hacen jalarme los pelos, pero los de inmigración me habían aconsejado que evitara su trato, consejo que consideraba sabio en vista de las atrocidades de que eran autores tantos de ellos. Mas el comportamiento de su hijo en la corte y la naturaleza tragicómica de sus supuestos delitos causaron que rompiera el bloqueo, y esa fue una de las pocas decisiones que he tomado en mi vida que no me pesan en absoluto.

Señora, yo sé que usted debe haber sufrido cantidades a causa de su hijo, pero puede tener la conciencia tranquila porque él siempre habló con mucho cariño y respeto de usted. La culpa no es suya. Yo sé que usted siempre se lo advirtió, no te apartes del camino por coger sendero, chivo que rompe tambor con su pellejo lo paga, etc. etc. La culpa de sus desgracias, según él, fue la cabrona calle donde se aprende la maldad. ¿Qué podía hacer usted sola y con tantos hijos? Darles consejos y soltarlos por las calles de la Habana para buscarse la vida. Enseñarles a mantener vivo ese instinto de sobrevivir a toda costa que los esclavos africanos trajeron al nuevo mundo, instinto que vino a manifestarse aquí en su deseo de tener un hijo aunque las condiciones no lo favorecían.

Cuando su hijo por fin me llamó varias semanas después del juicio para tomarnos la cerveza, me puse contentísimo porque pensé que ya se había olvidado de mí o que no quería trabar amistad conmigo. Recuerdo bien el día: una tarde lavada y almidonada de otoño, la mejor época aquí en el medio oeste. Crucé el puente sobre el Missouri, río anchísimo que ahora sirve de barrera entre el ghetto y los barrios blancos del norte. Claro que yo había atravesado el ghetto a menudo, pero siempre transitando por las autopistas y avenidas que están bien iluminadas y vigiladas por la policía. Hasta ese día, jamás me había bajado del carro en una calle del barrio negro, y tengo que admitir que si su hijo no me hubiera estado esperando sentado en la escalera del edificio donde vivía, creo que yo hubiese seguido de largo.

Señora, yo nunca entré a un solar de la Habana, pero no puedo concebir que sean tan deprimentes como estas casas de apartamentos. La pobreza es una cosa, pero estos barrios del ghetto representan algo mucho peor, esa actitud de qué carajo importa, qué más da. El letrero que Dante encontró a la entrada del infierno significa lo mismo. Es la vida sin esperanza, y sin ser sociólogo me explico por qué la materia prima de esa zona es el vidrio roto, fragmentos de un rompecabezas sin solución. Usted querrá saber cómo es que su hijo fue a parar allí. Pues bien, a los marielitos que habían estado presos, como él, allá en Cuba por delincuentes, los trasladan de las prisiones federales a lugares que llaman casas medias (o sea, mitad prisión, mitad hotelucho) para que aprendan a desenvolverse, bajo supervisión, en la sociedad ajena y se busquen trabajo de modo que no le cueste al agobiado pagaimpuestos norteamericano la manutención perpetua de inmigrantes indeseados. Una vez que encuentran empleo los sueltan para la calle aunque es obvio que no están preparados para triunfar por las buenas en una economía basada en el darwinismo spenceriano. Como la mayoría no habla, lee, ni escribe inglés bien, el único trabajo que encuentran es de lavaplatos o limpiamesas, y ese sueldo no da para el alquiler de un apartamento más o menos decente.

Su hijo fue a parar de cabeza a un edificio subvencionado por el municipio, situado en la 31 y Campbell, precisamente en el centro de la actividad cocainera. Con decirle que al apearme del carro me asediaron dos negritos adolescentes que querían venderme pastillas de crack a $5, porque según su hijo me explicó los únicos blancos que se aparecen por esos rumbos son drogadictos que van a comprar su vicio. En ese "proyecto", como les llaman aquí a las viviendas subvencionadas, conoció su hijo a la jeva de las pantaletas embadurnadas de sangre menstrual.

Ella había nacido y se había criado en tales edificios. Antes de mudarse al apartamento de su hijo, vivía con la madre inválida y una retahila de hermanos, hermanas y sobrinos de todas las edades. El padre estaba muerto hacía años; había sido alcohólico, les daba tremendas palizas a la madre (que por eso estaba inválida) y a los niños, y una noche el mayor se reviró y lo mató a martillazos. Usted quizás no pueda creer esa historia, pero le juro que es verdad, pues yo hice la investigación de la familia después que su nietecito murió. Porque yo estoy seguro (y su hijo lo intuía) que su nieto no falleció de causas naturales como lo indica el certificado de defunción, no. Sólo sabiendo la historia de esa familia se puede vislumbrar, aunque no entender ni mucho menos perdonar, la actitud que permitió a la joven madre matar a su hijo.

Señora, estoy convencido de que su hijo no estaba enamorado de ella, pero usted comprenderá que aquí los inviernos son infiernos y que su soledad tenía que ser la de un cimarrón en el monte. Por lo menos tenía un pedazo de carne al cual abrazarse por la noche, y sucedió lo inevitable. Ella salió preñada, y esa tarde de otoño cuando la conocí ya se le notaba el crío en el vientre. La sangre suya y de sus antepasados, señora, a través de su hijo iba a dar retoño en una tierra que en absoluto tiene que ver con la sabana africana o cubana. Pero su hijo estaba orgulloso de que su mujer estuviera encinta. Hasta ya había escogido el nombre que le daría al portavoz de su estirpe: Marielito (porque estaba seguro que sería varón), en honor al desdichado puerto que supuestamente le había dado la libertad.

Durante los meses que siguieron lo fui a buscar muchas veces. Me gustaba oírlo hablar. Resultó ser el informante de mis sueños. Oyéndolo, mi lengua materna recuperaba su elasticidad perdida, los fragmentos dispersos en la memoria se coagulaban en imágenes más vivas, más claras que las formadas otrora bajo los efectos de la mariguana. A través de sus palabras viví las horas triunfantes de Playa Girón, los días angustiosos de octubre, su participación forzosa en la zafra de los Diez Millones; a través de sus cantos la alegría de las rumbas callejeras, la risotada provocada por las congas de protesta contra las escaseces de la revolución: yo no quiero pollo, yo no quiero pan, lo que quiero es blume, pa tapalme el bollo.

Pero también sus comentarios me abrían los ojos a la vida en los Estados Unidos. En primer lugar, decía que, en efecto, los americanos tenían mucho dinero pero que no tenían corazones, al revés de los rusos. No entendía por qué aquí se gastaba tanto en construir carreteras en vez de fabricar casas para los pobres. Había dejado de comer pollo porque en su opinión la came de pollo aquí es sintética; nunca había visto una gallina viva en este país y además no es posible criar tanto pollo para abastecer todos los Kentucky Fried Chicken, como tampoco era posible criar tanto ganado para hacer los billones de hamburguesas que se vendían en McDonald's, las cuales las hacían de came, plástico y asfalto.

Pasaron los meses, y de buenas a primeras nace el chiquito. Su hijo me llamó desde el hospital para avisármelo y para pedirme que fuera a servirle de intérprete, porque había problemas y él no entendía lo que las enfermeras decían. Era bastante tarde y hacía un frío tremendo; le confieso que fui de muy mala gana. Estaban en el Truman Medical, que es el hospital para la gente que no tiene seguro médico, es decir los negros del ghetto. Él me estaba esperando en el vestíbulo y era claro que estaba muy agitado. Subimos al piso de maternidad y me señaló la incubadora donde pataleaba un bebito flaquito y pellejudo: "Baby Jones", porque como no estaban casados le dieron el apellido de la madre. Había nacido sietemesino, apenas pesaba cuatro libras y media y le habían metido tubos por todos los orificios del cuerpecito.

La enfermera de turno se acercó y explicó que el recién nacido tenía los síntomas de un crack baby. Quería decir, señora, que la madre era adicta a la cocaína y que el crío había heredado la adicción. Yo me quedé pasmado, porque su hijo no me había dicho que la mujer le metía a la cocaína. Le pregunté si él también la fumaba y dijo que no, que la había probado pero que se había dado cuenta que el camino de la droga conduce a un destino, la muerte, porque te matan o tienes que matar por ella; en cambio todos los hermanos de la mujer eran adictos y, aunque él se lo había advertido y le había pegado varias veces para que la dejara, no escarmentaba y aprovechaba cuando él estaba en el trabajo para saciar su vicio.

A la semana de estar en el hospital le desconectaron la tubería al chiquito y los echaron a él y a la madre para la calle, pues necesitaban la incubadora para otro bebito en las mismas condiciones. Cuando los fui a visitar al apartamento ese fin de semana, vi que el chiquito era un manojo de nervios y que no paraba de llorar. Su hijo lo cargaba y lo mecía con ternura, pero me fijé con pavor que la madre no quería nada que ver con él. Seguía pegada a la pantalla de la televisión como si no existiera. Ni le daba la teta, pues los médicos le dijeron que su leche estaba contaminada. En otras palabras, había perdido su instinto maternal. Era su hijo quien limpiaba y hervía los pomos, calentaba la leche sintética que les regalaban en el welfare y se la daba. Era su hijo quien le cambiaba los pámpers a Marielito cuando se ensuciaba.

No llegó al mes. Una noche, a eso de las dos, la llamada de su hijo me sacó de una pesadilla para hundirme en otra de la cual no había rescate. Estaba en la cárcel. Entre llantos me contó que al llegar a la casa de lavar platos a medianoche se había encontrado al chiquito como un trapo en la cunita y a la mujer en estado cataléptico, hipnotizada ante el televisor que nunca apagaba. Seguro de que ella lo había estrangulado o asfixiado porque la volvían loca sus interminables perretas, lo oyó a golpes con toda su fuerza y la hubiera matado si los hermanos suyos, que viven en el mismo piso, no se lo impiden.

Al principio, la policía pensó que su hijo había estrangulado al chiquito, y estoy seguro que, de haber sido cierto, lo hubieran achicharrado por ser marielito. Pero cuando las cosas se aclararon y se vio sin duda quién era la culpable, el certificado de la autopsia le achacó la defunción a esa misteriosa plaga que reclama a tantos angelitos negros del ghetto, la muerte de cuna. Y es que meter a una madre en la prisión por infanticida, de por vida, le cuesta al estado cientos de miles de dólares, y además la muerte de un negrito no representa una pérdida para la sociedad sino más bien un gran ahorro al welfare, así que qué carajo importa, qué más da que una madre negra mate a su hijo negro.

Señora, yo quisiera contarle lo contrario, escribirle que su hijo llegó a la tierra prometida y que, como yo, tuvo suerte, aprendió inglés, consiguió un buen trabajo y se casó con una mujer buena con quien tuvo tres hijos que triunfaron en este valiente nuevo mundo, pero la realidad es tan amarga y borrosa como el cafetazo que me he estado inyectando toda la noche, sin duda Charlie Parker se tragó noches aciagas como ésta que luego vomitó por el saxófago de fuego, pero yo no sé cantar blues para descargar esta honda tristeza, sólo puedo armonizar mi llanto interior con la lluvia fría y lenta que empezó a caer hace horas, vaciar mi dolor en esta carta que no sé cómo terminar porque se trata de un dolor circular como el pentagrama de un blues, la historia se repite, adiós mi amigo del alma, adiós.

Arturo Mantecón

An Imbalance of Humors

"Your phlegm is very tenacious . . . like glue. It clings to the inner lining of your lungs and is hard to dislodge. I'll write you a prescription for an inhalant—Ventolin. It will loosen your phlegm and make your cough more productive."

The thought of a more productive cough was almost too much for me to take. I had been coughing up a whitish mucosa for three weeks, coughing almost incessantly, coughing so much that my ribs had ceased to ache almost a week before. So copious was it that it struck me that my humors had become imbalanced. I even wondered if perhaps I shouldn't consult an Ayurvedic practitioner.

It was only after my phlegm had darkened in color (a sure sign of infection, I thought) that I had decided to make an appointment with Doctor Berlinda Flojo. I trust my Manila-born doctor, in spite of her peculiar tendency to suspect that every one of my ailments is due to parasites. She pronounced that I had bronchitis and prescribed the Ventolin, an antibiotic the name of which escapes me now, water by the bucketful, and plenty of bed rest.

I stopped working for a week and a half and took to bed and continued to cough, spewing out great sticky gobs of greenish brown phlegm. I quickly tired of running from my bed to the bathroom to spit my wad into the commode, so I kept an old plastic tumbler with a bit of water in it within easy reach. I would spit into this tumbler four or five times and then empty it out.

Wednesday, May 17, as I carried the tumbler to the bathroom, I stopped at the window to see what kind of day I was missing. There was a good wind blowing, and the sky was cloudless. The sun was almost at its zenith, its light overpowering and penetrating all and delineating everything it touched with an almost too extreme clarity. I averted my smarting eyes and glanced down into the shallow tumbler. I fancied I saw a kind of movement, a minute, quivering sort of flowing like unto a near-microscopic stream or rivulet upon the surface of my glutinous phlegm.

My first thought was that what I saw was merely the play of the sunlight reflecting off my mucus. I closed the blinds and examined the contents of the tumbler under the light of a small lamp by my bed. I still could discern what looked like a glistening thread or fiber, perhaps one-third as wide as a human hair, shimmering in a kind of flow across the otherwise inert phlegm. . . . Or at least, it *seemed* to flow. It started at one point and then simply ended. Despite its apparent movement in one direction, it did not extend itself beyond approximately three-eighths of an inch in length. Was what I saw a pulsing or tiny convulsion that seemed like a flux? What was this? A worm-like organism, perhaps?

I managed to find my magnifying glass, after some searching, and held it close to the mucus, peering through it and perplexed by what I saw. It is a good lens, and I was able to discern that this thin skein of movement was of a light bluish color, standing out clearly against the darker brown and green of the phlegm. It seemed to arise out of the mucus at one point and then to disappear into it at another.

Adding to the decided curiosity of this phenomenon, was the observable difference in the surface of the phlegm on either side of this thin blue line. On one side it was uneven and varied in topography, as should be expected; on the other, it was remarkably flat and regular. On the regular side, I thought I could discern, in several separate areas, tiny square shapes of a lighter green. Along the middle of the blue stripe, on the flat and regular side as well, was a blackish bit of color, about one-fifth the size of one of the periods on this page.

I was intrigued, and I was idle, so I decided to make closer inspections. I was convinced that I might see some interesting microorganisms. The previous year I had bought my son, Alex, a toy microscope for which he had no use or interest. It is a cheap and inferior plastic instrument, but it was all I had on hand. It can magnify an object to 75 times actual size.

I eased the phlegm from the tumbler onto a slide; then, to keep it from spreading, I contained the mucus using an ordinary rubber washer. I attempted to examine the phlegm by means of the indirect light provided by the microscope's mirror but found that the mucus was much too opaque. To remedy this problem, I took a small night-light that has a long cord and a metal clamp and attached it to the armor plate–studded back of a toy stegosaur (my son Andy's), which put the light at just the right height and at just the right distance from the microscope to illuminate the subject under the lens from above.

What I saw that day and the two days following affected me in a number of complex ways that I will attempt to describe in a cursory way elsewhere in this narrative. I would assume that my readers, especially those in the scientific community, are more interested in what I saw than in what I felt.

I trained and focused the lens on the bluish line. What I saw convinced me that it was a liquid stream, in appearance and behavior very much like a river observed from a great height—from a balloon or other aircraft, let's say. Far from flowing in a straight line, it traveled in gentle meanders, and at the crooks of some "bends" in its course, there were odd dots of pale blue standing alone like little lakes or ponds. I looked at one end of the stream and then the other. Indeed, it seemed to issue out of the surface of the phlegm, not at one spot, but from five discernible "springs," separate tributaries that eventually became confluent. At the other end, the stream flowed much more quickly and seemed to fall into a dark depression, about which hovered a white, mutable cloudy mass that I could not put into focus properly.

I scanned the surface of the mucus and was astonished by its "texture." It was exceedingly rough and varied. On the more "hilly" side of the "river," the "terrain" seemed to be covered with minute protuberances looking much like the tightly compacted florets of a head of broccoli. Even the smoother, flatter side of the river looked anything but smooth or flat. I found the pale green squares (there were five that I could see) and saw that in reality they were composed of other squares, alternating in blue and yellow like a checkerboard. I noticed that each of these checkerboard patterns had a thin white line radiating from one side. I followed one of these lines and found that it struck another thin line at a 90° angle. I carefully thumbed the slide to determine if this second line went to the river, and it was then I became so agitated by what I saw that I had to gasp to catch my breath.

The thin white line entered that blackish area abutting the stream that I had first seen through the magnifying glass . . . but this black area, really a mix of different colors, was wonderful! Its outline was uneven and angular. It was crisscrossed by a number of white lines. Its surface was rough with a jumble of diminutive geometrical shapes—mostly rectangles and rhomboids speckled with circular objects—the whole having a definite three dimensionality. And, still within its boundaries, there could be detected a tiny flickering as though it were the sparkle of white and yellow lights. It gave the impression, simply stated, of a great city seen from high in the air.

I don't know how long I squinted through the ocular lens; my excitement caused me to lose track of the passage of time, but eventually I became aware of the heat of the night-light on my cheek. Worried that the mucus would dry up before I could make further discoveries, I filled a spray bottle with water and gave the phlegm a misty shower from about a yard's distance. It was obvious that this was merely a stopgap solution of a serious problem. I recalled how my wife and her sister had made tamales some days before and how the fragrant steam had filled my lungs and given me great relief from my condition. My study is a small room. I shut the door, set a hot plate on a card table, and put some water to boil in the steamer my wife uses for tamales. I opened the window a crack so that the accumulation of moisture would not be excessive. A pot on the constant boil meant that I could not leave the house for any length of time, but this did not concern me as I had nowhere to go.

I was determined to obtain the best microscope that I could. I was considering buying one, when I remembered that my sister-in-law, Ana the medical doctor, had access to hospital equipment. As it so fortuitously happened, she had a binocular, oil-immersion lens microscope at home that she had "borrowed" from Kaiser Hospital. It was even equipped with an apparatus that could tilt slides by minute degrees, so that objects could be viewed at slight angles. Ana assured me that it was all right for me to have it for a while. The microscope was old equipment and would not be soon missed.

Of course, as soon as I was able, I wanted to focus in on the dark spot by the river. My brain had already been given over to the wildest speculations and imaginings, so it was with a relative *lack* of amazement, which in retrospect is truly amazing in itself, that I discovered the bustling town of crowded narrow streets, wide commercial canals, and its thousands of micro-humanoid inhabitants.

These creatures . . . these beings . . . these *people* looked identical to the human species. Were it not for the fact that they were microscopic, one would be compelled to say they *were* human. They were all similar in appearance in a superficial way; perhaps it would be more accurate to say that their differences were not striking, rather like a single "race" of humans: They had sallow to swarthy complexions, hair usually black sometimes chestnut brown, and, most rarely, coppery red (I would estimate one in one hundred, but I was only able to observe the hair of the children).

The males (I *assume* they were males; I saw no naked inhabitants of my phlegm) were clothed uniformly in baggy trousers and an upper garment with sleeves that ended at the elbow and that seemed to be a sort of "pull-over." They wore soft, brimless caps with a large limp peak that, without exception, was worn pulled to the left and over the ear. There was scarcely more variety in the women's clothing. Women wore either voluminous pantaloons that were pegged at the ankles, or trousers that were form-fitting in the calf and knee but much more roomy in the thigh and hips and that looked a lot like jodhpurs. Their upper garments were tight and long-sleeved and seemed designed to accentuate the breasts. They covered their heads with what had the appearance of snoods or else with turbans. Both sexes had their feet shod with a kind of snug, featureless slipper, looking like a heavy, padded sock with no visible soles.

The children were dressed indifferently in long pants and light, long-sleeved tunics. The boys and girls were distinguishable only by length of hair and general behavior. This appeared to be the uniform until early teen age. Every article of clothing, whether for men, women, or children, was of the same charcoal grey. The only exception was for infants who were wrapped up, mummy-like, in white cloth in such a way that only the head was exposed. Single babies were carried in an odd receptacle resembling a champagne bucket. Multiple babies rode in a kind of two-wheeled barrow filled with what looked like wood shavings.

The streets of the town constituted an irrational maze. (Their angle and direction seemed to be dictated by the irregular shape of the buildings, and no buildings were contiguous; they all stood apart.) They were narrow and well used. There were no sidewalks or banquettes. The streets could accommodate perhaps five people walking abreast. All the traffic was pedestrian; there were no vehicles of any description except for the litters and sedan chairs that some women would use. I never saw a man use one. As all the women dressed nearly alike, it was impossible for me to tell if the employment of such conveyances was the mark of superior rank or wealth, as it would be assumed to be so among our species.

In acute contrast to the crazy hodgepodge of streets, the canals were wonderfully straight and intersected at right angles to each other. The network of canals consisted of two sets of parallel waterways. Each parallel canal was roughly three-fourths to one mile distant from the other. (Of course, the reader understands that I am not talking about real miles but "scale miles," which I base on my own imaginary attribution of a height of "six feet" to any one of these homunculi.) Five ran to and from the river, and five crossed them, dividing the center of the town into sixteen perfect squares and leaving twenty odd-shaped sections at the city's boundaries.

The river was the source of the water (again, I *assume* it was water) for the canals. A massive levee some fifty feet high and one hundred feet wide stood between the river and the entire length of the city. Water was piped over the levee (I believe that only a pump could have made this possible, but I could not detect any such apparatus) and into the middle canal of those running from the river. This middle canal was the broadest of all ten in the system and fed the rest with its water. Within the borders of town, the canals were traveled by long narrow boats that were much like piraguas. The boats carried food and other merchandise to the sixteen covered markets to be found within the city. (I call these places markets, but, since they were covered, I couldn't see any transactions take place. I only know that goods were unloaded and that there was a constant stream of ordinary people flowing under the square, sloping red roofs. With few exceptions, the people went in unburdened, so barter can be ruled out. Either money was the medium of exchange or these places were distribution centers for goods that were available to everyone.)

Of the ten canals, only the broad, main artery left the boundaries of the city. This canal went out into "open country" and led directly to a large cultivated area some ten miles outside town. Before reaching this destination, the main canal branched out in two opposite directions in two places, so that four other cultivated fields were connected by waterway. These were the five green squares I had originally detected through my magnifying glass. The canals not only afforded transportation to and from the fields but also provided them with irrigation.

The large fields were composed of smaller plots that were alternately active and fallow. Some of the "plants" under cultivation bore a slight resemblance to those in the macrocosm; some were totally alien in appearance. Some were tall and lobed like nopales but were spineless and of a dusky pink color. There was one that was a smooth, blue sphere, about the relative size of a softball. One brown-colored species lay flat, amorphous, and tentacular, continuously oozing a kind of yellow sap. I observed and made detailed notes on fifty species. I have submitted these notes for publication to the *Botanische Jahrbücher für Systematik*

Pflanzengeschichte und Pflanzengeographie. One of the editors of that prestigious review, Dr. Joachim Grau, has given me his assurances that my work will be published this coming year.

Of the plants being cultivated, approximately 20 percent were being harvested during my observations. These were loaded onto barges and poled back to the town. The harvest was taken to a complex of six large, low rectangular buildings situated on the outskirts of town. The six buildings were laid out in such a way that their walls formed a spacious court. The court was hexagonal and open at opposite ends so that the main canal could run through. Inside the court, the canal widened into a kind of bay where the barges were unloaded and the produce put into smaller boats for transportation in the city. I suspect that the buildings were processing plants of some sort, as a quantity of the produce was taken inside them and numerous cylindrical containers of varying sizes were taken out and loaded onto the skiffs.

The river was perhaps one-half mile wide and rapid. Its five sources issued from great openings in the "ground" with tremendous force and quantity. The most impressive source sent water in a massive jet some 250 feet in the air. The river ended in a dive into an enormous crater approximately one mile in diameter. I could not guess how far the water fell, but the volume of liquid cascading into the abyss was at least equal to that of Niagara. The resultant heavy vapor obscured the crater to a great extent and rose high above it in a misty cloud.

The land on the other side of the river was uncultivated and thickly wooded. The most prevalent of the trees had a formal appearance much like an oak; but the trunks were carmine red, and the leaves were Prussian blue. Growing on the trunks of these trees were black, ring-shaped, fungal-like organisms. Amongst the abundant yellow bushes were purple, attenuated, limp-looking cones, the height of a man, with droopy or downcast extremities. Now and then, a long thin, worm-like creature would slither through the undergrowth. Twice or three times I thought I caught sight of a vague, scurrying animal, oppossum-sized with many legs, pig-pink and lightning fast. Otherwise, this forest would have been remarkably still, were it not for men.

Boats ferried parties of men across the river from and to the city every hour or so. The men would disembark in the wilderness and go off into the forest armed with pointed staffs. With these they would root around the trees and dig up white clods resembling truffles in all but color. Others would cut about six inches from the very tip-top of the aforementioned purple cones. The foragers would place their finds in sacks and carry them back to town. I saw no hunting take place, and it is my belief that the little people were vegetarians.

The buildings of the town were of many sizes and shapes, but almost all seemed to be rhombuses, that is to say they all had four sides. Few, however, were perfect squares or rectangles. There was great variation in the length of the sides and angles that they formed. Some buildings looked like triangles when seen under a magnification of only 250x, when in reality they were not. They were windowless, and all had but one door. They were all made of the same smooth, stony material. Their colors ranged from black to varying shades of grey to white.

There were five exceptions to the general rhomboid character of the town's buildings. These five edifices were found all together in a broad square (truly the town's only open, expansive space) near the center of the city. Four of the buildings were of the same size and were located at the four corners of the square. In the center was a building twice as big but identical to the rest in every other respect. Each white building was the shape of a kidney and was surmounted by a large ornament or decoration that looked like a rooster's comb.

These five buildings and this square were to be the scene of an occurrence the memory of which still makes my hair stand on end.

The blind, ponderous buildings of the city possessed little to please the eye. Their smooth blank facades would have made one assume that these microscopic people were unaesthetic and enthralled by the unlovely, but the public prodigality of beautiful, curious statuary contradicted.

Statues were at almost every intersection of streets in the town. They were without exception life-sized figures of people and entirely painted with life-like colors. Each one was unique, which led me to conclude they were effigies of real people. They were not set up on high pedestals. They were rooted to a low base not more than four or five inches high, so they did not loom over the passersby. This accentuated their verisimilitude. They did not seem to be statues but seemed rather to be ordinary pedestrians who had paused to ruminate.

On the plinths of these statues were engravings that were definitely not mere decoration. They had the recognizable regularity and sequence of written language. It is very difficult for me to describe the complex characters of the script. Some elements *reminded* me of Arabic, other features resembled the samples of written Korean that I have seen, but since I do not read a word of either language, it would be wise not to put too much weight on these perceived similarities. Regrettably, I did not think to copy what I saw.

The only other writings that I observed were on a sort of billboard that was to be found here and there within the town. Invariably, the signs displayed the same image and writing. They depicted a baby, a bald, fat-cheeked baby. The baby's mouth was opened wide, exposing a single, brilliant white tooth. Drool escaped at the corners of the baby's mouth. The baby's black eyes were narrowed in a frightful ferocity. The colors used were shiny and vivid—the pink of the cheeks, the black of the eyes, the blinding white of the tooth, and the gleaming transparency of the drool. What this dreadful image signified or was meant to convey is beyond me. The writing beneath each picture of the baby certainly gave me no clue.

It is a remarkable thing that when one's mind is entertained and completely absorbed in an exciting and fascinating enterprise, one forgets one's pains and ailments. During the forty hours since I had discovered the microscopic people in my mucus, I had so completely forgotten my illness that I had become virtually asymptomatic. As soon as I realized that I hadn't coughed for a day and a half, I started to cough. The cough resounded from deep within my lungs, a profound, spasmodic, gasping, croaking cough.

The microscopic people had been unperturbed by any noise up to this point, including the obstreperous drone of a next-door lawn mower, but my coughing fit had an immediate and radical effect upon them. The people in the streets stopped abruptly and with visible trepidation. They tilted their heads upward, making me absurdly uneasy as they looked and stared, seemingly at *me*.

After some moments of anxiously scanning "the skies," the people walked purposely to the five reniform buildings, converging upon them from all corners of the city. They thronged the plaza, and a number of them entered the large central edifice. Half an hour passed; then the doors were thrown open, and the crowd parted to form a corridor of tiny humanity. A man passed with slow measured steps through the doors into the open, bearing before him a staff with a kidney-shaped gilt ornament at the top end. Behind him twenty men bore a huge, uncovered palanquin decked with multi-colored fabric and branches of blue leaves. The palanquin bore the erect figure of a man with a beatific expression on his face, one hand upon his breast and the other outstretched in a beckoning gesture. The whole scene was strongly reminiscent of Semana Santa in Sevilla.

As I looked upon this icon, a faint feeling of nausea crept up on me, a feeling of uneasy recognition of the reality of the improbable. The figure's dark face, the thick lank hair, the indefinite jaw, the oblique, bushy eyebrows, the thin lips, the retreating chin, the long bulbous nose . . . it was I! An idealized me, to be sure . . . thinner in the face . . . thinner in body . . . but still, it was I. There could be no mistake about it.

The microscopic people carried my likeness in somber procession through the streets and toward the river. I will never know what their purpose and goal was, for a sudden catastrophe made an end of them all.

From out of the very pavement of the streets emerged a multitude of oblong, capsulate creatures, about the relative size of a cat or small dog, transparent and featureless save for a wildly beating fringe of filament-like appendages. The panic was universal as soon as the people saw the creatures emerge. They ran helter-skelter, but there was no escape, for the creatures were emerging everywhere at once like seventeen-year locusts in Spring. The creatures attached themselves to the bodies of the people and throbbed convulsively, quickly turning blood red in the process. The death agonies of the little men were horrible to see. Some brave souls attempted to fight the demonic creatures but were soon overcome by the sheer weight of their numbers. It was heartbreaking to watch parents try to shield their children to no avail. Many tried to hide in the buildings of the town, but the creatures passed through the walls as easily as they had through the surface of the streets. Curiously enough, neither the walls nor the streets were broken by their penetration.

In an hour it was over. All the inhabitants of the town lay pale and lifeless in the streets, in the fields, in the wilderness, and even in the boats in the canals. Then, all of a sudden, the creatures detached themselves from their now consumed fodder and simultaneously subsided from sight.

There are several things that I should have done.

I should have called in others to witness and confirm my discovery. But Leeuwenhoek did not think to look for witnesses for some weeks after discovering his microbes. It must be that he too was carried away and rendered oblivious to such details by the thrill of discovery. Besides, at the outset, I was made timid by the concern that others might think I was crazy.

I should have found some way to photograph my microscopic people. I subsequently learned that there are video microscopes that can project an actual image onto a television screen. Had I known, I would have done what I could to obtain one.

Since the annihilation of my microscopic men, I have examined many other specimens of my phlegm, but unfortunately I have found no other signs of life, let alone civilization. Perhaps I'll find other people in my phlegm, perhaps never again. Still, I cannot believe that I am unique. After all, there are *so many* people in the world and *so much* mucus. I would encourage everyone, who has the means, to secure a microscope and search the near limitless vastness of their own phlegm.

Erotica

They both worked in the cannery, and although they had known about each other for years—she was a friend of his cousin's wife—they did not meet until after he came back from the war. He had been in the Philippines, in Leyte Gulf, and had gotten through the worst of it without a scratch. Those who made it home came in on the same ship, and the neighborhood threw a block party for all of them. That's where they finally met. Well well, she said to him when his cousin introduced them, giving him an appraising once-over, which—to her surprise— did not fluster him, as she half hoped it would.

When the night shift at the cannery let off, he would accompany his cousin to meet the girls outside the ladies' exit. They would go to an all-night diner, the four of them, for breakfast and pie. He was not a talker. He rarely spoke. He would greet her with one deliberate nod of his head, followed by a kind of salute—a brief tap to his forehead with the index finger of his right hand. He would walk slightly behind her, just at her left elbow, pacing himself smoothly with her gait, attending to her while surveying the path before her for hoodlums or dog droppings. He would look her in the eye only upon greeting her and parting with her; at any other time he would look at her hair, or gaze at her hands. He did not touch her. He was a small, wiry man, intense in his gentlemanly manner, and intensely quiet—like his father had been—but not in a way that brought discomfort to those around him. He had the dark and flat *indio* features of his father, who had labored miserably in the coffee plantations in the old country before saving enough money to come down from the mountains to marry the woman he loved. His mother missed her husband terribly, and when tired, would often call to her son by her husband's name. Everyone had long ago stopped correcting her.

After four months of breakfast and pie at 4 a.m., he finally asked her out. He came calling for her one Sunday morning wearing his only suit, a wide-lapelled, baggy-pantsed get-up that he had bought during his zoot suit phase, and which embarrassed him to have to wear. He accompanied her and her family to mass. The two of them then took the intercity bus across the Bay Bridge and spent the afternoon together at the zoological gardens.

(There is a photo of them at the zoo in their Sunday best. She wears a light-colored summer dress, cinched at the waist, and fancy strapped heels. A large bouquet is pinned to her bodice, and the flowing skirt is caught by the camera pinned flat against her thighs by a breeze. He stands next to her at a slight inward angle, his left arm out of view behind her back. They are posed next to a scrawny tree. They are both smiling, squinting into the sun, the cage of some indeterminate animal behind them. Did he give her the bouquet? Who brought the camera? Who took the photograph?)

He bought her pink popcorn. They ate hot dogs, the mustard and relish staining his lapels and tie. He did not mind. When they entered the Cat House for the feeding of the lions, he apologized to her for the smell. At the Bear Grotto, they joined a crowd that was watching two brown bears in violent and clumsy copulation. Zookeepers with prods and water hoses were swarming into the Grotto in an attempt to separate the animals. The bears swatted and roared at each other, coupling and thrusting intermittently, then turning to snap at the keepers, who prodded them apart with poles and sprayed them with dousing streams of water. The crowd hooted and jeered until the keepers finally succeeded in isolating and herding one of the bears into a steel enclosure.

When it was all over, she turned to look at him. She gave him a steady and unwavering gaze, half hoping, once again, to elicit some blush or stammer. But he looked right back at her. When he escorted her home that evening, he asked her to marry him. She said yes.

So the story goes.

* * *

Their sex life was a good one. And the children they raised—a daughter and two sons—would acknowledge this unsettling truth only rarely to each other, and begrudgingly to themselves, carrying the collective record of their parents' ardor for each other like some shameful family secret. Sent home early from school one day, the daughter had caught them both at home—they had called in sick to the cannery—both in the bathroom, playing in the shower. The boys had come roaring into the house one Saturday after soccer practice and stumbled upon the two of them sitting stiffly next to each other on the sofa, their clothes in disarray, thumbing through an upside-down magazine. Returning home from their nights out together—a dance at the Cultural Center, a movie, a Feast of Saint Mary's dinner—it would take them a half-hour or more to get out of the car: the Oldsmobile sliding up just past the house, backing into the graveled car port; the motor throttling down and choking off, the headlamps winking out, and then . . . nothing, except the ticking of the cooling engine. The first time this happened the eldest boy had gone out to see what was wrong. Thereafter, none of them bothered to check again. Whenever they got caught red-handed—and they got caught often—they would be snappish and abrupt with their children for days following. The youngest boy grew increasingly indignant at bearing the brunt of these embarrassing episodes. It just wasn't fair, after all. Five of us in this dinky house and them going at it! Jesus Christ, what do they expect?

The children grew up, moved out, the daughter and eldest boy each settling into their respective marriages and families. The youngest boy went off to his war, and he, too, came home without a scratch. For a time, he slept on a cot in the basement of his parents' home. He finally settled into some steady work at a printer's shop, and earned enough to get his own apartment.

Nothing, of course, had changed between those two, he had reported to his siblings before moving out. You could hear everything, for Christ's sake!

* * *

She died first. At the gathering in his home after the burial, he went upstairs into his bedroom and closed the door. As the house filled with mourners—children, grandchildren, friends from the old days at the cannery, neighbors bearing casseroles and cakes—he changed out of his suit and into khakis and sneakers, a plaid shirt and V-neck sweater, a blue knit cap. He opened the door and came back down the stairs. He edged his way firmly through the crowd, and went out the front door. He walked the half mile to the mall and spent this day there. He strolled and browsed methodically, starting at the top level, circumnavigating every shop facing the central atrium, then moving down to the next level. When he got tired, he sat at a bench facing the central fountain, cleaning his glasses every few minutes to wipe off the spray from the water, listening to the ceaseless echo and hum of the crowds, trying to lose himself in their ambient noise.

On this day, he had established the rule for all who knew him: never speak of his wife again. Thereafter, if anyone ever spoke of her, he would simply get up and leave the room.

* * *

The oldest would on occasion invite his brother home for dinner. They were close in that reticent and uncommunicative way that brothers often are, their mutual silences conveying much more of their attachment to each other than any of their halting conversations ever could.

The oldest boy had done well. He had made a good life. He was a successful roofing contractor. He lived in a four-bedroom house with three and a half baths and a billiard table in the basement. He had five children, and all of them had either been to college or were anxious to go. His marriage was sluggish and comfortable. He loved his wife very much. They had sex twice a month, and more would have been nice, of course, but. . . . He had made a good life. But his younger brother had not done so well, had never settled on things. He was morbidly single, a virgin most likely, and was perpetually disgruntled about something:

his job, women, society. He had grown large and soft and unhappy from too many evenings alone in front of his TV. And so he was invited to his brother's home for dinner as often as he could be tolerated by his sister-in-law.

One evening, as the two of them sat having coffee on the front porch, the eldest brought up what had been niggling at him about their father for all these months after their mother died: What does he do now, I wonder?

What does that mean? his brother asked.

Well. You know how they were. I just wonder how he gets along now.

The youngest stared expectantly, his mouth open.

I mean, he must . . . take care of things on his own, right? You know, by himself? He cleared his throat, chuckled uncomfortably in the thickening silence, then said with exasperation: Come on, *niño*, you know what I mean!

His brother slammed his coffee mug down and snorted. He stared at his brother and snorted again. Then he tossed his cigarette into his coffee mug, stalked down the front steps and into his car, leaving his befuddled sibling red-faced and alone on the porch steps.

* * *

Later that night, in his apartment, he wondered too, of course, as he often did well before it had come up tonight. He snubbed out his cigarette in a coffee can on the floor, and rolled in his cot onto his side. He had grown accustomed to cots and sleeping bags; he could not sleep in a normal bed anymore.

When he was sleeping in their basement he had heard it all, through the ducts from the central heater. What would that house sound like now? What does he do now? Where does it all go?

* * *

She called her father one day to tell him she was coming by. She was in charge of the family albums, and her project was to assemble the photographic history, in chronological order. She had been working on the project for years, and had postponed it when her mother died, not wanting to bother her father with what he had always considered to be a ridiculous pastime. But it had now been over a year, and it was time to take up where she had left off.

He was working in the garden when she arrived. He was going deaf, and did not hear her drive up. Rather than disturb him, she used her key to enter the house. She went through the door off the kitchen, placed her purse on the counter, and entered the garage. She moved toward a stack of caved-in boxes when she stopped for a moment. The bedroom had always been off-limits to all of them. But she wondered now if he perhaps had forgotten about some photos in there. He always invited her to search the garage, which she had done numerous times before, always finding the occasional treasure—snapshots of her father bivouacked in the Philippines, out-of-focus crowd shots of her parents' wedding, a tiny, faded photograph of her grandfather posed before some immense gnarled tree, cradling a rifle. She often suspected that her father planted these rarities in the garage for her to find, that he got a kick out of feeding her photos one by one, and that he may have a nest of them somewhere in the house, a hidden source. He was a cagey one. She wouldn't put that past him.

She looked out the grimy garage window to see her father stooped over a rhododendron bed. She slipped back into the house and made her way upstairs to the bedroom. It was remarkable to her how unchanged this room was from her memory of it; this was probably only the fifth or sixth time she had seen it in her life. It was sparsely furnished, and dominated by an immense bed centered on the far wall—a four-poster maplewood frame, with a queen-size boxspring, and two down featherbeds, one on top of the other. There was no mattress. She had never noticed that before. She walked to the bed, placed her palm tentatively on top of it, and pushed. The featherbed gave, yet pushed back. She turned around, and eased her backside onto the bed. She did not expect the sudden lack of resistance as the cool ivory surfaces suddenly billowed up around her, engulfing her, seeming to pull her in. She gasped and struggled, her arms windmilling at the air until she finally clawed out of the thing. She skittered across the room, and watched warily as the featherbed returned to its original shape. Flushed and warm and feeling foolish, she continued with her task. She opened and closed bureau drawers, poked under the bed, rustled through the clothes hanging in the closet. She reached up into a top shelf of the closet, and felt the smooth surface of a box. She hopped once, twice, finally grasped the box by its top, and slid it out.

It was a shoebox. She opened it. There was a photograph, all right, a three-by-five photo of her mother and father, taken, apparently, at the zoo. But this she set aside as she pulled out the other contents, one by one: a large blue kerchief, folded and knotted into a blindfold; two terry-cloth bathrobe belts, knotted into loops; a small swatch of yellowed sheepskin; and a single, long, gray, bird feather. This last item she held up before her face. She stared in awe at it, as if she had never seen a feather before, as if she could never have imagined its utility here in this box, among the other accouterments, in her father's bedroom closet.

From where she stood she could see out the window and down into the backyard. The tiny old man was on his hands and knees, poking randomly through the soil with a spade. He had taken over the care of his wife's garden when she had fallen ill, and he was bad at it. He was a bad gardener, a garden's worst enemy. He had a black thumb. Everyone told him so. But he persisted, planting bulbs out of season, overwatering, weeding the flowering shoots and cultivating the weeds. He toiled every single day, and looked forward to it, compelled by some perverse instinct to care for his wife's garden even if it meant killing it.

She watched her father from the bedroom window, half hoping that he would stop poking in the dirt and look up and see her, that he would be neither embarrassed nor angry with her as she stood idly running her palm along the length of the feather, that in this unspoken way he would somehow pass on to her something—*any*thing—of what passed between him and his wife.

She put everything back into the shoebox and slipped the photo on top. She closed the lid and slid the box back onto the shelf where she found it. Slipping downstairs, she picked up her purse from the kitchen counter, closed and locked the side door, and walked around to the backyard, to greet her father as if she had just arrived.

Shangó's Rest

I am one of the Saints who sailed from Africa to the Caribbean world in the belly of a creaky caravel. The faithful took me along because I had the reputation of being an excellent prognosticator. Whenever flattered with sweet red fruit I'd predict the best of times to come. So it was thanks to me that they kept on living. In my own defense I have to say that I did not invent the future, I created it. Had they really expected a sad outcome to existence they'd have gradually stopped singing, dancing, and believing. One day the world would have become a silent place.

They knew me well. I did not demand much respect. I was playful, easygoing, and I had a sense of humor. But a Saint with only these traits just wouldn't be a real Saint, we also have to be scary. So there were things that were supposed to incite my wrath, and one of them was ending up with some human by mistake. In this case I was supposed to take the future away, make an anti-miracle occur. That's what the faithful decreed, I didn't make this rule, they did. In truth I just follow orders. Sometimes I even get tired of saying yes.

Shortly after crossing over I gave up my power of divination. One rainy night I chanced upon my brother Ogún dancing to the drums by the beach in the coconut grove, and I got terribly jealous. My envy was so great that I got carried away. I created the most furious of hurricanes. It was the first hurricane ever. It lasted two whole decades and was about to swallow the entire island when, fearing for my own well-being because I'm totally terrorized by the thought of death, I chose to have a talk with Ogún. Without the slightest pride I confessed this jealousy of mine. I too wanted to dance in the rain with snakes and dogs and iguanas. Could we do something about it? Luckily Ogún was in the same predicament I was. He wanted what I had. His one desire was to see into the future, while my one desire was to be rid of the responsibility of divining.

That's when we traded our gifts. So I haven't the slightest idea of what's to come, not even in the next ten minutes. Nobody expects me to vaticinate anymore. Now I dance, and I play the drums, and have total power over rain and thunder and lightning. Every single hurricane there has ever been can be blamed on me. I invented them. Oh, and I almost forgot, the rule still holds, if I end up with someone by mistake I'm supposed to unsheath my sword in anger. This just means that

I remain the owner of anti-miracles. At first I thought I could dump these on Ogún but he knew better, he hates blame, he refused them.

Many humans like me the way I am. I'd venture to say that I'm the most popular Saint. My power is deep and strong, like a jungle river, and my wrath is terrible. I know revenge, but I also know how to protect. So I get summoned fairly regularly.

The last time I got summoned I was looking forward to a few pleasure years and was planning to spend them in Nicolasa's kitchen eating her good meals, smelling her cigars, drinking her rum and Coke and listening to her pots and pans. I love it when Nicolasa does the dishes. And when she takes the silverware out and sets the table I'm convinced that even a Saint needs to feel safe.

It didn't happen. Everything went wrong. Nicolasa was very nervous. She wanted to buy groceries and that's all she thought about—Saltine crackers, eggs, cream, chickens, cheese, chocolate syrup, canned sardines—so she momentarily forgot about me. That's how I was stolen. That's how I ended up with a woman named Alma by mistake.

Now that it's all over and that Alma's grave is occupied, and silent, Nicolasa blames me, I blame Brígida, and Brígida blames Nicolasa.

It began innocently, like all wicked things. Nicolasa had summoned me to Union City, New Jersey, and I was looking forward to her feeding me indeed. You see, we've always had this deal, I provide the food and Mi Negra prepares it. Mi Negra, I call her, it's a term of endearment, she's the incarnation of my mistress Obbá, queen of the storms and of the gates of the cemetery, I really do love that woman. She may smell of onions, green peppers, frying oil, and occasionally of boiled cabbage, but that woman's really something, she can never make me angry, she can even mistreat me, for she's an earth mother, her body has given life seven times, and since she's either at the bodega buying groceries or in the kitchen cooking, she knows how to nourish those lives and make them thrive.

From morning till night she wears an apron, and she can feed three babies while she's preparing some other dish for the adults. Her legs have varicose veins that never quit hurting because she never sits down and probably doesn't even know what it feels like. Those feet of hers have never known pampering. They are as long as they are wide and make you think of radial tires. She's put them to good use and has been on them all her life.

Everything about her I like, even her old rope-soled slippers, her alpargatas. That's all she wears, and doesn't even bother to slip her big foot all the way in. She folds the back beneath her heel and those alpargatas go flip flop flop, flip flop flop when she's at her busiest.

At four o'clock in the afternoon, fresh out of the shower, she smells of violet water and talcum powder, but it doesn't last, she hurries back to the kitchen. I really do love Mi Negra Nicolasa.

This Negra here, who happens to be three-quarters white but remains my adored Negra, has been practicing the Regla Conga, my religion, since she was ten years old, and I've been loving her and protecting her since then. I seated myself in her head when she was just a tiny girl.

I only stopped protecting her when she sacrificed three years of power in order to keep her son Lucho from dying. These are rough neighborhoods here. Three men went to rob the bodega where Lucho worked and stabbed him in the stomach. Instead of taking the knife back out they kept turning it in there so he'd really hurt and die. The doctors had practically given up on him. The boy had no insurance and his guts seemed beyond repair. So Mi Negra prayed to Obatalá, my father, who specializes in rescuing people from the land of the Iku.

She went and got the seashells and the goat blood. She also killed seven guinea hens and performed all the necessary rites right there in the intensive care unit. It took a whole night, and that night robbed her of three years of power. Mi Negra was drained but the boy was saved. Not even the doctors could believe how well Lucho had recuperated.

It was a terrible ordeal for me, not to be able to protect her for the next three years, believe me, I counted the hours and the days. Helping her in any way would have meant going against Obatalá's orders, and we have enough family problems as it is. So I just had to stand back and let Mi Negra live those hard times. She was well aware of it, she too had a Catholic wall calendar just like I did, she too crossed out the days. She didn't even complain. Took it like mother earth. I swear, Mi Negra has character.

Terrible things happened to her during those three years. Her husband died suddenly one night and that was a great loss for both of us. Eulogio was a Negro Blanco, a real Black man with white skin on him, and he could make music simply by beating a frying pan with a spoon and a knife. He'd sing to all the powers, Babalú, Elegguá, and even Jesus Christ and the bosom of Abraham, depending on what he wanted. Mayombero he was born and Mayombero he died. One of my best soldiers.

Obviously he died leaving nothing behind, and by nothing I mean no money to pay the rent and to buy the groceries. No money for the funeral either. So Nicolasa had no choice but to go clean offices, apartments, bars, whatever, if it needed cleaning she'd clean it and quite a good job she did. At that time, and with the funeral costing six thousand dollars, Nicolasa was in such dire need of money that she even ventured into Manhattan to clean rich people's apartments.

After Eulogio died, Nicolasa's sister came to live with her because with all the cleaning she had to do Nicolasa had nobody to look after the children. The first month was fine, the two sisters managed the babies, the bills and the groceries. It was a busy life, but this didn't bother Nicolasa, as long as she could put food on the table everything was fine. What did bother her was this feeling that these times with her sister were simply borrowed times. She felt she could count the days between the now and the when it would be no more, but she could do nothing about it. What power could she pray to when she'd renounced all of them so that Lucho could survive?

Mi Negra lived and still lives in this three-story clapboard building on 36th Street right off Bergenline Avenue. Since there are so many bodegas and restaurants nearby the building's infested with rats and roaches. There's even a woodchuck who does the trashcans every night. Imagine that, a woodchuck in Union City.

Mi Negra's on the ground floor, in a dark dingy two-bedroom in a dilapidated building with stinky hallways. Whew! They smell of old soup and roach poison. Garbage too. So one day the upstairs neighbor called the department of sanitation and the landlady, who also owns the strip joint called *El Gallo de Colombia*, had no choice but to have these hallways cleaned up. She sent a guy over there to throw enough paint around so that the place would pass the department of sanitation inspection (they're not very strict), and the guy was supposed to do it as quickly as possible, which he did, he painted so quickly that he even painted over a roach. And this wasn't just any guy either, he was the cheapest laborer that the owner of *El Gallo de Colombia* could find.

On his second day there at noon he rings Nicolasa's doorbell to ask for a glass of water. Thank God Nicolasa wasn't there, she was cleaning apartments on the Upper East Side. It was her sister Chucha who opened the door and she felt sorry for this sweaty man and said, "Sure, come in, and wouldn't you prefer a cold beer?"

When Chucha turned around to open the refrigerator this man grabbed one of Nicolasa's knives from the kitchen counter and stabbed the poor woman in the back, then he turned her around, threw her on the floor and kept stabbing her.

The babies were all there. They were between the ages of one and five and they simply stared at him and he stared back. Then he looked around the kitchen for something else. Chucha was on the floor moaning, she was barely alive. He found a hammer and began to hammer Chucha's head until there was hardly a head left. There was blood splattered all over the place, even on the ceiling. Before he left he ripped the Saint Barbara medal off the chain around Chucha's neck and also took Mi Negra's bus quarters that were in a jar over by the fruit basket. At least he didn't do anything to the babies. When he was arrested trying to sell the little gold medal for ten dollars in a laundromat he said that the babies looked cute standing there looking at him and wondering what was going on.

Mi Negra didn't get home till five and you can imagine what she saw. God knows what the babies will remember. It's not fair and I never agreed to what happened.

So when the three years were up and I was ready to give Nicolasa everything in the world, Obatalá decided that I should be supervised otherwise I'd get carried away and make her win the Pick 6. That's how my brother Olofi and I ended up sharing the same gold crucifix. It didn't bother me. Olofi's so popular that he wasn't going to bother with a poor woman in Union City. He'd pretty much be absent most of the time, and into bigger and better things, like the Vatican.

Mi Negra didn't do the work herself. She had a Chinese man do it because a Chino's work is the most powerful in the world. Nobody can undo it except another Chino, which means that nobody can undo it. One Chino will never undo another Chino's work. Those people stick together.

It was a beautiful eighteen-karat gold cross on a gold chain that the Chino provided himself. The work cost one thousand dollars but Mi Negra had to do it. She didn't want any more bad things to happen and she knew that with this cross I'd be back and there'd always be food on her table. Besides, with her sister dead she couldn't work all that much anymore.

It took a lot of blood and guts to put that power in there. Then after the Chino gave her the crucifix she had to wait thirty days before wearing it. The rules are the rules, and Obatalá really wants people to stick to them. So she put it in the top left-hand drawer of her bureau, the one with the mirror, the nice bureau. You'd wonder what such a splendid piece of furniture was doing in a place like this. It really was a work of art, made of a tropical hardwood from Honduras. Nicolasa had gotten it as a gift from Señora Claudia, one of the ladies she worked for in Manhattan. When Señora Claudia had gotten tired of her old bedroom furniture and decided to change everything, she'd given this piece to Nicolasa who had always admired it. Even if it took up too much space in Nicolasa's bedroom, it was her prized possession.

During this thirty-day wait things got difficult again. After Nicolasa had spent every penny she had on the Chino's work she realized there was no money to go and buy groceries at the supermarket. So she scribbled a little ad on an index card and thumbtacked it to the bulletin board in that same supermarket where she was so anxious to spend money. For sale beautiful bureau Honduran mahogany $200. Exactly what she needed for a week's worth of groceries, Mi Negra is not greedy. At that time she was feeding six babies under six, as well as her two youngest daughters Yamilé and Bessabé, her niece Doris, and her son Juan Pablo whom she'd managed to get into college.

When Nicolasa got back home she began taking her little things out of the drawers. Bras kept in one piece with safety pins, raggedy underwear, faded nightgowns, and lots of handkerchiefs because Mi Negra is always wiping someone's nose and paper tissues just aren't good enough. Since she was supposed to refrain from touching the piece of jewelry that contained my brother Olofi and me she decided to leave it in the drawer until she found a safe place for it.

By the time the phone rang the bureau was empty except for the chain and the crucifix. A señora who happened to be shopping at El Sol del Caribe Supermarket that same afternoon happened to see the ad and wanted to come and see the bureau right away. And my worthy Negra was so eager to sell it! She got all nervous, she stammered, she even wondered if the price was too high. "Yes, of course, Señora," she said, "you can come whenever you want!"

Since this señora also lived in Union City and Union City is little she was there in no time at all. Brígida Pacheco was her name. She took one good look at Mi Negra and judged her poorly. Low class, she said to herself. Nicolasa showed her to the bedroom and I could hear Brígida Pacheco wondering why such a regal piece of furniture was wallowing in the mire of this building with these low-class people, and quickly coming to the conclusion that it was probably stolen, and regretting that her old country that she would probably never see again was full of low-class people like this one here, mixed bloods, half-breeds, mulattas. All these thoughts went through Brígida Pacheco's mind before she turned to Mi Negra and said, "I'll take it."

"Two hundred dollars," I made Mi Negra blurt out because she was ready to settle for less.

Brígida Pacheco chuckled. "Well," she said, "I can't give you the money right now. What if I come back tomorrow and this place has burnt down or you've disappeared?"

"I'll sell it to the first person who gives me the money."

I was the one speaking through Mi Negra, if not she'd probably have given it to Brígida Pacheco for half the amount and in exchange for her word.

They finally agreed that a twenty-five-dollar deposit would do it.

"No telling if I ever see my twenty-five dollars again," Brígida sighed. "No telling. God willing. We'll soon find out. Well, here's my name and number, could I have a receipt at least?"

"Sure, no problem, Señora."

Mi Negra got all nervous, a receipt was like a legal paper.

Brígida Pacheco promised to give Nicolasa the balance whenever she could arrange to have the thing picked up, which she hoped would be as soon as possible and at the latest tomorrow.

As soon as this Brígida woman left, Nicolasa was so happy that she began making a shopping list. By this time tomorrow she'd be at El Sol del Caribe Supermarket buying everything she wanted and that's all she could think about. Then she remembered Olofi and me. Where should she put us? It was important! Then she thought about the Saltine crackers that she'd forgotten to add to the list. She rushed over to the kitchen counter and scribbled it on the bottom of the list. Then she was back to thinking about Olofi and me. Where could we spend the next twenty-two days? Since the moving men were coming she didn't want it to be too visible. Had to protect us from the babies too, they were always getting into everything. What about the refrigerator? No. We need warmth. Had she added garbanzo beans to the list? Under the sofa cushions? No. We'd get crushed. Maybe she should get two or three chickens from the live poultry market and have a feast. Under the television set? She'd lose it. So she left us where we were for the time being, sure that she'd find the perfect spot for us the next morning before the moving men came. The truth is that the only thing that really concerned her at that moment was her shopping list. Paprika, green onions, cilantro, and what else? Milo. Yes, definitely, chocolate Milo.

Meanwhile, and this is what Olofi told me because I wasn't there, this Brígida woman was at home talking on the phone to her best friend, a false blonde with a French manicure named Olimpia, about the latest terrible thing that had happened in the neighborhood, which only confirmed the obvious, there were too many low class people around. It so happened that Lauro, the manicurist's husband, had been saving money for three years in order to buy a used Volvo. On Monday he'd finally gotten one for a good price and paid cash and proudly drove it to his building on Twenty-first and New York Avenue, right near this Brígida's, and apparently he was as happy as a little boy and had the whole family come out to admire the prized possession. A total of fifteen people were on the sidewalk ooohing and aahing over the car and wondering if it'd be bad luck to take it out for a drive, and just in case it would be they decided to wait until the next day. Apparently that night Lauro was so excited that he could barely sleep.

The next morning when he rushed out of his building to admire his new car, it was gone. Stolen. He hadn't even gotten the insurance yet. Apparently the manicurist wept when she told Olimpia this story. She said she'd never ever seen her husband so upset. She said he kept repeating, "Why didn't they at least wait a week?"

After hearing Olimpia's story this Brígida woman's comment was "Well, I hope that teaches this man a lesson about not being attached to material things."

"It's true, Olimpia," Brígida added, "the problem with the lower classes is that they want everything! That's why there's so much crime in the world! Anyway, you should see the bureau I bought today! From a mulatta of all people! It is beautiful! It must be stolen, I swear, because how would a mulatta get her hands on something like that?! It'll be delivered tomorrow, will you come over and take a look at it?"

It wasn't like Mi Negra Nicolasa to forget me in that bureau drawer but she had too many things on her mind, and forget me she did.

The next day Brígida Pacheco arrived at ten a.m. with the moving men and gave Nicolasa the hundred-and-seventy-five-dollar balance. Mi Negra couldn't wait for them to leave, and when they finally did she rushed to El Sol del Caribe Supermarket. It wasn't until noon, when she was cutting up onions and green peppers, because that's when she did all her thinking, that she remembered and immediately dialed Brígida's number.

"No, there is nothing in those drawers," Brígida said. "Are you sure you left it in there? Maybe the moving men stole it, no telling, you know how dishonest the lower classes are these days."

Nicolasa insisted, "Señora, please check again."

"I don't need to," replied Brígida.

"If you have it, please, you have to give it back. It won't be good for you and your family."

"You shouldn't be so attached to material things, Mulatta. And don't threaten me."

"Listen, Señora, that piece of jewelry has been worked on. I'm the only one who can wear it. It's not good for anyone else. I'm not joking, Señora."

Brígida chuckled. "That should teach you not to use a crucifix when you summon your demons," she said.

"How did you know it was a crucifix? I only told you it was a piece of jewelry."

"No telling. I guessed."

Mi Negra Nicolasa was a good woman. Her concern was not so much that I wouldn't be able to protect her now, for she'd already managed without me, and anyway, the three years were up, and, with me or without me, she had a right to get her power back. It was this woman Brígida that she was worried about. I wasn't even supposed to be in her house. So she tried to reason with that woman one more time.

"I'll call the police if you bother me again, Mulatta!"

That was Brígida's reaction.

By that time Nicolasa already knew, and I knew, that Brígida had decided to give the crucifix to her daughter Alma.

So Nicolasa left her onions and peppers on the cutting board, asked the neighbor to look after the children for a couple of hours and rushed out of her building. On the sidewalk her alpargatas were going flip flop flop, flip flop flop all the way to the Chino's house.

She explained what had happened and begged him to neutralize the crucifix he had worked on. The Chino said it was impossible. He couldn't do it himself. Only another Chino could do it and one Chino will never undo what another Chino has done. He explained that Chinos stick together and respect each other's work. So it was impossible. Next!

My name is Shangó. I was human once, just to feel what it was like. All I wanted was to bump into furniture and scratch my mosquito bites. But I was so unsuccessful as a human that I took my life. I've been terrorized by the thought of death ever since and if there is one thing that really incites my wrath it is talk about my self-murder. It should never be mentioned in Santería, and those who know me just call it Shangó's Rest, or Anti-Miracle.

As a reminder, my father, Obatalá, decreed that whenever I ended up with someone by mistake my past should repeat itself. One Friday afternoon in the late spring, Brígida's daughter checked into a Holiday Inn and shot herself in the head the next morning at eleven. She did try to seek help but all she got were answering machines where she left wrong numbers. The bullet didn't go across, it just stayed in the middle of her brain and turned in there, destroying all the fatty substance of consciousness. Just when she did it she thought about her two babies and lived to regret it. Violently she moved her head from side to side in one long, inalterable "no," her last statement. With the nerve strength she had left she pulled on the chain. She pulled so hard that the chain broke and I got tangled in her hair. It was one of the nurses at the hospital who untangled it and pinned it to her gown when her body was still shaking and her blood still warm.

The day after the funeral Brígida brought the cross back to Nicolasa. She only said, "It burns my hand." Ever since then, I've been sitting in Nicolasa's kitchen being ignored by Nicolasa. She thinks I did this so she's taken her affection away from me.

Today I want Nicolasa to know that she's wrong to blame me. I didn't even precipitate this sick fate. If I got tangled in her hair it was because of my fear of death. There's no explaining anti-miracles anyway. Why do some choose the road to silence, while others, like Mi Negra, just make life thrive? That's what Saints are here for. To explain grief. Not even Brígida deserved what happened.

When she understands, perhaps Nicolasa will take me back. I am nothing but a poor, lost, undernourished Saint without her.

Juan Armando David Acosta Posada

After the Rains

Now that the rains have stopped
I fashion this June the earth
a different entity.

And from the garden,
smells of damp soil
of earth newly revealed
enter these rooms:
a musky fragrance
publishing your absence.

So I turn from the window
aware of how silence
has filled in all the rest;
of how I am connected now,
more than ever, to things
limited and perennial,
a season gone astray,
somehow a brief summer.

Always I gave in to the dark
gave up so easily
believing in a certain happiness
in the far torn edge

of an undeniable hunger.
I learned to quiver in perfect rage
an elegy in air
the way we often speak
in the presence of water
gesturing the air into certainty.

But these long soft rains
have scarred the landscape.
Rain too is a form of death
and you gave back so much rain,
words full of doubtful certainty
and intervals of a disillusioned silence.

Dusk has fallen.
The sky seems bewildered
by an absence of clouds.
Far to the West
Late summer's light lingers.
The trees are rustling their August thirst.

About me shadows settle
awaiting the game of the absent
as I try to gather you
into an old way of dreaming.

But tonight you will rumor the dark
and tomorrow, tomorrow will somehow
insist that I want you.

Hunger

1

I want to carve
with hurried impatience
the hunger of others

and since your flesh refuses,
the hunger of my heart
is itself a bridge

between the terrible and the tender,
a bruise austerely dressed
in a deeper silence.

Mine is not a hunger for the world
but a longing for accidental things:
the light of January coming

at an unearthly hour,
learning new ways of living alone
and, of course, the simplicity of pain.

2

My hands busy now with so much absence
trace with more than love these wounds
as if seeking to purify the flesh.

Nothing I can tell you now
will say how much I missed you then.
And still disorderly you travel

these hours I have been given to waste.
Tonight, scraps of night air
take on the form of your body.

Blood makes its entrance
and your flesh, an aching for home,
transfigures the language of hunger,

reestablishes the wound as proof of ecstasy.
Hunger is the architecture of need.
And once again I seek the wound

the delicate wound
of rooms in silence.

In Winter

1

In the monumental, marmoreal,
stillness of winter
trees stand, nakedly silent,
dormant. And the hours,
taciturn, merge one with the other,
in the desolation of this season
that finds me trying to forget you.
My world could have been so simple . . . you see,
I have been writing poems to a stranger,
and my face is unfamiliar
as it stares back from the mirror.

2

On windows perspiring liquid frost
I write your name in big bold letters
through which this evening I can
see the moon. Full, pale,
frightened,
there beyond the mountains,
where the snow has already covered the
delicate pawprints of a fox.

3

The other day,
I stood at the river's edge,
watching gulls skim the frozen
surface of the water in search of food.
It was then I remembered the night we danced,
how my senses were assaulted by your smell
something vaguely wild, symmetrical,
like a vastness of pines.

4

While outside my window
it has begun to snow,
and somehow winter begins
to whisper softly of you over,
and over and over . . .

The Return

In the final act
of nocturnal and mysterious courtesies
your absence ratifies this silence,
re-establishes the order of dust,
of this flesh that must
inevitably retain us.

I unlearn things,
knowing there will be no harvest
in the absence of your voice,
which planted the seeds
to stave my hunger.

There is no order here.
My solitude paces to and fro,
a wounded animal awaiting
the season of your return.

You will come back
when the earth is full to bursting.
It will be an August
of yellow birds in air.
You will return
with autumn nipping at your heels,
bringing with you,
this long-awaited harvest.

Rane Arroyo

Blonde as a Bat

Me, I'm Ricardo and I was born blonde as a bat.

Sometimes you have to improvise—it's like being stoned and you know the saxophone inside your head is going to hit one perfect note that you know is going to just shatter your wisdom teeth—but it doesn't happen.

Then out of nowhere, a surprise.

Night gives you something else.

A moan.

A whisper.

A moon saying nothing, nothing at all but still somehow the sound it doesn't make hurts your ears.

I figure bleaching my hair is not a very big deal in such a big universe.

It's just that simple.

Why I don't have blue contacts for my eyes, that's another story and it's not that simple.

Maybe one day I'll bring pictures in of me as a kid.

There is one of me at Lincoln Zoo where I look like a runaway penguin.

I always knew I looked good in black—black pants, black leather coat, a black eye.

At school I used to pretend I couldn't pick out the state of Illinois from the other 50 states but I always knew which one it was—it's the only state that looks like a top that is about to stop spinning.

Once I used to cry whenever my top stopped spinning.

I wanted it to spin forever because I figured, even then, that forever must be longer than two or three minutes.

Yeah, my heart gets broken all the time.

I'm used to it.

I'm a romantic and I have to play any jukebox that I happen to see.

And I think about Sal Mineo a lot.

I wonder what he was feeling after *Rebel Without A Cause*?

Did he walk around the movie set thinking of ways he could spend all the money he was making now that he was a movie star?

The funny bastard is dead, right?

I mean in the movie, not in life—well he is dead in life but NOT to me.

Sal Mineo lives.

He's flesh and blood to me.

And I don't care if he had to taste James Dean.

None of my business.

A hero is a hero and you take your hero in whatever shape the hero shows up in.

Finding a hero is a tough business.

There were the fat Mexicans in the movies.

They could never be my heroes though they did dress in black.

They looked like my father.

Fatter.

You knew they were going to be killed.

Heroes never die in front of your eyes—it's a kind of universal law.

The rule says there can't be a camera in sight when heroes bite bullets.

Ricky Ricardo?

The human Cuban cigar?

He could have been a hero.

He had the looks and I bet he owned his own tuxedo too.

That's something.

But he married a redhead, a very famous redhead instead of a blonde.

She never taught little Ricky to talk Spanish and you know my name is Ricky and I knew she would have been a terrible mother if I had been her son which I wasn't and that's one thing I'm grateful for.

If little Ricky ever got lost in the streets of Havana, how the hell would he take care of himself?

What kind of mother is that?

What kind of hero lets his son get raised like that?

No—it was Sal Mineo, all the way.

He was dark.

You knew that he would have to fry his hair for hours just to get those smooth long waves.

He had eyes that were black as a blind man's moon.

He always looked up so slowly and he always turned away so quickly and that's because he had the kind of eyes that you could see through.

I don't have those eyes, but I do see things.

Sometimes when I ride a bus I can tell when a girl just got pregnant and maybe she doesn't even know it yet—but I do.

I hear the baby just knocking at the door to this world and I'm not talking about the world you see in the movies.

It's crying "Are there heroes out there?" And you better tell me the truth because I'll find you somehow and someday.

It stretches its little bat wings.
It thinks it'll be the one to finally put out the sun with its wings.
I tell you baby that my friend Sal Mineo tried putting out the sun.
I've tried it too.
Chase the sun and it'll just lead you to another sunrise, kid.
I'm blond as a bat and see how I'm on fire with every day I've ever lived.

Columbus's Children

I have stood at the corner of Broadway and Clark—what the poets in Chicago call *The Crotch of the Midwest*—and I like that because I have a crotch too—and on that corner I once had a fight with another Spanish man—tattooed on his knuckles was the world F A T E—I was dressed in clean clothes—invisible in a crowd of so many other people—Americans I call them—they call me Johnny because in Chicago that's short for Juan—I was lost among Americans—and then out of nowhere he bumped into me and I said excuse me—and he said that my mother had to rape my father to make me—and I said that his mother made food that gave nuns gas—and he raised his fists at me—and I raised mine—and I could just feel our mothers fall to their knees—suddenly filled with the need to scrub all the places their children have contaminated with their shadows—and a police car drove by and we both stopped fighting—and then raised our fists again—and I said Rico why are we fighting—then he punched me in the mouth because words were his weakest muscles—I saw blue cars drive right through flashing red lights—and I could see the neon light in the dentist's office across the street and I felt the pain of my first punch when I was ten years old—Georgie from across the way—he was a white boy in a Green Beret suit he would grow into—Georgie would spit at me—you stupid sixth grader—and I was in the sixth grade—and so was Georgie but he had been a sixth grader twice and at that moment I suddenly realized who had been smearing mud on our windows—my beautiful mother couldn't see outside to look at my father's garden—we were trapped in that house—and Rico hit me again because I wasn't hitting back—so I hit him—and the dance of angry atoms began—my friend I was with tried pulling us apart— think of the shame you give your fathers—fight them—not each other—but Rico, bleeding from where my fist pronounced itself, said where is your accent, where is your fucking accent—you talk American you are American—and then he jumped at me again—and the Great Ace guard looked out through a window and threw a dime at us—we could hear him laughing—how to stop—how to stop—I jumped at Rico—he jumped out of the way—we were really sweat dancing but then he pretended to twist his ankle—hey he said—you sure lucky your mother ate Mexican jumping beans when she had you—and then he ran across the street because the light had turned green and the Clark Street bus was coming down—I was breathing hard—the man turned around—grabbed his crotch with one hand and raised his fist with the other—I grabbed my crotch and became his mirror— then the bus left—and the fight was over—my friend who had tried breaking up the fight said to me—Ah hijo—hijo—I hadn't been anyone's son in a long time— not in Chicago, not in Boston, not in New York, not in San Juan, not in Salt Lake

City, not in San Diego—I hadn't been anyone's son—I hid the tears in my eyes—
Where shall we go Johnny and get coffee—I think my adrenaline glands are shot
to hell—I said to my friend—and he hit me on the back—saying a man is a man—
and I looked into a closed clothing store's windows—my eyes were still brown—
no one had slipped blue contacts into them while I was fighting—I had already
lost my accent—I wasn't going to lose my eyes—we are all Columbus's Children
I said—Yeah he said, Columbus just followed the direction his crotch led him to
and look at the women he ended up with—America—and we laughed and we tried
hiding the dance of our bones the best we could—we headed home, what we call
home—and the crowd swept our footsteps clean—we had never been there, at the
corner of Clark and Broadway—never—never—never—

Caribe Poems

I

English should be spoken with
a shovel instead of a tongue.
As if digging my own grave
with each phrase: Hello. Help.
This is an apple. How much
is a bus transfer home?
I bleach my black hair
to match my bones.

II

My parents are happier
than I am.

   They've kissed with
red lips in a blue ocean.

The time of their youths
before swimming to America.

   My conception
in a suburb of Chicago.

Guests stopped by and music filled
the house.

I sat in my room, brooding.

Later, much later,
I'd come downstairs and was
   forced to rumba.

III

You take the color
of the sea with you.
Even the paint
on the railing
is seriously gray.
It's the last thing
to hold onto;
I've lost sight of you.

Are you waking
in a room
that is as white
as the moon
I discovered
after you left?

IV

I wait for you by the burning road.
Overturned jeeps
melt into coral islands.
I string a necklace
of black and white days
when innocence was ours:
I'm sixteen again and again.
My hands tremble on a body
other than my own.
You teach me geography.
For love letters, I have maps.

Richard Blanco

Teatro Martí

Outside, I would close one eye and squint the other and count the bulbs in English while everyone stood for tickets. Inside Sarita Montiel awaited without subtitles. Always the semi-nude scene: Sarita in her porous eggshell skin, a perfect sienna mole under her left nostril, eyebrows penciled like Japanese ink strokes on silk, the soft balls of her painted feet seeping from under the edges of the sheets swirled around her contours like icing, propped on her breasts and elbows and crying with a Gallego lisp into a gross of satin pillows, believing there would be justice for her undeserved suffering. Justice because she loved; simply because she loved. We believed what she believed because there was little to believe in, and a lot to remember in 1972; and no place else to pretend on Saturday nights. Hovering in the dark, nestled in cracked vinyl seats, buttered over the aisles, we fostered our conjured justice, in spite of ourselves and our losses. While we ate smuggled *cocitos* and *cremitas de leche*, outside the fifty-eight frosted bulbs would flash in unison bursts of mint-white, like a beacon, on-off, on-off, signaling the '72 Malibus and the '67 Chevys whizzing by on Eighth Street to come in and wake us from the slow annihilation we pretended to ignore each Saturday and each day since *la revolución*, and to save us, too.

Lisa D. Chávez

In an Angry Season

They've gone to witness the river's mad
descent into spring. The heave and thunder
as the ice shakes itself from the shore,
the way the frozen slabs—pachyderm grey
and similarly sized—shear one into
another as the Yukon shudders awake.
From a hawk's height the pipeline bridge
mocks the river's riot and churn. Perched
there, they watch—then his pale hand
turns her tawny face to his and
they kiss, roar of loosed ice echoing.
They are both just nineteen.

And now they sit, hands clutching brown
bottles, in a one-room cabin turned
tavern. A wooden counter, scabbed over
with men's names. A naugahyde couch,
slouching by the door. One man at the bar,
face flat in a puddle of beer.
His phlegmy snores. The room choked
with smoke. The one they call Dirty Dave
is telling a story: "We picked up this squaw
hitching her way into town. Weren't no room
in the cab, so she crawled in back. I went after her.
I said, whatever you hear, boys,
don't stop this truck." Laughter. He grins,
gap-toothed and mean. Leers at the girl.
"I like it when they fight." She shivers.
Twists at a strand of her black hair.
Her boyfriend draws her closer.

Six men—they've been drinking
all winter. One girl. One nervous
boyfriend. A mining camp a hundred miles
or more from town. And Dave stares
at the girl. "What do you think of that?"

And she thinks: There is so much evil
in this world. And she thinks of her hand,
squeezing the bottle till it breaks, scraping
his man's face to bone with the shards.
And she thinks of the river, how in some
angry seasons it could not be contained—
bridges snapped like thread, whole villages
devoured by the Yukon's flood and fury.
And she hears the river shift and growl.

Young Widow Walking Home

Her shift ends just past 3 a.m.,
so she shucks the skirt
for a pair of wool pants,
tucks her tips away
and heads home. Some nights
she's drunk, but she always walks
alone. Other waitresses worry,
offer rides, but she looks
past them, faint shadows on a wall.

When she drinks, she thinks of nothing
more than scrunch of boots
in snow. Tonight, her mind leaps—
a restive dog on a leash.
She gazes at two birch, bent
close to breaking—an early snow caught
in their net of leaves. She wonders if
they'll survive 'til spring.
She thinks of her cold cabin,
the wood stove she'll fire up,
the bottle of brandy
by the bed. His hands.
His hands on the ax
last spring: swing, arc,
birch split clean.

A car glides by. Tail lights flash.
She's not afraid. Too many nights
she teases his loaded .44, tongue
lingering on the muzzle,
nudging the barrel
against the roof of her mouth.
She sleeps in his clothes.
He's been gone nine months, long enough
to have the baby they never conceived.

She thinks of it again,
him under the car, one toe poking
from his torn tennis shoe, the jack shifting—
no time for a scream—transmission crushing
his chest like an egg.
Like an egg, she thinks, his ribs
an ivory shell and his blood vivid
as the broken yolk.

Around the cabin, birch twist
into a snarl of bent trunks,
broken branches. She knows
she exists like them:
mute and unexpectant.

Art Coelho

Two Prices: No Yields

I

The farmer bragged
later   with a cool one
clutched in his hand
about the unearthing of human bones—
proud of his mean heartless dust
still rising up in the valley air,
kicking heritage square in the gut.

A suspension of shame
this moment when:
    forgotten ancestors
    old values
    last names and places
felt rows of slicing disc blades
    cutting into tombstones
    tumbling them
    and finally flattened
by the steel cleats of the Cat.

And the crumbling bones
remained on the surface
                exposing
a disturbance to the eye;
then mercifully gathered
by a kind soul
              for the coroner.

Now there's no way he can match
the bones to the plowed graves.
Nor can anyone resolve
the high cost of lost pride,
respect that has truly gone fallow
where ghosts do not have the last word.

II

The disc blades
eat at the abundance
of the melon crop, slicing
                    and burying
all but a sacrificed few.

    The remaining
    cantaloupes
    look like skulls
    in a lost battle,
    enemies of
    the market price.

No one to feed now,
no one to taste
his months of labor on the land:
the farmer braces himself,
wanting the saddened topsoil to offer
him another worthy dream beyond this
daily nightmare under the West Side sun.

Fertilizer
        ditch water
                sweat
the cost of a long season of toiling
haunts him, and kills
his hope for a future crop.

Gnats already raid
and dig into the tough broken skins;
the orange meat explodes
its cluster of seeds inside
towards the valley sun,
the cracks widen in the heat.

The ripe smell
          dripping
                    pungent
a different pair of eye sockets
staring back at the loss.

Ina Cumpiano

Metonymies

1

Last July, they loosened their grip, let go—
plum, sweet plum—until the grass
was bloody with the warm flesh. Months later
the finches, purple fruit, hide in what's left of leaves
so that only when they fly off,
      when the branches bounce back to true
is their presence known. They will not outstay
the leaves, the thin white light disclosing
those empty hands, the tree, against the sky.

2

This trip south, the egret questions the lagoon:
the white curl of its own back is the answer.
No matter how many times I return, this shallow inlet
to the sea will be here; and the egret, long gone,
will grace it with presence.

In "The Blind Samurai" the camera zooms
to the old man's clever ear: a double metonymy
that links our deafness to his danger. By the time
we catch on—snap, snap, footsteps
in the underbrush—
he has done battle and
bandits litter the forest like cordwood.

3

The camellia loses its head
all at once; it does not diminish
                petal by petal
so for weeks the severed blossom lingers
as moist as pain, at the foot of the bush.

4

If the police ordered me to evacuate,
what would I take with me?
Baby pictures, computer disks, the silver,
proofs of birth? The sun
would hang like old fruit until the smoke
gathered it in. Then: night in day, sirens,
and knowing that whatever I took
would hold in its small cup
everything I had ever lost.
So if the police ordered me to evacuate during a firestorm,
I would write your name on a slip of paper,
light it, and—
in those few hurried moments allowed me—
watch it burn, brush the ashes into an envelope
which I would seal and keep with me, always.

Yo, La Malinche

1. Native Tongue

Tecle, these seven women are for your captains, and this one,
who is my niece, is for you, and she is the señora of towns
and vassals.
> —A "fat cacique" to Cortés, as reported by
> Bernal Díaz del Castillo

I had no one name.
I was Malinalli, Malintzín, Doña Marina de Jaramillo,
Lady of Olutlán, Jilotepec, and Tequipaje.
From Coatzacoalco, my father sold me
as if I were daily cloth,
as if I were a clay bowl,
less than the grain of corn that is kept
for the next season, but after
I became
Malinche, *la lengua*,
Malinche, the *Tecle's* voice
Malinche, the tongued serpent pointing to the dismembered
bodies at the battle of Cholula,
Malinche, the traitor,
Malinche, *la chingada*,
woman of the *lope luzio*, Cortés's whore,
Malinche, Malinche.

My name for myself is wing.
My name for myself is loud silence.
My name for myself is spring-fed brook.
My name for myself is unknowing.
My name is My Name.

Who will speak up for Malinche?
Who will say she spoke as women speak,
in another's language
so that even when the eagle Cuauhtémoc
was caged that one last time
she had no words of her own that could warn him.

How could she have saved him?
How would you have saved him?
Would you have saved him?
How can we save ourselves?

2. Translating Woman

Everything I say is in a foreign language.
When I say *woman*, whose word is that
if not his?
And even the long howl in the darkness—*¡Ayyy!*—
is a code he has taught me.
Nothing, not *joy*, not *rain*, is my own.

I will make a language from stones.
One stone lifted from wet earth will mean *everything*.
The mark the stone leaves will mean *night*.

3. Martín's Birth

Soon, the war party Malinalli followed
would return to the great city;
soon she would seem, almost, to recover her tongue
but now, in her time,
Malinalli hid herself in the undergrowth.
Dappled by the fickle light, she was as silent as a doe—
only the sound of small twigs settling and breaking
under her weight.
No ancient *ticitl* would midwife this birth;
no neighbor wife would croon
        —The child will be a bird called quecholli;
          the child will be a bird called zacuán—
over and over, a naming like a prayer.
This time no reeds softened in the river for a basket;
no feathers were gathered to line it.
                The first pain
had been a garter snake that slithered, quick and sharp;
              now claws ripped at her belly.
     —The child will be a bird called quecholli
       the child will be a bird called zacuán,
       the child, the child.

Soon she would wash the child's bloody white skin in the river.
Soon she would wrap him in the folds of her huipilli.
Soon the soldiers would come to take him to his father.
Soon Cortés would name this cry of hers *Martín*.

4. My Dream of Ciuacoatl

According to Sahagún, the Aztec goddess appeared
at night, wailing for her lost children.

The woman lifts a rock high over her head
and describes
swiftly
the arc of the moon, the egg's curve,
as she brings the rock down to shatter
her children's skulls
as if the skulls were eggs, as if the light they gave off
were as insignificant
as the *luciérnaga's* pitiful, intermittent glimmer in a glass jar,
as if their skulls were as translucent as jars,
as if the jars were in shards already at her feet,
as if she walked through the shards,
as if she had shattered the children's skulls
in order,
in order to save them, in order to save herself,
in order to return the children to the dark of her body,
or to save her children from the dark of her body,
or in order to free herself from her body,
or in order to free them,
in order to say I never had them,
in order to keep them safe,
away from her saying I never had them,
and then
having taken pebbles from the round hollow of her mouth,
and placed them in her shoe to feel them as she walks,
she wanders, she still
keeps to the riverbank where the first rock lay
smoothed by the white tongue of water—
her name is what she does:
La llorona.

5. Bacalán

When Bacalán said this is my body,
I will do with my body
what I choose,
there was only that one choice . . .

And when the *adelantado's* soldiers found
the body
        where the stubborn woman left it
(the bitter root still clutched in her hand
as if she had treasured this little bit of stuff
more than
life and so her fingers had hung on to it)
they threw the body to the dogs like so much meat—
so that Bacalán's flesh would not speak
for itself any longer.

I am not as brave as you, Bacalán.
Daily I give myself away, Bacalán.
Piece by piece, they take me, Bacalán, so that
never again will I be whole
like you, Bacalán.

                Bacalán,
when de Landa tells your story
in *Relación de las cosas de Yucatán*
he gets it wrong, I think.
He says *She had promised her husband . . .*
not to have relations with any man other than him
and so no persuasion was sufficient . . .

Was it fidelity, I wonder,
or did you see the chance for once
to call your body back
as a *palomera* might welcome her pigeons
to their cote and settle them in
after their too-long flight over the battlefield.

Ramón García

Miss Primavera Contest

Saturday night at *La India Bonita's*
on 16th Street,
the jotos of the Mission
come looking for their Latin love,
come to celebrate their public secrets;
machismo and being maricón are blurred
as the tough cholo
dances with the drag queen,
it's almost surreal,
and the minutes continue to reel
like scenes from a Fellini film.
Somebody's Mexican mother
is there, just observing
with an indifference that reveals
she could be just as attentive
if she were anywhere else.
She must never have seen
Miss Primavera contests of this sort
back in her village in México,
but she must have seen things
just as wondrous
as Conchita lips-inking rancheras
or La Tina Turner dancing with the
legs of a sexy angel.
It's an art,
this messing with appearances,
and the old woman must know it,
to her, it makes perfect sense
that she should be there,
the mother of a Chicano drag queen,
baroque extravagance
and daring dramas

are her son's inheritances.
Shit, despite the Catholicism,
Miss Primavera's mother
must have been a little like
Miss Primavera herself, her son,
and deep inside this must please her,
for her hijo to turn out
so much like her
when she was in the Spring
of her life—a little bit Loca.

Rigoberto González

The Flight South of the Monarch Butterfly

They always return to make us hot here in Michoacán
Because they remind us of fire: they sputter like candles,
Expanding and shrinking their singed browns and reds
As they consume the air in November, finally tapering down

Into the shadows like burnt paper. What message
Do they carry on their wings, all the way from the north—
The place that gave them a brush of black opal
For weight, and touches of white to attract the clean

Clouds and fool the sun into sending its brightest rays
Through the mimic of holes? The butterflies settle their lit
Bodies on the naked tree, bringing back its autumn leaves,
Those breaths of orange that gasp before falling off again,

This time into the hands of winter. But here, winters
Are warm like *manzanilla* tea. Haven't we always known that,
Those of us who chose to stay within arm's length
Of our mothers? But for some women, sitting like stone saints

At their doors, these butterflies are calls for blessings
From their sons, the men whose names trickled down to thirst
Inside their mother's mouths. To them, the Monarch's eggs
Complete their prayers like rosary beads; they are flammable

Like the heads of matches. But we value the chrysalis of bone,
The blue shell that brought down the sky within our reach.
By March, when the Monarch leaves, a second fever
Strikes: the butterflies cluster like dreams; the trees

The women's sons once owned are set ablaze again; young boys
Raise their sticks like swords to cut them down in flames.
We all watch together as they drop: their explosions are bright
As fireworks without sound, yet loud enough to wake us up.

Ghost Story

I was only six when I began to fear
The dark's chilly thumb
It pressed down on my neck to feel
My pulse, and to ride the gush
Of echoes and shadows in my blood,
The footsteps my grandfather said
Would come as soon as I shut the door.

He called them ghosts.
They escaped from his tea-heavy breath
To inhabit the black corners
Like webs. But their silky muscles
Were as free as hands destined to rest
Somehow, on my shoulder,
Or in the hollows of my shoes.

These ghosts were invisible as words
And just as loud, taking over my room,
Making me its only prisoner
Like a tin cup makes a hostage
Of its coin: all walls at one time
And only when the occupant moves.
Many nights I hid under the covers,

Afraid to relax an arm, suppressing
A twitch for fear the mattress springs
Would call them to my bed.
Only my nose peeked out like a blind eye;
My nostrils were their only way inside
The sheets. My comfort was, that like Grandpa,
I could always breathe them out.

But my grandfather never stopped
Producing ghosts. He would let them crack
Their anxious bones each time he yawned.
While he slept in the room next to mine,
I could hear them sneaking out
With every snore. When they all left his mouth,
Grandpa had nothing more to say.

Years later, I'm learning to live with them.
They are part of me now, but only at night.
The ghosts wrap around my skin
Like the cloud of translucent winds
That envelops the full moon's curves.
The ghosts wedge their limbs into the black
Lines of my reflection when I walk by the mirror

At dusk. They have taken over my shadow
And are molding it to fit their needs:
I have a round back now, and my head
Is tilting forward with their weight.
My arms no longer rise above my chin—
But then, it was always useless
To cover up my ears, to conceal my face.

It all belongs to them; they have found
Their place inside me. Now, I, too,
Speak ghosts at the hour when darkness
Strikes as softly as bedroom blankets.
I, too, send out my voice to search out
My grandchildren's ears. They will keep me
Talking when I can no longer speak for myself.

Lola Haskins

De lo que yo me enteré/El Día de los Muertos

That secretaries in their tight red skirts
have skulls. That guitarists are
bones underneath. Judges too.
That skulls are made of sugar.
That I will be delicious when I die.

That we should make los muertos welcome.
That they like Pepsi especially. And
tamales. That they like to use heaps
of orange petals for paths. That
it is all right to bring a radio

(I get sleepy waiting). That Tío Pepe
was a funny man. My cousins sing
the way he did, weaving through
the graves, blowing kisses, almost
falling over.

Dear Tía

I do not write.
The years have frightened me away.
My life in a land so familiarly foreign,
a denial of your presence.
Your name is mine.
One black and white photograph of your youth,
all I hold on to.
One story of your past.

The pain comes not from nostalgia.
I do not miss your voice urging me in play,
your smiles,
or your pride when others called you my mother.
I cannot close my eyes and feel your soft skin;
listen to your laughter;
smell the sweetness of your bath.
I write because I cannot remember at all.

Moses of Echo Park

Part
this sea of pills
this ocean of distilled spirits
Moses of Echo Park.
Climb your hill
3rd street and Lucas
bring down your commandments
Thou shall persist
Thou shall endure
Thou shall survive
Thou shall outlive
Thou shall resist
Thou shall withstand
Thou shall continue
Thou shall outlast
Thou shall bear
Thou shall uphold.
Part
this sea of madness
this ocean of dreams
deferred
Moses of Echo Park.
Raise your staff
in the air
and cut the wind
'til it bleeds.
Strike down
false Gods
who ignore
your outstretched hand
begging for coins
and part this sea of piss
this ocean of cemented feces.

I listen to

Beny Moré's
danzones
and my thoughts float
over santiago de Cuba
this afternoon
while I water my lawn
and smoke a cheap
factory rolled cigar.
This afternoon
in America
land of the free
land of the brave
Beny's voice is sugar
his horns machete sharp.
Tumbadoras, congas, maracas,
rumba, fire,
slap, slap, slap,
this is all I have
all I know
all there will ever be for me
from the land of my grandfather
from the land of my father
from the land lost below
to the land of watered lawns.

Amalio Madueño

Ballad of Friendship through the Ages

After C.D. de Andrade

We've been friends since time began.
We always liked each other.
You were Olmec. I owed tribute.
You applauded me for my marriage.
I sprang in a fresh jaguar hide
To knife your brother-in-law.
We killed. We quarreled. We died.

Later, as an Aztec warrior,
Proud persecutor of Totonacs,
In the plaza of the great pyramid
I met you again—bound,
Climbing to the bloody sacrifice,
Dark priest waiting.
I made a desperate leap.
We both were skinned alive.

Next you were a Comanche renegade,
Scourge of the northern haciendas.
You set fire to the villa where I,
In the rotund name of the king,
Directed my soldiers against you.
We had to fight, through respect
For each other, our factions oil and water.
Your spear struck my heart
As my shot pierced you.

Later on, in happier days
I was a bolshevik and
You led the campesinos, rousing
The countryside. We collaborated
On the revolution. Our politics were dangerous.
We were shot at dawn in Puebla.

These days we're totally modern:
Tennis, poems, working out, jazz.
I'm doing some government work.
And you're a popular screenwriter:
TV specials, megadeals, jazz.
People wonder what we're up to.
Abrazamos en la calle. We are friends.

Sanctuary of Chimayo

> *Do we delude ourselves into thinking*
> *that we possess and command our own*
> *souls?*
>
> —C.G. Jung

While my touring friend peers the grounds
I shift in the hardened pew and wish
For my distant parents to arrive.
They'd come in smiling, looking good, limping
Slightly with years under their belts—years
Learning care is terminal. While
My new friend roams the flagstones, stepping on
The pilgrims with care, gazing the reliquaries.
Here, in the U.S.! Dark pilgrims
On Tuesday, praying in Spanish. Small photos
Beside discarded crutches—of children, mothers,
PFCs, glassy abuelitos—stare
Out at him and his nape tingles.
The white brocaded doll behind the glass
Frightens him with her eyes. The time
For clear thinking increases in the small
Room with cardboard sign and holy dirt.
I say, not knowing, "rub it on your face,"
As we bend to it like water, reverent.
Back in the pew I see them now above the altar
In wide summer . . . he shirtless in jeans,
Adonis in his twenties, the smooth skin
And mind Mrs. S. next door ruined us for.
Mom in her famous dress (the one that killed
The Greek lieutenant), paintbrush in hand . . .
What I have seen begins to sink in
As my astounded friend emerges from
The deep adobe shadow rubbing his arm,
Saying "damned if my arthritis isn't gone."

Arroyo

The arroyo is in the mind of the puma.
In its mind as the sun scatters
In its fur, in its eye
As suns whirl in dustdevils.

Antelope in the pools of dawn,
Rake the rim for his form.

The arroyo is in their minds.
Breathing with their vision they walk
As shadows of each stone,
Silent needles of thirst,
Exhaling a breath of weeds.

Shivering hunger follows them.
Thought and fear mix
In scratch and gravel drift,
Rolling downslope to settle
In the cleft of memory.

Julio Marzán

Grand Central Station

The Rican teen looked punch-drunk, stupid
as a stereotype, crusted notches
on his ears, fresh red nicks
on his nose, and a shaved scalp patch

spotlight on a still-wet wound. Maybe RIVERA,
black on his Army duffel bag,
and lost down from Upstate
he asked for directions still nervously pedaling

away from the line to his destination.
A hair-trigger pain
discharged in a glance,
his twin barreled eyes packed with pulverized words—

shy, confused, homicidal anger—
aimed along my outstretched arm and finger
toward his Bronx subway,
toward its lighted tunnel to an end with no light.

Volkswagen on Calle Cerra

Hjalmar didn't know he had turned right
to my street where life began:
beyond my pointing finger a storefront
once an uncle's travel agency,
a restaurant, a furniture store,
generations of Marzáns along both sides . . .
Now I can walk by unrecognized, it
having been that long, for instance,
that white-shirted pedestrian stepping back
to let his VW go by, is my father.

Hjalmar brakes. I insist he proceed.
"I think it's been ten years," I answer Gretchen.
The VW pulls out in first
as I put myself in reverse,
back up toward an angry memory
of when I tried to leave a number
the bald man fisted into a ball:
"I don't call anybody."

What if I had ordered "Stop,"
stepped out to an inquisitive stare,
a recognition, an ambivalent embrace?
Then his fatherly rebuke:
"You've been down here a month
and now you look me up."
That's when his bronze face
dissolves in smoky dusk,
as Hjalmar's eyes shift fast
from me to the road and back: "¿Todo bien?"
The sun, a fat cigar's red tip,
extinguishes itself in the bay.

Pablo Medina

The Apostate

To breathe fire
in this land is a conspiracy
of wrong.

The moon outside
wanes over yellowing fields.

Only the teeth of barking dogs
give light.

There is coffee
and phones ringing
and funereal smoke.

Na na, na na, sings a girl
on the road into autumn.
She stops, she turns, she goes.

Far away behind the hills—
birth, red earth.

Behind that
God's face receding.

The land is full of innocence
and comfortable slumber.
Na na, na na.
Few birds remain. The grass
is dying. The earth turns hard.

Sugarcane

can't cut
cut the cane
azuca' in chicago
dig it down to the
roots sprouting spray paint on the
walls on the hard cold
stone of the great gritty city
slums in chicago
with the mansions in the hole
in the head of
the old old rich left behind
from other times lopsided
gangster walls overgrown taken
over by the dark
and poor overgrown with no
sugarcane but you
can't can't cut
cut the water
bro'
from the flow and
you can't can't cut
cut the blood
lines from this island
train one by one throwing off
the chains siguaraya
no no
no se pue'e cortar
pan con ajo quisqueya
cuba y borinquen no
se pue'en parar

I saw it
say black a-frica down in the city
walking in chicago y
la cuba cuba
gritando en el solar
I saw it
say quisqueya
brown
uptown in the city
cryin' in chicago
y borinquen
bro'
sin un
chavo igual but
you can't can't cut
cut the water
bro'
from the flow and
you can't can't cut
cut the blood
lines from this island
train one by one throwing off
the chains siguaraya
no no
no se pue'e cortar
pan con ajo quisqueya
cuba y borinquen no
se pue'en parar

¡azuca'!

Yvonne Sapia

Del medio del sueño

My mother's face blushing
above me like a lung
checks my eyes to be assured
I am trapped somewhere
in the walls of my dream.
She glides in quietness to my dresser,
shifts the intimate fabrics around
like fresh evidence.
Del medio del sueño,
I am not so far that I cannot come back
to watch her wear down in purpose.

She thinks I have her food.
She thinks I listen at the bathroom door
when she washes what the doctors cut.
Sometimes she forgets who I am,
asks for the keys to the house.
Sometimes she forgets who she is,
asks to be walked to the ocean.

My father yearns to be patient,
then bites his fingernails
and sorrowfully turns to the television.
I pretend to go to sleep
and wait in the insomnia dark
for my mother and her suspicions
to verify the passing of nights
which permit few easy exits.

La desconocida

These clues to my identity are unmistakable.
Only the light portrays itself.
I am unable to recall
the street which turns out
to be my old neighborhood.
The familiar substance is the landscape
receiving a difficult winter.

When I turn around,
I am a contradiction.
I am not the one walking the dog,
I am not the one who lives the same life.
I am the one trying to avoid
stepping on the seams in the sidewalk.
I am the one searching for unreasonable things.

I have seen the angel of death
and thought of inadequacy.
I have studied the duration of sin
while lost in the long skirt of the night.
I am the one who has
a monster under my bed.

In the sequence of events,
mine is the name I have not memorized,
mine is the conscience I do not have.

Edgar Silex

Washington D.C.

it is not a place
where the dead can be buried
they would not rest like stones
it is not a place where the air sings
the Potomac licks blood off its banks
I have walked its red rivers
16th Street NW   Pennsylvania Avenue SE
I have seen the white stone faces staring
from marble sepulchres memorializing the sacred
names of slavers and lynchmen

I have heard moccasin bells
ringing the night   echodancing
against red brick walls and white columns
those dance steps were not my own
but those of Red Cloud
of Red Bird   of Hollow Horn Bear
of Standing Bear   of Ten Bears
of Santanta   of Muskogee
of Sauk   of Cheyenne   of Mandan
Choctaw   Blackfeet   Anacostan
Bear Clans   Fox Clans   *Ishi**
of clans whose names only the wind sings now

*Man (Ishi—Yana word)

by day   I can see crow people
perched in the windows of the Treasury
the Capitol   the Archives   I walk fast
this place is not for the living
when I walk over manhole covers
I can still hear the deceptions
conspiring whispers that steal
through catacombs   seeping up through street cracks
until they mix with the holy bloodstream
of women   children   and warriors
and the blood of others I am not familiar with

in the night
before the shadows of crows can be seen
in front of the Supreme Court
I have heard ephemeral pleadings
rattling the sarcophagus' doors
even the fish have swum downstream
to saltier waters that don't taste of blood

when I walk the red rivers
I am reminded of the dead who live here
I am reminded of the danger of ghosts
who breathe the black air walk in my nightmares
I know even the dead have memories
that is what keeps the spirits here
I know this is their city now
this is their City of Death

Leaving Cibola

El Paso, Texas, is the last place Francisco Vasquez de Coronado searched for the
Seven Cities of Cibola. He established two missions to convert the Indians. The
missions are still active as are the unconverted tribes.

no one has ever left here   not even Coronado
who came with delusions of cibolas
to claim a desert of gold
who can be found ragged and unshaven
waiting with other drunken Tiguas
in the soup line of the Ysleta mission

and the missionaries who came with him
to nail Indians to crosses
their ghostly voices can also be heard
near the river at night baptizing
young Indian women with their sperm

sometimes   in the desert sunlight
the red sand-ghost warriors will dance
in a swirl of dust devil happiness
as if time had changed nothing
as if the Pueblo Revolt had just ended

in the hot summer   if you look into the distant
mirages you may see
the conquistadores in their shiny armor
riding their horses toward the glint
of downtown glass monuments
they never found a single grain
of sacred dust   gold or otherwise

as I drive out of the mountainous arms
hugging this dust bowl   I see red
canyon fingers   soft palms of earth
cradling the lives of a hunched-over people
deluded by the illusions of America
of riches they cannot find
having already lost and forgotten
How to be Tiguas   Aztecas   Mixcos   Poconchis   Yaqui-Tepeus

in the rearview mirror I watch cibola
fading at night   glimmering like the sweat of my people
and I know where the gold is   and where it will remain

Franklyn P. Varela

Electric Cowboys

O when I was six
hissing tubes
and light chinks
gave me life
as I moved closer
to the mother warmth
of my Zenith Royal.
I was a child
held in the ecstasy
of time and technology
to behold electric cowboys
every afternoon
so when the Hop or Gene
even the singing duo
Dale and Roy
rode on palomino splendor
I knew
I honestly knew
I was in heaven.

O I would sit
seventeen stories
above Brooklyn concrete.
My small arms reached
for celluloid dreams
of electric cowboys
singing under
a whiskey sky
and when mama came home
I went for my gun
and shot her dead.
Death was a game played
in the desert valleys
of the synchronized west.

O my heart quaked
whenever my cowboys
met their deaths
but in their songs
ran notes I never heard
and the western song
became a dirge
with every Indian
and Mexican spent;
while I sat beguiled
in the shadows
of the flickering images
and when they rode
on the screen
I thought
I honestly thought
I was in heaven.

me-nudo

Hay vecinos que lo tienen todo,
y restaurantes con tufos perfumados
y aliños exquisitos.

Pero un menú sin menudo, no es menú.

¡Menuda mi sorpresa ante tanta
y nutrida menudencia!

Constelación

Una constelación se despliega
sobre tu cuerpo.
Mi tarea: trazar con astrolabio
distancias
y puntos suspensivos . . .

Under the Moon of Texas

I dance among the graves
and weep under the moon of Texas.
My tender talons frown
as, gingerly, I walk
on the forbidden ground
y respiro the dust of hidden truths
and lies in Texas.

Andrés sin tierra

Hay canciones que calan
hasta el hueso.
Igual que el frío serrano
de mi tierra.
Dígolo así, tan sólo por decirlo.

Yo, Andrés sin tierra,
no tengo más tierra ni sustancia
que la que llevo dentro,
allende el polvo que pesa
en mis pestañas y me cierra los ojos
a momentos,
y el otro, el del ombligo,
el que he acumulado poco a poco,
golpeando, a paso lento,
mi talón por todos los caminos.

Hay canciones, decía,
que calan hasta el hueso,
igual que el frío que baja de la sierra,
de los volcanes,
de sus crestas nevadas,
y nos abraza glaciales
las orejas.

Credits and Permissions

"Nuestra Señora de la Poesía" by Alfredo Arreguin first appeared in *The Americas Review* 23:3-4 (1995). Reprinted by permission of the artist.

"Sun Calendar" and "We Knew It" by Jimmy Santiago Baca appeared in *Revista Chicano-Riqueña* 10:1-2 (1982). Reprinted by permission of the author.

"El Pajarero" by Sandra Benítez first appeared in *The Americas Review* 21:2 (1993). Reprinted by permission of the author.

"Face—08", from *World Info Series* Copyright © Paul Berger, first appeared in *The Americas Review* 23:3-4 (1995). Reprinted by permission of the artist.

"1975," "Napa," and "The Antihero." From *My Father Was a Toltec and Selected Poems* (New York: W. W. Norton & Co.). Copyright © 1995 by Ana Castillo. Reprinted by permission of Susan Bergholz Literary Services, New York. All rights reserved.

"María la O" by Barbara Brinson Curiel appeared in *Revista Chicano-Riqueña* 10:1-2 (1982). Reprinted by permission of the author.

"Fuga" by Lucha Corpi first appeared in *The Americas Review* 15:3-4 (1987). Reprinted by permission of the author.

"The Hershey Bar Queen" by Elena Díaz Björquist first appeared in *The Americas Review* 22:1-2 (1994). Reprinted by permission of the author.

"After 21 Years, A Postcard From My Father" and "Bamba Basílica" by Alicia Gaspar de Alba first appeared in *The Americas Review* 16:3-4 (1988). Reprinted by permission of the author.

"Birthday" by Dagoberto Gilb first appeared *The Americas Review* 15:2 (1987). Reprinted by permission of the author.

"The Flight South of the Monarch Butterfly" and "Ghost Story" by Rigoberto González first appeared in *The Americas Review* 22:3-4 (1994). Reprinted by permission of the author.

"Luminous Serpent Songs" and "Coyote Woman Finds Fox at the Street Fair in Port Townsend," Copyright © 1995 by Inés Hernádez Avila, first appeared in *The Americas Review* 23:3-4 (1995). Reprinted by permission of the author.

Juan Felipe Herrera's "Photopoem of the Chicano Moratorium 1980/L.A." first appeared in *Revista Chicano-Riqueña* 10:3 (1982); "Outside Tibet" and "Selena in Corpus Christi" will appear in *The Americas Review* 24:3-4 (1997). Reprinted by permission of the author.

"Vaquero" Copyright © by Luis A. Jiménez, Jr. appeared in *Revista Chicano-Riqueña* 8:3 (1980). Photo courtesy of the National Museum of American Art.

"Curandera barriendo el susto" and "Tuna de nopal/Pedacito de mi corazón" by Carmen Lomas Garza first appeared in *The Americas Review* 15:3-4 (1986). Reprinted by permission of the artist.

"Gently Lead Me Home" by Jesús María Maldonado first appeared in *The Americas Review* 23:3-4 (1995). Reprinted by permission of the author.

"Hombre que le gustan las mujeres" and "El pantalón rosa" by César A. Martínez first appeared *The Americas Review*. 14:2 (1986). Reprinted by permission of the artist.

"Ellipse Round," "Spirit Las Mesas Round," and "Lapstrake" by Jesús Bautista Moroles first appeared in *The Americas Review* 15:1 (1987). Image courtesy Barbara Davis Gallery, Houston. Reprinted by permission of the artist.

"Sugarcane" by Achy Obejas first appeared in *Revista Chicano-Riqueña* 11:3-4 (1983). Reprinted by permission of Charlotte Sheedy Literary Services and the author.

"Pablo Neruda" by Naúl Ojeda first appeared in *Revista Chicano-Riqueña* 11:2 (1983). Reprinted by permission of the artist.

"La Jonfontayn" by Estela Portillo Trambley first appeared in *Revista Chicano-Riqueña* 10:1-2 (1982). Reprinted by permission of the author.

Alberto Ríos's "The Birthday of Mrs. Piñeda" first appeared in *Revista Chicano-Riqueña* 12:1-2 (1984); "On January 5, 1984, El Santo..." appeared in 13:1 (1985). Reprinted by permission of the author.

"Desire to Become a Storm" by Arnaldo Roche Rabell first appeared in *The Americas Review* 19:1 (1991). Reprinted by permission of the artist. Image courtesy of Lisa Sette Gallery, Scottsdale, AZ.

"Human Conditions #1" by José Luis Rodríguez Guerra first appeared in *The Americas Review* 23:3-4 (1995). Reprinted by permission of the artist.

"Running to America," Copyright © by Luis J. Rodríguez, first appeared in *The Americas Review* 17:3-4 (1989). It was subsequently published in *Poems Across the Pavement* (Chicago: Tía Chucha Press, 1989). Reprinted by permission of the author.

"Self-Portrait" by Patricia Rodríguez first appeared in *Revista Chicano-Riqueña* 11:3-4 (1983). Reprinted by permission of the artist.

"Laving Cibola" and "Washington D.C." by Edgar Silex first appeared in *The Americas Review* 22:3-4 (1994). Reprinted by permission of the author and Curbstone Press.

"Woman-Hole" by Carmen Tafolla first appeared in in *Revista Chicano-Riqueña* 11:3-4 (1983). Reprinted by permission of the author.

"Risen Christ" and "Dos Pedros sin llaves" by Luis E. Tapia first appeared in *The Americas Review* 21:2 (1993). Reprinted by permission of the artist. Image courtesy of Owings-Dewey Gallery, Santa Fe, NM.